JOHN POSTGATE FRS

Microbes
music
and me

a life in science

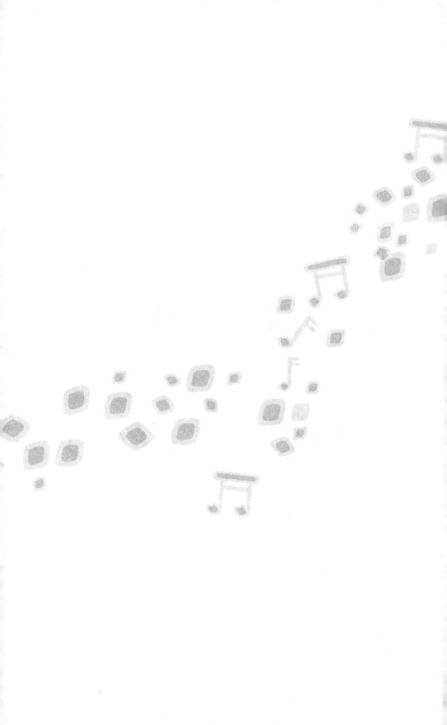

JOHN POSTGATE FRS

Microbes
music
and me

a life in science

MEREO
Cirencester

Published by Mereo

1A The Market Place Cirencester Gloucestershire GL7 2PR
info@memoirsbooks.co.uk | www.memoirspublishing.com

Microbes, music and me: a life in science

All Rights Reserved. Copyright ©John Postgate FRS

ISBN: 978-1-86151-100-3

Contents

Foreword

Foreword

Accounts of present-day science written for non-scientists exist in abundance; I have written a couple on microbiology myself. In fact, such works have become a genre in their own right and even merit their own literary prizes. But only rarely do they - can they - deal with the human side of research. After all, painful as the thought may be to the average researcher, in the long run it does not matter who added this or that bit to our edifice of scientific knowledge: all that matters is that it be reliable, based on sound and reproducible observations.

Of course, in the short run the reputations and abilities of the scientists who report new scientific findings obviously matter enormously - poor science will be neither believed nor funded - but in the end science is impersonal. Both formal and popular scientific writings generally strive to retain that impersonal approach; only in scientific biography and history may personality impinge. Which is as it should be.

Can it be its very impersonality that makes science so arcane, frightening or boring, to non-scientists? For very good reasons, proper scientific writing rarely gives any hint of more human questions. How is science actually done? What possesses anyone to become a scientist in the first place? What does it feel like to do scientific research? What, in fact, do people actually *do* in laboratories or research stations? What sorts of people guide and lead scientific advance? How do the fragments of knowledge garnered piecemeal all over the world come together in the ever-growing edifice of scientific knowledge?

These can be very interesting questions, and the answers differ according to the branch of science and type of scientist being considered. But the answers also have a lot in common, too, and can bear strongly upon the impacts and directions of scientific advance, not to mention the reliability of its tenets.

So this is not a science book (though a lot of science will creep in), it is a book about doing science. It happened that I reached manhood in the mid-twentieth century, just as the transcendent importance of science to our social well-being had become accepted by most Western societies and their governments, largely because of the very obvious contribution their scientific superiority had made to the Allies' victory in the then recent Second World War. Science had long ceased to be the province of amateurs; the profession of research scientist had come into being, and I became a professional scientific researcher myself. Hardly aware of my good fortune, I worked for half of my career through what proved to be a golden age of scientific research: the quarter century that followed that war.

Techniques, knowledge and even the social and professional environment in which scientists work have all changed again since those heady days, but the underlying spirit, the day-today frustrations and the occasional excitement of discovery persist. My story centres on a branch of biology called microbiology. This is the study of tiny creatures the majority of which cannot be seen without the aid of a microscope, but which have a quite disproportionate effect on our environment and daily lives. Most people know them as germs, the organisms that make one ill, but in fact relatively few types cause disease; the majority are beneficial, or at least neutral. It would not be appropriate to enlarge upon all that just now; certain microbes will appear in my story in due time. Microbiology as a distinct discipline within biology scarcely existed until the mid-twentieth century, but since then it has mushroomed. In illustration, in 1945 exactly 241 biologists who were especially interested in microbes came together and formed Britain's Society for General Microbiology, a learned society dedicated to the study of these beasties. By 1970 that society's membership had grown to 2900 and in the mid 1990s it passed 5000. That increase in membership, over 20-fold, reflects an explosive growth in research on and interest in the subject, which took place throughout the developed world during that period. I contributed my mite to that growth. But this is not an account of the development of the science, nor is it a proper autobiography. It is a subjective account of what it was like to play a small part in that intellectual adventure, especially of the people I met and the things I did. I have leavened it with an account of the tinier part I played in a musical revolution, which was fortuitously happening alongside.

Why, you may well ask, should you, the reader, have the slightest interest in a subjective account of a period of intellectual development which is already history, with outlooks and techniques that have already been transformed enormously by changes in social organisation, by the internet, and by the vagaries of popular taste and understanding? Well, there is a good reason. Scientific research shares with jazz a subjective exploratory quality (its practitioners are always seeking), and both blossomed spectacularly during the later 20th century. Yet like jazz, science became belittled and distorted by market forces as the twenty-first century arrived, so there are lessons to be learned. But I shall only hint at them, for this is not a nostalgic polemic, nor a call to reverse history. It is simply a personal account of a period of intellectual and cultural innovation which may yet prove to have been exceptional.

And it is not, I repeat, an autobiography (even if it is autobiographical in approach). But since I necessarily appear often in my story, it is only proper that I introduce myself briefly.

I was born in London, England, within the sound of Bow Bells, on June 24, 1922. My only sibling, my brother Oliver (1), was born a couple of years later. Oliver became famous, with artist Peter Firmin, for writing, making and presenting television films for children. They were very good. Often, in later life, people would say to me, "Are you the Postgate? I just loved *The Clangers*". Or perhaps it would be *Ivor The Engine*, *Noggin The Nog*, *Bagpuss* or another of Oliver and Peter's sensitive productions that they loved. But I, by then quite a large frog in my own frog-pond of microbiology, was not envious; I was happy for him. My father was Raymond Postgate (2), classicist, historian, novelist, gourmet, socialist writer and propagandist, broadcaster and journalist; he was a widely known polymath of the mid twentieth century. Somewhat to his dismay he became most famous in the fourth of these contexts: he founded and edited for many years *The Good Food Guide,* an annual compendium of British restaurants based on customers' recommendations. In consequence I had also to accustom myself to being asked to advise on good places to eat, and I was once elected to a wine committee because I bore my father's surname.

He had an academic background, and his father had been a distinguished classics don at Cambridge (a co-founder of the Classical Association) and later Professor of Latin at Liverpool University. My mother, Daisy, had no academic background; she was from London's East End, daughter of George Lansbury (3, 4), Labour Member of Parliament for Bow and Bromley (London) for very many years and sometime Cabinet Minister and Leader of the Labour Party. Daisy was Lansbury's Private Secretary throughout much of my boyhood, and I became quite familiar with the rooms and corridors of the House of Commons, as well as with several of the Labour MPs. My parents moved to the suburbs of North London when I was about two years old and my brother and I were brought up there, first in Hendon, later in Finchley.

My family background, then, was political and literary. Famous names from the earlier twentieth century worlds of politics and left-wing literature often visited our home, usually taken for granted and unremarked by Oliver and me. There were no scientists among my aunts, uncles and cousins and, though one or two of my parents' friends were scientists, they came as primarily political associates. So in my domestic environment I encountered only a casual interest in scientific matters. In taking up science I followed in none of my then extant family's footsteps (a great-grandfather, my namesake, had been medical; he was a Victorian reformer who battled food adulteration (5), but it was in no sense a rebellion on my part. I was not reacting against their interests; I shared them, though perhaps to a relatively modest degree. As I shall in due course tell, it was just that science took me over.

(1) *Seeing Things, An Autobiography.* Oliver Postgate, 2000, Sidgwick & Jackson.

(2) *A Stomach For Dissent. The Life Of Raymond Postgate: 1896-1971.* John & Mary Postgate, 1994, Keele University Press.

(3) *The Life Of George Lansbury.* Raymond Postgate, 1951, Longman's Green & Co Ltd.

(4) *George Lansbury. At The Heart Of Old Labour.* John Shepherd, 2002, Oxford University Press

(5) *Lethal Lozenges And Tainted Tea: A Biography Of John Postgate (1820-1881).* John Postgate, 2001, Brewin Books.

CHAPTER ONE

The run-up

When I was a youth my parents would tell the story of the night when my Aunt Margaret (Cole) sneezed the lights out. It must have been a winter evening in the later 1920s, when I was around six or seven years old. We lived in a small semi-detached house on the North London suburb of Hendon (4 Elm Close), and my parents were entertaining guests, including Aunt Margaret, in the front room (which doubled as my father's study). Animated and probably political conversation was abruptly silenced when Aunt Margaret inadvertently emitted a very loud sneeze, at which all the lights in the house went out. Torches were found, candles were lit, and as calm returned a small boy was disclosed whimpering in the adjacent dining-and-play room where he had been left to amuse himself before bedtime. It was me. It transpired that, having recently learned something of the binary nature of electricity, I had wound a short length of copper wire around an ordinary torch bulb and inserted the two ends into the two holes of a live mains outlet in the wainscoting, expecting the bulb to light up. The consequent blinding blue flash and *phutt* sound, followed by total darkness, had dismayed me and induced tears - but done me no other harm. I believe I had caused a subsidiary fuse to blow, for it was soon mended; my parents were so surprised that I do not recall being punished, only admonished.

The coincidence of the timing of my experiment with Aunt Margaret's sneeze was just one of those absurd improbabilities that make trivial events memorable. But in retrospect it all shows that I already had within me the makings of an experimental scientist. Nevertheless, for the first dozen years of my life it did not enter my head that I might one day study science at a university. Universities were remote and expensive places populated by undergraduates; wealthy young men who wore top hats or blazers and who held annual boat races and amusingly riotous dinners involving duckings and champagne, events which were diligently recorded in the columns of the evening papers. I was vaguely aware that my father had been at Oxford University, but I knew little about it (I later learned that he had been sent down during the First World War for reasons arising from his conscientious objections to military service). As far as I was concerned, neither of my parents nor any of my teachers conveyed to me any suggestion that I might seek a university education - my parents were short of money, of which quite a lot would be needed, and not since its foundation had anyone from my secondary school, Kingsbury County (just outside the North West boundary of London), gone on to higher education. So I was untroubled by such considerations and, although a bright boy, I was neither academic nor hardworking. I was also uninterested in any form of organised sport, so I spent much of my boyhood following up my boyish interests, which happened to be my pet animals and my chemistry set.

I would happily write of my pet animals, whom I knew and loved almost personally. They included an itinerant population of tiddlers, sticklebacks, newts, tadpoles and water beetles, culled from two productive ponds in the grounds of a local sewage works. These, I regret to have to say, did not survive well, but I learned a lot about pond life: the hideous 'nymphs' of dragonflies, water fleas, the strange zig-zagging larvae of mosquitoes, nasty leeches which (we feared wrongly) sucked one's blood, baby newts with feathery gills, water boatmen and so on. More serious were goldfish (in a sink in the garden); the family cat (which soon learned to fish for my goldfish, thus arresting any tendency on my part towards ichthyology); a multiplicity (I choose my word) of rabbits; some guinea pigs; tame white mice (whose cage, however, was secretly invaded by lecherous males of the wild variety, so that they unexpectedly produced offspring which were neither tame nor white); tame white rats (happily un-invaded); grass snakes, tree frogs and slow worms in a so-called vivarium (these escaped rather easily and inspired terror in the next-door neighbours); green, striped and sandy lizards, similarly housed; free-range tortoises, none of whom survived for long. Missing from my menagerie were birds (I objected to caging) and a dog (my father hated them). As I said, I knew and loved each one of them and it says much for the tolerant outlook of my parents that I was permitted these friends.

Indeed, by the standards of the British in the 21st century, my parents were remarkably relaxed about most aspects of daily life. My mother smoked cigarettes and had done so even before I was born; they both drank alcohol - my father liked wine and my mother liked gin - and we had no lock on the medicine cupboard. I recall at about the age of five I got a taste for syrup of figs, a widely-used mild purgative for constipated children; finding the bottle casually left on a bedroom mantelpiece, I drank the lot. The drastic consequences caused amusement more then reproach.

In my later sub-teens I lived on my bicycle, riding with circus-like competence (no hands, jumping kerbs and so on), without helmet or kneepads, mending my own punctures and putting back the chain after minor accidents. The brakes were highly inefficient, since replacement brake-blocks made serious inroads on my few pence of pocket money, so the soles of my shoes acted as (unreliable) brakes. I bumped, abraded and cut myself - around the age of nine a piece of gravel lodged beneath the skin of my knee for a couple of years before emerging spontaneously. My friends and I could be out all day, and ate anything, stale or fresh, sharing bottles of Tizer (a sweet fizzy drink), licks of ice cream or chips (if anyone was rich enough to buy two pennyworth). For a change of scene we would buy half-return tickets to the next station on the local underground (Edgware, Highgate and Morden Line, now London's Northern Line) and take tube trips back and forth along the local network - until recognised and chased off by a local official. We did what we fancied, and got wet, muddy, tired or exhilarated; we just had to be sure to get home before dark, preferably uninjured. And no one locked their doors (this was in the North London suburb of Hendon in the 1920s), so we usually walked in and out of friends' houses as we chose. Even at eight years old my parents, or our housekeeper, would send me to the local shops for this or that, and I would walk alone on Saturday mornings to the children's cinema show (Buster Keaton, Charlie Chaplin, Felix the Cat etc), and cycle alone to school on weekdays. We had no car; had we had one, there would have been no seat belts.

The Hendon scene in general was rich with interest to a child of lively curiosity. Up a series of back-alleys towards the North, then across the main road past St Mary's church, was the brow of a hill overlooking Hendon Aerodrome. There one could sit on the grass and watch the coming and going of RAF biplanes – they all had two wings in those days – and with enormous luck an airship might come over. Well, only twice, actually; both the R100 and R101 floated past, but I do not think either called in at the airport. However, one never knew.

Then in the opposite direction, at Golders Green, reached by open-top omnibus, clanky trams, they of the reversible wooden seats, became replaced by strangely silent, enclosed trolley buses. At home we had a domestic ice box in which to store perishable foods, recharged weekly by the fish man humping in a huge block of ice from his cart where it and its brethren kept the fish cool and fresh. He wore a leather sheet on his back and gripped the ice on it with a huge pair of metal callipers, backing up to the thick-walled box. A tough and chilly job. Great was my excitement when his services became redundant and we acquired the oh-so-modern Frigidaire, which mysteriously used electricity to generate coolth (the obvious opposite of warmth). And gradually the actual townscape changed: muddy roads became tarmacked streets, lined by rows of three-up, two-down houses very like ours, which spread into adjacent farmland; along the main road appeared a rash of 'Belisha beacons', orange-globed poles echoing zebra stripes painted across the road; carts pulled by huge furry-hooved horses became a rarity, displaced by the 'mechanical horse' and pantechnicon. Even the townscape's all-pervading smell of horse manure changed.

How I relished the white heat of technology, both fascinating and useful! Often explained by those invaluable sources of general knowledge, cigarette cards, which my chums and I collected and swapped. Before the age of 11 I attended Woodstock, an inexpensive private school in Golders Green; my parents found the fees somehow because the nearest council school was rather rough. In this I was fortunate, because the school, though very English in character, was truly multinational; my fellow scholars included Japanese, Indian, Dutch, German, English (Jewish, Christian and one budding atheist), so I grew up with no colour prejudice. Indeed, my best friend was Indian and the runners up, so to speak, were Japanese and Dutch. Knee-jerk anti-Semitism was the norm in 1920s Britain, more prevalent among the teachers than the pupils, and I became mildly infected by it. Happily my parents soon disinfected me.

But I must not digress into details of my childhood. For one thing, my brother Oliver has documented much of our childhood experiences in his autobiography, which I cited in my foreword. My message here is that my parents were remarkably trusting and tolerant, allowing me free rein; tolerant, too, of my amateur chemistry.

In 1933, when I was about eleven, we moved from Hendon to a large Victorian house in Finchley. In the same year I passed my 11-plus examination and transferred to Kingsbury County School, some seven miles away but readily accessible by bus or bicycle. Woodstock School proved to have been a bit of a crammer (I had taken that in my stride), and I had done two years' Latin, two years' French and a brief course of physics, whereas my fellow Kingsburians had done none. This, regrettably, was a recipe for laziness in class. I had also pursued my hobby of chemistry, in a shed at the side of our new house, so I was dead bored when my teacher spent the whole of my first term's chemistry chuntering on abut washing soda – sodium carbonate. However, I found a like-minded friend whose name was Winks. Unlike all the rest of my schoolfellows, he had no nickname and I do not recall anyone using his forename, whatever it might have been. (There was, probably still is, an unspoken consensus whereby children revise their fellows' given names, but our peers must have considered that Winks' surname, unaltered, was superior to any nickname they might invent.) Winks was a mild, bespectacled boy, a budding stereotype of an academic, and

I hope he went far in life. In his company, and sometimes with another pyromaniacal friend Wiggle (actually Cyril Weighell), and on my own, I made some fairly dangerous fireworks and some fairly revolting gases, burned off an eyebrow and suffered acid and alkali burns. Once in Winks' home, while his parents were out, we attempted to make nitro-glycerine. We used the correct textbook synthesis, albeit in odd equipment (an old teacup) and obtained the oily product expected. However, it failed its major test: we tried to set it off by touching it with a hot coal wired to a long rod, but instead of exploding for us it merely decomposed with a great hiss and masses of brown smoke (nitrogen dioxide). We were disappointed; I now know that we were incredibly lucky, because we had actually made about 5 ml of nitro-glycerine - a dessertspoon full - which was sufficient to blow up ourselves and the kitchen had we detonated it successfully. I can add that we bought the necessary chemical ingredients without difficulty from the local pharmacist for a few pennies; today a couple of schoolboys could not buy them at all. I think that was our most dangerous enterprise; despite our enthusiastic ignorance, not I, nor Winks, nor our families, nor any visiting tradesmen, suffered permanent damage.

I also developed an interest in radio, constructing first a crystal set and later a primitive valve receiver; these played an important part in my cultural life, as I shall record in due time. In addition, undiscouraged by my early experiment, I graduated to manipulating the electrical supply of our house to provide, for example, extra power outlets, and a fitted light over the mirror of my mother's dressing table. I think my parents' tolerance of my activities stemmed from a sublime ignorance of their technological bases, because these were in fact highly unsafe lash-ups. But no disasters ensued. (Unlike the time when my brother Oliver modified the electric bell to make it audible throughout our rather large house. It worked well until the system got damp, then it electrocuted the postman, because Oliver had put the mains current through the bell push. Happily the postman recovered quickly after administration of hot sweet tea, and the system was demounted after a threat by the Post Office to cease deliveries.)

The reader will perceive that, albeit uncanalised, I was confirming my earlier hint of a bent towards either a science or technology. Unfortunately, I pursued these hobbies at the expense of my more formal studies; I found it easy to improvise, so I skipped lessons when possible, ducked such homework as I could and generally behaved like an average uninterested schoolboy, a frustrating nuisance to my teachers but a cunning one, because I could usually come up with an excuse or misleading response. I rather enjoyed pitting my wits against pedagogical authority; for example, I had worked out an ingenious way, using an undated letter from my doctor, of avoiding gym and sports. This was so effective that, after a while, the appropriate masters had, I believe, forgotten about me. I also ceased attending music classes quite early on - the school buildings were large and rambling enough for a pupil, even a tall, conspicuous one, to disappear for an hour or so fairly easily: into a laboratory preparation room, into a store room or out to the cycle sheds for example. I regret to say that I introduced certain schoolfellows to strong drink, in the form of cider and (most luxurious) Spanish vermouth. And gambling: I ran illicit draws among them on certain notable horse races, the Derby and the Lincoln, keeping a small profit for myself and a friend, who was my runner. Illegally, I skipped school lunches and spent my 'dinner money' on such junk food of the day as was available in Kingsbury's shopping area: saveloys, jellied eels and all sorts of the cheapest tooth-destroying confectionery. But this happy nonconformity could not go on forever; the crunch came when I failed to reach 'matriculation' standard in my School Certificate exams.

This statement probably requires explanation. In the 1930s, all schoolchildren in the maintained or 'State' schools were examined around the age of 11, in transition from primary to secondary education, and allocated to schools according to their academic achievement. A few years later they would again be examined, at 15 or16, to obtain the 'General Schools Certificate' (GSC) - like the more recent 'O-level' - to certify that they had been educated to a reasonable standard. If they did well, they would also have qualified for 'matriculation', which meant that they had overcome the first hurdle towards a university education. Few took the achievement in that sense; for most it was a pass to a better-paid job because 'matric' was one up on a plain GSC, widely called 'school cert'.

I muffed matric, largely because of poor English papers. However, my teachers and my parents - and indeed I - thought that I should ignore this setback and should go on to the next stage, the so called 'Higher Schools Certificate' examination (corresponding to the more recent 'A-level') because, if I obtained my HSC, I'd score matriculation without having to re-sit my GSC. So, after a homily from Mr A G Tracey, my Headmaster, on the need for hard and sustained schoolwork, this was agreed. In keeping with my scientific tendencies, I chose to concentrate on Chemistry, Physics, Botany and Zoology.

I wish I could write that Mr Tracey's homily had the required effect, but I shall never know, for this was 1939 and the Second World War intervened. Between the end of my school certificate year and the start of the next, Britain reluctantly declared war on Nazi Germany and most schools were plunged into the chaos of evacuation. Those in or near places likely to be bombed were closed and their pupils were sent into the countryside, to be billeted on local families and to attend local schools. Kingsbury was not, in fact, in an evacuation area, but my parents chose to evacuate me, and together with Oliver, who attended a grammar school at Woodside Park, North Finchley, to Totnes, Devon, where a family friend, one Kath Starr, was willing to house us, and where a school was willing to accept us. The School was part of an *avant-garde* community at Dartington Hall, the brainchild of Mr and Mrs Leonard Elmhirst, and it boasted all sorts of artistic/cultural enterprises (weaving, glass working, progressive farming, music, painting, ballet; it is still a flourishing concern today). But the famous - notorious to some - progressive school to which we went has not survived.

Although many unexpected events, some admirable,

some absurd, formed part of my abrupt transfer from North London to Devon, I must eschew side issues and stick rigorously to my theme. Dartington Hall School, Headmaster a famous educationalist W B Curry, prided itself on its lack of rules so, after a few weeks testing and teasing the staff, eliciting no response, I sobered down and started to do real work. I formed reasonably friendly relationships with the biology and chemistry masters who were, respectively, David Lack, expert on the biology of robins, and Boris Uvarov, who compiled a dictionary of scientific terms. I rejoiced, too, in the freewheeling cultural environment of Dartington Hall itself. But an academic problem loomed: my choice of HSC subjects was too specialised for the school. Wheels were therefore set in motion and after a few months I transferred, rather reluctantly, to Hele's School, Exeter, and was housed by my uncle Richmond Postgate who was living and working as an Education officer in that City.

My reluctance proved to be well founded. Hele's was a long-established all-boys school (all my schools had hitherto been co-educational), which modelled itself on the public school it would have liked to be. It had even adopted the Harrow School song as its own. It was a dark and forbidding edifice located up a hill from Exeter St David's railway station (the building has since become part of Exeter University and the school itself seems to have been absorbed into the local comprehensive system). Discipline was strict and schoolwork had absolute priority. Emphasis was on success in examinations. The school uniform, a dark suit, was *de rigeur*. I made a number of innocent mistakes at first, but my association with Dartington, plus wartime exigencies, combined to protect me from severe retribution. For example, I was wholly unaware of the sensation I caused by turning up on my first day wearing brown corduroy trousers, a green shirt and a bright yellow tie - I was a somewhat fancy dresser at that age. I got away with similar garb for a few weeks, until a message of reproach was sent to my uncle. A scratchy suit was duly obtained for me from the Fifty Shilling Tailors, an economical source of such garments for growing adolescents. I think the school had some difficulty in working out how to cope with me, a relatively senior eccentric youth from London via Dartington, but, with guidance and some admonishment from the Headmaster, Mr. A E Nichols, Hele's School and I settled down together and I more or less conformed.

For me, the valuable feature of this establishment was that, for the first time in several years, I was not automatically the bright boy of the class. I was surrounded by pupils who worked really hard and many of them knew more about my subjects than I did. They even discussed topics from their lessons outside school hours - which would have been regarded as unthinkable by my erstwhile Kingsburians (though not, actually, by the Dartingtonians). This, combined with some science teachers who were very good indeed, undermined my leisurely attitude to schoolwork and, for the first time in several years, I started to work hard myself.

Kingsbury County School regarded itself as forward-looking, with an easy-going attitude to school rules, discipline, comparative grading and even curricula, within the constraints of the national examination system. Under Curry, Dartington Hall was earnestly progressive: the school was a medium for self-expression, rules were anathema, education was a co-operative and non-competitive process etc. My brother Oliver, who was also a bright boy but who had been getting pretty bad reports from his grammar school in Finchley, flourished, blossomed indeed, in all sorts of creative ways at Dartington. I had reacted to the freedoms of Kingsbury and Dartington by skiving: I did the unavoidable minimum of work unless it happened to interest me. It took the traditional discipline and competitive outlook of Hele's to turn me round, and I owe that school a great deal for doing this relatively painlessly. Important Message: there is no universal formula for educating children.

I passed my HSC with credit but no great distinction. Yet my mentors reported that I was university material. The long-suffering uncle with whom I lived had received his call-up papers summoning him into the RAF, so I could no longer remain in Exeter. Duly I returned to my parents' home in London, and re-joined Kingsbury County, now as a 'scholarship' pupil (their first ever). Absurdly, considering the motives that had sent me to Devon in the first place, I arrived back neatly in time for the Nazi blitzkrieg on London and other cities.

Again I must discipline myself, for a schoolboy's view of wartime London would be a distraction from my major theme. The truth is that, being young, I rather enjoyed the day-today existence. I was physically undamaged, though sometimes scared; our house and my family survived with nothing worse than broken windows, when a small bomb landed a few houses down the road from us. Most of the family, now augmented by two aunts (Oliver was still in Devon) slept in a shored-up cellar on improvised beds, with the domestic cat, which was fun. I commuted to school on a bicycle, ready to dive into a ditch if I heard the very recognisable sound of a German aircraft overhead; I joined in stints of fire watching at school, which allowed us free range of the gymnasium and its apparatus, on which we devised elaborate clambering games. Like most other Londoners I was adequately but far from abundantly fed, though we all developed a tendency to drool at the sight of meat. I was perhaps more than usually politically aware, and I abhorred in principle the very idea of murderous conflict; I also hated the often threatening and sometimes catastrophic wartime news - which I nevertheless followed avidly. But there was nothing to be done about it; we all adjusted to the threatening circumstances and I, protected by still being young, resilient, and relatively carefree, found happiness breaking through the gloom rather often.

At Kingsbury there was no one accustomed to teaching at the level I needed, but I had acquired my own academic momentum and, given freedom of the labs and what amounted to occasional tutorials, I worked. I pored over curricula and old scholarship exam papers from Oxford, Cambridge and London Universities, I practised answers, I looked things up as often as I discussed them with my teachers; I became almost a professional examinee; I certainly lost all fear of examinations. I duly sat scholarship exams for all three - the London one took place in the Prefects' room at Kingsbury, the others at Cambridge, then Oxford. I failed two but, miracle of miracles, I obtained a minor Exhibition (a kind of junior scholarship) at Balliol College, Oxford.

Swing – a new passion

Here I must introduce a musical obsession which has brought continued but largely welcome complication into my life, providing a sort of counterpoint to my scientific career. My immediate family was not musical; my father knew the usual two tunes, with the difference that, because he was a staunch socialist, the first was *The Internationale*, not the National Anthem, and the other was all the rest. My mother, however, had a true voice. She had a repertoire of dismal Victorian songs ("Don't sell no more drink to my father, it makes him so rough and so wild..."; "If you knew those tiny fingers, beating on the window pane, would be cold an' dead tomorrow...") with which she would regale her very young offspring (my brother and me) after Sunday lunch, often reducing us to tears. But she had a musical problem: she did not distinguish the melody from its first harmony and as often as not sang the latter. Thus I, and no doubt my brother, acquired a rather approximate sense of melody. This did little to help my own musical background and when, at quite a young age in my preparatory school, I was ejected from the choir because its mistress discovered where the strange buzzing noise was coming from (I was singing merrily, with abandon, indeed), any interest I might have in school music began to wane.

There were other deterrents, too. A later music mistress was a ferocious lady with wild, dark eyes, given to thrusting a severe face at one. "That's a bre-e-e-eve," she would intone, as a breath scented lightly with Phul-na-na cachous swept over her cringing pupil.

And we would feel right silly when, ostensibly to inculcate a sense of rhythm, she would cause us to stand up and recite: "Tafatefi, tafatefi tafatefi...."

And comparable cries, the inwardness of which escaped me and most if not all of my schoolfellows. Do they still inflict the 'tafatefi' on budding musical intelligences, I wonder?

I came to hate all forms of school music except some of the hymns we had to sing at morning assembly, and these I pretended to dislike, because to me religion was sissy - and illogical. However, it seems that some musical bent within me had to find an outlet and I came to love the dance music broadcast every afternoon at 5.15 by London National radio in the 1930s; I would rush home from school lest I be too late to turn on our 'wireless' in time. I became quite expert on the relative merits of bands led by Jack Hylton, Jack Payne and Henry Hall (I list them in the order of merit assigned by the school *cognoscenti*); later I learned that there were other bands broadcasting at night, which I was not allowed to stay up for. But I, crafty, had made myself the crystal set of which I wrote earlier, wherewith, aided by an earphone under my pillow, I made the acquaintance of 'hotter' bands, led by Roy Fox, Harry Roy, Lew Stone or Ambrose, for example. But though I knew the words and tunes of a lot of popular songs of the day, and could even gasp out an approximation to some on a mouth organ, I was still almost non-musical. Like today's pop fan, I was aware only of the words and the beat. Melody, harmony and rhythm passed almost unnoticed.

Sophistication began to dawn in the later 1930s when older friends introduced me to a new musical craze which was sweeping the USA: swing. I at once embraced it, for the entirely adequate reason that both my parents and my school objected to it. In retrospect I realise that it was the novelties, not the swing, which I listened to: the funny singing and cryptic asides of Fats Waller, a swing version of *Loch Lomond* by Maxine Sullivan, a hot rendering of *Three Blind Mice* by the Milt Herth Trio. However, at some time I came by a record of *Bugle Call Rag* by Benny Goodman's Orchestra, the leading swing band of the period, and I still remember the morning when I played it, not for the first time, and realised that the squeaky instrument (which I did not then recognise as a clarinet) was playing something quite special; something much more complicated then the simple melody which I well understood, yet something which made me want to jig around and which cried out to be played again. That morning, aged about 15, I crossed some sort of aesthetic threshold. I played the record again and again, sometimes just Goodman's solo, until my mother cried out at me to stop. That morning I became addicted to the music we now call jazz. I have happily never recovered.

(By a marvellous coincidence, years later, one of the very few notes I have ever written for the covers of jazz record issues was for an RCA Extended Play reissue of Benny Goodman tracks which included *Bugle Call Rag*.)

Exiguous though my pocket money was, and short as were the supplies of swing records in wartime, I saved up, scrounged, and amassed six or eight such records of my own - heavy, wax 78 rpm records by the bands of such as Duke Ellington, Count Basie, Muggsy Spanier and Artie Shaw. Shaw was the chief rival swing clarinettist to Benny Goodman. But I could not remain just a listener for long. Soon I developed an ambition to play my own swing. My mouth organ I regarded as inappropriate and anyway, my idols had become clarinet players; what I now yearned for was a clarinet to learn to play.

Clarinets, even second hand ones, were right out of my financial reach, even had my parents been sympathetic, which they were not. However, a wealthy friend of my parents, perhaps thinking to inspire me to musical expression, had given me a cheap but real piano accordion as a Christmas present a few years earlier. I had progressed with it hardly at all. (Oddly, it features in a portrait painted by the Australian-Bloomsbury artist Stella Bowen, a family friend, and was used as an illustration, with me aged about 13 pretending to play it, in her fascinating autobiography *Drawn From Life*, Virago Press ed. 1984). In a local second-hand shop there were no clarinets, but there was an ancient cornet, lacking springs to operate the valves (wherewith, for the uninitiated, one changes the note being played) but otherwise seemingly intact. Negotiations took place, and I traded in my accordion for it. Thus did I become, in 1941 and aged 19, the proprietor of what was probably the last remaining Bell's Acoustic Cornet, dated 1862 and having valves in a long-obsolete sideways-on position. Blackened with age, until I polished it lovingly to a shining, if pitted, silver; unplayable, until I incurred the fury of my mother by vandalising the springs of her vacuum cleaner to make new valve springs; exhausting to blow, for I never had any tuition in how to blow such an instrument. It wasn't a clarinet, but I came to love it, and we struggled through many years together.

Preparing for Oxford

The particular Exhibition which I had been awarded appeared at the end of Balliol's published list of available awards as "Possibly one Williams Exhibition". It was a source of great pride to me, to my family and to Kingsbury County School. Only after I had been an undergraduate for several terms did I learn that the authorities reserved this particular award for the occasional oddball: for candidates who were not up to much in their exams but who showed signs of academic potential. I was still proud.

There were two more hurdles to leap. In those days one had to pass an examination in Latin, called Responsions, to be admitted to Oxford University. With the aid of a tolerant, almost spherical Latin mistress called Miss Baker I brushed up enough Latin to get through, despite her absent-minded but distracting mannerism, while talking, of dangling her silk handkerchief up and down in the rather noticeable cleavage of her bosom. I also needed quite a lot more money than the £40 p.a. of the Williams Exhibition. Middlesex County made me an award of £30 p.a. plus fees; my grandmother covenanted £15 to me which, since I paid no tax, was brought up to £30 by the Inland Revenue; a different uncle rallied round with an allowance; my parents, although impoverished, scavenged, and thus I amassed the (to me) amazing sum of £200 p.a., the amount recommended by Balliol as the minimum needed for materials and living expenses.

By July of 1941, all I needed to do was to survive the war until October, since I was still under age for military service from which, anyway, my science scholarship would have exempted me. I registered at the local employment exchange in case war work (preferably paid) of a temporary character appeared. None did, so I hung about with school friends, holidayed with my parents and survived. Oh yes, I also took another exam - a qualifying exam for an honours degree in science at Oxford. I hardly noticed it; I passed.

CHAPTER TWO

Balliol

I arrived at Balliol with a trunk, a black Wedgwood teapot, a bottle of crusted old port given to me by my father, a new set of dissecting instruments and some other paraphernalia appropriate to a freshman embarking upon a science degree. It was October of 1941. The miasmal damp which settles upon Oxford for two thirds of the year was already there, but it was warm, the sun shone and the colours of the trees and quadrangles and the soft sandstone of the syphilitic-looking heads enclosing the Bodleian were beautiful; even the blackened Victorian gothic of Balliol College, so reminiscent of London's St Pancras Station, was an enchantment. I was starry-eyed, and it mattered nothing that my room was damp and icy, with no washing facilities and remote from lavatories. I was utterly, indescribably delighted to be there at all.

It is difficult now to convey the glamour of simply being an undergraduate, and the popularity among the lay public those fortunates then enjoyed. The ugly student image of the late 1960s and after, militancy, intolerance, drugs, low academic standards, even crèches and mixed colleges, were not part of our imaginings; our excesses were occasional drunkenness, the late-night grope with an acquiescent undergraduette (an expression culled from the *Daily Mirror*) which (very rarely) led to a most unwelcome pregnancy, or staying out after hours; or (for the very daring, with the aid of conspirators) staying out of college overnight. We accepted that we were there primarily to learn, be we Marxists, conservatives, atheists, evangelists, libertines, socialites or just plain idle.

Not that we were short of distractions from our academic work. I arrived for the last couple of terms of an Oxford which was to vanish with the war, never to return. But in the autumn of 1941 the war was only beginning to affect Oxford life: a few dons had disappeared into the Forces or into secret work of national importance; the selection of meats for lunch was limited; port was only available on Sundays. But it was still a marvellous world of theatre, political clubs and debates, the Rhythm Club, punting, parties with lovely young ladies (and some strangely ambiguous young men), afternoon tea on the lawn (anchovy toast, China tea, scones and jam); College beer from pewter tankards in the sunset before dinner; talk, talk and more talk, far into the night. I took to the life exultantly. I made myself rather ill, but did not mind - it gave me a Byronic, hollow-eyed appearance.

But, and it is a crucial but, I got on with the science. It was with some surprise that, during the first week of term, I found myself in the Honours School of Chemistry, reading for a degree in that subject. This was odd because, though I had taken scholarship papers in chemistry as well as zoology, it was zoology that I had intended to study and to that end I had spent precious funds on a lovely new set of dissecting instruments. I raised the matter with my tutor; the conversation went something like this:

"When shall I get to do some zoology, sir?" (I had not yet gained confidence enough to use my Tutor's given name).

"Oh" - pause- "Yes, they said your zoology paper was your best. But your chemistry was rather weak. You had better brush that up."

Unfamiliar with the Oxford system, I agreed. Eighteen months later, I asked the same question again.

"Oh, certainly. You can attend some zoology lectures if you like - and courses if they'll fit in. Now, about the Debye-Hückel Theory..."

By then the chemistry schedule was so intense there was no hope. I gave in and became a chemist - though later I did take some optional biochemistry to keep up a biological lifeline.

My new dissecting instruments, you ask? They did some good: I sold them at a hungry time after my first degree, when my Exhibition and grant money had run out. They provided me with several plain but nourishing meals.

And how about my crusted old port? My father's gift had been badly shaken on its journey to Oxford and now had disagreeable flaky things like tea leaves floating in it when poured out. (Experts know these as 'beeswing'; they are flakes of the 'crust' that forms within an aged bottle of good port.) However, man's ingenuity triumphed: filtered through a clean handkerchief into a tooth glass (a slow process) and dispensed from there, it was quite delicious and impressed my new friends mightily.

The tutor who had thus eased me effortlessly into becoming a chemist, for which I am now extremely grateful, was Ronald P. Bell, known to all as Ronnie. Already a distinguished physical chemist, his special expertise was in homogeneous catalysis.

What's that? I shall try to explain.

When you mix two chemicals, as it might be two gases or two solutions, sometimes they interact and form new chemicals, sometimes they don't. If they do interact, 'react' in the jargon, they might do so very quickly or very slowly. When they react slowly, you often find that a tiny amount of a third, perhaps quite different, chemical makes the reaction go much faster. That third chemical is called a catalyst. (The word catalyst has now of course entered vernacular English in all sorts of contexts.) If the catalyst is in the same physical state as the other chemicals - if it is a gas catalysing the reaction of a couple of other gases, or a solution catalysing reaction between two other solutions - then the process is called homogeneous catalysis. If it is in a different state - a platinum wire is a catalyst for several reactions between gases - the process is called heterogeneous catalysis.

Ronnie had done much of his earlier research in Denmark, and had by then become a leading world authority on how the first class of catalytic reactions took place: on the detailed way in which the reacting and the catalytic molecules interacted with each other.

It was an austere specialism. But Ronnie was an austere

scientist. He was of small build, almost gnomish in appearance, with an almost paralysing shyness of manner - until he had actually embarked upon a scientific discourse. He certainly imbued his pupils with comparable austerity right from the start. Wartime exigencies had led to the doubling up of tutorials, by which I mean that each weekly session with one's tutor was shared with another undergraduate of the same year; a staff to student ratio of 2:1 instead of the pre-war 1:1. Not much of a hardship compared to modern teaching ratios! So I shared tutorials with one Christopher Longuet-Higgins, a scholarship undergraduate from Winchester College (about whom more later), and our first assignment was to read and study two long and immensely tedious papers, published about the turn of the century, concerned with measuring the weight of a hydrogen atom relative to an oxygen atom. This measurement was in fact an immense task in its day, requiring the most meticulous cleanliness of equipment, scrupulously careful weighings of highly purified silver, painfully exact measurings of gas volumes, all to discover a number which was, by 1941, taken for granted by even the most elementary text; a number, moreover, which could be measured with greater accuracy by newer methods then unknown to those early scientists. The only light relief was an episode, solemnly reported in one of the scientific papers, wherein an operative put his foot through the apparatus and ruined weeks of work.

For a person of my impatience, this was the dullest imaginable introduction to the Honour School of Chemistry. We used up the best part of two sessions on this stuff. I now realise that Ronnie's intention was to impress on us from the beginning the need for meticulous accuracy and perfection of experimental design in science. He certainly did that.

Then, suddenly, I was plunged in at the deep end: we got cracking on thermodynamics (a topic of which I had never previously heard), quantum theory (of which I had read popular accounts but gained no inkling of its mathematical difficulty), and the theory of solutions, of the two kinds of catalysis. These are part of the hard core of chemistry, and jolly heavy stuff to boot; I shall not attempt to explain them. I floundered but, rescued quite often by Christopher, I kept my head just above water.

I remember late in my first term writing a rather hurt letter to Mr Tracey (who had taught me mathematics as well as being my Headmaster at Kingsbury) reproaching him obliquely for letting me go up to Oxford without having heard of a partial differential function (an aspect of the calculus much used in thermodynamics), nor of the Laplacian operator (an elegant but subtle function used in wave mechanics). He was much amused.

Ronnie's shyness outside the lecture room and tutorial was reflected by his almost total lack of small talk. One never had idle chats about arts, literature, politics, music and so on - perhaps an occasional comment on the weather or the war before getting down to chemistry, but that was all. However, he took certain aspects of his relations with the undergraduates seriously. It was his custom to invite small groups of his pupils to tea once a year, at his home in St. Cross Road. This was a ceremony much feared by experienced chemistry undergraduates, for there they would discover that Mrs Bell, likewise, had very little small talk. So, once the weather and one or two parochial matters had been disposed of, there tended to be long, uncomfortable silences. On one such occasion I had a bright idea.

"I heard a jolly funny story the other day," I said.

Everyone brightened up and I embarked on it.

I no longer recall the actual story. What I do recall, still with a nasty quiver inside, was my traumatic realisation, some way into the story, that its *dénouement* was highly obscene, quite unsuitable for the occasion in this far from permissive era. In my anxiety about the flagging sociability I had momentarily forgotten this detail.

I did the only thing possible; I pressed on but invented a new ending, an ending of such awe-inspiring banality that it did not raise a flicker of even polite mirth from anyone. Thus ended any thought I might have had of being the life and soul of parties - I was no social catalyst.

Actually, in other circumstances, Ronnie might have enjoyed the story. For another of his half-dutiful sociabilities was to accept, when offered it, an invitation to a periodic party held by the Junior Common Room of Balliol, called the 'JCR Smoker'. This was a fascinating tradition, a part of a now-vanishing culture exclusive to the Anglo-Saxon male, one which the admission of women undergraduates to the college in the 1970s must have altered drastically, probably abolished. It was a masculine party with lashings of beer and, for the many who in those days wanted it, tobacco. Indecent stories would be told, obscene recitations spoken, lewd chants and songs sung. The songs, recitations and stories were highly traditional - material of similar character was later collected and published during the permissive 60s and 70s as 'Rugby Songs', 'Raunchy Stories' and so on. Balliol had its own special repertoire of 'Balliol Rhymes' which have also been collected and published, I believe.

The proceedings were often witty or surrealistic and always hilarious. The Dean and a few of the more friendly of the dons would generally be invited along and would enjoy and encourage it for its traditional continuity and as a means of dispersing some of the mischievous energies of youth. At JCR Smokers everyone had a great time. Many made themselves sick - a macho measure of the party's success - and Ronnie would be seen to be enjoying the merriment hugely - "grinning like a copulating dog", in the words of one of his pupils (later a Professor of Chemistry at Hull, W. E. (Gus) Higginson).

Ronnie was too shy to be aggressive or dominating; he was austere for most of the time but totally without pomposity. He could become 'one of the boys' on occasion, yet he was a superb and intensely critical scientist, concerned with inspiring the ability to learn rather than with teaching *per se*. The ideal tutor; in fact, I think only one of the dozen or so pupils who joined him during the three years 1940 to 1943 did not later become a professor or achieve comparable distinction. That is a tremendous record, even for Balliol. His election to a Fellowship of the Royal Society, the highest British distinction a scientist's research can earn, in 1944 made rather less impact on me than it deserved because I had become acutely aware that my finals examinations were imminent that summer. In later years Ronnie would have liked to become Master of Balliol, but, although he was a strong candidate, another was appointed when the opportunity arose in 1964. It must have been disheartening – I am told he had turned down an Oxford Professorship in order to remain a candidate for the Mastership. After a couple of years he accepted a Chair of Physical Chemistry at the University of Stirling in Scotland and remained there, even after retiring in 1975. He died in 1996. Only then did I learn that, throughout the time that he had been tutoring me and Christopher, he had also been an important figure in wartime scientific intelligence, periodically called upon by the military to question scientists who escaped from Scandinavia about the civil and military situations in their countries.

Freddie King

The Oxford system was, perhaps still is, firmly based in the College tutorial system. In terms of economic use of teaching talent, this was an amazingly expensive way of educating people, but one which was highly effective. The University laid on lectures, and practical classes if appropriate, in a myriad of subjects. But one's education was primarily the responsibility of one's tutor, who would guide one's reading, prescribe and criticise one's essays (every Balliol chemist was required to produce two essays a week), ensure that one attended the practical courses and advise one on what lectures to attend. But there was no formal obligation to attend practical classes and lectures; at least one chemist (from Trinity College) went through his three years without ever attending a lecture, and he obtained a first class degree. But he was quite exceptional; in fact not even the most recalcitrant chemistry undergraduate doubted that practical courses were absolutely essential, and there was strong moral pressure on us to make use of the University's lectures. Ronnie, for example, would question us on them occasionally.

In a wide-ranging subject such as chemistry, it was not unusual for a college to provide a second tutor who specialised in a different subject area and in our case Balliol provided its chemists with F.E. (Freddie) King, whose job was to teach us organic chemistry, in contrast to Ronnie's physical chemistry.

(By universal consent, the third major branch of chemistry, called inorganic chemistry, was left to take care of itself, by way of a two-year marathon set of lectures, two a week, given by a very famous, by then rather ancient, chemist, N.V. Sidgwick.)

Freddie resembled Ronnie only in being rather shy and not given to small talk. He was of moderate height, rather handsome with somewhat square, well-formed features and resembled a minor film actor just becoming known called Ronald Reagan, although Freddie's build was stockier. His chemistry formed an unnerving contrast to Ronnie's. Organic chemistry, I should explain, is a study of the chemistry of compounds constituting, or more often derived from, living matter. It is the chemistry of the element carbon, which is a basic element of life itself (at least on planets such as ours), and there are literally millions of different carbon compounds known. In contrast, there might be a couple of million compounds of all the other 92-odd elements added together; their study is called inorganic chemistry, although many of them do combine with carbon and so form part of organic compounds. The border between organic and inorganic chemistry is fuzzy; let us set it aside and accept that there are so many millions of carbon compounds that they constitute a branch of chemistry of their own.

Ronnie's physical chemistry was logical, formal and mathematically precise, concerned with rates at which well-established reactions took place in various conditions, and the reasons why. Freddie's science was so far from logical that it was almost intuitive. Given a certain organic compound, how might one make another organic compound from it? What sequence of reactions might one follow in the laboratory? One would look at the structure of the starting compound, guess the sorts of reactions it might be persuaded to undergo, then guess the conditions in which they might take place. You may ask (if you have got this far), what possible basis might there be for such guesses? The answer is: previous experience. Over a century's chemistry had led to the build-up of a repertory of organic reactions, mostly named after their discoverers: the Grignard reaction, the Scraup synthesis, the Schotten-Baumen acylation, the Reformatsky reaction, Schiff's base formation and a hundred others. The aspirant organic chemists had to know what these reactions were and gain some sense of when they would work and when they would not. Freddie seemed to know by some sort of instinct, and this, in fact, was what he tried to instil into us. He did this by requiring us to do immensely time-consuming essays on how to perform carefully prescribed organic syntheses, usually choosing ones which we could not easily find in textbooks or even scientific journals, and then, in tutorials, explaining to us in painful but rarely clear detail why our suggestions were never quite right. I say never; actually, I got some right myself because I began to get some feeling for the subject. Christopher, who had an intensely precise and logical mind, very rarely did so - which, I may now admit, I found something of a relief because he was always a few jumps ahead of me in the more philosophically amenable physical chemistry taught by Ronnie.

Freddie's tutorials were, I am sorry to say, mostly hard slog over tedious detail and he talked with a dry, uninflected intonation, as if suppressing gloom over our lack of organic intuition. This did nothing to bring a spark of life to the subject. Yet I soaked up some sense of the subject and acquired passable expertise in this area - which proved to be an asset when I later chose to learn some biochemistry.

Outside tutorials, Freddie always seemed to be abrupt and in a hurry. Yet he was very kind and tolerant. One time during my first year I had overdone things and was put to bed by the college nurse with 'flu. (Actually, I had a bad cold augmented by a gargantuan hangover). Freddie called into my room, as I had had to miss a tutorial, and presented me with a bottle of orange squash - nectar in those times when wartime exigencies had caused oranges and their products to vanish from the shops. Freddie later went on to become a Fellow of the Royal Society and a Professor at the University of Nottingham, before moving into Industry to achieve great heights in the hierarchy of British Petroleum. He died in 1999.

Christopher Longuet-Higgins

I must tell more about my fellow tutee, Christopher Longuet-Higgins, since providence caused us to traverse the Honours School of Chemistry side-by-side, so to speak. He came of a clerical family, an ascetic young man with apparently two obsessions in life: mathematical science and classical music. He was polite, of sober habit, benevolently non-political, a Christian in a highly intellectualised way, an outstanding natural scientist with an enviable grasp of advanced mathematics, seemingly already familiar with the greater part of the first year chemistry and its mathematical basis, having read it for fun. Happily he was also blessed with a lively sense of humour and an enjoyment of the absurd, for otherwise I do not see how he could have tolerated the association with my nonconformist, atheistical, leftist, often ill-informed but none the less pompous, somewhat bumptious (ie: typical undergraduate) behaviour. But in fact we got on very well and were good friends outside our chemistry studies as well as within.

Christopher had a formidable intellect. Here is an illustration. The element boron (a component or borax, used in eyewash) ought to have a simple chemistry because its atoms have a valency of three. What this means is that they behave as if they have three hooks with which to stick to other atoms. (They do not have real hooks, of course; their ability to stick to other atoms and so form compounds is really a matter of sharing electrical charges, of which each boron atom has three available). Hydrogen, continuing the metaphor, has only one hook so, if a chemist makes a compound of boron and hydrogen - a boron hydride it would be called - it ought to have one boron atom to three hydrogen atoms. In fact, boron forms lots of hydrides, with two, three four and more boron atoms surrounded by hydrogen atoms, but perversely they all contain more than three hydrogen atoms per atom of boron. How can this be? The question had been bothering chemists for several years. In one of his essays, Christopher proposed, on theoretical grounds, a set of original structures for the boron hydrides, which no one else seemed to have thought of. They fitted in with a newly emerging concept of chemical bonding; he and Ronnie Bell did some appropriate calculations and they seemed plausible, so they published a joint paper. These structures are now universally accepted.

To tidy up the theoretical basis of an area of chemistry and produce an original paper while still a second-year undergraduate is quite an achievement but Christopher was very English and very modest about it. I would tell people about it rather proudly (since he had discussed it with me and perhaps interpreted my wise nods as understanding), so Christopher mocked me gently with a rhyme in the form of a clerihew, a form of comic doggerel, which was then cultishly popular:

"I thought I knew most

But Post

Gate knows more on

The hydrides of boron."

Despite his modesty, Christopher was not above a spot of lifemanship. His fascination with mathematics was shared by another good friend of mine, one Ivor Robinson (most inappropriately a medical student at the time). In those hungry days a queue of undergraduates would form on the steps of Balliol Hall before lunch, in which Ivor and Christopher would exchange a strange rubric:

"a2b4c4d3", one would say.

Pause.

"a3b4C3d4", the other would reply.

Pause

"a4b3C3d4".

Pause - and so on.

Then, occasionally, one would say, "Got you!"

And both would nod.

They claimed to be playing the old game of Noughts and Crosses, but in a four-dimensional matrix. Who could say they were not? I still wonder whether they were.

Christopher provided a very high standard of chemical understanding for me to try to live up to. But my life would have been impossible had he not had one small Achilles' heel. It so happened - perhaps because of my self-training with Winks - that I was quite good at practical chemistry; a bit sloppy and impatient perhaps, but on the whole my experiments worked. On the whole Christopher's did not, and though I do not know why his often failed, it gave me the only edge I had on him. So when we shared an experiment, as often happened in the practical classes, I would do most of the manipulations and Christopher would do most of the sums. Thus we were an effective team and each learned what he could from watching the other. We also shared lecture notes if, for some reason, one of us missed a session. And Christopher was happy to explain more theoretical things to me; I learned an approach to thermodynamics (called 'functional thermodynamics') from him, not from the formal lectures and tuition, and it stood me in good stead later in my finals examinations because it is actually simpler, and much quicker to write down, once you have got the hang of it.

Christopher and I went our separate ways after sharing tuition for three years, when it was time to embark upon the research stage of our degree course. After that his career was meteoric: Balliol made him a Junior Fellow once he had taken his degree (first class, naturally); four years later, at the age of 30, he became Professor of Theoretical Chemistry at London University, moving to a comparable Chair of Chemistry at Cambridge two years later. He became a Fellow of the Royal Society at the unusually young age of 36 and later achieved one of the Royal Society's few and very select Research Professorships; his *curriculum vitae* began to accumulate a marvellous collection of academic honours and distinctions. Within a few years we had lost touch, but we met again a few decades later when he moved to the Biology School of the University of Sussex. There he and a computer worked together doing research on brain function, that is, cognition, memory and so on (including, I am happy to note, response to music). A far cry from physical chemistry perhaps, yet he had by then acquired considerable distinction in Cognitive Science. He died, an outstanding and cultured scientist, in 2004.

Sandy Ogston

Alexander G. Ogston was Dean of Balliol during my undergraduate days. A biochemist universally known as Sandy, he was a friendly, outgoing personality with a ready, if slightly coarse, sense of humour. Tall, bearded and pipe-smoking with a lined, rather long face, he lived in a Dean's residence in one corner of Balliol quadrangle with his equally friendly wife, Lisa, and two tiny daughters (the latter became thoroughly spoiled, I suspect, from the avuncular attentions of many of the undergraduates). Sandy, as Dean, was responsible for discipline within the college, for the wartime Air Raid, Fire and First Aid Precautions, with their sometimes eccentric undergraduate teams, and for teaching and lecturing, not to mention his biochemical research. Yet he was always accessible to those with problems - or even those who sought a companion for a chat and a beer - and he carried his chores and authority with such effortless amiability that none of the undergraduates thought of him as other than one of the gang.

I had had some brushes with authority during my later schooldays and I took some time to get used to Sandy's informality, but, once appreciated, it made a deep impression upon me. He taught good science; his decisions with his Dean's hat on were reasonable; he had no need of deference. The old adage that respect is earned, not commanded, is very true and I have since seen many in positions of authority making asses of themselves, or generating antagonism, through unnecessary pomposity or formality.

In my third year the opportunity arose to learn some biochemistry and, since I still hankered after biological themes - though my early desire to be a zookeeper had vanished - I accepted this option, even though it meant doing extra work, which would not help me get my degree. There was, by the way, no degree course in Biochemistry at Oxford in those days; my course was a special one offered to chemists interested in moving in a biochemical direction; it was mounted by the Department of Physiology and Sandy gave me some tutorials. By then a fairly self-confident young chemist, I was bemused by the uncertainties of biochemical knowledge, by the ambiguities resulting from experiments on living or partly living material, by the imprecision of biochemical analyses. So, required to write an essay on a difficult and complex topic such as fat metabolism, I would read as much as I could get read in the time I had allowed myself - always insufficient - and write a self-consistent rationalisation of whatever information I had succeeded in absorbing. Sandy found the results surprising and sometimes hilarious, and I later learned that he kept one or two of my essays to show to others as examples of how not to approach biochemistry. Yet he was very tolerant and kind to me, gently redirecting my thoughts and tactfully disclosing salient gaps which I had failed to notice.

Tutorials with Sandy took the form of an informal discussion of matters related to one's essay, with frequent digressions therefrom, but with the hazard that he was constantly attempting to kipper his pupils with pipe smoke. That he failed in this endeavour was largely because he would start to light his pipe, with a special petrol lighter which produced a huge flame (from laboratory solvents, I wonder?), but then would get involved in saying something and it would go out. Then he would bang it loudly, but almost unconsciously, on a metal fender beside his chair, before tamping down the original tobacco and starting to re-light it. He did not, in the event, produce much smoke or use up much tobacco - which must have been an economy, given wartime shortages - but his pipe play, coupled with a sort of hesitancy while he mentally perfected what he was about to say (a most impressive ploy, this), provided an almost surrealist sideshow to tutorial sessions with him.

Sandy was a physical biochemist: he was involved in the study of the physical behaviour of substances comprising living things. His speciality was the use of a device called the Svedberg Velocity Ultracentrifuge to study such properties. For example, proteins (such as the albumin which makes white of egg gooey) consist of very, very big molecules composed of lots of atoms, chiefly carbon (they are organic, of course), oxygen, hydrogen and nitrogen atoms, all bundled together. Proteins usually dissolve in water but their molecules are a tiny bit denser than water molecules. So, if you spin a solution of a protein in water at a tremendous speed, in a strong tube, centrifugal force pushes on the water, keeping it in the tube, but it pushes on the protein molecules rather harder, and they slowly sediment to the bottom of the tube; a bit like a fine mud settling in a pond by gravity. From the speed at which various proteins sediment one can obtain information about the size and shape of big molecules, and this was the sort of thing Sandy did. Small, high-velocity ultracentrifuges are commonplace in laboratories these days, but in the early 1940s I think Sandy's was one of only two in Britain. A Swede called Svedberg designed it, and it was monstrous. It occupied two rooms in the Biochemistry Department and was located in one of them, bolted with gigantic bolts to four thick steel rods set in an enormous block of concrete, built into the laboratory foundations. The spinning part or rotor was encased in thick, hardened steel and had a corkscrew-like end; it was set, and kept, spinning by squirting oil under high pressure at the corkscrewed end, the whole operation being under vacuum to avoid air resistance. A noisy pump pumped the oil. It had a cooling system and a means of taking photographs of the sedimenting solution (very ingenious, this) as well as a means of measuring how fast it was going. It took several hours to reach maximum speed and several hours to slow down again; it might be run full out for twelve or more hours. It was operated from the next room, the operator peering over a wooden block for protection. The reason for this was that it spun rather faster than the muzzle velocity of a shell emerging from a gun and so, if it got out of balance, it would shake itself to pieces and probably explode. Apparently Svedberg's original had once done so and an assistant had received a severe blow on the head from a bolt, a blow which could have been avoided, had the wooden block been there. Hence the Svedberg design thereafter included a wooden block.

The Leonardo Society, Balliol, June, 1946

John Postgate, A G Ogston

Pears, Chernievsky, Cohen, G Kennedy, Wheatley, Lloyd, Grant, Burns, B Fiddes, Wilkinson,

Christopher Longuet-Higgins, Leech, Smithies, Frost, Moss, Aitken

The whole set-up recalled the bridge of a ship. Sandy, with beard, pipe and polo-necked sweater, was Captain. One Rupert Cecil was First Officer, while a graduate student or two were crew. When the pump was throbbing and Sandy and associates had embarked upon a run, the noise, the oily smell, the hours kept and the general mayhem were just like a long sea voyage.

Sandy had taken a chemistry degree from Balliol around

1932 and, after research at Balliol and later in London, had realised the value of the ultra-centrifuge as a result of a spell with Svedberg himself in Sweden. He returned to Balliol as a tutor in 1937; during the current war, I learned later, he undertook research for the military, helping in a programme of research into antidotes to poison gases and also advising on the design of compact food rations for troops. He was elected a Fellow of the Royal Society in 1955. He left the Oxford Biochemistry Department in 1959 and spent a decade as a Professor of Physical Biochemistry at the Australian National University in Canberra, before returning to become President of Trinity College, Oxford. He, too, collected a stack of honours, including (not many of us score such a one as this) a Hall of Residence at Trinity named after him. When he finally retired he moved to the University of York; he died in 1996.

Jazz

I told earlier how I not only became a 'swing fan' but a budding swing musician during my last years at school. I had also learned more about this music, notably from two excellent programmes put out by the BBC, and I now recognised my 'swing' as a modern, rather commercial, variant of the much more subtle and varied music we now call jazz. I pass over the sufferings of parents, friends and neighbours as I practised my 'bloody bugle' (as my mother called it), even during air raids, or played my abrading swing records at odd hours. We all survived and I arrived at Balliol with somewhat more than I said earlier in this chapter: included in my paraphernalia was a case of about a dozen swing records, followed a term or so later by a cornet which I could hardly play but was determined to practise.

I said I never had any tuition in cornet playing. That is quite true. In addition, since I had skived off music lessons for most of my secondary school career, I could not read music. Not a note; nor can I yet. I was therefore a trifle thwarted by all those dots on lines when I bought a book called *125 Hot Licks For Trumpet* by Louis Armstrong, who was by then replacing Artie Shaw as my prime idol (later Bix Beiderbecke replaced Armstrong). I comforted myself with the myth, and it is a myth though I firmly believed in it then, that the great jazzmen of New Orleans were all self-taught musical illiterates. In this belief I was encouraged by a fellow undergraduate, Martin Milligan, a communist who happened also to be a near-genius as a jazz pianist, able to improvise most complex solos in any key. He, too, had no time for written music, but then, he had been blind from about nine months old.

Aided by Martin, I worked out a way of learning to play jazz trumpet which I can with the greatest confidence advise aspirant jazz trumpeters not to follow, though many did and will probably do so in future. I disregarded all such matters as scales, embouchure, and the special pitch in which music for trumpets and cornets is notated; I just blew, starting, like many another aspirant, with the chorus of *Basin Street Blues* in piano B flat. This melody is especially useful because you can get through four bars of the theme on only one note, and do a whole chorus with about five. I graduated therefrom to tunes with more notes, simplifying them as 'free improvisation on the theme' if there were too many notes close together. Then I moved to the next easiest key; I think it was by way of *Georgia On My Mind* in E flat (it is more usually played in F, albeit written in G). And thence to greater things.

Balliol had restricted hours during which undergraduates might engage in music practice, but they had not bargained for an aspiring jazz cornet player. Freddie King was reported to me as having expressed the hope that I might learn a tune other than the *St. James' Infirmary* which I was currently murdering (I was amazed and delighted that he had recognised it); a near crisis came when the American Ambassador, John Wynant, being entertained to lunch by the Master of Balliol, walked with other guests across the quadrangle to the accompaniment of a halting version of - guess what - *St James' Infirmary*. I heard that the Senior Common Room discussed whether to impose special restrictions on my cornet, but all I received was a reproach from Sandy.

At the end of their first year most undergraduates were required to move into lodgings in Oxford town, because a Government agency had requisitioned part of the College. I think my cornet may have been one of the reasons why I, unlike Christopher, was not one of the few privileged to stay in College. However, Balliol did not free itself of my serenades; my landlords and landladies - I moved around a bit - unanimously refused to permit cornet practice in my lodgings. What to do? The ever-tolerant Christopher had a piano in his room and sympathised with musical aspiration even if he had no time for jazz. To the chagrin of his neighbours he allowed me to keep my cornet in one of his cupboards and practise in his room, often with Martin on piano - provided he himself was out.

Students are very tolerant of their own, if not of others. I was enabled to make progress as a jazz musician. I also made progress as a chemist. After three years I took my final written examinations. I did well and qualified for an Honours degree though, as I shall shortly explain, it was not yet classified. But I had overcome a major hurdle and could now embark upon the research phase of the degree. Thus did I come under the direction of another powerful scientific influence: Professor (later Sir) Cyril Hinshelwood.

Hinsh

The future Sir Cyril Hinshelwood, already recognised as one of Britain's most distinguished physical chemists, was something of a legend even among Oxford's substantial quota of remarkable personalities. He had spent much of his career doing experiments on the way in which gases interact chemically, and, with insight and originality, he had used his findings to reshape theoretical understanding of their behaviour. Most of that research had been done in the old chemistry laboratories at Balliol (still there, but derelict, by the time I joined the College; now vanished, having become part of the Senior Common Room). Part of Hinshelwood's legend held that, in the early 1920s, he and two other researchers had had a serious laboratory accident in which a highly poisonous vapour from an organic compound of mercury was released. One researcher died, one went mad, and the third - Hinshelwood - lost his teeth and hair but became Dr Lees Professor of Physical Chemistry.

I had religiously attended all (or perhaps I should say most) of his lectures on the kinetic theory of gases, a series notable for their lambent clarity, but our first direct encounter occurred during a practical class in the University's Physical Chemistry Laboratory, known to all as the PCL, which Hinshelwood headed. I no longer remember what particular experiment we were doing but, as usual, Christopher Longuet-Higgins and I were sharing one. A Dr Danby was overseeing the class, but on this occasion, as sometimes happened, the Professor paid the teaching lab a visit. I should explain that the Oxford Honours Chemistry degree is taken in two chunks, occupying four years in all: the first three comprise Part 1, a conventional programme of lectures, tutorials and practical classes, at the end of which the student takes 'finals', a series of written and practical examination papers. On the results of this a degree is awarded (or not, as the case may be). But the degree is not classified until Part 2 is completed, a fourth year devoted essentially to research culminating in a short written thesis. Both Christopher and I had opted to take our Part 2s in the PCL, Christopher with Ronnie Bell, me with Hinshelwood. My own choice stemmed from my lingering feeling for biological matters: I had learned that Hinshelwood had an ongoing research programme in which he was applying, with great success I was told, the principles of chemical kinetics to the multiplication and variation of bacteria. There was room for a Part 2 student in the team and the research area seemed to promise a reasonable compromise between chemistry and biology. Ronnie Bell had therefore mentioned my interest to Hinshelwood.

The reason for the Professor's visit to the teaching lab became clear when he came up to Christopher and me and spoke.

"You are Postgate, then?" he said to Christopher.

I regret to say that our undergraduate sense of humour took over at this point.

"If you say so, sir," said Christopher, with Wykhamist politeness.

"I'll be Longuet-Higgins, then," I said to Christopher, though clearly enough for Hinshelwood to hear.

"Are you Postgate, then?" said Hinshelwood, turning to me.

"Oh!" I said, and turned again to Christopher. "Aren't I Longuet-Higgins?"

"If I'm Postgate you must be," he replied.

"How do you do?" I said, offering my hand.

"How do you do?" Christopher replied. We shook hands.

At this point the charade stopped, because Hinshelwood's tolerant smile was wearing thin. I owned up to being Postgate, apologised for our play-acting - which he dismissed with a wave of the hand - and he told me something of his research on the kinetics of bacterial growth, of the project he had in mind for me to do for my Part 2.

All this occurred before our final examinations, and some weeks before I actually joined Hinshelwood; in August of 1944, actually, because one of the exigencies resulting from the war was that one was expected to work in the long vacation.

The laboratory where Hinshelwood conducted his research on the kinetics of bacterial growth, the 'bug' laboratory, was on the first floor of the PCL close to his office. It was much like many another physical chemistry laboratory except that it had a tiled floor so it felt rather like a public lavatory, an impression enhanced by a light smell of phenolic disinfectant which pervaded it. There was rather little in the way of specialised equipment: some glass-fronted thermostats and a central bench with Bunsen burners, tripods, some large flasks, a stock of largish test tubes with cotton wool stuffed into the top as plugs. These plugs served keep out extraneous microbes yet allow sterile air to be bubbled through any liquid within the tubes. There were a few microscopes, against one wall was a still which generated distilled water continuously, there was a sink, and spaces for writing notes. But it was clean and reasonably spacious with big windows and, in the thermostats, held at 40°C, were the plugged test tubes within which, in solutions of sugars plus salts, grew *Bacterium lactis aerogenes*. The tubes were constantly, though silently, bubbled with air from a compressed air system, conveying a sense of endless activity.

Hinshelwood, or 'Hinsh' as I could now refer to him (though not directly), had several other research programmes going elsewhere in the PCL building, as well as his teaching and college obligations, but bacteria were his favourite research topic at the time. Nevertheless, he was often busy elsewhere, so the day-today running of our bug laboratory was left in the hands of Duncan Davis, a married postgraduate who was preparing for his doctorate. He had charge of me, Arthur James (also from Balliol) and, senior to both of us and already well into a research programme, J. M.

Pryce. We newcomers had nicknames provided by Duncan, who alternatively addressed us with the prefix 'Man'. Thus Arthur James was 'Man James' or 'Bløndie', I was 'Man Postgate' or 'Ål' (note the Scandinavian vowels - used by Duncan in honour of the great Danish kineticist Brønsted and the Swedish scientist Ångström). Pryce was only 'Man Pryce' as I recall. Duncan was a good-natured *major domo* who maintained cleanliness, co-operation and reasonable apportionment of routine chores with good humour, setting the necessary example by his own capacity for hard work. He also seemed to find me intrinsically funny, with my still naive socialism, my corduroyed Bloomsbury-ish appearance, my disposition to see philosophical/political implications in almost everything, my love for jazz. I took this as it came.

Hinsh had started his research on bacteria before the war because of the tremendous success of his own developments and simplifications of the kinetic theory of gases. In essence, he had developed an impressive mathematical description of the properties and chemical reactions of gases based on the statistical treatment of gas molecules, a treatment that was valid because gas molecules are very, very small and they come in very, very large numbers. It had dawned on him that bacteria, albeit much larger, are still very small and numerous, so the growth of their populations ought to be amenable to comparable statistical treatment. By the time I joined him, he had had some success and already published several papers on the regular growth of cultures of his pet microbe and had embarked on a study of their adaptation to new environments: how they acclimatised themselves to changed food sources, or acquired resistance to antibacterial drugs. It was probably this latter feature, with its implications for the treatment of infections resulting from injuries in wartime, which led to the research being regarded in high places as having adequate priority for funding and for me, Bløndie, Duncan and all to be 'reserved' from military service to carry it on. Yet the relevance of the detailed programme to the war was remote. His pet microbe was, happily, a totally harmless soil organism. It was, as I said earlier, *Bact. lactis aerogenes* (actually already reclassified by taxonomists as *Aerobacter aerogenes* and due a few years later to be renamed yet again as *Klebsiella aerogenes*; taxonomists are allowed to muck about with the first (generic) names of microbes, which have a capital letter, but not with the second (specific) names). However, he had done a little work himself on a microbe called *Bacterium coli mutabile* (now known as a strain of *Escherichia coli*, the famous *E. coli*) studying the way it switched from growth with glucose to growth with other sugars such as lactose; he wished me to do parallel experiments with his main workhorse, *A. aerogenes*.

Theoretically, I found the prospect interesting and exciting. In practice it was hell. The way I studied the question was to measure the rates at which successive cultures grew with a new sugar (eg lactose) after transfer from glucose. To do this, in those days, one had to take small samples of the culture at intervals and count the number of bacteria in them under the microscope. This was slow and tedious because you had to know exactly what volume of culture fluid you are counting. The field of a microscope is actually minute, both in area and depth, the volume you can count is also tiny, so a very special and expensive calibrated microscope slide called a haemocytometer was required, and it had to be set up perfectly and kept scrupulously clean. Moreover, the phase-contrast microscope, which enhances the visibility of tiny objects, had not yet been invented, so the bacteria had to be stained with a dye or they would have been virtually invisible. In addition, the bacteria had to be killed or they tended to swim about, thus confusing the observer. The way to do this was to heat them to just below boiling for a moment or two - if you heated them too long, they coagulated like a dumpling, fouling up the count. The haemocytometer slide had a barely visible grid engraved in it, so that one could be sure not to count the same bug twice and also be sure to count a similar area every time. One had to count over 200 cells for the result to be statistically valid, so one rapidly got an eyestrain headache, until one learned to 'rock' the focus while counting. Even so, I would be quite dazed after a few hours' work and could not look at an old-fashioned Critall-type window without seeing illusory bacteria distributed among the panes. Today there are electronic counters which will do this work in seconds, painlessly - but that's the way with scientific research.

Actually, within a couple of months I became quite unwell, convinced that I had tuberculosis or a brain tumour (but actually suffering from common stress-induced hypochondria). Fortunately a friend was going to Tintagel and I fudged up a reason to escape for two weeks to join him there. (That was where I first met Ernst Chain - more about him in the next Chapter.) I returned feeling much better, by which I mean subject to no more than my usual quota of mysterious hypochondriacal ailments, and my research began to make some degree of progress.

At this stage, Hinsh began to take real rather than formal interest in my results. Although amiable, he was a shy, austere figure, uninterested in small talk or even in the more mundane problems of research. He was of thin, almost skeletal build, bald and ascetic looking with lined, pale features. He always looked unwell, and it was said that this was a result of his pre-war mercury poisoning, but I do not remember him being overtly ill during my year with him. Unmarried, his life centred on the PCL and Trinity College SCR. He was the ideal mentor for me at that stage of my career. Almost every morning he would come into the laboratory and ask how the experiments were going - and this ensured that I kept at my research. Then, whether or not I had made progress, we would have some discussion about the actual and potential implications of the work. He was constantly producing new ideas and suggestions, many of them useless in practice but nevertheless valuable because they broadened the mind.

An example: one morning I was particularly fed up because my cultures were behaving completely inconsistently, sometimes failing to grow, at other times growing at divergent rates in what were supposed to be identical conditions. I suggested, as a rueful joke, that their growth was determined by the phase of the moon rather than by anything I did. Observing that I had meant it frivolously, he at once took this suggestion seriously, pointing out that the phase of the moon might well reflect fluctuations in the incidence of cosmic rays, that these undoubtedly had biological effects and that such effects might indeed be magnified and detected in the sorts of experiments I was doing. We then got on to the possibility of 'mitogenetic rays', a discredited hypothesis of growth-promoting biological radiation, which some Soviet scientists had proposed several years earlier. I disputed this hotly, until I spotted the twinkle in his eye - but by then my morale was restored and I learned one of the important lessons of my scientific career: think laterally and leave a small portion of your credulity open to even quite absurd ideas. A good scientist must always be extremely critical and sceptical but, equally, he/she must never be totally dismissive.

Hinsh was impatient of mundane obstacles. At an early stage of my research I needed more compressed air lines for my cultures, which meant a larger glass manifold than I had scrounged from Man Pryce. In those days, students did not have access to the services of a professional glassblower; we had to make our manifolds from soda glass tubing, which broke or distorted very easily and which shattered spontaneously if cooled impatiently. I had found myself singularly incompetent at making these manifolds ("cows" we called them) and had thus set up fewer cultures than was scientifically desirable. Discovering this, Hinsh wasted no time: he had me watch him make a six-fold 'cow' and gave it to me, with the clear, though unspoken, message not to waste any more time over trivialities.

I think Hinsh shared Duncan's view that there was

something slightly comic about Postgate. There was always an element of teasing in his discussions; he also took pleasure in revealing his connections with Imperial Chemical Industries, for me a wicked symbol of Monopoly Capitalism, and in gently chiding my populist ideas about the Social Function of Science. Again he was right: on the one hand, for all its faults, ICI did a lot to support basic science in universities long before Government intervention was financially serious; on the other, science is not going to be of much use to 'People' or to anyone else unless it has a sound academic basis.

Despite his austere and shy manner, he had a well-developed sense of humour. On one occasion, to tease Duncan, who was thinking of joining ICI (he did so in the end, and became a most distinguished senior manager, borrowed by Whitehall on occasions), I had typed on the communal typewriter a short, bogus message to the group, as if from someone in ICI, but patently in German-English with overtones of spying and corruption. I no longer remember the contents, it was short and parochial and probably not all that funny. I left it there for the gang to see. It was still there when Hinsh came in and caught sight of it. Instead of asking who wrote it, he simply read it out aloud in a deadpan voice. There was then no need for him to ask; when he finished and looked around the lab, there was I, purple with embarrassment, with the rest of the lab grinning quietly. He considered me to be sufficiently reproached.

On another occasion my adolescent sense of humour stretched his tolerance too much and I escaped less easily. I had come in late on a Sunday to inoculate some cultures for the following Monday and had found the still overflowing on to the floor, where it had made quite a large pool. I turned off the still but I was in a hurry, having some urgent engagement of a non-scientific character, so I did not mop up. Instead, and here I made my mistake, before departing I scrawled and left conspicuously in the middle of the lab a note saying 'WE 'AVE BEFLUDDED US'.

Next morning, it seems, Duncan arrived to find Hinsh in the lab with mop and bucket, cleaning up for us with a face of thunder. When I breezed in, rather late as usual, I received a well-deserved tongue-lashing from Duncan about my irresponsibility, my insulting attitude to the team and to the Professor, my tardiness, lack of true scientific motivation etc., etc. I was duly and rightly ashamed (and many years later, as a Professor myself, I, too, have performed menial tasks which others have neglected, to shame them into remembering that they are part of a team. It doesn't always work.) Anyway, Hinsh did not visit us again that day. Notice that he wisely left it to Duncan to discipline me, another lesson in leadership which I found useful later on: running the lab was Duncan's brief, however annoying the episode was to Hinsh at the time; his was not to intervene unless I became awkward or persistent. I was fairly soon forgiven.

Hinsh had been something of a renegade in his time and also had a somewhat impish sense of humour; he greatly enjoyed, and recommended to us, a little book, which was then considered to be rather naughty, called *The Specialist*; it was the fictional reflections of a mid-Westerner who specialised in making lavatory seats. I believe my shy nonconformism elicited a chord of sympathy, quite unconsciously, at times. He was always very friendly to all of us in the lab and seemed pleased to see us in the street. He had us to tea at Trinity, sometimes for a discussion meeting, and on one occasion the lab held a dinner for him at Balliol. I organised it; these were austere times and interesting food was very hard to come by, so I obtained some headless pigeons from the Biochemistry Department, where they were being decapitated for experiments on brain metabolism, and prevailed upon the College chef to cook them. They were good, if tough; Hinsh, not knowing their origin, was pleased and impressed.

As I said, Hinsh and his bug lab formed a close and friendly community. Yet after I had finished my Part 2, within a couple of weeks of my leaving to work with Donald Woods in the Biochemistry Department, he ceased to acknowledge me if our paths happened to cross, in the street for example. I was surprised and a little dismayed - after all, I had obtained a good degree and we had written a joint paper. But I learned that others found the same thing - it was a matter of single-mindedness and desire not to be distracted by mundane courtesies. In fact he did ask, in a friendly and interested manner, after my postgraduate work at a meeting a couple of years later, in circumstances in which he could hardly avoid recognising me.

A complex personality, combining shyness, austerity, dedication and an immensely powerful intellect, Hinsh was perhaps one of the last of the Giant Polymaths. He was fluent in several European languages and had adequate Russian and Mandarin Chinese. On one memorably absurd occasion the Communist Party, then highly respectable because the Soviet Union was our wartime ally, had arranged a ceremonious visit of a Soviet soldier to Oxford City and University. At a crowded assembly in Balliol Hall, it fell to Hinsh to greet the soldier on behalf of the University, which he did in fluent Russian. The soldier was a fearsome lady called Lieutenant Ludmilla Pavlichenko; she had killed, we were told, a substantial number of Germans. One hoped she was impressed by Hinsh. We were.

He was interested in, and expert on, Chinese ceramics. He liked classical music (but had no time at all for my beloved jazz). He was middling to left in politics but not especially involved. He was deeply interested in philosophy but had no time for Marxism, though some time for the Logical Positivism, which was in process of replacing soft-core Marxism in my own political outlook. He was extremely well read and a dozen or so years after my association with him he achieved what I imagine must be a unique academic distinction: for a time he was simultaneously President of both the Royal Society and the Classical Association. He was also a sufficiently good amateur painter to mount his own successful exhibition towards the end of his life. Oh, and he was knighted in 1948.

I became aware of these many accomplishments only gradually because, in the British way, he did not advertise them at all. To me on a day-today basis he was simply a high-powered scientist with a penetrating mind and a wholly convincing theory about how bacteria adjusted themselves to changed environments. I, in common with my colleagues in the lab, had not the slightest doubt that his theory was right and that it told us something important not only about bacteria but about the nature of life itself.

What a pity, then, that he, and therefore we, were wrong.

I shall now try to explain why, because it has an interesting bearing both on his quality as a polymath and on the way scientists think. As almost everyone knows these days, all living things carry, in virtually every cell, entities called genes. These are complicated chemicals called DNA which carry the blueprint of what the organism is like: they specify whether a child will be male or female, have blue or brown eyes, the right number of fingers and so on; they programme the life of a plant, the colour of its flowers; they prescribe whether a microbe will make people ill or not. Genes specify what living things are in minute biological detail. Within cells, genes are strung together in spiral chains, knotted up in one or more bodies called chromosomes. Human beings have forty-eight. In sexual reproduction, chromosomes from each parent are mixed and the offspring carries a complement of genes from both parents, thus ending up with biological resemblances to both. Most creatures can make minor adjustments to changed environments - people bronze in sunshine, get fat if they eat too much, achieve unusual dexterities - without their genetic make-up changing. Major adjustments - such as bacteria acquiring resistance to penicillin - result only from changes in the genes. These occur only rarely; they are called mutations.

Bacteria can make remarkable, indeed spectacular,

adjustments to new environments, becoming resistant to drugs or learning to use entirely new chemicals as food. Hinshelwood had himself demonstrated some impressive examples of this ability. In the 1940s there was still reasonable doubt whether the genetics of bacteria were similar to that of higher organisms and Hinshelwood did not believe that bacteria had either chromosomes or genes; he was satisfied that their flexibility, which was already known to be remarkable, could be accounted for entirely in terms of the physical chemistry of their metabolism and that genes, and mutations therein, were not involved. Hard pressed, he might admit that possession of genes by bacteria was not impossible, but he considered the idea that they might be present a scientifically unnecessary irrelevance.

These views, which I have necessarily oversimplified, were plausible and widely accepted among bacteriologists in the early 1940s, but as that decade progressed they became increasingly at variance with the thinking of those with any deep involvement in these matters. When, by 1950, the nature of heredity in bacteria was becoming clear and both genes and chromosomes had been demonstrated within them, Hinshelwood's views had become positively capricious. Yet he modified them only marginally despite such clear advances in biochemical and genetic understanding of bacteria.

Why? Partly because he had no patience with, or confidence in, biologists and biochemists. He was himself a chemist *par excellence* and chemists are an arrogant species of scientist. In my little way, I was, too. Chemists are used to clear and unequivocal findings. They work with pure chemical compounds, of defined structure and properties, and they expect well-designed experiments to yield clear, unequivocal results. Biological variation, at once the plague and the fascination of biological research, is anathema to a chemist, who feels at heart that the vagueness and lack of finality which inform even the most constructive of biological publications must, in some way, indicate poor experimentation. So Hinsh rarely consulted biochemists about his science and he read biochemical and microbiological journals rarely and selectively, disregarding papers that seemed to have no positive bearing on his own interests. He also submitted his own papers to non-biological journals, so that biologists did not referee them - for otherwise many would certainly have been rejected. In the early 1950s he did his reputation some harm by rediscovering and publishing a set of phenomena which had essentially been discovered and well documented in the late 1930s (for specialists I mention that they concerned the Citric Acid Cycle), an especially odd circumstance because one of the country's leading experts on such phenomena, Professor of Biochemistry R. A. Peters, was, like Hinsh, a Fellow of Trinity College. They must have met and talked in the Senior Common Room; but not about science, it would seem.

Although, as I said, Hinsh did adjust his views somewhat in the light of developments outside the PCL over the years, he did so grudgingly and with obvious reluctance. This was a pity because, though he was wrong in his broad view, he was in fact right about some of the detailed quantitative responses of bacteria to moderate changes in environment - they are well capable of non-genetic acclimatisation - and this aspect of his work tended to be discounted along with the rest.

What would cause so brilliant a mind to disregard so firmly the wider context of his own research, as well as the regular criticisms of his peers? Some would say the arrogance I have just mentioned; some would say impatience - that he could not be bothered with contradictory detail; some would say single-mindedness - that he could not see the wood for his own special tree. These may have been contributory factors, but I think that the real cause was aesthetic. His theory of bacterial growth and adaptation was beautiful - the scientists' *cliché* for it in those days was 'elegant'. It was a mathematical and intellectual construct which was simple, based in good physical chemistry, and self-consistent; it matched in minute detail the painstaking quantitative experiments conducted in his laboratory, experiments which were so tedious to do (as well I knew) that few others even thought about repeating or extending them. It was intolerable that his lovely intellectual edifice should be wrong, and the intensely human Hinsh resisted remodelling it for as long as he could.

I learned another lesson while, over the following few years, I recovered from Hinsh's influence: that all the best scientists have to be a little like that.

CHAPTER FOUR

Ernst Chain and record mania

I mentioned a few pages ago that during my year with Hinshelwood, I felt ill and took a short break at Tintagel with a Balliol friend. He was a medical student who had been seriously ill with tuberculosis, not uncommon in those days, and had been advised to take a holiday. He had invited me to go along with him for company. So I borrowed an advance on my grant from my parents and, braving the rigours of the Great Western Railway, we set off for a hotel at Tintagel, where he had booked us a double room.

In those days homosexuality was an aberration which most people grew out of and, unlike today, nobody thought twice about two males sharing a bedroom. But since homosexuality has become politically correct these days, I must make it clear that we shared for reasons of economy; our friendship was wholly platonic.

It was late autumn and, though I have never revisited Tintagel, I still remember the menacing Gothic atmosphere of the place, with its autumnal skies, its stark rocky outcrop, enhanced by the Arthurian legend. Such holiday season as existed in wartime was effectively over, so there were few people in our hotel, and there was little to do except walk, climb rocks, talk, eat and sit in the bar of an evening, drinking cider at about 2d a glass. All this suited us very well indeed, and we filled the time doing just that; we walked, talked about politics, arts, philosophy, sex - my friend had long discarded his virginity and I had not, so he was anxious on my behalf - but regrettably not jazz, because my friend did not share my obsession, though he tolerated the 'hot fountain pen' I had brought with me and played occasionally.

Hot fountain pen, you ask? Imagine a descant recorder (if you can't do that, you won't be interested in this bit anyway - move to the next paragraph), imagine it with its mouthpiece sawn off and replaced by a clarinet mouthpiece, with reed. That was essentially the instrument invented by one Adrian Rollini, a distinguished American jazzman of the twenties, though I think his version used a sawn-off penny whistle in place of the recorder. Mine had been bought at a shop just north of Oxford Street in London and it had a range of about an octave, sounding rather like the low register of a clarinet. On it I could play a few simple melodies in the single key of C.

My friend was recovering fast and began to yearn for feminine company. In Tintagel, it seems that Saturday nights were drinking nights, and our hotel was a favoured rendezvous for the locals, so the Saturday evening a couple of days before our departure was a big evening. Much cider was drunk and songs were sung. The hotel guests miraculously included a youth who could play the piano, exclusively in C, but what better key for me? We astonished the locals with a couple of shy duets - just enough to establish ourselves as good chaps while not interfering with the singing and competitive sport (bar skittles). Over there, however, was the local charmer, a pretty young Somerset girl with long eyelashes, dark flashing eyes and a pleasing, if marginally over-abundant, figure.

Ah! The mystery of youthful interaction! How my friend and I came to be either side of her as the evening wore on I do not quite recall; it was indeed an inappropriate juxtaposition since we both had steady lady friends back at Oxford. However, there we were, all three singing lustily, and at least two of us lustfully. Closing time duly came and - the story of my life - I found myself bidding farewell to my friend and our young lady, since without my noticing he had somehow established that he would escort her home. Bemused and somewhat sozzled, I returned to our room, to await his return with doubtless prurient details of his conquest.

When he returned, sooner than I expected, my friend seemed less than delighted. It transpired that Maud (that was not her name) had certainly been more than just acquiescent; she had returned my friend's advances with distinct enthusiasm. The night had been dark enough for reasonable privacy, though not pitch black, but after certain overtures familiar to the young in comparable situations, the problem had been damp ground, due to a recent shower. However, he and Maud had found a seemingly secluded wall just off the road and progress had been fine: she had permitted agreeably intimate fondling and, indeed, had responded by placing herself in jeopardy had she been one to take Deuteronomy 25 seriously. My friend had every hope of a gratifying fruition of his plans when, raising her head unexpectedly, she said:

"'Night, Dad."

My friend, startled, observed a passing shadow on the adjacent road, which responded:

"'Night, Maud."

And continued its journey. The lady seemed inclined to resume, to my friend's pleasure, but within a few seconds:

"'Night, Mum."

"'Night, Maud."

Then it was:

"'Night, Fred."

"'Night, Maud."

"'Night Ron."

"'Night, Maud."

Every few seconds, interspersed with encouragingly enthusiastic amatory activity. However:

"'Night, Jean."

"'Night, Maud."

Was followed by:

"Oi must go now."

And, despite my friend's remonstrations, go she did, explaining that her Dad and Mum, two brothers and sister had all "gone on" now and she was expected home. Bewildered as much as frustrated, even forgetting to make a further rendezvous, my friend returned to his chaste couch.

It was at Tintagel that I first encountered a small busy man, in his late thirties, of Central European aspect having the flat, faintly Mongol features which I associate with Slavs. We got talking in the bar one evening and he asked me what I did. Flushed with Hinshelwoodism, I told him I was doing research on tiny creatures called bacteria, which caused disease. I added that I was particularly interested in the way in which they learned to resist disinfectants and anti-bacterial substances. My new friend - my Oxford chum was out somewhere - expressed considerable interest and said that he, too, was a microbiologist. Delighted, I then told him about a new drug which I had just heard of called penicillin, which was tremendously active; a cure-all, a wonder drug which would revolutionise medicine. My companion agreed that there was a need for such a drug. Warming to my theme, I told him that another microbe - a mould - produced it and that there were difficulties in extracting it. My companion seemed impressed so, hinting without actually saying that I might myself be involved, I discoursed on the general importance of drug resistance in medicine and the need to study penicillin resistance. At this stage my friend indicated that he had some modest experience of penicillin and was, indeed, doing research on its preparation and use at Oxford. He introduced himself as Dr Chain - a name unfamiliar to me - and invited me to visit his laboratory when I returned.

My friend from Oxford then came back and our

discussion turned to music, in which Dr Chain was very much interested. Regrettably, his interest did not extend to jazz, an aberration, which I endeavoured to correct with a long account of jazz as an urban folk music, and a promise, which he received with apparent goodwill, to lend Dr Chain a few books on the subject when I came to visit him in Oxford.

Dr Ernst Chain, only a couple of years later, shared with Fleming and Florey the Nobel Prize for the discovery and isolation of penicillin. He was also a classical pianist of professional calibre. Yet he had listened to this brash, self-important youth who cheerfully, and unrecognizing, gave him what must have been a pretty garbled account of his own research subject and who also attempted to revise his musical tastes, and had listened with such modesty and politeness that it was not until I got back to Oxford that I realised who he was and what he had done. Even then, he let me down most gently, accepting the loan of jazz books and returning them after a decent interval, showing me his laboratory and the old milk churns in which the first pilot-scale production of penicillin was performed. More than that, it was the start of a lifelong, though intermittent, friendship.

In later years Dr Chain became more and more important and in due course gained a knighthood; he became known as a turbulent man of scientific politics yet, if our paths crossed at a meeting, for instance, he always had time for a brief chat about family matters and music, as well as about science. When I met him at Tintagel he was tired and in low spirits - he told us he was on holiday because he needed a rest. Perhaps the company of a couple of educated but self-absorbed undergraduates were what he needed, for we walked, ate and drank beer or cider together a few times. He seemed cheerful enough, but later on, particularly after he had married Anne Beloff - whom I came to know later as a fellow postgraduate student - and after they had had their first son, Benjamin, I saw the real Chain: a bundle of energy and enthusiasm. I remember particularly his lectures on penicillin, which would start off calmly enough but would end up with Chain talking volubly, gesticulating, almost dancing to the board and back, leaning forward, propping himself with both hands on the lectern or bench, to emphasise a point. It was impossible not to be carried away, and it must have devastated administrators and businessmen when he later took up proselytizing for applied microbiology. In private he could be scathing about pretentiousness or incompetence; he had no time at all for the British civil servants who had lost the patent rights for penicillin to the USA; he had little time, I fear, for his fellow Nobelists. Some scientists were becoming anxious about the way use of penicillin seemed to be leading to the appearance of penicillin-resistant strains of microbe; this would make him cross because he felt, if I remember correctly, that (a) it was not true and (b) if there was an instance in which it was true, it arose from of incompetent use of the drug.

In other ways he could be very kind and tolerant. Several years later I gave a paper at the 3rd International Congress of Microbiology, held in Rome, invited by Chain, who was by then Director of a World Health Organization research centre housed in Italy's principal laboratory for applied microbiology in Rome. There were some distinguished presentations, and I was scarcely known as a scientist, yet, in casual conversation, he more or less apologised to me for the low quality of some of the papers accepted by the Congress, saying that he believed such an international gathering should be a forum for anyone who felt they had something to say. He took time from many pressing formalities to show me, with great pride, his laboratory's fermentation equipment.

I met Chain on another memorable occasion many years later. He was by then Professor of Biochemistry in charge of a marvellous, all stainless steel, fermentation plant at Imperial College, London, and again he took time to show me not only his giant gleaming vessels but also, gleefully, his private living quarters on the top floor of the lab - where we had a drink.

Chain was obsessed with the value of science to society, and he (rightly) accepted me as a supporter. He took every opportunity to emphasise the importance of applied science to social welfare and the need for society to support its scientists. But he was impatient, almost aggressively enthusiastic and given to overstatements, both dismissive and supportive. Naturally he became a Fellow of the Royal Society and when he died in 1979 his maverick, turbulent career, affectionately documented by his colleague and fellow penicillin worker Sir Edward Abraham, made one of the more entertaining of that Society's Biographical Memoirs of deceased Fellows: as I am sure he would have wished, for he added colour to the scientific community wherever he happened to be.

Jazz records

From my account of the way I bludgeoned Chain with books about jazz, the reader will rightly deduce that I had become a jazz bore. Jazz lovers are an obsessive lot, and for the majority of them the centre of their lives is their collection of jazz records. When I brought my precious dozen or so 78 rpm records to Balliol with me, I naturally took my Viva-Tonal Grafanola, a portable wind-up gramophone with a heavy acoustic pick-up, which provided startlingly loud, distinctly low-fidelity reproduction which my friends either greatly admired or hated. I was proud, shortly after arriving at Balliol, to become College Secretary of the Oxford University Rhythm Club; there I met fellow jazz devotees, some still good friends several decades after, and heard visiting jazz groups: Johnny Claes (trumpeter) and his Clae-pidgeons; the Feldman Brothers with a 13-year old drum prodigy (Vic Feldman, billed as 'Kid Krupa' after the celebrated US swing drummer, Gene Krupa); a contingent from the band of Harry Roy (one of Britain's 'hottest' dance bands at this time); the black trumpeter Leslie 'Jiver' Hutchinson, who bowled the audience over with his rendering of *St. James' Infirmary*... These were exciting events for me, which further fired my ambition to be a jazz musician myself, but I enjoyed equally the record sessions where we played our records to each other, discussed which soloist played what, argued about the relative virtues of Chicago and New York styles of jazz (the New Orleans style, seminal to all other jazz, had amazingly not yet received widespread recognition), talked knowledgeably about the blues (the basic musical form of jazz), worried about the plight of American Negro musicians within their racist society - and so on.

Like all obsessives, we had capacious memories for detail. We knew the dates and personnel of recording sessions (some even knew the matrix numbers given by the recording companies to the pieces recorded), could identify most jazz soloists by ear, and we had often contrived to hear literally all available recordings by our favourite groups. We bothered record shops, spending hours in their listening booths, for, in those days, shops allowed customers to hear records before buying them, and they would order records which they did not stock and which, in those days of scarcity, were hard to get. We sought out rare or deleted records in junk shops, we envied the few who, with contacts in the USA or US army, managed to get hold of much coveted US issues, including the US Army's wartime V-discs. And, naturally, we had to tell people about our pleasures. This was fine for other jazz buffs but a great bore for the rest. Pryce of Hinshelwood's laboratory, however, had a most effective put-down. One day I arrived in the afternoon having bought a rare recording by one Jelly Roll Morton, a celebrated pianist from New Orleans, which Taphouse's record shop had succeeded in obtaining for me after a long delay. I was exultant and was explaining to my colleagues the importance of both Mr Morton and my achievement when Pryce walked in. Seeing a record beside me, and ignoring the conversation so far, he picked it up, slowly and carefully studied both sides, then handed it back to me, pronouncing:

"Ah. I see Man Postgate has purchased a foxtrot."

It was the perfect stopper. The themes played by Jelly Roll Morton's band were indeed labelled 'foxtrot', but that was profoundly irrelevant to the record's quality as jazz and to my delight in it - as Pryce well knew. There was nothing for me to do but shut up and get on with counting bacteria.

I once brought my cornet into the laboratory, thinking to practise it in the evening. Which I did - once. Dr H W Thompson, distinguished infrared spectroscopist, had clearly been working late; he stormed up from the floor below and told me forcefully to stop. I did. Probably just as well, because he proved later to be my oral examiner for Part 2 of my Honours Chemistry degree. He had not forgotten the episode but was by then quite genial about it; he opened the *viva voce* by saying:

"Well, Postgate, I see that you have managed to get some research done in between practising the trombone."

For once I suppressed my lifelong pedantry and did not correct him. After all, my mother still thought my cornet was a "bloody bugle".

The oral examination was a success and my thesis was deemed good. My degree was classified first class. Rarely have I been so astonished.

The Duck

As my year with Hinsh drew to its close I began to think about what I might do next. Like most of my undergraduate contemporaries, I adhered unquestioningly to the anti-industrial culture; I took the view that no undergraduate worth his salt would consider joining private industry except as a last resort. I extended this view to public service. The regular Civil Service, I felt, might be acceptable for Arts graduates, but the Scientific Civil Service was an organisation for routine analyses, troubleshooting in sewage works and the like; scarcely to be taken seriously by real scientists. It took me but a moment's thought over these far-reaching matters to conclude that it was academia for me. I was quite wrong, but that comes later.

A career in academic science in the mid 1940s required a research degree, so I looked around for a postgraduate position. I was getting bored with Oxford; after four years I felt I had sampled all it had to offer, and the only other

University a Balliol man could think twice about was Cambridge. In fact, I rather fancied Cambridge, having gleaned a hint of its character when I visited it in 1941 and tried, unsuccessfully, to win a scholarship to Trinity Hall. Sandy Ogston knew Chibnall, Professor of Biochemistry at Cambridge, and it seemed that his Department included some microbiologists, so Sandy arranged for me to visit that Department.

Thus it came about that I scraped together the train fare and set off for Cambridge, slow train via Bletchley, calmly conscious of my effortless superiority as an experienced researcher, to see whether I liked the 'Other Place'. It did not enter my head to find out in any depth what sort of research they were doing. Otherwise I might have discovered that they were collectively perhaps the best group of biochemical microbiologists in the UK, headed by one of the subject's most distinguished research workers, Marjory Stephenson. She proved to be rather a formidable lady, tall and grey, the author of a seminal book on bacterial metabolism (which I had not read, no one having pointed it out to me) and she was noticeably, if courteously, put out by my substantial ignorance of the research of herself and her colleagues. Nevertheless, she and they treated me kindly, passing me from hand to hand and telling me something of what they were doing, and they received with tolerance my Hinshelwoodian outlook and consequent gratuitous advice on what, instead, they ought to be doing. I do not think I disgraced myself entirely, for I later learned that they would have considered finding a studentship for me had I produced but a single scientific reason for wanting to move to Cambridge. But the only reason I gave was the honest one: I fancied a change of scene. I remember Chibnall receiving this remark in some perplexity; he politely agreed that to move around was scientifically quite a good thing but observed that it was helpful to have some appropriate scientific theme in mind.

Needless to say, the question as to whether I liked Cambridge did not arise. They did not offer me a place. I wish I could say that my scientific arrogance had been struck a blow, but it was not so. I felt that Cambridge had shown narrow-minded concern with detail.

However, once again Providence intervened. One of Marjory Stephenson's younger associates, Dr Donald D. Woods, had just accepted a position in the Oxford University Biochemistry Department and was setting up a group to do microbiological research. Wheels were set in motion, Sandy exerted influence again, and Woods agreed to take me on - as his first-ever graduate student.

Transferring from Hinsh to Woods was, for me, a traumatic experience. Hinshelwood was a quick-thinking, scintillating intellectual, charismatic in his austere way, decisive, highly cultured with wide interests outside science, haughty about other groups' work. Yet he was prone, I fear, to the touch of sloppiness in experimental design which can afflict even the most brilliant scientists when they are overconfident of the rightness of their views and impatient to complete the supporting data. Woods was, in most ways, the diametric opposite in personality and outlook. He was a big man, slow-moving and slow-talking, slow in reaching decisions and apparently slow-thinking; wholly absorbed in microbiology with no interests outside the subject, at least, none that I became aware of; he also possessed an encyclopaedic knowledge of the relevant literature and was meticulous, as I later learned, in the design and execution of experiments. His sense of humour was schoolmasterish; he had no small talk and was awkward in the social graces. I later came to learn that he was also extremely kind and good-natured, as well as very patient both with colleagues and with the science itself.

A small but significant illustration. As I was finishing my work with Hinshelwood on the adaptation of *Bacterium lactis aerogenes* from using the sugar glucose to using another sugar, lactose, for growth, it seemed possible that a short paper might be written about it, but that it would be a much better one if comparable experiments had been done with *Bacterium coli mutabile*, too. Within a trio of weeks, Hinsh had done the experiments himself and got the results he expected. In due course, the first scientific paper of my life appeared in print, in a journal called *Transactions of the Faraday Society*. In contrast, I spent two years working under Woods' direction on the adaptation of a bacterium called *Acetobacter suboxydans* to resist a sulphonamide drug (more about why later) and, many months later, I drafted a joint paper on my findings. These, I can now say with confidence, were good and relevant - over fifty years later their equivalent had not reached print. Yet Woods was not wholly satisfied. Extra experiments, which I had not had time to do, would have led to a better-rounded paper; he could not quite bring himself to agree to publication without them. By then I was busy earning a living elsewhere and could not do them. I redrafted and reshaped the manuscript so as to leave the new questions open but clear; yet Woods remained indecisive. Fourteen years later, after his untimely death, his secretary found the still unsubmitted manuscript among his papers and returned it to me. It remains with me still, unsubmitted and unpublished, in a trunk with old experimental notes; a tiny monument to Woods' perfectionism.

Happily, I gained something valuable from this experience. I had, at the end of my research career, two or three more draft manuscripts of my own which I never submitted for the same reason: they were just not quite good enough for me to wish to see them in print. Yet these days I see several poorer ones in most issues of every scientific journal I read.

Actually, my transfer to Woods' supervision was eased by our common agreement that I, trained as a chemist, was far too ignorant of general microbiology to embark upon a good doctorate project. Woods therefore arranged for me a special studentship of £250 a year from the Medical Research Council, under which I spent the whole first year learning Microbiology and biochemistry, jointly tutored by Sandy Ogston and Donald Woods, and doing no research. This seemed to be an excellent arrangement, and I agreed to it enthusiastically; it promised considerable freedom of action for me and therefore time for such serious matters as jazz, politics and girls, as well as for boning up on what was for me a fascinating science.

However, there was an immediate problem: I had completed my Part 2 in June, my exhibition and other awards had run out, and the MRC grant did not start until September. It was the mid 1940s and my parents' finances were at a very low ebb, my father's wartime job having come to an end; though I wanted to get on with reading up the subject, I needed to live and eat. I possessed a few textbooks and these could be sold for the second-hand market to Blackwell's Bookshop for sums ranging from 12/6d to 25/-, and by patronising the British Restaurants (sources of cheap, government-subsidised meals from the wartime years which still operated in Oxford) I could eat for a week on 15/-. I sold a few, mostly with little sense of loss because they were accessible in libraries or else somewhat out of date, but I regretted parting with my 'Buckingham Prize' from Hele's School, Exeter, a zoological work by then of no scientific value to me but embossed with my name. I also regretted, and still regret, having to part with Hinshelwood's own book on chemical kinetics.

After a few weeks, however, this source of funds began to run out and things became seriously tight. With a puritanical sense of shame, because poverty, like religion, is something well-bred people only talk about in the abstract, I plucked up courage to see Sandy about my plight. As a result, Balliol College generously made me an 'eleemosynary' grant of £30 to see me through the rest of the vacation - a most welcome, indeed princely, sum which solved my problems for the foreseeable future. I still wish I had asked earlier. The College later awarded me War Memorial Studentship of £100 to assist with my tutorial year which, although a great honour, was but a short-lived pleasure because the MRC thereupon subtracted £100 from my grant.

In the autumn of 1945 I started on my year's study of chemical microbiology. It involved attending lectures and classes in a variety of University Departments; I took a pathology and bacteriology course for medical students, I attended their biochemistry lectures, I injected mice and measured physiological responses of vivisected cat organs on smoked drums in a pharmacology course, I looked at protozoa with zoologists (but this course petered out rather soon - I think the teacher found me an arrogant chemist and a distracting bore). I even went on a botanical expedition to Boars Hill to seek fungi; this I greatly enjoyed, as well as my discovery of the eruditely *risqué* systematic names that mycologists have invented for their pets. Twice weekly I reported to Woods or Ogston, with notes, questions and the occasional essay. I was reasonably assiduous, partly because I was truly interested but mainly, I regret, because I soon found out that Woods would discover if I was not - by a strange osmosis he seemed to know the content of all the courses he prescribed without ever being there.

But I did manage to crowd in quite an active non-scientific life as well. 1945-6 was a good time to be relatively free in Oxford; the bulk of the survivors of the war were returning or had returned to complete their courses, or take up new ones. Some I knew; some good friends were dead; a few chose not to return. College life was still austere, probably more so than during the war because supplies of 'lease-lend' food from the USA had ceased and such delicacies as spam fritters (quite delicious in those hungry days) disappeared forever from College lunch. But new activities started and old ones revived. I had become bored with student politics and scarcely noticed that the little squabbles, which had so preoccupied my fellow socialists and me during the war had, as befitted their essential triviality, succumbed to *forces majeures* in the surge of idealism following the Labour landslide of 1945.

The arts began to flourish again; The OU Dramatics Society revived and the name of one Ken Tynan, with his Experimental Theatre Club, began to be noised abroad. So did both amateur and academic philosophy; I became deeply influenced by logical positivism, courtesy of A J Ayer's seminal book, *Language, Truth and Logic*, and have never looked back. I already had a moderately uninformed interest in painting; I tried my hand at some phoney surrealism, even having a one-off shot with oils. Happily the familial frankness of my brother Oliver, himself trained at Kingston School of Art, put a stop to any further aspirations in that direction. My own paintings were terrible, but I still enjoy looking at other people's. I was accepted into a revived Balliol club, the 'Leonardo Society' (see picture in Chapter 2. It has since died out but still existed in the 1980s), where we read and discussed papers on almost anything, providing it was intellectually stimulating.

And periodically we dined. Often I was out of my depth, but I could improvise and dissimulate - and something usually rubbed off. I was also one of a very select group in Balliol (Christopher Longuet-Higgins was another), who called ourselves 'The Owls' and read poetry to each other; my taste for poetry was, however, transient and I already favoured the comic or bizarre. I was a member of a short-lived Balliol club called 'The Society For The Abolition Of Tuesday' which, with comic constitution and rituals, existed solely for frivolity and a couple of good dinners.

I remember a nightmarish episode when, in March 1945, with J P 'Johnny' Johnson, also a recent science graduate and a good friend, I hired two Canadian canoes and took a weekend off to go camping up the Thames into the river Evenlode. All went well, and our return was speeded by the fast-flowing spring water. Arriving near Oxford Prison some six hours before our canoes were due to be returned, we decided to 'navigate the drain'. This was an old Victorian drain conduit which went right under the centre of Oxford City and which was said to be navigable; there were stories of pre-war punt parties being held down there.

We found the entrance, close to Oxford Prison, easily. The current swept us along. But the water was high and we had insufficient room to manoeuvre our paddles. Our only lights were a candle each, which we stuck to the prows of our canoes once we were out of the wind, plus a few matches.

All went well at first. I was in the lead and we heard traffic and voices as we passed under a ventilation shaft several minutes into the drain. I believe it lies close to Carfax, more or less the town centre. But soon the ceiling became worryingly low, and we had to crouch down in our canoes. A short time later disaster struck: my canoe hit something, stopped abruptly, and my candle fell into the water, plunging me into pitch-black darkness. Almost at once Johnny's canoe hit mine and his candle vanished, too. L

Lighting one of our precious matches I saw that I had hit a pipe which lay transversely across the tunnel and, worse, that immediately beyond it the ceiling lowered again, down to within inches of the gurgling black water.

I think that pipe was our salvation. High spring water had almost filled the drain. The current was strong and we would probably have been drawn under and drowned. We had only a couple of matches left, so we took turns at smoking cigarettes, lighting one from the other, exploiting the glow for occasional glimpses of our surroundings. We still could not use our paddles; we had to lie on our backs in our canoes and propel ourselves hand-over-hand on the roof, ignoring as best we could damp, squashy patches, and tickly things that ran down our arms into our sleeves. Fear overrode my horror of spiders.

It was painfully slow and quite ghastly. Our relief as we glimpsed light from the entrance, some 45 minutes later, was tremendous.

It had been an idiotic thing to do - but we had a good tale to tell afterwards. Johnny took it all stoically. I had a sort of delayed shock: about a month later, I began to have nightmares about the trip, which returned occasionally for several years.

These were heady times, but the greatest thing for me was the increased opportunity to play and hear jazz. There were parties; dances and the pre-war Commemoration Balls were being revived. Among the returning military were several good jazz musicians; some had brought rare American jazz records. Soon there were enough jazz musicians around for the Bandits to undergo binary fission; like a bacterium, we split into two progeny, the OU Dixieland Bandits, led by me and playing a traditional kind of jazz, and the OU Bandits, who played more modern jazz and actually used written music (anathema to me, of course).

My relatively footloose year under Woods' direction allowed me freedom to run the Dixieland Bandits and play quite a lot, so when the time came for me to start regular research in the laboratory I was able to dovetail the music into my days fairly efficiently.

Shortly before my preliminary year ended, Donald Woods was involved in, and arranged for me to attend, one of the most useful gatherings of my scientific career; one which has a small but important place in the history of British microbiology. The Cambridge group of microbiologists decided to hold a summer school in microbiology, the prime movers being Marjorie Stephenson, Ernest Gale, Woods, Sidney Elsden (an alumnus of the Cambridge group, by then at Sheffield University) and probably others. The idea was to bring the participants in the school up to date with recent developments in chemical microbiology, and the list of lecturers' names read like a roll call of the British 'stars' of microbiology. It included the four organisers just mentioned plus B C J G ('Gabe") Knight, H J ('Bill') Bunker, Frank Happold, W E ('Kits') van Heyningen and several others. The lectures ranged from excellent to very good and there were demonstrations of research techniques, such as the use of the then fashionable Warburg manometer. (This was an ingenious but thoroughly awkward device, which was of amazing versatility for studying any physiological process which involves exchange of gases - as most such processes do - breathing, for instance. It was ideal for investigating populations or cultures of bacteria, which have a great propensity for producing or absorbing gas, and people who had mastered its basic clumsiness became so dedicated to it that they were known to put off, and even fail to do, experiments which could not be done in 'the Warburg'). The summer school included a few graduate students among the participants, but most were older than me with a few years' research experience. I formed several long-lasting friendships with scientists at this summer school and many participants later became pillars of the Society for General Microbiology or of its smaller progenitor, the Society for Applied Bacteriology. One personality whom I met first here was a Mr K R Butlin, a merry, laughing character with a devastating stammer; he will have his own chapter later.

Woods' intention, and that of the Cambridge group, as he made clear to me, was to upgrade the quality of non-medical microbiology in Britain. In this they succeeded quite remarkably; the spin-off as participants returned to their home laboratories, with new ideas and outlooks, was perceptible even to me in later years. And I know well that many participants still remembered this summer school, and its successor at Oxford a couple of years later, as a seminal experience several decades later. To the best of my knowledge the organisers got nothing material out of it beyond hospitality and some expenses. Their motivation was wholly altruistic, arising from dedication to microbiology - a motivation typical of the Cambridge group and of Donald Woods in particular.

I started on my doctoral research with Woods in mid August of 1946, in two rooms on the ground floor of the University Biochemistry Department. My first duty was not one which would be well received by today's graduate students; it was to help paint the walls and ceiling of one of these rooms. Indeed, I mildly resented this chore but was reduced to silence because Woods and his senior colleague Bob Nimmo-Smith also helped - as did Woods' efficient girl technician, Kathleen.

The two reasons why we all briefly became painters and decorators were quite simple. This particular room had been a small experimental animal room (called the 'rat room') and smelled of it; it was therefore full of the spores of microbes and in a wholly unsuitable state for microbiology until it had been thoroughly cleaned. But more urgent was the fact that Professor (later Sir) R A Peters, Head of the Department, had indicated vaguely that Woods could have the room - he was desperate for research space - and had then gone away without confirming this offer. Someone else might grab it, so a rapid take-over was necessary - which Woods successfully effected.

A digression about Professor Peters. He was a very friendly, accessible Professor, in no way alarming or severe. But he was always busy. Therefore he tended to conduct conversations fairly briskly and on the trot, walking along a corridor, away from a lecture or back to his own laboratory. His laboratory was located on the top floor of the Department, a tedious climb even for the young, and there was a special lift, reserved for him, with room for just one person, to take him there from the ground floor. It so happened that the entrance to the lift lay just between the doors to the old rat room and Woods' main lab, well within our earshot. I recall several occasions on which the slow-speaking Woods lumbered up the corridor talking to Peters, who duly entered his lift and, pressing the button before the conversation was finished, slowly vanished, his final remarks disappearing completely as he ascended to the heavens. I think the confusion over the rat room arose in this way; Woods was less than enthusiastic about it but, such was his natural discretion, he voiced no criticism - at least, not to me.

Even with the extra room, Woods' little microbiology group was chronically overcrowded: the two rooms housed Woods, who worked at the bench himself, me, Bob and Kathleen, very soon joined by June Lascelles of Australia and John Polding, an Englishman who had been working in Sudan, plus his technician. I was allowed slightly over a metre of bench for my own use, with a cupboard underneath, plus access to the refurbished rat room, now reserved for aseptic work with cultures.

June Lascelles

June Lascelles arrived in 1947 from Sydney University, financed by a 'Royal Exhibition of 1851 Overseas Research

Fellowship' - a most prestigious award. Severe-looking, firm-minded and plainly dressed, she fitted in with the Unit's ambience at once, taking to Woods' dedicated outlook and tolerating the crowded conditions well. She was usually in the lab of an evening and much of weekends (as were Nimmo-Smith and Woods. I, not the most earnest of research students, was rarely there). The Unit was a good-humoured group, but outside the laboratory June did not care for Oxford University; she considered it snobby, puffed-up and aristocratic - I have forgotten her frank Australian phraseology. She would tease me about my Oxford accent, but she put up with being called "colonial" in return, and we became long-term friends. I shall tell later how that friendship led me to one of my most important scientific discoveries. Her research at the time concerned the involvement of a then new vitamin, folic acid, in microbial metabolism.

In later years she became a world authority of a group of coloured bacteria that live by photosynthesis, as green plants do, and went to work in laboratories on the West Coast of the USA. She ended up as a Professor at the University of California, Los Angeles (UCLA). By then June and I met only at rare intervals over the years, at scientific meetings, but I remember particularly visiting her when I passed through Los Angeles in 1977, because I was due to give a seminar at UCLA. She met me at the airport without, rather to my surprise, a car, explaining that she hated LA traffic and never drove more than two miles. She used a bicycle for average journeys. We took the airport bus to Westwood Village where she lived, in a little cottage among the near-skyscrapers, rather English in style, with its own small garden, but within walking distance of the University. Apparently her home was much coveted by developers but she was firmly settled and, with typically Australian independence, avowed that she had not the slightest intention of giving it up unless she chose to return to Australia - which she had in mind to do when she retired. We talked of science and old times. The picture, from about 1950, shows Donald (left), Mrs Alison Woods (centre) and June (right).

My research

Back to 1946. My research project, as I mentioned earlier, was to study the adaptation of a microbe called *Acetobacter suboxydans* to resist the sulphonamide drugs. This was not just any old microbe; it was one, which needed a vitamin called paminobenzoic acid (which I shall abbreviate henceforth to 'pAB'). I shall explain the logic of the choice forthwith.

The sulphonamide drugs had been discovered and developed in the early thirties. They were an absolutely invaluable group of medicines which, in the pre-antibiotic days of the thirties, had revolutionised the treatment of bacterial diseases such as classical pneumonia and puerperal fever; during the then recent Second World War they had worked marvellously with gonorrhoea and war wounds. What they did was simply to stop many kinds of infecting bacteria from multiplying, without harming the patient at all. The patient's natural resistance then disposed of the non-multiplying bacteria and the disease regressed, often spectacularly. Woods' major claim to fame at the time I joined him was that he had elucidated, a few years earlier, the way sulphonamide drugs did this trick. He had discovered that various body fluids such as blood, or extracts of cells, could negate the action of sulphonamides, which means that they could prevent the drugs from stopping bacteria from multiplying. He then found that a well-known chemical, the one I called pAB, would do the same thing. He also found that amazingly small amounts of pAB worked. So he predicted that pAB was a vitamin: one of a class of substances which are essential, often in tiny amounts, for growth of both bacteria and higher organisms - like the familiar vitamins B C, D and so on which are needed by humans. And he also guessed that bacteria mistook sulphonamides for pAB (chemically these substances have certain resemblances) so that, in trying to use them in place of pAB, the bacteria gummed up their own works. Both ideas were proving to be absolutely right.

My *Acetobacter* was chosen because it had recently been shown to require pAB for growth: as far as this microbe was concerned, pAB was a true vitamin and it could not multiply without being supplied with a trace of it. It was also sensitive to sulphonamides, the amount it tolerated being entirely conditioned by the amount of pAB one allowed it. Still absorbed by the general topic of adaptation after my experiences with Hinshelwood, I was sure that I could 'train' the microbe to resist excessive sulphonamide. If I succeeded, how would it manage for pAB? Would it learn to make it? Or to manage without? Or what?

I no longer know whether this project was my idea or Woods'. I think it was largely mine but nursed and influenced by him. Anyway, it raised good scientific questions and was in a way complementary to Woods' and Bob Nimmo-Smith's research project: they were trying to work out in precisely what way deficiency of pAB 'gummed up the works' of sensitive bacteria, and they were making good progress in this direction. My plan also had a certain wider relevance: sulphonamide-resistant gonorrhoea had appeared towards the end of the war in Europe and any information on the topic of sulphonamide resistance might be medically valuable.

I chose to 'train' my bacteria in the way I had learned from Hinshelwood. His procedure, which had been used by bacteriologists in the 1920s and 30s, was to take a culture and inoculate portions into several culture tubes containing fresh growth medium, all but one of which also contained an increasing range of concentrations of the drug being studied. Usually each successive tube would have twice as much drug as the last. After incubating for two or three times as long as the drug-free population had taken to grow, the tube containing the highest concentration of drug that the bacteria had tolerated was selected, and its population was used to inoculate a new set of cultures with a higher range of drug concentrations. The tube from that range which had the most drug-resistant population provided the inoculum for a third, even higher, range of drug concentrations. And so on.

In that way, Hinsh and his colleagues had been able to build up the resistance of *Bacterium lactis aerogenes* to the antibacterial substance proflavin some 2000-fold. Today, microbiologists no longer 'train' bacteria so laboriously; they treat their bacteria with mutagenic agents, chemicals or radiation, thus making mutants which (generally) get there in one. But neither Hinsh nor I would have any truck with mutants, nor was Woods confident that mutants might not be odd in all sorts of other ways, so I adopted the gradualist approach, keeping the concentration of pAB constant but trying to push up the amount of sulphonamide tolerated by my sub-strains. I also set about trying to train *A. suboxydans* to do without pAB at all, thinking that this might alter its sulphonamide resistance interestingly.

My experimental plan had a further advantage, for one delighting in the social turbulence of post-war Oxford. I could come into the lab, spend a couple of hours setting up my 'training series', attend to a few chores - such as cleaning glassware as part of my duty rota, and helping to prepare communal sterile equipment or solutions. Then I had nothing to do until my cultures either grew or didn't, so off I went, to play music, talk, punt, have coffee and do all the very important things of student life.

I have always been very efficient in the lab, quick at manipulations and, except when under stress, accurate. But I was not well trained and in certain ways I was distinctly slapdash. Donald, for I could by now address Woods thus, was slow, deliberate and meticulous. This led to the most difficult feature of our relationship: a clash of work patterns. Donald was in the lab at all hours, except when lecturing or otherwise teaching. I, like many a student, tended to stay up late for all sorts of non-scientific, barely academic reasons, so I usually got up late, sometimes with a hangover, and always arrived at the laboratory last. I might also disappear for the odd hour or two during the day and I tended to vanish about six - though I might reappear for the odd hour or so in the evening if cultures needed setting up for next day. I might come in at weekends (from Saturday noon to Monday morning), but on a similar basis: for the odd hour or so. Usually I'd find Bob, Donald or June there and greet them cheerily before departing.

Donald put up with this flightiness for about six weeks and then decided action was necessary. One day, after a discussion of my progress, he embarked upon a serious talk with me, to the effect that he did not think I was spending enough time in the lab, that if my present research left time available I should use it to expand the range of my studies or do more kitchen duties (communal washing-up, sterilisation etc.), that I lacked dedication, that the MRC was not subsidising me to frivol around... and so on. All in his slow, mumbling voice, clearly gloomy and embarrassed. To say that I was hurt and dismayed would be an understatement; I had had no suspicion that my performance was in question. I was also appalled by the seeming humourlessness and philistinism of Donald's outlook - for was there not much else in life besides science? Did not a researcher need time off for thought and inspiration? And did he not appreciate my celebrated efficiency? I made these points and he was unimpressed; but the terrible thing was my sneaking realisation that there was something in what he said.

I wish I could say that I revised my ways with good grace. I certainly revised my ways but our relationship had soured: I felt restricted, spied-upon and bossed around by a censorious slave driver and I grumbled accordingly to my non-scientist friends. They sympathised. Today I can see that mine was a grossly unfair response to what was a kindly meant, if clumsy, way of setting me on the path to being a good research scientist. An effective way, too, and he must have hated having to tell me off at all. But graduate students are especially prone to take a paranoid view of their mentors; my sense of grievance attenuated over the succeeding months but never quite vanished during my stay with Donald. I should add that, observing a rapid improvement within days, Donald forgave me quickly and, I fondly believe, never suspected the depth of resentment he had stirred.

I could not feel overtly angry for long because, despite Donald's tendency to take a gloomy view of things in general, the microbiology group was a cheerful place, making real scientific progress with difficult problems; he was popular if exasperatingly slow at times and, despite my own problem, all regarded him as a working colleague and guide rather than a master-figure.

The work was indeed difficult. The key substance, pAB, is, as I said earlier, active at very low concentrations. It is present in almost everything: chemicals as supplied by commercial suppliers, tap water, the organic broths and extracts used to make up culture media for bacteria, human sweat and even fingerprints, dust, hair, the cotton wool used to plug culture vessel. In order to do experiments involving pAB one had to ensure its absence to start with, and this involved an elaborate routine of chemical cleanliness. Details would become tedious here, but here is a hint of the labour needed.

Glassware (such as flasks and test tubes) had to be washed in hot concentrated sulphuric + chromic acid, a hideously dangerous mix to get on yourself or your clothes, then washed repeatedly in tap water followed by twice in water distilled from an all-glass apparatus, itself previously washed with acid-chromate. Then dried, in a special oven kept free of dust and organic matter. Specially-cleaned stoppers and wrappings had to be used. Specially pure reagents, often recrystallized by one of us using our specially clean equipment, were used to make up culture media; all stocks to be kept in acid-chromate-washed vessels. Finally everything had to be sterilised separately from ordinary bacteriological equipment and media.

This procedure, devised by Donald and typical of his

meticulousness, was logical enough: it amounted to destroying, or removing as best one could, any contaminating pAB from everything one used. It was also a tremendous chore, which we performed communally, sharing a rota of cleaning duties (Donald's usually but not always taken by his technician - as was proper). If it was carried out carefully, one could obtain cultures, which were deficient in pAB, but, even so, they were not devoid of it. By this I mean that an inoculum of a microbe that required pAB would multiply in the 'clean' medium, but only a little; if one added a trace of pAB, the multiplication increased about tenfold and the extent of multiplication was proportional to the amount of pAB one added. Not a perfect experimental system, but one we could all make do with.

The acid-chromate treatment is not, I believe, nowadays permitted for routine use in laboratories, the Health and Safety at Work legislation, which sets laboratory standards, having excluded it. Apparently it can cause dermatitis in some people in addition to the hazards we knew of. Happily we all survived our weekly duties unscathed.

Another lesson Donald taught me was to set up all experiments in duplicate and to do them at least twice on two different days - plus a third time if there was any discrepancy at all. This, too, can become a chore and, in later life, I sometimes lapsed, but only with pilot experiments, never with crucial ones.

Well, my research had its ups and downs but I made the sulphonamide-resistant strains that I had planned to; I also studied some other pAB-requiring microbes. The results were interesting and moderately innovative; after some eighteen months I could see the shape of a doctoral thesis emerging. At some psychological expense, however. Donald's austere outlook and example did not suit my grasshopper mentality. I was in fact as obsessive as the next scientist, but I needed rests and distractions to keep up my morale and alertness. Yet now I felt guilty about such *congés*. I am sure that is why I was frequently unwell, subject to dizzy spells, abortive attacks of putative 'flu, dyspepsia and all the trimmings of what is now recognised as mild anxiety neurosis. Neither I nor anyone else saw it that way - which is probably just as well, because no treatment was available; tranquillisers were a couple of decades ahead. But there were many occasions when the veils lifted, sometimes capriciously. Here is one. There was a disastrously cold winter in 1946-47, with a terrible fuel shortage in addition to familiar post-war shortages. For six weeks Oxford's streets were barely passable to traffic because of the snow, and supplies of domestic gas and electricity were minimal. By then I lived in a self-catering single-room apartment in Wellington Square, a squalid place but my own, albeit shared with a family of mice. (I did not mind them except that one would sometimes get trapped in my waste paper tin and would wake me up at night with its scuffling.) Electric fires and cookers were banned, but I cooked my rations for breakfast and supper on a paraffin stove. Paraffin was like gold but somehow, John Polding had access to some and kept me supplied. Privation distracted me and I remember the surprise with which I realised, cycling merrily through ruts of snow to the laboratory one bitter but sunny morning, that I was feeling uncommonly well and rather happy.

I set about writing my thesis, with the concomitant discovery of experiments, which I ought to have, or thought I had, done properly but which were not quite right and had to be repeated. I worked like a beaver, putting my thesis together and doing the missing experiments while discussing it regularly with Donald. He seemed happy enough, if not actually delighted, with its scientific content, as well as with a burst of maths (a residue of Hinshelwood's influence), which I incorporated into the Discussion section. But I found him unhelpfully pernickety about the writing - he would mumble on about a paragraph or section but was not precise about what was wrong with it; all he would actually say was that it was unclear, vague or out of place. Since it usually seemed to me both logical and clear, I pressed on without paying much attention. It was over a year before I got an inkling of what he had in mind. Meanwhile I was typing it myself, to save money, on an Olivetti italic-only typewriter given to me by my father (a rare and curious, but cheap, machine) and time was pressing - my grant would soon run out. I needed and was seeking a job, for it was clear that there was none for me at Oxford; I was also contemplating marriage as well as continuing to run the Dixieland Bandits. In the event, time did run out. In the autumn of 1948 I got a job and I got married, but my thesis was not complete and, because of the pressures of both, it was a year before I finally finished it. So, more about that in another chapter.

Donald saw to it that I attended a few meetings of the

Society for General Microbiology, a newly formed learned society, which I enjoyed greatly but with some vicarious fears: alarm at the thought that I might one day have to get up there and speak myself. For I had discovered, as I had long suspected, that I was utterly terrified of public speaking. I would shake with abject fear and my voice would quaver; to ask a question at such a meeting would have required a level of bravery which I could not possibly have reached. This was odd, because, as Secretary of the Junior Common Room in my undergraduate days, I had had little such difficulty and was considered quite a wit, both spontaneously and in my writing of minutes. I had got a hint of this terror during my political activities, finding myself prone to unexpected nerves in a debate or discussion, but by now it had become nightmarish. It was the only reason why I never sought a university post: the very thought of lecturing made me feel ill. I now believe that this was a family predisposition which became hardened by my general anxiety state but, whatever the cause, dread of public speaking remained with me, waxing and waning, for some 25 years. I avoided teaching and lecturing obligations whenever I could and, as I shall tell, took up a career in professional research.

Consistent with my phobia, I avoided giving a Departmental seminar during my period in the biochemistry department and when, in the summer of my last year, Donald organised a second summer school in microbiology, this time at Oxford, I volunteered to make the domestic arrangements and so escaped any teaching function. It was a good school and my affairs went smoothly except when Professor Winkler of Holland, a distinguished microbiologist fond of things English, walked after dinner with some lady microbiologists back to their hostel, Holywell Manor, then a temporary residence for students of St. Hugh's, a College for women. They invited him in to continue their talks, but, to his and their astonishment, the porter refused to admit him because of a rule that no men were allowed into women's colleges after 7 pm. Happily their sense of humour came to the rescue and Professor Winkler returned to his own hostel, still a fervid anglophile if somewhat bemused. I apologised on behalf of my University but could do nothing.

It was at this summer school that I learned from Sidney Elsden of Donald's nickname, the Duck. I actually never heard it used at Oxford; it seems that he had acquired it in Marjorie Stephenson's group at Cambridge where, as an allusion to Walt Disney's animated cartoon character Donald Duck, Sidney and others had put a celluloid duck in his constant-temperature water bath. Remember Donald Duck? Brash, fast-talking, cunning, ebullient and emotional, yet always the ultimate fall guy? Never was a nickname less appropriate - or was that the point?

Musical interlude

Everyone (I trust) knows that jazz is basically a non-written music primarily played by ear and to a large extent improvised by the musician as he or she plays. I write 'primarily' because jazz themes and arrangements have usually been written by someone, sometime, and I write 'basically' because, especially in public performances, the 'improvisation' is often a modification of something thought out and played before rather than something wholly new. Yet there is a spontaneous quality pervading all good jazz, the major feature which distinguishes jazz music from orthodox Western music; other trademarks, such as its idiom and 'swing', are terribly important, but they are secondary.

Improvising together means that everyone playing must know the basic theme properly, and also have some reasonable anticipation of what their colleagues will play. For its first two or three decades of its history, this presented jazz musicians with little difficulty, because the jazz idiom was fairly easy to pick up, being rather stylised, with straightforward themes and harmonies. Collective improvisation was rather formalised and not very difficult. But during the later war years a serious challenge emerged: a new jazz style was developed in the USA called 'be-bop', later abbreviated to 'bop'. It was a way of playing which confused many older-style jazzmen because its themes were complex and technically difficult, and its idiom was rhythmically and melodically convoluted. Its name, be-bop, was onomatopoeic: an echo of the choppy rhythmic phrasing which was part of the new idiom. Some thought it liberating and embraced the new modernism with delight; others turned their backs on it in dismay or distaste. And if musicians were divided, audiences were positively schizoid; there were near-riots between modernists and traditionalists in France in the late forties.

This dichotomy afflicted the Bandits. As I mentioned earlier, it divided into two bands, the more traditionally-minded Dixieland Bandits, run by me, and the Bandits proper, more modernistic, even 'boppy', in approach, run by Dennis Matthews, a pianist. The two subdivisions were cool about each other (though a couple of Bandits played with both factions) and they gained different followings among the undergraduates. Happily, there were enough opportunities for both groups to play as frequently as our obligation to study permitted.

The Bandits proper had a problem, which did not bother the Dixieland Bandits. They needed written music. In pre-war days, apparently, the Bandits had possessed music stands with elegant insignia on the front. However, by early 1943, when I assumed responsibility for the by then defunct Bandits, I had no knowledge of them, nor would I have had any interest in them since I could not read music. My sole inheritance seemed to be a mysterious debt of thirty shillings to the National Provincial Bank, of which I learned only after a few weeks, and my major concern was then to avoid being held personally responsible for it. I no longer recall how the matter of that debt - which would have been crippling to me - was solved; I suspect the bank manager took pity on me and wrote it off. But the music stands were remembered by several of the returned servicemen after the war and, representing as they did quite a substantial cash investment, were a serious matter to the modernist faction of the post-war Bandits. The debt remained a mystery, but the music stands were recovered.

For the first couple of years of the war, the Bandits had been run by one Frank Dixon of Magdalen College, classics scholar and accomplished saxophonist and clarinettist; I had heard him play with the Bandits in my earlier Rhythm Club days. One of his preferred tunes was called *Angry* and I thought he performed very well; I had been deeply impressed by his talent, though I was less than keen on his disposition to quote *Colonel Bogey* rather often when improvising. Later he was briefly well known as a presenter of jazz programmes for the BBC. It transpired that, on his departure from Oxford some time around 1943, the music stands had followed him to his destination, Leeds, whither a search party from the modernist Bandits duly went and recovered them.

The returning servicemen altered the atmosphere of Oxford dramatically. As the war had progressed it had become a quiet, thinly-populated University, peopled mainly by scientists plus a leavening of Arts students who were deferred from, or unfit for, military service, and short-course visitors from the British, and later US Forces. Numbers at the four women's colleges, plus the Society of Home Students (later St Anne's College) had been less affected by the war, so there were proportionately more women undergraduates in the university - probably about 700. There was little to eat or drink, little in the way of theatre or social life, few punts on the river, few (and austere) parties. The local cinemas were well patronised; otherwise the main undergraduate activities centred on the political clubs, planning for the Brave New World. After mid 1945, the University rapidly filled up with men (and some women) returned from the war, remarkably (and understandably) mature in outlook, anxious now to leave their wartime experiences in the past and resume, and some to assume, the gentle and scholastic life amid the dreaming spires. Neither post-war austerity nor, for many, their own experiences, actually allowed the return of pre-war Oxford life, but change the Oxford scene they did.

As I wrote a couple of chapters ago, cultural and social activities burgeoned on all sides and, despite the exigencies of my post-graduate studies, I and my group of Bandits, managed to join in quite a lot of them. My own cornet playing was still rudimentary, though I could improvise within limits, and so could my equally amateur clarinet-playing friend, Paul Vaughan. He was an admirer of one Frank Teschemacher, a jazzman associated with the Chicago style of the 20s who had died young; he played spiky, agitated music, which Paul emulated, and had quite a cult following. (Paul later became a broadcasting personality, presenter of programmes and documentaries for BBC TV and radio, and occasional writer; he deserted jazz to become a good amateur classical musician). But we were fortunate enough to include some good, experienced musicians. Notable among these were Mervyn Brown, later Sir Mervyn Brown of the Foreign Service, who was (and is) an excellent tenor saxophonist and clarinettist as well as a useful occasional pianist. His tenor playing carried overtones of Bud Freeman, yet another famous Chicago jazzman. Mervyn could also read music, which few of the rest of us could do, and he more or less directed our music - or at least added some structure to our anarchic musical tendencies. Our double bass player was Mike Samuels, later Professor of Old and Middle English at the University of Glasgow, who was also outstanding for an amateur; he was a rather serious, mature man, very critical of drummers, whom he requested (usually unsuccessfully) to play quietly so the bass could be heard. Mike was prone to melancholy, not only about the band and its quality but his health, life in general, and the cumbersome nature of his instrument - which usually meant he had to be provided with a taxi fare. Our drummers, of which we had three at various times, admittedly had a cavalier attitude to dynamics and, sometimes, to tempo.

We had two principle pianists. The first was my early

musical mentor, Martin Milligan, who was amazingly talented, but he left Oxford in about 1945 to take up a career in keeping with his Marxist principles: as a lecturer for the Workers' Educational Association. It is an indication of his talent that the piano at Ruskin College, where we played for regular 'hops', was badly in need of tuning and played half a tone flat. Wind instruments such as the cornet, clarinet and saxophone could not be tuned down to match it, so whenever we played, Martin stayed in tune with us by fingering a semitone sharp. It made no difference at all to his fluent playing.

When he left, we were lucky to find an immediate replacement in David Clinch, who was a convincing follower of the style of jazz pianist Teddy Wilson. Musicians such as these carried the less accomplished of us along, and saved our reputation when the dancers required us to play such non-jazz dances as waltzes, tangos, rhumbas and so on - which we did, if with ill grace. I had learned three waltzes (one old-fashioned), two tangos and a rhumba by heart especially for such occasions.

We would play for private parties. We were sometimes booked for College dances - at one disastrous dance at Somerville College the band almost disintegrated because our musically trustworthy (but otherwise less dependable) tenor saxophonist, Mervyn, had double-booked himself and so departed at half time to play with the modernist Bandits. I mentioned that we often played at Ruskin College; by some quirk of the University Statutes, Ruskin was the only College in the University which was allowed to hold casual dances without obtaining Proctorial permission. We were not allowed to play for non-University functions, though we were sometimes asked to, because this would have been to intrude upon the local Musicians' Union's patch.

Actually some of the 'town' musicians liked us, and would 'sit in' with us - join in with the band for the fun of it - if opportunity arose:

"You chaps really know how to swing," said a saxophonist from one of the city bands enthusiastically. He had joined us (actually for a fee of about ten shillings) for a special occasion and relished his escape from the chores of playing dance music from printed arrangements. He spoiled it by adding quietly, "Even if you can't handle your instruments", a remark that added greatly to the melancholy of Mike, our bass player, who was the only one to hear it apart from me. Mike could handle his bass as well as any professional.

We sold ourselves, so to speak, on our enthusiasm, and when Commemoration Balls came back, many Colleges took to booking the Bandits - Dixieland or modernist - to play in the interval. 'Commems' as they were called, were expensive, all-night evening-dress shindigs with champagne and delicious food, for which nationally-known dance bands would be booked. We were delighted to be invited to play, because we would waive a fee in favour of a free double ticket (most of us could not possibly have afforded the necessary five to eight guineas), thus being able to bring along our girl friends, consume marvellous comestibles, play the music we loved and fraternise with 'name' musicians from London.

I recall, as leader of the "interval band", being invited to take champagne with the College Dance Committee in the company of the leader of the main band, Sidney Lipton, one of the most celebrated West End bandleaders. He was friendly enough to me, but uninterested when I left fairly soon in order to play in my band's set. The Bandits were playing merrily and noisily some 40 minutes later as a few of Mr Lipton's musicians drifted back - and it became clear we had sympathisers among them. Indeed, by the time the Maestro himself returned a marvellous, boisterous jam session was in progress, with the Bandits plus several jazz-minded members of Lipton's own band. His expression was thunderous - recollect that jazz was still a far from reputable music, especially among non-jazz dance musicians - so the professionals crept shame-facedly off the stand, we finished off quickly and Sidney Lipton took over without even the conventional acknowledgement expected on such occasions - such as: "A big hand for the... er... College Bandits..."

We usually had a somewhat disruptive effect on these visiting London bands. Tommy Kinsman, a popular 'society' bandleader, was more tolerant of us and craftily provided total contrast by going into a highland reel after our stint. Another, more sympathetic, occasion was when the late Nat Gonella, a pioneer trumpeter in the history of British jazz and a follower of Louis Armstrong, brought his own dance band to the St. Johns commem. This time we had a permanent effect on the evening's programme because, seeing the reception we got with our crude jazz, Gonella started playing jazz as well. I am not sure how the dancers made out, but both the Bandits and Gonella's men had a marvellous time, taking in rather a lot of champagne in the process. That evening included my one and only appearance in public as a jazz singer: urged on by equally inebriate colleagues, I sang a song into the microphone in which I expressed the wish that I might shimmy (a kind of dance) like a certain Kate, whom I claimed, quite falsely, as sibling. I have always had a weak, almost counter-tenor voice; I cannot think that my performance was impressive and I had the good taste never to repeat it. I like to think that no one minded.

Alcohol was (and is) the main hazard of playing jazz. There is always an element of touch-and-go about taking a jazz solo - will it work out? Will people like it? A little alcohol deadens both the nervousness and the critical faculties, but the temptation is to go on and have a little more, especially as playing jazz is always thirsty work. Well, we were young and physiologically tough; but conversely, strong drink was scarce and not always of high quality. At the Oriel College dance of a certain year a wine cup was served, one of those horrendous mixtures of wine, spirit, fruit and sugar widely favoured at the time because it would disguise the taste of even the nastiest wine. It seemed rather innocuous to the palate; not very nice - our guitarist said it reminded him of Dr Fenning's Fever Cure (a distinctively nasty-tasting medicament which is now obsolete, I believe). However, it was drinkable. Also, nothing else was on offer. The dance was going with a swing, the Bandits were playing well - so they believed and so the audience seemed to agree - when we were asked to play a popular novelty dance called *The Hokey-Cokey*. This, actually, presented us with no serious problem: the simple melody somewhat resembles a slow version of a traditional jazz number called *Muskrat Ramble*, so we followed our usual practice of playing that song slowly. However, to depart from the melody by taking a jazz solo would have confused the dancers and, after a dozen or so choruses of the same thing the band, though not the dancers, were getting bored. I do not know quite who had the idea of substituting a vocal chorus of *Lloyd George Knew My Father*, sung to the tune of the hymn *Onward Christian Soldiers*, I suspect the tenor saxophonist Mervyn, but we did just that - until I spotted the College Chaplain dancing past, eyeing us in some perplexity as if sensing something slightly out of place but not yet sure what. We rapidly segued into our emergency fail-safe mode: if things go seriously wrong, we all switch to playing play *Dinah* in A-flat. We brought it off, still maintaining the *Hokey-Cokey* tempo. It sounded terrible, but again no one seemed to notice. We'd never have managed it sober.

Later that night I learned the lesson every jazz musician must learn as soon as possible: if you must drink, pace your drinking. Sustained by the euphoria of musical creation, and perhaps wine cup, I was fine on the bandstand but, as I walked happily back to my lodgings through a deserted Oxford in the small hours of the morning, I was on three occasions perplexed to find myself apparently face to face with a grey wall. In fact I was not; each time, after appreciable reflection on my position, it transpired that I was flat on my face on the pavement. No one was about, so I picked myself and my precious cornet up and carried on, eventually reaching my bed - dusty, confused but largely undamaged. I remember little of the following day.

Unlike, I expect, our guitarist. He was an excellent

musician, batty about Dixieland and an admirer of Muggsy Spanier's Ragtime Band, a formative influence on all of us. Also, importantly for us, he emulated a Chicago jazz guitarist called Eddie Condon, a marvellously firm rhythm guitarist who actually never took a solo; he also played the relatively rare four-string guitar. So did our guitarist, Paddy; he too eschewed solos and played a four-stringed instrument. His enthusiastic cry of "take five!" - meaning take five choruses - as Mervyn took off on a tenor saxophone solo was a great stimulus to all.

Paddy was then decidedly Christian, and to many Christians jazz was still devilish music. He had resigned from the Bandits once on the grounds that "it is not God's will that (he) should play in a jazz band", but he had later crept sinfully back. However, at a certain Keble College commemoration ball his worst fears must have been confirmed. Late in the evening he went for a rest to the room set aside for the band, only to find it occupied by one of the front-line musicians without his trousers on, and a young lady in process of replacing her brassiere. She was a nice, well-endowed girl who had been introduced to him earlier and she bade him enter with friendliness and goodwill. Seemingly (for I was not there) he ran in dismay from the building. However, dedicated jazzman that he was, he was back for our next set.

Paddy later toured the world as bass singing classical songs. He spent only about a year with us, but again we were lucky in that Jim Hartley came back from the war and replaced him. Jim used the electric guitar, which he played with a natural talent and style. He had a very good ear for harmonies but could rarely name them, so, when arguments arose, as they usually did, about the harmonic structure of a tune, he would say, "This is the chord", and strum it. He would be right, sometimes exasperatingly so, but we would then have to argue about what the chord was that he had strummed. His solo style, being somewhat modernistic, helped to make the Dixieland Bandits musically less hidebound than they might have been. Today the band would be, more correctly, described as a 'mainstream', not Dixieland, jazz group.

Like Mike the bass player, Jim was given to melancholy about the band's repertoire and performance, not to mention about life, sex and politics. I knew that, on rare occasions when both Mike and Jim were smiling, it must be a great session...

We were enthusiasts, but we certainly needed stamina. In my last term at Oxford I played at four commems in one week. It was too much, and I took to returning to my lodgings between our sets for a couple of hours' sleep. Other Bandits were, it seems, to be found asleep in odd corners of the relevant colleges. Miraculously, when it was our turn to play, we all turned up on time, rarin' to go - and I managed something like a day's laboratory work in between.

Actually, such moments of mild debauchery were rare. We might normally play at a couple of formal dances a term, so we had to seek other opportunities to make our music. Undergraduates were not then allowed to go into pubs, but we did so, secretly, choosing pubs with pianos and tolerant landlords, so that we could have jam sessions - drinking beer and improvising jazz before a small gathering of supporters. Occasionally we had to stop and vanish, when word reached us by the undergraduates' bush telegraph that the University Proctors were on the prowl.

Some literati

Among our supporters were a couple of undergraduates who fancied themselves as blues singers, and who would sing with us when we played the blues or blues-based songs. Perhaps I should explain that the blues is one of the basic songs of jazz; it is a 12-bar motif capable of almost infinite variation, which has provided the harmonic and thematic basis of at least half the jazz repertoire since the music's inception. The major theme of *St Louis Blues*, if you happen to know it, is a perfect example of the blues.

The late Kingsley Amis, one of the most distinguished and amusing writers of the latter half of the 20th century, was to me simply a friend, fellow jazz fan and occasional blues singer. He was one of our more staunch supporters at these informal pub sessions, though it was quite clear that his enthusiasm was selective; he tolerated my distinctly primitive cornet playing but Mervyn's tenor and clarinet playing were (justly) the real attraction. Rather pale of complexion, with fair wavy hair and a somewhat daunting, curmudgeonly personality, Kingsley held strong opinions about jazz, as about most things, but I was never quite sure whether he was mimicking a view (or accent, which he did brilliantly) in mockery or expressing his own considered opinion. On the whole he liked the same kind of jazz as I did, but we had our differences: he enjoyed the jazz of Art Tatum, a pianist of exceptional technical brilliance whom I found far too decorative and flowery. But Kingsley's blues singing was convincing and far from flowery.

Blues singing was probably the only thing Kingsley had in common with another very talented young writer, the late John Wain, though later (in the 1950s) Wain and Amis were classified together (to their surprise) in the 'Angry Young Men' school of writers. John was then a rather sallow, scholarly-looking youth with sunken, penetrating dark eyes. On one occasion he summoned me and a couple of other Bandits to his rooms in Longwall Street because he had a trombone-playing friend visiting and a jam session seemed in order. It was only a moderate success: typically, given our level of musical achievement, the trombonist could only play comfortably in the key of C whereas I was awkward outside B flat or F. And our repertoire barely overlapped; we had little in common but the blues. So we played the blues in C at several tempos, John sang and I struggled with a few jazz phrases. He sang the blues well.

It does not detract from my admiration for both of them to record that, in later years when both Amis and Wain were famous, these old contacts gave me a conversational gambit, which I valued greatly. If, in literary company, the conversation turned to the literary works or views of Amis or Wain, I was in the rare position of being able to remark:

"Wain? Amis? Oh yes. Sang the blues with my band at Oxford. Not bad at all..."

A true statement, if excusably misleading: neither sang at any of our public performances.

Another great jazz fan of the time, though not an especial supporter of the later Bandits, was the late Philip Larkin. He possessed a remarkably comprehensive collection of the recordings made by a jazz clarinettist called Pee Wee Russell. A colleague of the aforementioned Eddie Condon, Russell was another Chicago jazz musician who came to prominence in the early 1930s, one with a most individual, almost eccentric, musical imagination. He would develop solos and themes in extraordinary directions, using a characteristic tone, sometimes squeaky, sometimes throbbing or growly - he was almost the jazz equivalent of a surrealist in painting. Larkin, like most of us, thought him marvellous; I recall going to Larkin's lodgings above a shop in Walton Street sometime in the mid 40s, to try to interest him in an attempt to revive the University Rhythm Club. He had a dark, overheated room with a portable wind-up gramophone, set on a table, which was covered with a heavy cloth to damp the sound. A shy, rather intense young man, already he seemed to be slightly balding, with a large, bespectacled, bean-like head. I failed in my mission, but spent a marvellous hour listening to him expounding upon, and illustrating from records, the diverse moods of his beloved Pee Wee.

Some thirty years later, after giving a seminar to the Biochemistry Department at the University of Hull, I had the pleasure of dining with Larkin and going over much of it again (though without records) - a gathering arranged by our host, Professor of Biochemistry Eddie Dawes, who thereby displayed his great good nature and tolerance. He had no special interest in jazz himself, and for such unfortunates there is no greater turn-off, as I learned early in my monomania, than two jazz lovers reminiscing and exchanging prejudices. Larkin, by then the University's Head Librarian, had become the distinguished poet known to almost everybody, as well as a respected if controversial jazz critic.

I had no real idea of the literary aspirations of these early fellow jazz fans. I myself had journalistic rather than literary aspirations and had got some political stuff published in a magazine called *LEFT* as well as, more important to me, being mentioned in the *Melody Maker* (the professional dance musicians' national weekly) by jazz pundit and columnist Max Jones. ("Well-known student of jazz John Postgate writes...." he wrote, in a resumé of letters he had received). And when I managed to sell an enthusiastic article on the history and development of jazz to a paperback series and it was published (Penguin Parade vol 2, 1948), my literary friends went out of their way to congratulate me, looking at me very narrowly indeed.

A coda

The Dixieland Bandits did achieve transient fame in the outside world. In 1947-8 the traditional jazz revival was well under way in Britain and we got to play at some London jazz clubs and for some parties in the metropolis (clandestinely as far as the University authorities were concerned, of course). We appeared twice at Cooks Ferry Inn, a sprawling pub somewhere on the North Western outskirts of London, which was the residence of the nationally renowned jazz band of Freddy Randall. Here we were complimented by some visiting Australian jazzmen, members of the Graeme Bell Band. We performed once, very briefly, at the club of the then up-and-coming trumpeter Humphrey Lyttelton in Windmill Street, where his clarinettist Wally Fawkes had a kind word for us. Once we appeared at a jazz club in a pub in Barnes. We were a hit on each occasion, even at Barnes, where we played badly, but in those days anyone who could get a jazz-like sound out of an instrument was likely to be a hit. It is ironical that Mervyn Brown, perhaps our most accomplished jazzman, was the least enjoyed because he played the tenor saxophone. In the 'trad' enthusiasts' canon of the time, tenors were not wholly respectable jazz instruments. Once, when I was trying to fix up a booking at a place in Leicester Square, the organizer offered to find a trombonist (the trombone was respectable) to replace our tenor for the proposed session. I demurred. We did not get the booking.

Amazingly, several tracks that the Bandits had made as private recordings were issued commercially, in 2002, on an historical compact disc of 'Oxford Jazz through the Years - 1926-1963' (Raymer Sound RSCD 763). Two tracks included me!

I learned another lesson. Playing jazz to a lay audience, it does not matter how good your music is, the audience will not notice - unless it expects it to be good, in which case it won't notice if it isn't. Yet even now, over sixty years on and having played until quite recently, I could never adjust to that precept; I continued to be dismayed when audiences fail to notice something good, and bemused when they cheered something just trite or trendy.

On course for reality

My time with Donald Woods ran out. As well as getting my research programme more or less finished, though with my thesis still incomplete, and also playing jazz, I had needed to look into the matter of earning a living. I fancied a research job, preferably a position without teaching commitments because of my fear of having to lecture. Guinness, brewers of the famous Irish stout, were recruiting staff for a new laboratory which they intended to set up to do basic research on brewing yeast, so at their invitation I visited their headquarters in Dublin. This was my first-ever flight in an aeroplane and I discovered another life-long phobia: I was frightened. But gradually I got used to the roar and rattle of our twin-piston-engine machine as it progressed, slowly and at a fairly low altitude, over these green islands; terror receded and I saw with astonished revelation that Wales, for instance, actually looks from high up like its map in the geography books.

The plane was over an hour late and I was politely reproached (as if I had any control over the matter) but forgiven and fed a late and alcoholic lunch, before being shown over the brewery. There was a marvellously aristocratic feel to the place. Its managers were called 'Brewers' (may be still, for all I know - I rather hope so) and their dining room was like a London club. The only time I have ever seen a footman in proper 'flunkey' dress was outside Lord Iveagh's room, when I was taken to meet him briefly. I was looked after most hospitably; I spent the night in their Georgian guest house in St James' Gate near the brewery and was deeply impressed that the bottles of Guinness on the table were dated and changed daily, whether used or not, so that they were always at their peak age of two months.

Fascinated as I was, I did not fancy the science which they had in mind, nor, in fact, did a certain hierarchical structure in the company appeal to my youthful egalitarianism. "We don't join the same tennis club as our staff, of course" said one of the Brewers. The one thing I liked was the salary: the pay of £800 a year, muttering about £900 when I seemed reluctant, was princely when the going rate for a new post-Doc in academic circles was £500 to £550 pa. But philosophical principles won and I turned down the job, gaining only a usefully inflated sense of my worth. Offering a fairly routine research job with the MRC at Hampstead, North London, the laboratory head was shocked when I mentioned £800, repeating twice: "That's much too much, far above your market value". They offered £500.

I did not go there either, though the science promised to be fairly interesting. I applied for a job in Alexander Fleming's laboratory at St. Mary's Hospital, Paddington, which provided me with my one and only direct contact with the discoverer of penicillin. I had an enormous regard for his work, and was a trifle disappointed to find a small, dour man with a northern (Scottish?) accent who did not seem much interested in what I had been doing. To put it tactfully, our minds did not meet; I was not at all impressed by his laboratory nor, in truth, by his rather vague scientific plans; appropriately, he did not want me. My friend Ernst Chain was of the opinion that I did well not to go there.

Good fortune intervened in the form of K R Butlin, the microbiologist I had met at the Summer Schools in Chemical Microbiology at both Cambridge and Oxford. He had a small research group located in a laboratory at Teddington, to the South West of London, working on the involvement of bacteria in the corrosion of metals. His work was very much concerned with practical matters and he wanted a biochemically-orientated young microbiologist to complement the applied work with some basic research on the relevant microbes. Of immediate concern to me was the fact that the rate of pay of Scientific Civil Servants at my age and level of qualification was around £500 pa. I was still dithering over Guinness, Butlin seemed to want me, and, with the support of the then Director of the laboratory in which he worked, Dr R P Linstead, he managed to fix for me a sort of personal Fellowship which would pay me £600 pa and enable me to work with his little team. I will not admit that the money tipped the balance, but it certainly left me happier with my emerging decision to decline Guinness' offer.

So I decided to go and work with Butlin at Teddington. But there were a couple of other matters to be seen to first.

The first was that I had decided to marry. I had undergone, for enjoyed is not the right word even though I would not have missed it for worlds, the largely sexual turmoil, the hopes, frustrations and delights of adolescence, superimposed upon a rather humdrum reality. I had been in and out of love with several young ladies, first at school and then at the University, and remotely with a couple of film stars, some of whom (not the film stars) had returned my affection. I had known the agonizing optimism of "will she? won't she?"; the trauma of being rejected; the compulsive selfishness of rejecting. As part of my youthful disdain for convention, I was impressed by the idea of free love, though opportunity for examining this conviction persistently eluded me. Yet I had vivid imaginings of a happy bachelor life with a succession of rich, voluptuous mistresses. In reality I found the world peopled with pleasant, even beautiful, young ladies who had their own, rather different, ideas of how their lives might develop.

All these dramas, fraught as they were with mundane absurdity rather than erotic incident, must await a proper autobiography, or perhaps better remain untold; it is sufficient to record that I had some years earlier fallen for a student of English from St. Hilda's who was both intelligent and good-looking. Her name was Mary Stewart, a raven-haired brunette (who in certain ways reminded me of me one of my preferred film stars, Jane Russell, though not, let me add, in her acting ability; Mary's would turn out to be greater). We got on well together in all appropriate ways (including that of companionship, so often forgotten by the young of today) and had enjoyed a steady relationship; the prospect of prolonged separation concentrated our minds, as they say. Mary had by now graduated, and was employed but not committed; she agreed that we should marry. We were old-fashioned enough to seek permission of our parents and, in the late autumn of 1948, we were duly married at a North

London registry office. After blueing a third of my father's wedding present on a week's honeymoon in Paris (total cost: £30), we together faced the next problem: where to live?

London in 1948 was suffering from a catastrophic post-war housing shortage. Rents were controlled at low levels; flats were very scarce and were rarely obtainable except on payment of an exorbitant (and illegal) premium called 'key money', an unpleasant means of exploiting the gratuities of demobilized soldiers. Consequently many newly-weds had to spend months, sometimes even years, in lodgings or (worse) in a parental home. But again Butlin (or rather his wife, Helen, this time) solved our problem: she miraculously found us a flat near Teddington, at a legal rent and without a premium. So, after a month in lodgings, amazed at our luck, Mary and I were able to move into a real home of our own.

My third problem was less easily solved. How, where, to play jazz in south-west London? I started hanging around jazz clubs in the West End when I could spare an evening, or cycling to jazz clubs in Hounslow, in nearby Richmond or Kingston. There was lots of jazz, most of it more stolidly traditional than I really liked, but there were also lots of decent cornet or trumpet players around, and no one wanted me.

Well, not quite no one. I met a few of the London jazz revivalist musicians, though I rarely got to sit in with their bands. However, hanging around a jazz club in Newport Street near Leicester Square underground station, I got talking to an aspiring trombonist by the name of Chris Barber. This was early in 1949; he was not happy with the band with which he then played, led by a rigidly traditionalist trumpeter called Ken Colyer, and he sought to form another.

I am almost sure that the clarinettist was to be one Cy Laurie, whom I had met a few times, but my memory may be faulty. However, I was to be tried out as the cornet player.

I often wonder how my life would have developed had I got to the planned try-out rehearsal. But I was having persistent intestinal troubles and, a couple of weeks before the date; I went unexpectedly into the Manor House Hospital, Golders Green, for emergency removal of my appendix. By the time I had emerged and become fit enough to take up the cornet again, a trumpeter had got my (potential) job. Chris Barber and his band (without Cy Laurie, who became famous in his own right) went on to fame and fortune as one of the leaders of the British traditional jazz revival, a household name, with hit records, a pop star income and (at least according to the fan magazines) jet-set life-style. His band became very good and his later lead trumpeter, Pat Halcox, became outstanding. Playing constantly, would I have become famous, rich and musically excellent too? Probably not; more likely I would either have been sacked for musical incompetence quite soon, or have collapsed with some kind of physico-nervous exhaustion.

Why the latter? Because, I later came to realise, my vague illnesses, intestinal disturbances, fears and anxieties of several years' duration were ay least in part stress symptoms, resulting from conscientiously trying to do too much all the time, doubtless exacerbated by an eccentric post-war diet. For I did not recover well from my appendectomy and, within months, was shown to be the possessor of a small but active duodenal ulcer.

Mary and I were both devastated. She because she "had not thought she would marry someone with an ulcer" (having made that remark, she buckled down and made the best of it). Me, because I was furious, insulted even, to find myself to be the sort of person who got ulcers, as well as being dismayed, when I read up on it, by the then intractable nature of this disorder. In those days the role of bacteria called *Helicobacter* in gastro-duodenal ulceration was not suspected and the means of controlling the patient's response to duodenal ulceration were either medically primitive or surgically devastating. Today, antibiotics and/or inhibitors of acid secretion render this condition trivial for the majority of patients; in 1950, under my nice, elderly doctor, my lot was a boiled fish plus milky slops diet with thrice-daily dollops of a suspension of bismuth carbonate. He took heed of the psychological component of this condition; he laced my bismuth with sodium bromide, and enjoined me not to worry so much and to restrict sexual intercourse to once a month at most. (As man-to-man he spoke: "Do find an opportunity to explain to your wife why; she might think there's another woman".)

I had been married and in my job with Butlin's group for about six months when the ulcer was diagnosed. My colleagues at the laboratory were sympathetic and supportive, and I arranged for a supply of milk to replace my share of their customary morning and afternoon cups of tea. Mary and I adjusted; she now had a clerical job in the Head Office of Thames Launches, a Twickenham firm that ran riverboats. I stuck fairly closely to the diet, persuaded my doctor of the virtues of aluminium hydroxide (without bromide) fairly soon, tried not to worry and sustained his other precept for just one month (I think). Nevertheless, I nursed that ulcer for two or three years, even carrying heavy bottles of antacid through the Libyan Desert.

But I have got a few months ahead of my story. Let me now introduce Kenneth Rupert Butlin and his team.

CHAPTER SEVEN

Butch

The Chemical Research Laboratory was a Government research laboratory employing about 180 people at Teddington, on the Western outskirts of Greater London. It was located within the grounds of (in 1948, within the same barbed wire as) the National Physical Laboratory or NPL, a much larger organisation of some 1200 employees. The NPL, founded partly by the Royal Society in 1901, had an international reputation for good, meticulous science with a practical background. CRL's reputation, on the other hand, was modest: its science tended to be steady and useful, though useful to whom was not always clear.

Amid this rather plodding community there were one or two nuclei of energy and enthusiasm, none more notable than Butlin, known to almost everyone as 'Butch'. Slim, balding, bespectacled, of rubicund complexion, exuberantly friendly, he was already one of Britain's leading applied microbiologists, an expert on industrial fermentations. And what was a microbiologist doing in a chemistry laboratory, you ask? So did many of the chemists, sometimes resentfully. In fact, there had been microbiologists at CRL since 1933, doing research on the chemical activities of industrially-important microbes. The probability is that, since microbiology was not a well-known science in those days, the Powers That Were in government could not think where else to put these inconveniently unclassifiable scientists, with their chemical reagents which happened, perversely, to be alive.

Butch had been at CRL since 1933. A Cambridge graduate, he had earlier worked on industrial fermentations in the Argentine, and later studied the acetic acid bacteria which are responsible for vinegar fermentation, continuing to study these microbes at Teddington. During the recent war he had worked in a team culturing edible yeast, for use as a food supplement. At the end of that war he had inherited a tiny research team of three (himself included), plus two support staff, working on sulphate-reducing bacteria as part of the Corrosion of Metals Group. The reason for this seemingly illogical placement was that sulphate-reducing bacteria quite often cause corrode iron and steel. My joining, as an academic Research Fellow, was the first step in his plan to expand his team into a larger, autonomous Microbiology Group, a plan that he carried through successfully over a decade.

Butch's successes, both personal and professional, was achieved in the teeth of a serious obstacle: he had a terrible stammer. He was not at all self-conscious about it, and he was dogged: he would not be helped with a word. One very soon learned to get on with something else while he struggled to say what he wanted to say, which might take some seconds - and a second can be a long time in such circumstances.

Though I know Butch hated his stammer - we never talked of it, though we became close friends as well as colleagues - I think he sometimes enjoyed the comedy occasioned when his words were not those expected. A group at the NPL used to put on musical evenings, with amateur talent, which was usually impressive, though not always. On one such occasion, as an aspiring young trumpeter of limited competence (not me) was making a real hash of a trumpet solo, Butch was clearly moved to make a confidential comment to his neighbours.

"I could f...f.... f...", he started.

It is difficult to whisper with a stammer; inevitably those around him began to pay attention.

"I could f-f-f-fuck it better than that!", he finally remarked, distinctly audibly.

But I fear he did not enjoy another occasion, when things became so farcical that I had to leave the room. At an early stage in my time with him, I shared his office. One day a distinguished soil microbiologist, Dr Jane Meiklejohn, visited him. She, it transpired, also had a speech problem but, whereas Butch had difficulty in starting certain words, Meiklejohn had difficulty in ending them - the last syllable would seem to resonate on. Each made the other worse as they sat facing each other, pop-popping and wa-wa-ing like two defective motorcycles. Young and inconsiderate as I was, I was seized with mounting hysteria and felt suddenly obliged to remember some urgent work in the adjacent lab.

However, such was Butch's openness and amiability that most people, me included, rapidly learned to take his stammer in their stride. People also enjoyed his outgoing, relatively uninhibited nature. It could have disconcerting consequences. I recall a comic episode, which involved June Lascelles, my erstwhile colleague and friend. In public, June and I were both shy and easily embarrassed; for instance, we had both suffered stomach-churning anxieties when due to talk at an International Congress of Biochemistry in Brussels in 1952. Around 1954, in a period when the Royal Society had its rooms in Burlington House in London, Butch and I went to a meeting of the Society at which June was present. Butch thought highly of June, and they sat together. However, Butch had a regular problem in lectures: whenever the room was darkened for slides, he was likely to fall asleep. Inevitably this happened again, but this time he remained asleep when the lights came back on. However, he soon emitted a snore so loud that he woke himself up with a start. He looked round in wild surmise, as did everyone else in the room, and June, much embarrassed on his behalf, blushed bright pink. In consequence, as poor June realised instantly, everyone thought it was she who had snored.

Mary and I lived in Twickenham, about two miles away from the laboratory. In 1950 she left Thames Launches for the NPL and was editing the NPL's house magazine, *NPL News*. This meant that we would both set off for the same destination each morning - though not always together, because my timekeeping was less assiduous than hers. We rode our bicycles, or took the bus in wet weather, for to possess a car in one's mid twenties was extremely rare in those early post-war days, even for two working partners who together earned a relatively high income.

CRL was one of several research stations financed and governed by the now long-disbanded Department of Scientific and Industrial Research (DSIR). This body was a true Civil Service Department and its headquarters and its stations were run on the stuffier of Civil Service lines. (One of its more outward-looking Headquarters staff once explained to me, sadly, that, if Ministries wanted to rid themselves of their more rigid, less competent Civil Servants, as they tended to in the post-war reshuffles, they would get them transferred into the DSIR). Staff at CRL were expected to work "conditioned hours" - notice the overtone of rigidity in that official terminology - from 9 to 5 from Monday to Friday, and 9 to 12 on Saturday; there was a book in the entrance hall which staff, on arrival in the morning, were expected to sign, entering the time on an adjacent column; at nine o'clock, the Porter/Doorman would draw a line and those that signed in late, below the line, would, in due course, be obliged to make up time or lose pay. Staff also had to sign out at the end of the day, but extra time spent at work at the end of the day did not make up for time lost at its beginning. After the independence of Oxford I found all this regulation amazing - which shows how innocent I was of the normal conventions of the nation's workforce - and I should have found it all most irksome had I not been working on a Fellowship basis and therefore not been required to sign the book. I was rather bad at getting going in the mornings at home, so I tended to arrive at about 9:20 and to leave late -

though I soon learned that the porter/doorman would be less than pleased if I stayed on after 5:30, when he was supposed to lock up. In fact, my privilege did not make a lot of difference because, as I learned after a couple of years when I transferred from my Fellowship to the Service, the staff had made a fool of the system: they signed the book but entered the time as 9:00 until about 9:20, when the obliging doorman got round to drawing the line.

This practice had a predictably absurd consequence a few years later when a young student came to do a short-term vacation job with Butlin's group. He, regularly arriving a little late and innocently signed the book at the correct time, thus throwing the cosy system into chaos. His unwelcome honesty generated considerable turbulence in the laboratory, of which he was largely unaware; until, after a couple of days, he was spoken to - at the instigation of the Administration, who did not wish to be bothered computing all the minutes lost by the more leisurely staff members. The young man, who went on to become one of Britain's most distinguished microbial geneticists and a Professor at Leicester University, was still telling the story in the 1980s.

Reducing "The Book" to a mockery was entirely admirable and had the support of the laboratory's seniors, especially Butch, because research, even pedestrian research, cannot be done on a nine-to-five basis. But I can understand the Administration's dilemma; it was at CRL that I first encountered real, dedicated skivers: people who did not arrive until a moment or two before the doorman drew the line, who then spent 20 or 30 minutes hanging up their coats and chatting, who took long tea breaks, who started to clear their benches or desks around 4:30 so as to be at the door, ready to sign off and go home, promptly at five. They would use every day of the Civil Servants' generous allowance of annual leave and they would also take the whole statutory allowance of uncertificated sick leave, whether they were actually ill or not. Not all that numerous, they were accepted and set a sort of norm for the laboratory's atmosphere. They were usually quite strong Trade Unionists and I am sure they felt proud of themselves for extracting every possible privilege in selling their labour to the exploiting bosses. They thus engaged my youthful leftist sympathy - though I was given pause by the thought that their 'bosses' were the community, not a lot of bloated capitalists.

When I joined them at the end of 1948, CRL's microbiologists comprised Butlin, who did no bench work himself and had his separate office; Molly Adams, an experienced microbiology technician skilled at isolating strains of sulphate-reducing bacteria; and Butlin's younger assistant Margaret Thomas, who was engaged in a programme of testing their resistance to disinfectants, antibiotics and anything else Butlin might think appropriate. They worked in the main lab, as did I, helped by two friendly but rather elderly gentlemen: George, who prepared culture media and sterile materials, and also washed up laboratory glassware, and Dave, who helped wash up, did heavy work and - very important this - made tea for us all twice daily.

I buckled down to bench work the day I arrived, to the astonishment, I later learned, of some denizens of CRL, who expected new staff to take a month or so to settle in. Molly and Margaret showed me how they grew sulphate-reducing bacteria, which was no easy task in those days, even for a trained microbiologist. They would not grow in the presence of oxygen, so one had to culture them in vessels from which air was excluded. There were various ways of doing this; for research purposes, one would set up test tubes with solution of appropriate nutrients, inoculate them from a previous culture (or a natural source) in air. To exclude oxygen the tubes went into a strong glass jar which would then be sealed with a special brass lid, then evacuated and filled with a mixture of hydrogen plus a little carbon dioxide from a gas cylinder. Next, the jar would be taken to a terminal where a low-voltage current would be passed into two terminals in its special lid. The current heated a small cylinder of platinum gauze inside the lid which was intended to ensure that the hydrogen burned up any traces of oxygen that might remain in the jar. After twenty or so minutes the jar would be removed to an incubator where the cultures would grow - or not, if that was the point of the experiment. When one wanted to inspect the cultures, the jar had to be opened, the culture tubes would be re-exposed to air, and the whole rigmarole would need to be repeated.

The idea behind that hot platinum gauze was, as I said, to catalyse the removal of residual oxygen. The idea works well for most anaerobic bacteria, but with sulphate-reducing bacteria it has the snag that they produce large quantities of hydrogen sulphide when they grow, and this rapidly 'poisons' the platinum: it coats the metal surface so that it is no longer a catalyst. Butlin and colleagues had thought of this; to overcome it they had George keep up a supply of discs of cotton wool, as wide as the jars, soaked in a chemical that would absorb hydrogen sulphide and dried. They would place one of these pads between the catalyst and the culture tubes, the idea being that the hydrogen sulphide would not reach the catalyst. The absorbent chemical, lead acetate, was highly poisonous, but health and safety regulations in laboratories were not what they are today and we all survived by handling the discs gently, with tongs.

Brashly, I pointed out that only minute amounts of hydrogen sulphide are needed to poison the tiny amount of platinum in those catalysts; surely enough it would sneak round, if not through, the lead acetate pads in a matter of minutes, once the cultures started growing. Politely my new colleagues agreed that I might well be right, but that the procedure worked. So I, too, adopted the ritual. I am still sure that I was right: that our platinum catalysts became poisoned from their first day of use and that we might just as well have played a flute to the jars as to heat up dud catalysts. But, like Molly and Margaret, I accepted the precept 'if it works, don't mess with it'. It can be a useful maxim in research.

The conventional recipes for media in which to culture sulphate-reducing bacteria did not enable the microbes to grow in sufficient numbers for me to do biochemistry with them, so I set about devising improvements - seeing if there were any special ingredients which I could add to the nutrient mix, which would cause more cells to grow in a reasonable volume of culture. I had some success, but Butlin was not altogether pleased. He already had Molly and Margaret working on growing these bugs in one way or another; that his new researcher from Oxford should also start working on growth was not what he had in mind at all. Moreover, he had invested in that expensive and fashionable piece of apparatus, the set-up of delicate little flasks and tubes called Warburg manometers, which were then widely used in biochemical and physiological research. They were invaluable in their day but are now totally obsolete. Butlin, Molly and Margaret had used the apparatus once, with highly unimpressive results. He had expected that I would use them, but I, innocently, had hardly looked at them. After hinting for a few weeks he could contain himself no longer, he virtually ordered me to do some experiments with the 'Warburgs', as we called them.

I asked what he wanted me to do with them. I do not recall his reply, but it was to the effect that he did not know, but that I was there to know what needed doing, and to "use those b-b-bloody Warburgs!"

So I did. In the mornings I would set up growth experiments; in the afternoon I 'played Warburgs'. Very soon both techniques began to pay off, and I found ways to link them, so that my findings with one technique complemented those with the other.

There is a lesson here. The truth is that I had been mentally lazy. I had worked on one or another aspect of bacterial growth with both Hinshelwood and Woods, so ideas for the sorts of experiments that needed doing came easily to me. But I was not adding much to what Butch's group had already done; I needed a metaphorical push to make me think beyond my habitual research outlook. This, I now know, is a major problem among research scientists, especially as they grow older: they are, sometimes barely consciously, reluctant to adopt unfamiliar techniques and approaches, especially when familiar ones seem to be going nicely. Butch had no clear idea what might be learned using Warburgs, but he was sure that, since it was a largely untried technique in the context of sulphate-reducing bacteria, it could not fail to yield new and important information. He was right. For myself, I realised the underlying message only slowly, but in later years I was careful to guard against such inertia in myself, and, when I reached a senior position in research, I too would urge associates into exploring new areas and techniques even if I was less than clear myself where they might lead.

At Teddington I began to make progress. Within a few months I had made a real scientific discovery, one worth reporting in a letter to the scientific journal *Nature*. Butlin was pleased and I was delighted. Donald Woods, whom I consulted, thought I was rushing things but he was not actually discouraging. I began to write my first original, albeit brief, scientific paper, but to explain what it was all about I must introduce the sulphate-reducing bacteria more formally, so to speak, and explain what I, a distinctly academic scientist, was doing among a tiny team within a group studying the corrosion of metals.

Sulphate reducers

Scientists have very subjective attitudes to other scientists' research. Once, during my time with Hinshelwood, I was queuing for lunch at Balliol, and I told Bruce Fowler, a fellow undergraduate and medical student, that I was working on *Bacterium lactis aerogenes*. Though a medico's training involves a lot of science, he was nevertheless astonished, incredulous even. Thus he spoke:

"How can you *work* on *Bacterium lactis aerogenes*? Either it's *Bacterium lactis aerogenes* or it isn't. What work is there to do?"

I tried to explain that I was studying the way in which it acclimatised itself to new types of food. He found this even more absurd.

"Who wants to feed *Bacterium lactis aerogenes*? Couldn't you at least study something useful?"

I think I was left opening and shutting my mouth like a goldfish. To Bruce, who later became a distinguished London physician, the only microbes that mattered were those that caused disease. He might have conceded, had the queue not moved, that something with a bearing on disease might be learned by studying bacteria that did not cause disease; but he would have regarded it as a devious and ill-judged approach.

Yet even that argument would have wrong-footed our discussion. On a different occasion I explained to a sixth-former with a scientific bent what I was doing with Hinshelwood: that I was working out how a microbe adjusted itself to a new environment. His view was different from Bruce's; he was deeply impressed.

"You are probing a basic secret of life, aren't you?"

I preened myself. I tried to look profound. I agreed.

Actually, the truth lay in between. Philosophical romanticism - probing a basic secret of life - was a primary motivation for me, for Hinshelwood, for Woods and the rest of us; of that there is no doubt and I do not think I ever met a biological scientist of whom that was not in some degree true. But if, in pursuing our inquiry into such matters as the ways in which a living thing adjusts to change, we were to turn up something of use to medicine, industry or society, how delighted we should be! But the chance of that was fairly remote, at least within our immediate research programmes, and it was the inquiry itself which motivated us from day to day. Both the possibility of a glorious practical discovery and the dramatic overtone expressed by my sixth-former friend became suppressed in our minds in the ongoing, pedestrian routine of daily experiments.

I imagine such considerations apply to all science. But if scientists themselves take such divergent views of what their colleagues are doing, it is hardly surprising that administrators and laymen have difficulty in grasping how research works, how vague its objectives are and why the researcher's actual day-to-day operations more often than not seem barely relevant. The administrators at CRL felt that they had grasped what Butlin's group was doing: he was trying to stop some perverse bugs from corroding buried gas and water pipes, a problem they could understand because it did, and still does, cost Britain's industry immense sums of money in repairs and other losses. They had even learned to take the term 'sulphate-reducing bacteria' in their stride. But ask them what that name implied, and they would have been baffled. I fondly believe that they recognised that I had some function, but what it might be was as obscure as the name of the bugs I worked on. Molly and Margaret were doing the work related to corrosion and I was definitely not; I had been brought in to find out more about the inner workings of these bacteria. That was the formal, and principal, reason why I was there at all.

From a purely scientific viewpoint, these bacteria are quite fascinating. You and I, and all the living things we see around us, plants and animals, need the oxygen of air to live and breathe. Without it we die very quickly. The sulphate-reducing bacteria will not grow in air; the oxygen of air puts a stop to their metabolism. There are several groups of bacteria like this; microbiologists call them anaerobes, and most obtain energy for growth and multiplication by breaking down organic matter. They flourish in places which air does not reach readily, in the middle of a compost or dung heap, for example, where they are protected from oxygen by the respiration of other, air-breathing, microbes. Many anaerobes cannot multiply at all if air is present; they become dormant and sooner or later die in air. How do they survive at all, then? You would be surprised how many air-free environments there are on this planet, in river and pond sediments, marine sediments, rich soils, animals' guts, heaps of decaying matter such as leaf litter or manure, sewage plants - they have plenty of long-term habitats. Many anaerobes are of considerable medical, environmental or industrial importance - but this is not a textbook. The sulphate reducers are odd in that, though they hate oxygen gas, they conduct a special sort of respiration for which they need oxygen atoms. Where do they get them? Sulphates are compounds of oxygen and sulphur, which are widespread in soil and water; these bacteria split the oxygen atoms off the sulphate, use them for respiration, and leave the sulphur atoms behind as a substance called sulphide. The technical description of the process is 'the reduction of sulphate to sulphide' - hence their name.

I shall describe the intricacies of sulphate reduction a little further in due course, but at the moment I am leading up to my first-ever scientific paper.

What I had done stemmed directly from Donald Woods' work. I told in Chapter 5 how Donald had shown that sulphonamides worked because the bacteria confuse them with a vitamin, pAB, which they must have in order to multiply. Could I, I had asked myself, confuse the sulphate-reducing bacteria by offering them something which they would mistake for sulphate, and which would gum up their works in a comparable way? Trained as a chemist as I was, the answer was obvious: try selenate. Why is that obvious? A chemist knows that the element selenium is very like sulphur in its chemical properties: though it has an altogether bigger atom, it forms the same sorts of compounds, and selenates have similar chemical structures to sulphates except that a selenium atom replaces the sulphur. Amazingly, no one had tried this before. I had set up appropriate growth and Warburg experiments and discovered, delightedly, that sulphate-reducing bacteria not only failed to reduce selenate, but that selenate blocked their ability to reduce sulphate. Moreover, the silly things were so confused by selenate that a little selenate would block the reduction of a lot of sulphate. This was quite unexpected; you need a lot of a sulphonamide to block the utilisation of a little pAB, because the bugs have a high affinity for their regular vitamin. I had discovered what was then the most powerful antagonist of a metabolic reaction known. It may still be for all I know.

I wish I could say selenate was as useful as it was scientifically interesting, but selenates are rather poisonous substances to use in the real world, especially as agents for preventing underground corrosion. But metabolic antagonists were in subjects around the end of the 1940s and my paper, my very first, my own, paper, was accepted and published, a contribution to fundamental scientific knowledge.

I had proudly entitled it, "Competitive Inhibition of Sulphate Reduction by Selenate". Ray Tucker, CRL's deputy administrator, with whom I had formed a bantering friendship, told me he was impressed by the title. He understood the words 'of' and 'by', he explained, but the subtleties of the rest eluded him.

Butch, too, was pleased. I had produced a small but novel gobbet of basic science, which was what I was supposed to do; my little publication pleased academic microbiologists and brought transient glory to the Teddington group. I extended the work in various directions, I successfully devised a new medium for growing lots of cells; additional creditable academic papers were in the offing. I had opened up a channel of basic research at CRL, and Butch could now proceed with his subsidiary reason for having me there: he began to think out ways in which he might exploit our new understanding of sulphate reducers to get more independence for his group of microbiologists at CRL. His first step would be to get away from the emphasis on corrosion, which was the official justification for his whole research support.

Providentially, a consequence of post-war industrial expansion provided Butch with the lever he needed: British industry found itself running out of elemental sulphur, and it seemed possible that microbiologists working on sulphur bacteria might have ways of alleviating that shortage. But before I embark on that story, I must tidy up a few of my own affairs.

A lesson in English

I had left Woods with my doctoral thesis unfinished. Partly this was because there were some experimental loose ends, which I had hoped I might tidy up at CRL, but that had proved impracticable. Butch would not have objected, but I was much too busy and anxious, working myself into my new job. The only thing left was to be open about the loose ends and hope the rest, written up nicely and logically, would pass muster. Woods thought it would.

So in the evenings, in our flat, I typed out my thesis on the sitting room table, using three fingers (I could not type, nor could I afford a typist). I used an old portable typewriter lent me by my mother. The neighbours downstairs complained, but were mollified when I bought a thick felt mat which, placed under the typewriter and supplemented by a blanket, damped the tap-tap-tapping. It made the operation sort of squashy, which enhanced the inaccuracy of my typing, but I was in a hurry. I was also nursing my duodenal ulcer and, for a couple of months, I was immobilised by having to have an appendectomy. Altogether I was in poor physical and mental shape, despite the fact that my research at CRL was going rather well. No one read the script of my thesis for me (Donald might have been willing, but I was in no mood for what seemed to me his vague nit-picking). I bashed on, threw a thesis together and submitted it, the copies in spring-back binders (although the regulations stipulated 'bound') to avoid the expense of having it bound professionally.

Duly at the end of 1949 I was summoned to Oxford for my *viva voce* examination. My examiners were Dr G P Gladstone, a distinguished medical microbiologist, and Dr S R (Sidney) Elsden, a distinguished non-medical microbiologist of biochemical slant: a wholly appropriate choice for the character of my research project. They were friendly but distant; they seemed to be strangely preoccupied with ambiguities in a few of my sentences and seemed almost wilfully to misinterpret points which I had made. We got round to discussing some of the science and I felt I defended my corner well enough, but it was a long and gruelling experience and I emerged feeling somewhat wrung out.

I was chatting to old colleagues in Woods' laboratory later, when Donald himself called me aside. He told me I had failed: the examiners had let him know informally that they would recommend that my thesis be rejected on grounds of poor presentation.

I was devastated. Bob Nimmo-Smith and the rest had a party planned for that evening, but I could not face it. I left Oxford for home by the next train, telegraphing my regrets to my old colleagues from the station.

Looking back from a lifetime later, that result was well deserved and necessary. I had had no training whatever in written self-expression since early adolescence. I had been obliged to scribble down lecture and teachers' notes, to write essays and answer examination papers, at tremendous speed with little attention to syntax or thoughtful phraseology. My background reading had been the published literature of chemistry, still rich in convoluted writing derived from its Teutonic heritage; I could not distinguish good from bad writing and I wrote almost by free association, expecting my readers to be on my own wavelength, as tutors, teachers and colleagues often are. I had no thought of those who might not be. I was a fast, lazy writer.

Butlin was sympathetic. He offered to look at my thesis. After one brief look at it he must have reached the conclusion I have just outlined; it remained unopened on his desk for the next three months, after which time, having to some extent recovered from my shock, I surreptitiously reclaimed it.

I still did not clearly understand what was wrong until Mary, with her degree in English, took the matter in hand and laboriously went through it with me, sentence by sentence. It was a revelation; I came to realise that it was full of errors of grammar and syntax, fraught with ambiguities, over-condensations and circuitous expression. And the presentation was often illogical, with backtracking and confusing side issues. There was convoluted writing, which sometimes reflected confused thinking. There were misspellings and too many typing errors: even the title page had sported, unnoticed by me, the non-word 'microorgansims'. The references were not set out consistently and some were wrong; the information accompanying tables and diagrams was inadequate. In short, it was a sloppy product, produced in haste and read through uncritically.

Mary was totally non-scientific, which was probably an advantage because she not only saw the obvious faults but caught defects which a microbiologist might have let slip by. Her criticisms added up to another devastating experience, but one which educated me in a way my formal mentors had wholly neglected. I got the message. Several years later I would become a severe and respected Editor of *The Journal of General Microbiology*, a researcher widely admired for the high quality of my scientific writing, and the scourge of my colleagues' reports and papers - entirely because of Mary's ministrations in 1950-51. But the immediate problem was the recasting and resubmission of my thesis. To the dismay of the neighbours downstairs, who had had three months' respite, I got out the old typewriter and tap-tap-tappitted once more.

I had the new edition of my thesis properly bound, after Mary had rechecked it, and then I resubmitted it. I was so terrified of the *viva* a few weeks later that I could hardly bring myself to enter the room. But it was short and friendly. I sailed through. In due course I paid appropriate fees and could call myself Doctor John Postgate.

The sulphur bandwagon

By late 1948, when I joined Butlin, British industry was just picking up from the parlous economic conditions of the immediate post-war years. Sulphur is an extremely important raw material of industry; indeed, it is an odd fact that the economic state of a developed country can be judged by the amount of sulphur it consumes *per caput*. Sulphur consumption is a curious index of industrial activity because in fact the sulphur, which is consumed hardly ever, forms part of the final product. True, sulphur is a component of rubber goods, of some medicines, plastics and fertilisers, but by far the greatest quantity is converted into sulphuric acid, and consumed during the processing of industrial products. There are few heavy industries that do not use sulphuric acid at some stage in their manufacturing processes, but almost always at an intermediate stage, so that the sulphuric acid eventually goes down the drain, not into the product. In 1950 Britain needed something like 200 000 tonnes of sulphur a year to make sulphuric acid for its slowly reviving industry, and was not getting it. Most of the world's sulphur comes from the USA, especially Texas and Louisiana, and the deposits of sulphur in those states were being exhausted faster than new ones were being discovered. So there was a shortage, and the price of sulphur was going up to levels which the penurious British could not afford, especially as they had to pay in precious US dollars.

The crucial matter for Butlin's plans was that industry does not have to make sulphuric acid from elemental sulphur; it can be made from sulphides and, especially easily, from hydrogen sulphide, which is a gas. And hydrogen sulphide is what the sulphate-reducing bacteria make from sulphates. The idea of using bacteria to make hydrogen sulphide on an industrial scale, for conversion into sulphuric acid, had been considered during the war, as part of a search for resources that did not have to be imported, but the idea had been discarded because the bacteria were much, much too slow.

In my experiments using Warburg manometers I had been measuring rates of sulphate reduction, and I found that I had some numbers which altered the picture. I was using fairly dense populations of sulphate-reducing bacteria, which had been harvested freshly, and concentrated from one of my new, productive culture media. Instead of organic matter, such as the conventional sodium lactate, I provided them with hydrogen gas wherewith to reduce sulphate. This was because others had established, and I had confirmed, that the rate and amount of hydrogen they consumed was a precise measure of the rate and amount of sulphate reduced to sulphide. It was much easier in the lab to measure rates of uptake of hydrogen than either disappearance of sulphate or formation of sulphide, and in research one always tries to take the easiest way.

The important point for Butlin was that my bacteria were sensationally active. They reduced sulphate about ten times as fast as those that had been studied earlier. I could get them to function another seven times faster if I contrived to harvest cells that were still multiplying: a seventy-fold increase at their best. The reason was that my cultures had grown very quickly, usually overnight, so the cells in the population were all young and vigorous. My predecessors had used populations, which were two or three weeks old.

For my part, I took this result casually: it was what I had hoped would happen, because I knew that microbes often show immense metabolic activities when they are, or have recently been, multiplying, but that they simmer down rapidly. I had wanted fresh, active cultures so I could get on with my experiments quickly.

However, my numbers, when scaled up, brought the industrial production of sulphide using bacteria into the realms of feasibility. Butlin, seeing a route towards making his research team independent, proposed to the DSIR that his group abandon part of its corrosion programme and start research on such a process. Naturally, I was pleased, too, and helped to do the scaling-up sums. After all these years I can admit that we got them optimistically wrong, not only with a slipped decimal point (we caught up with that quite quickly), but we did not know then that figures obtained using hydrogen did not fairly measure the microbes' activity with more ordinary substrates; these never supported such impressive activity. No one noticed these flaws. The DSIR and the Board of Trade passionately wanted a process, which would save dollars anyway. All agreed that we should go ahead; if things continued to look promising, more money and staff would be forthcoming.

All sorts of questions now arose. For example, might there not be better, faster bugs than the strain I was using? It had been isolated before the war from a corroding pipe at Hildenborough in Kent. Why not seek and test some new ones? But where from? There were sulphur springs in various parts of the world, where bacteria were known to be responsible for forming the sulphur naturally. Would some of these microbes prove to be super-bugs?

Butlin had come across a report by some oil geologists, which described a trio of lakes, fed by sulphur springs, near El Agheila in North Africa. They lay on the border separating Cyrenaica from Tripolitania, in what is now Libya. Apparently at least one of the lakes produced elemental sulphur in sufficient quantities for the local Arabs to market it (they sold it for veterinary and medicinal purposes). At that time Cyrenaica and Tripolitania were separate countries, still under a British Military Administration in the aftermath of their liberation from Italian domination during the Second World War. Butlin suggested to the DSIR that a sulphur lake might be a good place for a visit, especially if the army would rally round with help. Astonishingly, for he had not expected the idea to be taken seriously, they agreed; arrangements with the local administrations were made and, in the spring of 1950, he and I were sent to North Africa to bring back samples from the lakes from which we could isolate sulphur bacteria.

Tripoli

The four-hour flight from chilly London Airport to Tripoli, in a British Overseas Airways York aircraft, through a thunderstorm over Spain, did nothing to ameliorate my fear of flying. Happily the noise and vibration of its piston engines made conversation impossible, so I did not have to talk to Butch; I could wallow silently in my private cold sweat. But the euphoria of arriving, alive, and sensing the warmth, the strange sounds and smells of the North African night, almost compensated for my ordeal. Tripoli, seen next morning from the balcony of the Uaddan Hotel (Tripoli's poshest, still an Officers' Club at that time), was beautiful, with palm trees lining its harbour, blue sea and sky, almost traffic-free but for horse-drawn gharries. The town was sunny, dusty and smelly (a blend of warm horse urine and eucalyptus - one got used to it).

We were a few days early for the weekly flight to Benghazi, from whence we were to make our expedition to the lakes, and we had a few arrangements to make in Tripoli: inquiries about the sulphur lakes, some official visits; things moved at a leisurely pace in that part of the world. We went to a local Agricultural Research Station; we had talks with the British Administrator, and with the US consul. The latter, Mr Orray Taft, was an enthusiast for developing the region and wanted us to report the existence of potash deposits to the North. This was far from our objective, but we dutifully included it in our report. As best I know, it passed completely unnoticed. Butch was always rather frank about matters of health and regarded it as something of a conversational gambit to tell all and sundry that I had a duodenal ulcer - to my embarrassment. The consul expressed himself impressed that I proposed taking my ulcer on an expedition into the desert. Happily my digestive system worked well and my recollection of Tripoli is more of eating and drinking than of science. Though liberated from the Italians, Tripoli retained its Italian *ristorante* together with their proprietors, so the food, coming after Britain's post-war austerities, was marvellous. At the Romagna Restaurant, Tripoli's best, we had *tournedos* and *zabaglione*, my diary reminds me, a rare treat after years of British austerity and to hell with the ulcer... Butch and I were warming to scientific fieldwork.

A couple of fragments. At a cocktail party I asked His Excellency the British Administrator, "What is the major industry of the local Arabs?" "Theft," he replied mildly. I was young, and a little shocked by his cynicism. At Sidi Mesri, outside Tripoli, the Agricultural Research Station, directed by a Mr Wordsworth (related, he said, to the poet), had virtually no staff. Lovely, expensive precision balances and other desirable scientific equipment, left by the Italians, were deteriorating for lack of use and maintenance.

We went into the old Arab quarter to visit an Italian

scientist who had written a paper about the El Agheila sulphur lakes several years before the war. He was delighted to see us, but had little English; as we had no Italian at all, communication was limited. The old town pleased Butch mightily, but it rather alarmed me and I disappointed him by refusing to return for a walk-round at night.

After three or four days it was time to catch the Air Malta plane to Benghazi. That airline, which was not then party to the International Air Agreement, used sparsely refurbished wartime Dakotas, noisy and slow. It was a 90-minute flight and the one steward, male, served coffee tasting of paraffin in paper cups. But the flight went so smoothly over the Gulf of Sirte that I plucked up the courage to answer a call of nature and visit the loo at the tail end. Once in there, and duly positioned, all hell broke loose: the aeroplane seemed to leap and plunge about the sky, and my unease was enhanced when I realised, as I was peeing, that I could see the desert below through the hole at the bottom of the pedestal. I did not then understand, and it would have been no comfort anyway, that we had just finished crossing the sea and were feeling turbulence as the plane encountered air rising from the warm land. I returned to my seat as fast as I could, lower garments a bit damp, and spent the rest of the journey in misery while my neighbour, indifferent to the bumping like the rest of the passengers, talked to me incessantly and incomprehensibly in Maltese. The steward, whom I consulted during a moment of calm, explained he owned a cinema in Benghazi and he was urging me to pay it a visit during my stay there.

The Galloper

If things had moved slowly in Tripoli, they were almost at a standstill in Benghazi. The Commercial Secretary, Mr Livingstone, who was our local contact, was sorry, but there was no transport available to take us into the desert. He would continue with representations, but for the while there was nothing for us to do but to wait; perhaps, he suggested, we might visit the beach, and look at the local souk. The Officers' Club, another commandeered hotel, had excellent food and friendly Arab staff, and the town and beach proved to be agreeable; we found some congenial fellow guests. So there was more eating, drinking and lounging about. Butch did not complain, though I was a bit prone to youthful impatience.

However, within a day we had met the one man who seemed to know what to do, and be able to do it. Colonel Evans, known locally as 'The Galloper', was a retired Colonel who, however, retained connections with the Military Administration; in what way was never clear. He was the man who would show us the way to the sulphur lakes. He was fit and wiry, of indeterminate age (someone told us he was over 70), and he visited us at the hotel to invite us to accompany him to the beach. We travelled in his Land Rover, actually one that the army had assigned to him, and learned that we should certainly get our transport, but that a high-ranking official was due to come through that weekend and the local military, fearing a cut in their transport facilities, wished to be able to say that they had boffins from the UK, sent on a vital scientific mission, held up in Benghazi for lack of transport.

He was right. After four days of relaxation on our part, the appropriate official having come and gone, Livingstone told us that the army had found a 15-cwt truck and a Land Rover, with drivers, which would be available to us for a week or so. The Galloper helped us to draw camping equipment, fuel-operated cooker, water carriers, beds and so on from the army stores, as well as advising us on provisions. Butch made me responsible for choosing the food, just specifying that I include 24 cans of beer and a bottle of gin (gin for him - I was off drinking spirits). The Galloper also recruited an interpreter and a cook to accompany us, saw us safely started on loading the truck, and craftily left Benghazi, having arranged to meet us next day at Adjedabia, some 200 miles south in the desert. This ploy was necessary because 'They' might otherwise requisition his Land Rover to replace the one assigned to us.

All went smoothly. Early next morning our party set off for El Agheila: Butch, me, the driver Taher and our interpreter, Safi El Din El Said (as he wrote his name down for me) in the Land Rover: Awad, the second driver following in the truck with Ashour, the cook, perched among the luggage in the back. (Ashour was a 'fellah', which meant the other Arabs treated him rather like an untouchable; it would not have done for him to sit in the cabin with Awad.) We also carried a portable laboratory, like a wooden coffin, which had been constructed for us at CRL, and, of course, our personal belongings - including my ulcer medicines.

I must not let this become a travelogue, but here are some brief impressions.

The road was dusty and potholed; there was a 40 km/h gale blowing us along, it was hot, I was nervous. But I relaxed as we trundled steadily through mile after mile of seemingly uninhabited scrub desert: not sandy, but stony with sparse bushes, stretching out flatly in all directions. Buildings were few and derelict, no areas of cultivation were obvious; instead the desert was a machinery graveyard from World War 2: burnt-out tanks, wreckage of crashed aircraft, other unidentifiable metal debris, were scattered all over the place, every hundred metres or so. Forgotten metal skeletons, rusting slowly with no sand to inter them decently. Our only sight of human life was a camel caravan, some distance to the east of the road, making its way north.

Around midday we found some shelter, from the wind as much as from the sun, by a disused building, and paused so that Butch and I could have some lunch out of tins - the Arabs did not eat during the day - and by dusk we reached Adjedabia, triumphant, but none the less relieved to find the Galloper, his driver, his Land Rover and his dog awaiting us.

Adjedabia was a tiny settlement surrounding a well, with a few Arab inhabitants; Ashour made us all a good dinner and was rewarded with a can of beer and we slept in a disused building on camp beds.

Up at dawn and on to El Agheila, a hamlet with a dozen or more buildings, for breakfast by an old Turkish fort. We were introduced to the Mudir, a sort of Mayor, who welcomed us - and regretted that we could not stay and be sociable.

We then left the road to cross apparently featureless desert, to seek the principal sulphur lake, Ain-ez-Zauia. The

Galloper and his driver disagreed over the route, which conflicted with our military map; Galloper protested; driver said (in Arabic) that he wanted us to take the "main road", pointing south; Galloper laughed and gave in - no road, main or minor, was discernible to our European eyes. Later we bogged down briefly in quicksand, but the four-wheel drive of the Land Rover got us out.

At last we reached our destination. From a small escarpment we looked down on the sulphur lake Ain-ez-Zauia, gleaming in the sunshine: a bright, pastel blue jewel among the scrub, topped with a rare clump of vegetation at one end. (The blue colour is due to colloidal sulphur in the water).

The lake became less attractive as we got closer; it smelled strongly of bad eggs (hydrogen sulphide) and was surrounded by treacherously deep gelatinous mud, black with pink flecks and stinking. But to Butch and me it was wonderful. With the Galloper and our Arabs we set up camp upwind from the lake, then Butch and I explored, discovering the sulphur deposited all over the bed of the lake, green- and red-tinted sulphurous pools here and there around it, strange floating protrusions of gelatinous mud with gas inside, crystalline encrustations of calcite and salt round the edge. To us it was thrilling. Galloper, his dog and two of the drivers took a more practical view: they plunged in and swam, for the water is warm (32°C), slightly saline, and believed locally to be health-giving - as, like the spa waters of Bath or Leamington, it probably is.

The sulphur lake of Ain-ez-Zauia

The Galloper saw us settled and left us late that afternoon. Ashour saw us fed and we slept exhausted, though the night was cold. Next morning Butch was astonished that my commissariat had included canned orange juice for breakfast. He did not like the idea at all. Then he remembered the gin; it is the only time I have seen a stiff gin-and-orange consumed for breakfast.

That day was spent in examining the lake, collecting and analysing samples. There was a slight clash at the start because Butch's way of doing things was unsystematic and inefficient, but when I started telling him what we should do I was firmly put in my place - he was the boss. But there was plenty of time and we got a fairly representative set of samples to take home. We did some chemical analyses and microscopic examinations and even caught some tiny fish which lived in a pretty poisonous out-flowing stream. (Because of their resistance to hydrogen sulphide they proved to be of interest to ichthyologists and J L B Smith, the South

African scientist who later discovered that 'living fossil' the coelacanth, wrote a little paper on our specimens.)

Next day we returned to El Agheila, intending to visit some other lakes, but that had to be put off because the Mudir proposed a gazelle hunt - in our Land Rover, it transpired - and there was also a wedding party in the settlement that evening, to which we were invited. Our party shot no gazelles, though we actually spotted one, but we had a fine trip, visiting Mussolini's absurd monument (Marble Arch to the British Eighth Army) on the border of Cyrenaica and Tripolitania. The local water was said to be good and our Arabs insisted we taste some; Butch politely suppressed his preference for gin. Later we visited a Bedouin encampment to hire a guide to take us to the other lakes, a procedure requiring a drink of Leben (soured milk) and the tea ritual: three rounds of strong black tea, the third flavoured with mint. In the dry, dusty climate the astringent brew of the Senussi Arabs was very refreshing.

The wedding party, to which we went after supper, was a jolly affair in a hut near the old fort. Tea, not alcohol of course, was offered, with drumming on inverted enamel bowls, singing - keening to our European ears - and shuffle dancing by our hosts. No sign of any women. Every now and again a guest would go outside and shoot a rifle into the air as a sort of private celebration. When we left after a couple of hours it was still in full swing.

The following day was occupied by visits to three other sulphur lakes in the region, all rather like Ain-ez-Zauia, none so productive of sulphur. At one stage we had to drive across an uncleared minefield where our guide insisted on walking ahead of the Jeep. Our driver, who liked to get a move on, was contemptuous of our guide's timorousness - until we saw an actual mine a few yards to our left. But the high spot of the day was the evening's entertainment.

A feast

Safi, our interpreter, had cousins among the local Bedouin and they invited us to supper in their tents. We were delighted to accept. I had actually been letting a beard grow but Safi insisted I shave. Butch and I smartened up as best we could; we picked up the Mudir, who was a fellow guest, and set off on a 25-mile drive to their encampment in the desert. Butlin's stammer caused him to be viewed with great respect by our hosts, for his pronouncements, made with such difficulty, had to be of substantial importance; he was, rightly, given a cushion as we all squatted on the carpet, with the Mudir on one side and our principal host on the other, both of us having a direct view out of the tent to the desert (and, I noticed, in good view of whoever it might be who looked across the blanket separating us from the women. These we never saw, but they all had a good peek and giggle at both of us).

Bedouin hospitality took its time. Two glasses of the sweet, astringent but very welcome tea were spread over some two hours of chat, largely gestures and laughter because Safi's powers of interpretation were woefully inadequate to such an occasion - his English amounted to about fifty words. But it seemed that we were being told rude stories and we managed to laugh uproariously and slap hands at the right places. Occasionally the conversation was less frivolous; I was disconcerted to discover that the admiration the Senussi so clearly had for us British was at least partly due to their belief that we had invented the atom bomb. Thus we were truly great warriors. I had sufficient courtesy to suppress my youthful priggishness and look pleased.

In due course our attention was drawn to a youth carrying a cuddly lamb past the tent. This, we learned, was to be our supper; letting us see it was a polite way of assuring us that the meat would be fresh. Any ambivalence we may have felt was overcome by mounting hunger - made worse by the realisation that the lamb would take another couple of hours, if not more, to cook. Another glass of tea, minty this time, and another hour passed. Jolly chat continued, but tummies were rumbling. Then, suddenly, an old, very silent Arab in the corner of the tent produced an enormous belch. Butch, with a hoot of delight, pop-popped a bit and produced an even more monstrous belch himself - to the delight of all assembled, who slapped hands and rolled about with laughter. Butch was very pleased with his social success - as was everyone - and also relieved internally. Later we had some dates as aperitif and (much) later a little boy came round with a pitcher of water and a remarkably dirty-looking towel, and it was indicated that we might wash our hands prior to the main meal.

At last it came, preceded by a certain amount of giggling behind the curtain: two plates (instantly recognisable as borrowed from our camp), heaped with almost everything you find inside a sheep (I said everything), fried; plus knives and forks, and boxes for Butch and me to sit on, all from our camp. I realised that, as guests of honour, we were supposed to eat this fry-up, watched by the rest. After mildly demurring, we tucked in.

Butch endeared himself to his hosts by finishing his whole plate; I couldn't - there were some worrying pieces of anatomy there (though not the apocryphal eye) and I only managed half. But my failure proved to be no solecism for, after repeated assurances that I had had enough, the Mudir had a go at my plate, then it was passed round and everyone had a bit, the plate arriving finally at the small boy, he who had earlier brought us hand-washing water, who consumed a remaining lump of congealed fat with every sign of pleasure.

Even more socially successful was Butch's insistence that the boxes, knives and forks be then taken away: for the rest of the meal we English would eat like Arabs, using our hands and squatting on the carpet. This we did; we lolled on the carpet while a washing-up sized bowl containing a sort of date pudding came under the curtain, followed by hot roast joints of the lamb (by then indescribably delicious and welcome; and there must surely have been more than one lamb among the dozen of us). To start with, we rolled balls of pudding politely (a technique demonstrated by our interpreter to me and by the Mudir to Butch) and tore strips off the joints with our fingers, conveying them delicately to our mouths. But soon, following Butch's example, we began to grab lumps of pudding and gnaw directly at the joints. Our hosts perceptibly relaxed again.

When one had finished, the correct thing seemed to be to roll on one's back and belch, at which the little boy would run up with his water and horrible towel. The Mudir finished first and set the example; Butch got the idea and, with another monstrous belch, rolled out of the meal. I, to my shame, could only manage a feeble, palpably forced, *gurk*. But it was received with goodwill and I duly washed my hands.

Then it was time for strong, sweet tea again - three cups, the third minted. Butch asked for an Arab song. He could not have made a request more pleasing to his hosts. One of them keened in quartertones for some considerable time while our interpreter struggled to convey the sense of the song - it seemed somebody did something to somebody and somebody else was sad and so was somebody else, or perhaps the first somebody. A timeless theme. We looked solemn and applauded. Then, inhibition-ridden Englishman that I am, I was thrown into a convulsion of embarrassment by a request for a song from us. But ever-reliable Butch leapt in; his obsession with opera sustained us and he sang an aria from Aida, in a stentorian but accurate voice, astonishing his hosts not only by his volume but also because he did not stutter at all. He never did when he sang.

We returned to our camp at El Agheila well after midnight, giving the Mudir a lift. Several of our hosts came along for the ride, because it had been such a good party; the Arabs and Butch sang some more. Ashour, a little glum, had been watching over the camp - as a fellah, he had not been invited.

We were up at dawn, as usual. Every knife, fork, plate and box was clean and back in its place at our camp - we saw neither their going nor their return.

Benghazi again

We broke camp next morning, bade farewell to the Mudir and set off for Benghazi, giving lifts, for some of the way, to our guide of yesterday and to the only woman we encountered on the whole trip. She had appeared from nowhere and Safi explained that she was a Gypsy, which was why she did not cover her face. We were able to buy eggs on the way and Butch again impressed our Arab colleagues by commanding seven each, fried, for our lunch. We reached our hotel by early evening, but the truck with all our equipment had not kept up. In great anxiety we telephoned the Galloper, who assured us it would be safe. It was. The driver and Ashour had decided to stay the night in a village outside Benghazi, where the contents of the truck would be safer. As Safi explained, urged indeed, our Arab friends would happily and profitably dispose of the equipment if Butch and I would care to donate it to them, but he accepted our excuse that it belonged to the Army. "You too afraid of Army!" was his mildly aggrieved comment.

Next day the truck duly appeared. We returned it and our equipment to the Army, paid or tipped our Arab friends as appropriate, distributed the remains of our supplies - tinned food, canned beer, bumf - among them, and wrote references for them all. Then back to our hotel, a bathe in the sea, and we rejoined the social whirl of post-war Benghazi: dinner with Mr Livingstone and friends.

We had to wait another three days for the next flight to Tripoli. Butch's striking personality and friendliness ensured that we did not lack entertainment. I do not recall exactly how we came across a young English-speaking Greek, John Vrouzes, but he befriended us and took us on an excellent overnight trip to Cyrene, to see the remarkably abundant remains of a Roman city, with stops in both directions at his family's winery at Beda Littoria. And as if that was insufficient, he insisted that next day we should lunch with his family; a friendly occasion involving a magnificent repast which lasted from 1.30 to 4 pm. Fortunately my digestion was in good shape, because it was our last whole day in Benghazi and hardly had we returned to our hotel for a brief rest than we were due to be guests of our British hosts at a special dinner at the Vienna Hotel - and at both meals it would have been most discourteous not to eat heartily. I appreciate that old menus can be a bore for those who were not there, but our consumption on that 11th of May 1950 was so monstrous that I may be perhaps be forgiven for recording it:

Lunch:
Hors d'oevre Ouzo
Stuffed vine leaves
Veal cutlets and potatoes White Beda wine
Hare and fried liver
Chocolate mousse
Bananas
Coffee

Dinner:

Fish and beetroot

Soup

Beef olives Rudesheimer

Steak and artichokes with spinach

Chicken and cucumber

Patisserie

Pears and Apricots

Coffee

Bloated and pleased, we flew next day to Tripoli and the Uaddan Club. There were five more days to wait before the next flight to England, and again entertainment seemed to be the order of the days: cocktails, being dined out, being shown the Arab markets. I bought a pair of leather sandals, a form of footwear which was then quite unobtainable in Britain, at a shop just inside the Old Town; they later proved to be made largely of cardboard, cunningly covered with thin leather so that I did not find out until the first time they got wet after my return home. My purchase of nylon stockings (like gold in post-war Britain) as a present for Mary was happily more successful.

But we did fit in a little science. Mr Wordsworth arranged to have a capped artesian well opened for us at Sidi Mesri; it was a spectacular sight, my first experience of hot, smelly, subterranean water gushing to the surface amid clouds of steam. We took a water sample and later Miss Adams found thermophilic sulphate-reducing bacteria in it.

By a remarkable and happy coincidence, an old Oxford

friend and jazz lover, Jim Silvester, signed into the Uaddan a few hours after our return from Sidi Mesri. He was travelling on behalf of a multinational firm. I introduced him to Butlin. Jim had an expense account, and we had access to official transport, which we were positively encouraged to use for sightseeing. We joined forces and had a splendid three days; I recall particularly a trip to the spectacular Roman ruins of Leptis Magna (where I photographed Butch and Jim sitting on the remains of a communal loo, see below), and a couple of marvellous meals at the 'Romagna'.

All too soon we had a farewell dinner with Jim, managed two hours' sleep at the Uaddan, and caught the 03:35 BOAC York for London. We arrived, "bronzed and Godlike" in Butch's words, to be met by our anxious wives - only our earliest letters had reached them. While we had been eating strawberries on the sun-baked patio of the Uaddan, they had had snow, even though it was mid May.

Aftermath

We had taken many samples of water, sulphur, slime and mud from the lakes, and even done some analyses and microscopy beside Ain-Ez-Zauia. The lake samples proved, as expected, to be rich in sulphate-reducing bacteria, as well as other kinds of sulphur bacteria, and we were able to show, with little room for doubt, that most of the sulphur in the lakes was being formed by these bacteria in combination. The coloured bacteria were of a type which make use of sunlight, rather as plants do, to make organic matter, but unlike plants, they have to oxidise sulphides to sulphur at the same time. These were the bacteria which made most of the actual sulphur; the sulphide was being generated by the sulphate-reducing bacteria, making use of organic matter (formed by the coloured organisms) to reduce calcium sulphate dissolved in the artesian water. We were able to reproduce the process on a small scale in the laboratory. But there were lots of other interesting bacteria around, including some that were doubtless involved in the process, and I wished, and still wish, that we had been able to do more about them. However, our somewhat simplistic account of how sulphur came to be formed in the lakes proved to be substantially correct: a Canadian scientist, Professor Thode, had devised a method of telling whether sulphur was formed by bacteria or by geological processes by examining specimens in a device called a mass spectrometer. (For those who know some chemistry, he measured the ratio of sulphur isotopes in the specimen; there is always an excess of the lighter isotope if the sulphur has passed through a biological system). In Thode's hands, our specimens of sulphur from the lakes were very clearly of biological origin.

Quite soon we were able to report to the DSIR that the lakes were indeed producing sulphur biologically, and their publicity department produced the customary little research bulletin for the press. Such bulletins were DSIR's way of letting the taxpaying public know where its money was going and providing the science correspondents of newspapers with material. If their bulletins reached print at all, it was usually as short pieces, perhaps only a few lines after the sub-editors had made cuts, filling space on inside pages. Sometimes a fuller article would appear in a specialised magazine. What no one had foreseen was the excitement that the press release about our trip generated. The sulphur shortage was at its worst, and suddenly the press found itself informed that a remedy was at hand - or so it interpreted matters. "Boffins Make Sulphur with Bugs!" cried one of the headlines. Butch and I were in the tabloids, 'quality' papers and magazines not just in Britain but all over the world; Butlin was deluged with enquiries about how many tonnes of sulphur our bugs had made so far, whether they could buy shares in our company, and so on. I was required to do not one but two tremulous broadcasts about our work, for the BBC's *Radio Newsreel*; I was also offered a well-paid job to help set up a sulphur-producing plant exploiting hot springs in Iceland. Everyone thought the sulphur shortage would be alleviated next week, if not tomorrow.

It so happened that a Cabinet Minister, Richard Stokes

of the Board of Trade, was at the time visiting the USA to negotiate increased sulphur quotas for British industry.

"What do you need more for?" his opposite numbers in Washington asked, "Haven't you got boffins making it for you with bugs?"

An urgent message reached DSIR HQ from Washington to play down the publicity about our research programme.

The photo shows (L to R) Butlin, HRH the Duke of Edinburgh, and Postgate in April 1952, on an occasion when the Duke visited CRL to be shown its research in progress. We used it that year as a Christmas card, captioned "How much Sulphur have you made so far, then?"

Back at CRL

Gradually it transpired that the Libyan sulphate reducers were no more active than our domestic strains. It was also clear that the process, as it took place in Libya, was much too slow to be of any use to heavy industry. But the excitement remained. My own work had shown that the bacteria could work much faster in the laboratory than they seemed to do in nature, and the prospect of developing a reasonably rapid microbiological process remained serious. Butlin was promised more staff and space to develop such a process and it remained a major part of the group's research programme for the next nine years. It was very much Butlin's pet theme – though he did no bench work himself, somewhat to the relief of his assistants, Sylvia Selwyn and Don Wakerley.

By the late 1950s they had worked out a process based on sewage and calcium sulphate as feedstocks for a bacterial fermentation generating hydrogen sulphide. For this research, deliveries of raw sewage were generously provided by a sewage works a few miles away at Mogden; this had to be homogenised before use and Sylvia, an attractive and fresh-faced young lady, took in her stride the preliminary removal of used condoms, plastic fragments and other relatively indestructible matter from the daily delivery, commenting, with true scientific detachment, on the interesting fact that the major recognisable component of her research material seemed to be hair.

Their process was eventually tested, successfully, on a pilot plant scale in collaboration with the London County

Council. But nothing more came of it. By then, the late 1950s, the sulphur shortage in Britain had receded. New sulphur deposits had been found, and also several major industries had gone over to making sulphuric acid by processes which did not require either elemental sulphur or hydrogen sulphide. Demand for elemental sulphur had slackened while the material actually had become more plentiful, and its price had dropped. The bacterial process did not become economic for the UK or Western Europe, though comparable processes were used on small scales in the USSR and Czechoslovakia in subsequent decades.

CHAPTER NINE

A fundamental advance

As far as my own work was concerned, the trip to Libya had been something of a holiday from my more basic research, so I was happy to return to more rarefied problems. Nevertheless, I was sometimes called upon, or allowed, to advise on the sulphur-from-sewage project.

As I told earlier, I had been studying the rates of sulphate reduction by my pet bacteria, and its inhibition by selenate. This kind of work progressed well; I was also busily working on the organisms' carbon metabolism, as well as trying to extract the enzymes involved in sulphate reduction; and I had an assistant, Joy Grossman, to help. I had published some decent papers on the metabolic chemistry of sulphate reduction, and the reputation of Butlin's laboratory had benefited. Our fame began to spread internationally: scientists in Europe, the USA and Japan would write letters or ask for reprints; occasionally they would arrange to visit us. DSIR was pleased. Butlin achieved his ambition of severing his connection with CRL's Corrosion Group; DSIR assembled a special Advisory Committee of distinguished microbiologists to oversee Butlin's research plans (I was the Committee's secretary); his Microbiology Group got a new building and yet more staff; it was enabled to embark on new projects, some unrelated to sulphate reduction - more about all that later.

I had mastered the art of growing the bacteria in bulk, using a culture medium which did not turn black. That detail needs explaining. Small amounts of an iron compound were traditionally added to media used for cultivation of sulphate-reducing bacteria because the dissolved iron reacts with the sulphide to form a very obvious black precipitate of iron sulphide, a quick chemical indicator of sulphate reduction. But most cheaper grades of chemical reagent contain iron as impurity so, even if one did not add extra iron, routine cultures produced cells which were black, because they were coated with iron sulphide. For my kinds of experiment, this black colour was an interference, and I had devised media in which the cells came out their natural pinky-white colour, with no contaminating iron sulphide.

Back in Oxford, in Woods' laboratory, my old colleague June Lascelles had just received a device called a Hartridge reversion spectroscope. It is now, I think, completely obsolete, but in those days it was tremendously valuable, because it enabled one to look at any reasonably translucent material and see if it made a difference to the spectrum of light shone through it.

This, too, may need explaining. If one looked at plain electric light in the instrument, one saw the white light split into the colours of the rainbow: red, orange, yellow, green, blue, indigo, violet. This is an ordinary spectrum. If one put a thin green leaf in the way, so that the light shone through, three strong shadows in the form of dark bands in the red zone would be seen. These are due to the chlorophyll, which makes the leaf green (one would see other, less pronounced bands, too). Any spectroscope would do this. The thing that made the "reversion spectroscope" special was that, by optical wizardry, it contrived to show two spectra back-to-back against each other: red over violet and violet over red. The operator could make these spectra move relative to each other, and could line up a band so that it stretched neatly across both spectra. When that was done, a gauge on the side of the instrument recorded the precise wavelength at which the dark band appeared. June was highly delighted with her new toy, using it to measure the wavelengths of absorption bands - as they are called - in cells of photosynthetic and other bacteria.

When we next met she asked me if I would like her to have a look at sulphate-reducing bacteria. I agreed, and duly prepared a thick suspension of my clean bacteria and posted them to her in a sealed, carefully packed medical bottle. Sulphate-reducing bacteria grown my way were the only kind that would have been of any use to her because they were not an opaque black mass. Light certainly did get through: a few days later, June rang up to tell me, frank-speaking Australian that she was, that I was a lousy microbiologist because my culture was contaminated with aerobic bacteria.

I was dismayed. I had certainly had problems with contamination in the past, as had everyone who worked with sulphate reducers, but this was my carefully checked and cosseted working strain. What made her say that?

She told me. She had seen two clear bands in the yellow-to-green range of the bacterial spectrum, which vanished if one shook the cells in air, but returned slowly if the suspension were left stagnant. Behaviour typical of substances called cytochromes, found exclusively in air-breathing creatures. They are red proteins involved in respiration by aerobes as diverse as people, plants and yeasts. In particular, the wavelengths of the bands matched closely those of a particular, quite common, cytochrome called cytochrome C. But sulphate-reducing bacteria did not breathe air; they were anaerobes. Indeed, they could not multiply in air. And it was a matter of biochemical dogma - and experience - that anaerobic bacteria did not have cytochromes. Ergo, I had sent the wrong bacteria.

I was demoralised. Could my population really have been impure? Could it have become contaminated in the post? There was only one thing to do: recheck a culture and take it to Oxford myself.

In the event I took three different, carefully checked, strains to Oxford about a week later and, to the astonishment of June, Donald Woods and me, all three contained something that looked and behaved like cytochrome C. There was also a faint, unchanging third band, in the red part of the spectrum, and Donald could see a fourth in the orange range which in truth neither June nor I could make out. But at least the Oxford microbiologists were convinced that a cytochrome was present in this species of anaerobe. We were also able to get a better measure of the wavelength of its stronger band and in fact it was slightly different from that of yeast or muscle cytochrome C. (Later Donald's fourth band proved to be real: a breakdown product of the substance responsible for the third band.)

Well, I may have satisfied my old colleagues that there was a genuine cytochrome in what was a genuine anaerobe, so threatening to undermine the textbooks, but there were other hurdles to cross.

The fountainhead of all knowledge about cytochromes at that time was the Molteno Institute at Cambridge, which housed Professor David Keilin and his colleague E F Hartree. They were responsible for most of the available knowledge of cytochromes and their functions, as well as for the dogma of their absence from anaerobes, so my next duty was to get Keilin's seal of approval, so to speak.

Duly a visit was arranged and I went to Cambridge with specimens of live cells and, because I had succeeded in preparing some, a pinkish extract of cells containing a solution of my cytochrome. Keilin, a small, bird-like figure in a white lab coat, received me with polite scepticism and conducted most of the conversation through Hartree, who actually examined my material as I looked on. Both at once agreed that a cytochrome was present, leaving unspoken their doubts whether my culture was pure and, if so, whether it was truly an anaerobe. But in one afternoon I learned more about my cytochrome than I had in the previous few months.

Their micro-spectroscope (an ancient instrument: nothing so modern as a reversion spectroscope had yet penetrated to their laboratory) was on a bench between two doors. Keilin would make a suggestion to Hartree and then walk out of the door. A little time later he would return through the other door to hear what had happened, perhaps take a look at the spectrum, make a new suggestion, and vanish through the first door. Hartree showed me chemical derivatives of the cytochrome made by treating my cells, sometimes after boiling, with nitrous acid, with pyridine, with carbon monoxide, cyanide and so on. The details no longer matter: the upshot was that all agreed that I had a c-type cytochrome, probably a new one. They also agreed that there was something odd absorbing red light.

I returned to Teddington with my morale much restored, even though Keilin still thought my bacteria must be aerobic. (It later transpired that the cytochrome reacts spontaneously with oxygen, giving a false impression of aerobic respiration.) By mid 1953 I was certain enough to mention the cytochrome in a review paper presented (at the invitation of my friend Ernst Chain) to an International Microbiological Congress in Rome (at which almost everybody was too busy to notice its significance) and in 1954 I produced a couple of short communications on it at meetings of the Biochemical Society. Independent confirmation came from Japan, where a trio of scientists headed by a Dr M Ishimoto had discovered a similar cytochrome in their strain of sulphate reducer - more about that in chapter 10. I called it cytochrome C3; the other substance, responsible for the red absorption, I called desulfoviridin. My research was much helped by the fact that Butlin had deployed some of his extra staff to study the continuous culture of sulphate-reducing bacteria. This entailed growing cultures continuously night and day, in order to obtain basic data for Butlin's sulphur production experiments, and their apparatus produced a steady stream of bacterial culture from which cells could be harvested. Otherwise all would have been sterilized and poured down the drain. Thus I had plenty of material to work with and was able to purify the cytochrome and desulfoviridin substantially, and also to make preparations of cells, which told me quite a lot about what the cytochrome did. (Desulfoviridin remained an enigma for another fifteen years, before it proved to be an enzyme involved in one of the steps of sulphate reduction.)

Cytochrome C3 and desulfoviridin did my and Teddington's academic reputations a power of good, because the biochemical world, including ultimately Keilin, saw that a hitherto well-established principle of biochemistry had now to be revised. Cytochromes began to be found in other anaerobes, too; indeed, a certain Martin Kamen, working on anaerobic photosynthetic bacteria in California, independently reported one hard on the heels of cytochrome C3, in 1964.

DSIR's press office tried manfully to explain our epoch-making discovery to its clients. "How much sulphur will this - er - cyclogroan make?" they asked, as they quietly shut their notebooks. But it did get mentioned, in mock astonishment, in the comic weekly magazine *Punch*.

Thus was discovered the first cytochrome to be found in an anaerobe, amid disbelief even among those who first saw it. As momentous discoveries go, the wider public found it less than riveting. But in the little frog-pond of microbiological biochemistry it caused gratifying excitement. Not only was its origin unexpected, but I had discovered that some of its properties were curious, too. All cytochromes are proteins, and their molecules include the metal iron (actually, it is the iron which makes them red, as it does in haemoglobin, the iron-rich protein of blood). Cytochrome C3 was redder than most, and it proved to have more iron than any others. It seemed also to withstand brief boiling - most proteins disrupt when heated, to coagulate like hard-boiled egg. And its ability to react directly with oxygen was unusual. So there is an irony in the fact that gradually, over the next thirty years, research by others showed that I was wrong in almost every detail about it that I reported. In the first place, the material which I believed to be pure was not: it was a mixture of cytochrome C3 with two other, different cytochromes, all three having closely similar absorption spectra. Other scientists have since sorted them out and they prove to have distinct biological functions. Secondly, cytochrome C3 was not as stable as I had thought, and a step I used in purifying it caused my final product to include a fair amount of heat-damaged material. Thirdly, I claimed that my 'pure' protein had two iron atoms per molecule; today it seems that the other impurities must have interfered with my analyses, because pure, undamaged cytochrome C3 is now known to have four per molecule.

Ah well! That is research for you. All can be excused because, in the mid 1950s, the laboratory techniques necessary to reveal those errors were simply not available, and Ishimoto's and my findings certainly provided the basis for exciting advances in microbiology and protein chemistry over subsequent decades.

More personalities

Cytochrome C3 had given me brief *entrée* to the laboratory of Keilin, one of Britain's most distinguished biochemists, but the contact did not develop further, either in a professional or a personal way. On the other hand, even before that discovery I had begun to be known among microbiologists and biochemists as someone who was doing interesting research - remember that most were scarcely aware that sulphate-reducing bacteria existed in those days - and I began to form new friends and colleagues, both at scientific meetings and by correspondence, as well as having travelling scientists invite themselves to visit me at Teddington. Now, gradually, I became part of the wider scientific community.

Bill Bunker

Probably the least alarming of the Great Names that I met

was Henry James Bunker, known to everyone as Bill. When I was a graduate student I had heard him lecture on the sulphur bacteria, and I realised that he was one of the handful of international experts on these creatures. He had been one of the original group of microbiologists at Teddington before the Second World War, and, as well as working on several other aspects of applied microbiology, he had initiated the Teddington group's research on sulphate-reducing bacteria, as well as on other kinds of sulphur bacteria (Butlin had come to sulphate reducers later, after his work with acetic acid bacteria). During the war Bunker and Molly Adams had worked on bacterial attack of fire hoses: they discovered that sulphur in the rubber, present from the vulcanising process, enabled special kinds of sulphur bacteria to grow, and these formed destructive sulphuric acid. It was a serious problem for wartime fire services; drying out the hoses carefully could control it. Bunker, Molly and Butch had also participated in the wartime project to grow yeast as a food supplement. By the end of the war Bunker had gained a substantial reputation as an applied microbiologist, and he had deserted sulphur bacteria for yeast and had taken a research position with a major brewery.

Bunker was none the less a senior researcher on sulphate reducers. In fact he had published only a few original papers on them himself, but in 1936 he had written a short monograph on sulphur bacteria, which everyone agreed was still, in the 1950s, the best source of information about sulphate reducers. Woods had had me read it as a graduate student.

A few months after I had joined Butch, I learned that the Great Bunker planned to revisit his old haunt. I was duly introduced to him. Far from being formidable, he was an immensely friendly, disarming character. He was rather short, rotund, balding and bespectacled, and seemed always to be laughing. I was told that his nickname 'Bill' had been acquired at school because, already tubby, bespectacled and cheerful, he bore some resemblance to Billy Bunter, anti-hero of a then popular schoolboys' magazine, *The Magnet*. He had a seemingly inexhaustible fund of comic anecdotes and jokes, as well as an impressive knowledge of the nitty-gritty of bacteria in the everyday world (not in medicine, but in corrosion, industrial processes, dairying, brewing and so on). Happily he also had a gratifying respect for the more fundamental things that interested me, though rarefied academic matters were not his speciality. I recall the occasion when we first met, when I had recently discovered the effect of selenate on sulphate reduction and was all agog with it. (To save flipping back to Chapter 7, I remind you that selenate poisons the process in rather a special way.) Triggered by some remark he had courteously made, I had launched upon a detailed explanation of the phenomenon and of its fundamental significance until, after a minute or so, I realised that my audience was looking a bit glazed. I brought my discourse to a tactful end. "It's going against nature," he said, shaking his head with a mock-pedagogical expression.

Bunker was a valuable source of really practical information, and I was in touch with him often. He also was, microbiologically speaking, most clubbable. At various times he was President of each of Britain's three Learned Societies dedicated to microbiology, also President of the Institute of Biology and Fellow of several Institutes; by the end of his life his *curriculum vitae* included 48 distinguished or honorific positions, including an honorary doctorate from Brunel University. (He had served on Brunel's Council for many years and they had awarded him an honorary doctorate; "I have been Doctored!" was his exultant cry when he told us his news.) Despite all the trappings of distinction, he was a warm, even humble, man, wholly lacking in pomposity. His lectures were informative and amusing. He found himself particularly in demand during his brewing period because he usually brought samples for his audience to taste. Because of his fund of anecdotes and jokes he was frequently called upon for a speech after dinners associated with his various offices, including, as I shall tell in the next chapter, the Society for General Microbiology. Indeed, Bunker must have spent many man-hours dining ceremonially and performing appropriately, usually accompanied by his secretary and consort, Marie Travers. (Bunker's wife had died prematurely; Bunker and Marie were both Roman Catholics and circumstances prevented them from marrying for many years.)

Towards the end of his career, Bunker left brewing and became a private consultant in applied microbiology. He was actually rather annoyed about having to make the change, because the obligation was more or less thrust upon him when the brewery employing him was taken over by a large conglomerate with but minimal interest in research. But it all ended well; consultant microbiologists with his special expertise were few on the ground and he received many commissions. And, for his new work, his wide circle of microbiologist friends was especially useful (even I, with my predilection for abstruse and academic science, was able to provide him with advice or information occasionally).

Circumstances so rearranged themselves that, late in his life, he and Marie were able to marry at last; by that time both had become personal friends of my wife and me to the extent that my family, living by then out of London, visited Bill and Marie at their home in Twickenham whenever we could. Marie's lunches were memorable occasions in the lives of our three young daughters. Bunker died in 1975, greatly missed by the microbiological community as well as by his friends and family.

Sir Hans Krebs

Professor Krebs, who had moved to Oxford University from Sheffield in 1954, was probably the country's most distinguished biochemist. He had come to Britain as a refugee from Nazi persecution before the Second World War and had made his name in the late 1930s by discovering the chemical steps by which cells convert their food to carbon dioxide, thus obtaining energy.

Food is not burned, like wood on a fire; it is broken down stepwise by living cells, so that as much energy as possible can be obtained from it. For every aspect of life - walking, thinking, growing, keeping warm etc - energy is needed. Though the major components of food (proteins, carbohydrates and fats) start off by being broken down differently, they all end up as one or two of a very few simple organic chemicals, and these undergo a fascinating sort of rondo or cycle, losing some carbon dioxide each time the cycle turns. I do not want to burden with formulae readers who are unfamiliar with them so here is a brisk run-down, which you can skip if you wish.

Imagine that a key breakdown product is compound A. This reacts with a compound, which I shall call J to form a compound B, and that reaction gets it into the cycle. B becomes C and then loses carbon dioxide to become D. After that it will be changed again and again by special enzymes in the cell, becoming successively compounds E ,F, G, H and I, losing some more carbon dioxide on the way. Finally compound I will be converted to compound J, ready to react with some more of compound A and start the cycle over again.

Krebs identified all of the compounds in the cycle and thus discovered what became known to biochemists as 'the Krebs cycle' (today it is known by the more precise name of "the citric acid cycle", for that is the identity of the compound which I designated B in my explanation). When he first worked it out, it seemed as if living cells had devised an almost capricious way of decomposing organic matter. Today scientists understand the cycle's role much better, and can marvel at the beautiful way in which it fits into the wider scheme of cell metabolism, ensuring the smooth and economical working of all air-breathing life forms.

Krebs' cycle occurs, as I have just indicated, in all air-breathing cells, from plants and humans to bacteria, but it was not known to occur in anaerobes. I was interested in what happened in sulphate-reducing bacteria and, while I worked on cytochrome C3, Joy Grossman was working, under my guidance, on how a strain of sulphate-reducer tackled malic acid, one of the compounds in Krebs' cycle. We had reason enough to know that Krebs' cycle did not occur in our bacteria, but we gradually obtained evidence that some of the other components of the cycle did crop up while malate was metabolised.

When our work was nearing its end, I remember taking Joy's notes home one weekend, together with bits I had done, to try to make sense of our findings. Though I had dismissed the Krebs cycle as irrelevant, I still remember lying on the floor, late at night, stiff and uncomfortable and surrounded by paper, and realising that it would all make sense if a kind of short cycle took place. I put pen to paper and drafted; I wrote to Joy (who had left me to get married; she retired from research). I had concluded that a mini-cycle did indeed take place, involving the repeated inter-conversion of two components of the Krebs cycle, and that this mini-cycle linked the breakdown of malic acid to the reduction of sulphate. I also proposed that the metabolism of substances other than malate were linked to sulphate reduction by way of this mini-cycle cycle. Our evidence, crude and old-fashioned as it would seem today, seemed sound: Joy agreed with me and we submitted a paper on the work to the *Journal of General Microbiology*. It was published about a year later - the usual delay for such a paper.

I was at once flattered and made uneasy, and Butlin was much impressed, when, some weeks after our paper appeared, a letter from Sir Hans arrived asking me to visit Oxford and discuss it.

Sir Hans was a small and energetic man. He received me kindly, and showed me around his newly-built research building, which had grown up beside the Biochemistry Department where I had earlier worked with Woods. He was especially proud of a rather terrifying continuous lift called a 'paternoster' which he had had installed: one had to leap in as it came up to meet one, and begin stepping out as it reached one's floor. He asked my opinion on several matters of contemporary biochemical interest and received my views with consideration; I gradually relaxed. I even maintained a polite difference of opinion on a fine detail of the physical chemistry of sulphate reduction, and he introduced me to a colleague who put me right. We talked about my paper in a general way - he seemed to have no scientific criticism of it, but some useful ideas about its implications. I told him the recent news about cytochrome C3, which interested him. In all, it was a most pleasant and instructive visit, and I left having undertaken to send him some information about work at CRL on ion-exchange resins, a topic largely unrelated to anything we had discussed.

As I returned in the train, it slowly dawned upon me why I had been summoned. During my visit Krebs had told me something of his earlier research on his own cycle, and had reminded me that, in the mid 1930s, he had discovered, and published a paper on, a succinate-fumarate cycle in liver tissue. It was this discovery which had ultimately led him to his full cycle. I realised that I had neglected to refer to that piece of research in Joy's and my paper (in truth, I had taken it as read, subsuming it into the complete cycle, to which I had indeed referred. I had forgotten its relevance to my findings). I do not doubt that, at least in part, he had summoned me because he wished to be sure that I, a relative newcomer, knew that my mini-cycle was not the first of its kind to be proposed.

But I must have born up quite well. We met and even corresponded occasionally over subsequent years, always in a friendly manner. Towards the end of his life, in the late 1970s, when he had retired but was still active, the local biochemistry students invited me to give a seminar in his erstwhile Department, and he made a point of joining me at the dinner afterwards. Apart from an interest in my work, which I am sure was genuine because it involved some interesting new biochemistry, he had another agendum: it seemed that he had heard of my fondness for jazz and wished me to know that a niece of his was a popular country and western style singer called Olivia Newton-John. Country and western music is not far from jazz. He died in 1981; he had seemingly preserved every document of his life, even air tickets. A great man.

Robin Hill

A famous researcher whom I sought out myself was Robin Hill of Cambridge. He was another great biochemist, in his case with a special interest in plants. He had done outstanding work on the way photosynthesis works (the so-called 'Hill reaction' remains a cornerstone of our understanding of the process). During that research he had uncovered, among other important substances, a new C-type cytochrome called cytochrome F. It played a part in photosynthesis, and his paper on the subject was a masterpiece of how to characterise a new cytochrome; I cribbed it openly when I later came to write my own major paper on cytochrome C3. Although sulphate-reducing bacteria do not photosynthesise, and are not in the least like plants, I could see some analogies between his cytochrome F and cytochrome C3. So in 1954 I arranged to visit him to discuss the matter.

Unlike my visits to Keilin and Krebs, which had had their awkward moments, this encounter was a success almost from the start. Robin was intrigued by 'my' cytochrome and anxious to hear all about it. But he also proved to be such a surprising person that my normal diffidence was quickly undermined. For one thing, he acted as if he were even more diffident than me. The details of that first meeting have largely faded from my memory, but I recall an early stage, soon after I had arrived, when conversation was not flowing all that comfortably. We were standing around in his laboratory and I offered a somewhat careless interpretation of one of the properties of cytochrome C3. Robin looked extremely uneasy and, backing away from me, obliquely suggested that I might be wrong. Suspecting that he was right, but anxious for clarification, I leant towards him and asked him to explain further. He did so (he was indeed right), but in the process backed right out of the door of his own laboratory into the corridor. He was, I think, edged back in again by someone outside who wanted to get past.

To me it seemed as if Robin was acutely embarrassed at having to offer a criticism to a stranger. But in later years I realised that his diffidence was more of a mannerism. He had in fact not the slightest hesitation about offering criticism if criticism were necessary. And often it was necessary, and not only with me, because in discussion he would grasp a point and see its further implications with disconcerting rapidity. Beneath that appearance of shyness lurked a firm and incisive mind, one determined to get to the root of both intellectual and practical matters.

My first sight of his laboratory revealed another confusing feature of Robin Hill's personality. It was quite a spacious, high-ceilinged room, with pipes along the walls and in need of a lick of paint, like most well-used university labs. But virtually all the flat surfaces, that is, the benches occupying the major part of its four walls and, as I recall, a central table, were covered with used glassware. I saw beakers, racks of test tubes, dishes, flasks; almost all covered and with something in them, most of them grey on the outside with accumulated dust. To lean on the bench, or to perch on it, as he often did when talking, he had to push a few aside. Guests, of course, would not dare to do this, and would lean gingerly against the edge of a bench. Nevertheless, the vessels must have become well scrambled over the years. I discovered later that he was almost incapable of throwing things away; what I saw before me was a sort of shrine to the experimental history of cytochrome F, and of many other substances. I never established whether he knew what every receptacle contained; I suspect he did. I suppose he simply must have had a grand clear out now and again. I had always maintained that a sloppy laboratory indicates a sloppy mind, but the mind I then encountered was about as un-sloppy as one can get. Well, I have not given up my belief entirely, but I am compelled to admit that exceptions exist.

Once Robin and I had sensed each other's measures, so to speak, we got on well, though I remained in some awe of him, both then and at our several later meetings (he died in 1991). On that first meeting we had a long and, for me, most useful discussion of cytochrome C3 and its significance. Where Keilin and Hartree had shown me how to establish the facts about cytochrome C3, Robin Hill set me on the path of understanding their implications.

There is a postscript to this story. Over a decade later I had moved into a different research area and had become Assistant Director of a laboratory dedicated to studying nitrogen-fixing bacteria (microbes which are of special agricultural importance because they can use nitrogen gas from the atmosphere and thus augment soil fertility). I shall write more about that in Chapter 20. I was taking on new staff, and hired, more on her referees' recommendations than on our uncomfortable interview, a shy, almost inarticulate young postgraduate called Susan. She was a microbiologist who had recently graduated, at a rather later age than is usual and with but moderate distinction, from the University of Reading. We duly agreed a research programme and she got going on it. Gradually her lab filled up with used flasks, beakers, culture tubes, agar plates and specimen bottles, as well as bits and pieces of continuous culture apparatus. And gradually Susan's samples filled up the communal deep-freezers, rightly eliciting protests from her colleagues. Her project proved difficult and it moved slowly, but I had chosen the right person: despite discouraging experiences, even the odd weep, she persisted doggedly and made real progress. My major problem was getting her to write her work up for publication, or for the doctorate for which she had registered: she would always find that there was another piece of uncertainty to be cleared up, and the thought of glossing over a point did not enter her head. At laboratory discussion meetings she was usually silent, but if anyone said something, which did not quite make scientific sense, she would, almost apologetically and usually obliquely, point out a simple but cogent flaw. Gradually the eager beaver, talkative high-flyers on our research staff began to be respectful of Susan and to pay close attention when she spoke. She obtained her doctorate, wrote good papers and stuck to her guns; now she has become one of the country's most distinguished microbial physiologists. Her surname - have you guessed? - Is Hill; she is Robin's daughter, and her lab was still messy when she reluctantly retired. There is something in genetics, you know.

Claude ZoBell

Once the Second World War had ended, scientists could begin to travel about the world again and visit each other's laboratories, often prompted by international scientific meetings, which had naturally gone into abeyance in wartime. Scientific research resumed its international character. The first wave of travelling scientists was largely American, simply because US nationals had readier access to travel funds than most, but gradually other nationalities began to travel, too. Butlin's laboratory, although hardly a major research Institute, began to attract a share of visitors from overseas.

An early visitor, who came in 1953, was Professor Claude E ZoBell - the capital letter within his surname is correct. He speciality was the study of microbes in the sea. The sea covers a habitat which is fraught with sulphate-reducing bacteria, especially in near-shore and estuarine sediments, and ZoBell had published several descriptive papers on them; he had also sent Molly Adams some of his cultures. But he had not always used pure cultures, by which I mean cultures free of contaminating bacteria, which were not sulphate reducers, so I had found his papers a little difficult to assimilate, a problem compounded by their (to me) convoluted sentence structure. I was chastened to discover that he talked as he wrote, verbosely and elaborately in a flat Californian accent. I think he found my Oxford English and oblique, deprecatory way of talking just as odd.

A dapper gentleman, he had married his secretary and she, accompanying him, had continued her secretarial duties. She spoke hardly at all, and during discussions with various member of our group, ZoBell would rap out, "make a note of that!" and she would dutifully inscribe something in her notebook. This arrangement made the somewhat feminist

Molly and Margaret restless. Actually his interests had much more in common with theirs than with mine; I fear that my biochemistry left him somewhat fazed and scientifically we found rather little common ground. But I found him fascinating on the subject of oil companies, with whom he had many dealings (sulphate reducers are very important in oil technology). They provided him with much financial support, but he had no illusions about their research competence or their secretiveness. He was a Mormon, we learned, but I formed no impression of that side of him; I was simply surprised at what seemed to me strangely enlightened, if optimistic, ideas about the way in which American capitalism was likely to develop: he expressed the opinion that its destiny was a uniquely American kind of socialism - a word which, in those days, most Americans could not bring themselves to speak.

Claude ZoBell died n 1989, the father figure of marine microbiology.

Fujio Egami

One of the more distinguished Japanese biochemists of the 1950s was Dr Fujio Egami, and it was in his Department at Tokyo that Dr Ishimoto had discovered cytochrome C3 around the same time that I did. The Japanese, like the British, were not liberal with travel funds for their scientists, and Ishimoto and I never met. But Egami was able to travel now and again, and in 1954 he made a visit to Butlin's laboratory, largely to tell me of his colleague's discovery. He brought me a typed translation of a note by Ishimoto on the cytochrome of sulphate-reducing bacteria, which had just been published, in Japanese, in a rather obscure periodical called *Seikagaku*. Butlin and I had reported cytochrome C3 (though not named it) at an International Congress of Microbiology in Rome in 1953, and Egami had heard of it.

Egami and I had much to talk about. He was himself an expert on rather more orthodox bacterial cytochromes, quite apart from his knowledge of Ishimoto's doings, but unfortunately he had very little English and I, needless to say, had no Japanese. So we sat together rather solemnly and communicated in a kind of gesticulating Pidgin English. I do not know how much he was able to take back to Ishimoto about my work, though I showed him what I was doing and where I had got to; I learned something, too, of Ishimoto's progress, in particular that he was having some success with the purification of cytochrome C3 using substances called ion-exchange resins - a technique that I had also adopted.

Egami was an enthusiast for Esperanto, a wholly artificial language which had been devised as an attempt to create a truly international means of communication. It had something of a cult following in the mid-Twentieth Century among those who were convinced of the potential of such a language for international understanding and peace. I had looked at its vocabulary and grammar in my youth, but I had come to prefer its rival, Interlingua, because it had Latin roots which made it easier for me. In the event I had learned neither (wisely, it seems, since both virtually disappeared and English, in various forms, has become the effective *lingua franca*).

Anyway, Egami was always seeking, and rarely finding, fellow Esperantists; I must have been yet another disappointment to him. I think he was rather generation-conscious - I was as young as his pupil Ishimoto - and he found communication rather too difficult for other than formal intercourse. But the fact that cytochrome C3 had brought a Japanese professor of international renown to Teddington greatly pleased Butlin, if only because it bewildered the more earth-bound administrators of the DSIR.

I met Egami again in Australia in 1960, at a meeting on cytochromes to which I had been summoned - more about that in Chapter 17. Again he sought Esperantists among the Conference delegates, again without success as far as I know. He seemed to me to be an austere and formal person, and I formed the impression he found that some Western behaviour patterns stressful.

Here is a tale of East meets West. Professor Drabkin, a conference participant and very distinguished elder of research on cytochromes, was, like most Americans I know, in mighty sociable form at breakfast. On our first morning he joined the same table as Egami, and I was there too. Sighting kippers on the breakfast menu (they must have been imported; the Australians do not have herring to make into kippers), he announced loudly that whenever he was in England (the English character of the Hotel Canberra must have confused his geography briefly) he always ate kippers. So he ordered a pair. He ate them with relish, heads, skin, bones, tail and all, chatting to us the while about the merits of breakfasts and travel. I caught sight of an expression of exquisite dismay on Egami's face as Drabkin rambled on, the tail of the last kipper disappearing into his mouth, and then sat back replete, to light a pipe of smelly American tobacco and smoke it over us.

In later years Egami and I exchanged some letters about microbial evolution before he died in1982. A sensitive man.

Bob Burris

At the University of Wisconsin at Madison, USA, Dr R H (Bob) Burris was the biochemical half of a partnership with microbiologist P W (Perry) Wilson, which led the field in research on biological nitrogen fixation. Nitrogen fixation, as I mentioned a page or two earlier, is a process whereby nitrogen in the atmosphere is converted into fertiliser for plant growth; certain kinds of bacteria are the only living things that can bring it about, so it is of tremendous practical importance. It is also of great academic interest, partly because the process itself involves some surprising chemistry, and also because, even among bacteria, not many types can do it, which is odd considering that it matters so much.

I knew a bit about nitrogen fixation and of Burris and Wilson's work, though it did not obviously impinge on my own studies. (I little knew in the 1950s that nitrogen fixation would be my major research topic for the last quarter century of my professional career.) In 1956 Burris had recently described two new cytochromes, which he had found in a nitrogen-fixing bacterium called *Azotobacter*; he named them cytochrome C4 and cytochrome C5, in succession to my C3.

En route to Cambridge he visited Butlin and me, largely to talk about cytochrome C3. Somewhat overawed in anticipation of meeting him, I found him gratifyingly ordinary and down-to-earth, a natural research worker who was interested to talk about day-to-day bench problems as much as more speculative matters. He had the rather monotonous, uninflected manner of speaking which is not uncommon among inhabitants of the Midwest of the USA, leavened by a dry sense of humour. Altogether he was a man of erudition and common sense. We spent a constructive morning together; he took some photographs and survived a canteen lunch. When he left I advised him to cross London by the Waterloo and City underground railway because not only was it then an effective, if little known, way of reaching the mainline railway station for Cambridge from Teddington: it was also a fascinating relic of turn-of-the-century urban transport. He did as I advised, and sent me a postcard from Cambridge thanking me for putting him in the way of a remarkable experience. (The line has been modernised since then.) However, our research paths did not cross again for many more years and it was not until the mid 1960s that I began to meet him regularly and came to know him much better.

C B Van Niel

Professor C B Van Niel of Pacific Grove, California, was something of a microbiological guru. A most distinguished scientist, despite a remarkably small list of publications, he had been born in Holland and had migrated to California to take up a university post in the 1920s. He had been trained in microbiology at the Technical High School in Delft (equivalent to a British polytechnic), which had a reputation for outstanding non-medical microbiology. The City of Delft is hallowed in the annals of microbiology. It was there that a Dutch microscopist, Antoni van Leeuwenhoek, saw bacteria for the first time in 1676 and, by reporting his observations to the Royal Society of London, initiated the branch of biology which is now called microbiology. Some 200 years later a pioneer of modern microbiology, M W Beijerinck, worked at the Technical High School; he discovered the sulphate-reducing bacteria, among several other environmentally-important microbes (including *Azotobacter*). His pupil and successor at Delft, A J Kluyver, carried on the theme of non-medical, environmental and applied microbiology, and Van Niel, who was a junior contemporary of Kluyver, carried the Delft tradition to the USA, specifically to the Hopkins Marine Station in Pacific Grove. There his summer schools were justly famous among microbiologists. For many they provided their first experience in depth of microbes in the natural environment, and many of the more creative microbiologists of the later twentieth century, particularly in the USA, have affirmed their debt to Van Niel's summer schools. I regret that I never managed to attend one.

Van Niel was reluctant to travel, so he was quite a catch when, in the spring of 1955, he agreed to come to England to give the prestigious Marjorie Stephenson Memorial Lecture of the Society for General Microbiology, combining it with a tour of Europe including, of course, Delft.

I met him for the first time at that gathering, which took place at the Royal Institution off Piccadilly in London. Donald Woods introduced me to him; he was tall and slim, an athletic man of middle age with flaxen hair and an austere, quintessentially Dutch face. He gazed at me with piercing blue eyes for what felt like several seconds, and then pronounced, slowly and deliberately, "John Postgate"; finally he shook my hand. It was almost as if he had been waiting for many years to meet me. Only later did I learn that he usually did this when introduced to someone new: he prided himself on remembering people's names and this was his way of imprinting them on his memory. At the time I felt a combination of inadequacy and hubris, but things soon eased; I recall sitting and talking microbiology in Green Park, in the spring sunshine, with him, June Lascelles, Donald, Sidney Elsden and doubtless others, during a lunch break.

On another sunny day in the week after that encounter, when Butlin was out from the lab, I was summoned to DSIR Headquarters in London for some official business. The cause of the summons I have wholly forgotten; only that it was an inescapable nuisance. As I bicycled out of the gates of the laboratory compound - it was mid morning, and I needed to go home and tidy up before setting off by train - I saw a man and woman having trouble with the gatekeeper, for visitors need appointments at Government laboratories. Then I recognised one of them as Van Niel. He had come with his wife to visit us. I stopped.

What could I do? A visit from him was not to be taken lightly, but he had come without notice (hence his difficulties with the gatekeeper) and Butlin's laboratories were almost empty because it was Easter holiday time. Certainly there was no one who could look after him and his wife properly. I explained the position as best I could – it must have seemed arrogant, my explaining that there was no one worth talking to around – and urged him to visit Hampton Court, a short distance away by bus, and to return next day. Coming from freewheeling California, I do not think he quite understood the exigencies of DSIR's bureaucracy, but he took my advice – and did indeed return, expressing himself delighted by Hampton Court. How fortunate that the English spring was beautiful that year!

What we talked about next day I no longer recall. Our conversation covered a wide range and I simply remember being deeply impressed by his knowledge and experience of exotic microbes, mostly bacteria, which do peculiar things in nature: not only the sulphate reducers but creatures that grow on iron salts, or at high temperatures, or in strong salt solutions; those which use sulphur or sulphur compounds, some of which use sunlight in curious ways. And many others. I knew something of all of these, of course, but to meet a scientist to whom they were everyday experience was fascinating. We discussed some peculiarities of the sulphate-reducing bacteria; he told me he had a source of cultures of a very rare kind of sulphate reducer back at Pacific Grove and that, if I ever got to the USA, I should visit him and examine them. I resolved to do so – and ultimately did, as I shall tell later.

His actual lecture to the Society had been something of a disappointment, at least to me (though that did not diminish my respect for the respect with which my seniors regarded him, so to speak). The Society requires such lecturers to produce a manuscript for publication at about the time of the lecture. Van Niel had dutifully left one with the Editors of the Society's journal and vanished into Europe to continue his tour. Unfortunately, it was not set out according to the journal's conventions, and it also lacked that most important feature for a scientific publication: a list of references. It fell to me, by then a new member of the journal's editorial board, to track down and compile the references that ought to have been there. I hope he was impressed by the journal's editorial services!

Professor Kluyver

In 1951 the great Professor Kluyver of Delft himself called upon Butlin, and I remember being invited to join them. He had recently been made a Foreign Member of the Royal Society, an honour conferred on very few scientists, and was in a good humour. An imposing, gaunt figure, with that slow way of speaking that anglophone Dutch people quite often have. We had some discussion of my research and he was teasingly critical of a short paper we had just published - knowing full well that I was primarily responsible for it. In truth, I am not sure how well I defended my corner, but I was gratified that he had not wholly dismissed our little contribution. I was left with the impression of a remote headmaster-like figure, basically benevolent but austere.

Jacques Senez

In 1951 the CNRS, the French equivalent of DSIR, sent one of their younger microbiologists, Dr Jacques Senez, to Britain to experience British research, preparatory to establishing his own research group on sulphate reducers in Marseille. After a brief stint at Cambridge with Ernest Gale, he came to Teddington to work alongside me and my assistant Joy Grossman for two months. He was somewhat older than me and, when he arrived, he was clearly disconcerted by the amount of research I had got done, some of which extended work he had himself published. However, he rallied, and we got down to collaborative research, dividing our efforts so that we did not overlap too much. He was energetic and entertaining, and taught me a method of analysis called Duclaux distillation, which, although almost obsolete, actually proved to be very useful to me.

He and I had an arrangement whereby we spoke English for scientific and laboratory matters and French at meals and on social occasions, a good way for both of us to improve our rather modest linguistic abilities. Our collaboration continued after his departure and for several years we kept each other informed of our progress in detail, and would exchange manuscripts of our papers, for comment and criticism, before submitting them for publication. We continued our linguistic convention in our later correspondence: English for science, French for gossip.

Senez later became more of an operator than a researcher; an influential if controversial figure in Science

Politics in France, as well as on the international scene, and he managed to generate criticism and even antagonism among his peers. However, the details elude me because by then our research interests had drifted apart and we met and communicated only rarely.

Starka

In 1957 I had a visitor from Czechoslovakia, a rare species because that nation's communist régime was very strict about whom it permitted to travel abroad. Jiri (George) Starka had done some work on sulphate reducers in 'medicinal muds' and I was pleased to meet him, particularly so when he proved to be a charming and cultured man, with a good command of English, a liking for good food and wine and, above all, for jazz. I took him home to dinner and we played records; he was much pleased by some records I possessed of a traditionally inclined band led by one Graeme Bell which, hailing from Australia, had played in Prague during the late 1940s. The Australian jazzmen's visit had taken place during a brief period when jazz was acceptable to communist régimes, being then regarded as an essentially proletarian music, which was therefore to be encouraged. A few months later I received from Starka a letter of thanks from Czechoslovakia, adding that he had sent me a gift, a 78 rpm record, which I should collect from the Czech Embassy in London.

Doing so was a rather alarming experience. Someone was clearly suspicious: five different men, all of rather sinister aspect, came to talk to me about it, each one requiring the story from the beginning, before the disc was handed over. For a jazz lover it was a rare possession, though the band sounded uncommonly like Graeme Bell's.

The reason underlying the Embassy's wariness was that the communist states behind what was then known as the 'Iron Curtain' were suffering from a constant if modest leakage of talented individuals - academics, writers, scientists, technicians and so on - to the West. They guarded against such escapes by ensuring that the travellers' families remained at home. Yet they had to remember that talented travellers were not only good for the countries' international reputation, they learned things that might be useful to a country's defence or well being. Starka was privileged; he was allowed out a second time to attend an International Congress of Microbiology in Stockholm in 1958, where we renewed our friendship and explored the town together - but we both knew that his wife and family were being carefully watched in Prague.

Starka changed his research area and we lost touch to some degree. I heard from him in the later 1960s after he had once again been released, this time to work with Senez in Marseille. Somehow he had contrived to get his wife and family out to visit him just as hard-line communists had ousted, with Soviet help, a relatively mild regime in Czechoslovakia. He decided to remain in exile. I was able to point him towards a job opening for a microbiologist at the then new University of Kent, but in the event he found a position at the University of Marseille, where, despite terrible homesickness for Prague, they all remained for the rest of his career. A gentle man, and a good teacher, his story is typical of many scientists from the Communist side during the 'Cold War'.

Our advisers

Prompted by Butlin, who wished to ensure that his group was not wholly overseen by non-microbiologists, the DSIR had set up an Advisory Committee on Microbiology (with me as Secretary) to keep tabs on our research. Each member visited us at one time or another, collectively amounting to quite a galaxy of distinguished British microbiologists. All were impressive personalities. In 1952, the committee included microbial geneticist Guido Pontecorvo of Glasgow, an amusing, no-nonsense scientist whose incisive criticisms seemed somehow softened when delivered in his inimitable Italianate English. His speciality was then the genetics of moulds, though later he moved into cancer research and became Director of one of Britain's most famous cancer laboratories. Then there was microbial nutritionist B C J G ('Gabe') Knight of Reading, with his alarming bushy-eyebrowed stare when something silly was said or done. He was also an authority on a weird group of jelly-like bacteria now called Mollicutes, an authority on French literature and a staunch socialist. He will reappear in my story as a senior Editor of the *Journal of General Microbiology*.

My one-time examiner Sidney Elsden, good-natured but tough, came to see us; so did Bill Bunker, amiable and well informed on applied microbiology as usual. David Henderson, Director of MRE, the biological warfare laboratory at Porton, was on the committee, a firm-minded Scot with a low explosion point when it came to administrative bureaucracy; and Donald Woods, slow-talking perfectionist as ever, was Chairman. Later dairy microbiologist L A Allen and industrial microbiologist P W Brian joined the committee. I remember Brian, who worked for ICI, informally expressing regret that his group had discovered giberellin, a fascinating plant-growth promoter made by a mould, because it was proving commercially profitable and his group therefore was obliged to study its production and exploitation, and could no longer get on with the basic research, which they really enjoyed.

Butlin's group had numerous other distinguished visitors during the 1950s, from home and abroad, and in 1952 we shared with the rest of CRL the visit from the Duke of Edinburgh mentioned at the end of Chapter 8 - I usually acted as Butlin's spokesman because of his stammer. To detail all our visitors at Teddington would be wearisome, though one or two will appear later in this book, but I must mention two more, neither of whom concerned Butlin in any way. Jazz, not science, brings me to these.

Peter King

I had found a few aspiring musicians in the environs of my home in Twickenham, and had prevailed upon the sports pavilion of the National Physical Laboratory to have jazz evenings about once a month, at which we would play. I could usually summon my old Bandits friend Jim Hartley on guitar; I had found Jack May, a drummer, among the NPL's maintenance staff (who talked incessantly); excellent double bass was played by Roy Whitehead, a research chemist from the local sewage works at Mogden - which supplied Sylvia Selwyn with sewage, incidentally; a couple of clarinet players from the locality were Jeremy Counsell and Alan Shaw. Sometimes pianist Norman Day, also from the locality, who would in due course run a regular London jazz band, joined us. And an excellent guitarist who worked at CRL, Solly Isaacs (brother of a famous British professional guitar player, Ike Isaacs), condescended to play with us a couple of times; and so on. The personnel was variable, depending on whom I could persuade to turn up, and variable, too, was the quality of the performances. But we were popular enough - audiences generally expected jazz to be ragged. One time in 1957 Peter Tulett, an enthusiastic if then rudimentary trombonist (he later took up the guitar), asked if he might bring along a friend who had just started playing the alto saxophone - he had had the instrument for but a few months - ten, I believe. Naturally agreed, anxious to help a struggling beginner. He appeared with a spotty, reticent youth of about sixteen called Pete King.

We played our first number. The boy was brilliant. We were so astonished we could hardly play ourselves. He seemed to have total command of his instrument and melodically he blew rings round us all. His inspiration had been Charlie Parker, the twisted musical genius nicknamed 'Bird' who developed bebop, and jazz seemed to well out of him. Rarely have I, and the others, felt more inadequate. But we rallied, and had a wonderful session, even if our small audience that night was a little baffled by what was going on. I possess a very lo-fi recording of some of it, dubbed later from a reel-to-reel tape, which Tulett had borrowed for the evening. Even today the musicality of young Pete King shines through our amateurish strivings, but the stimulus he provided is still audible - we excelled ourselves.

I met him some twenty-five years later. By then he was famous as one of Britain's top players of the alto saxophone and he happened to be appearing as star musician at a Jazz club in Brighton. Of course I went along. It may have just been showbiz courtesy, but I believe he remembered me; anyway, I was able to give him an audiocassette of the NPL session as a reminder of the company he had once kept, and watch him smile wryly as he listened to some of it on a Sony Walkman cassette player, which he had with him. Well, he took it in good part.

George Melly

Here is another resounding name from the British jazz world. It was about 1948-9, soon after Mary and I had married, I had joined Butlin and we and moved to Twickenham, that I first came across pianist Norman Day. I was anxious to play jazz again and he wanted to play too. He suggested we form a trio with a then guitarist of our acquaintance, John R T Davies (who later achieved distinction as a jazz multi-instrumentalist and professional restorer of ancient recordings). We rehearsed a couple of times at a pub on Eel

Pie Island in Twickenham, then one day Norman phoned me and said he had found an aspiring jazz singer who would like to join us. "He's not very good, but he's uninhibited; would be a useful front man," said Norman. So he came along to a rehearsal. He sang blues and some jazz oldies in a sort of vaudeville style with energy and confidence; Norman's assessment of his style was not far out. His name was George Melly. He had brought with him his sister, Andrea, who spoke not a word to anyone but who jive-danced whenever and to whatever we played. George fitted in nicely, and Norman and I felt ready to go public, now as a quartet. We would seek gigs.

However, fate intervened. At the same time a trumpeter living in neighbouring Hounslow, Mick Mulligan, was putting together a full-sized jazz band. He needed a pianist and a banjo player or guitarist and would accept a singer. So Norman, John R T and George all joined Mick Mulligan's Magnolia Jazz Band. I was left, forlornly holding my cornet, figuratively speaking. Mulligan's band did well as traditional jazz became increasingly popular during the 1950s and Melly became famous as a jazz singer and entertainer, as well as broadcaster, writer and art critic, noted for his flamboyance, his Bohemian life style and outlook. Sadly, he died in mid 2007.

Norman and I can claim a tiny part in launching him on an unsuspecting public, I suppose.

CHAPTER ELEVEN

Meetings and papers

Meetings of one kind or another are the life-blood of scientific progress. All the main sciences, and many of their branches, have their own Learned Societies, which are organizations that hold meetings for discussion, and which often publish a Learned Journal dedicated to their subject. They are run by elected volunteers, though most have a small office with some paid staff, and they are financed out of members' subscriptions, sometimes augmented by charitable grants. A few lucky ones supplement their incomes through the sales of their journal to non-members and libraries.

In the early Twentieth Century, despite a couple of International Congresses and one dedicated journal (in German), few biologists, let alone other scientists, used the name microbiology or recognised it as a distinct subject. Microbes did crop up at meetings of societies devoted to a variety of disciplines, microscopy, bacteriology, agricultural science, pathology (medical, plant or veterinary), algology, mycology, zoology or general biology come to mind, as well as in chemistry, physiology, and, occasionally, at meetings of industrialists concerned with brewing or pharmaceuticals and the like. A move to create a society for all British scientists whose main interests centred on microbes, and so to consolidate and advance the subject of microbiology, arose in the 1930s, but it only came to fruition as the Second World War ended. It was signalled by the event mentioned in my preamble: the formation of the Society for General Microbiology (SGM for short) in 1945.

The timing proved to be just right: I told in my preamble how its membership grew over the next few decades from an initial 241 to over 5000. The Society soon started its own Learned Journal (which quite quickly began to earn money), but perhaps its most valuable function in those early years - from about 1945 to 1955 - was simply to hold its meetings, at which a motley gathering of two or three hundred specialists would come together and talk to each other about microbes. Gradually a communality, a kind of fellowship, developed; the members began to think of themselves as microbiologists rather than as bacteriologists, pathologists, hygienists or whatever, and concomitantly departments and even schools of microbiology began to come into being in universities and polytechnics. Microbiology crystallized as a distinct scientific discipline; no one today doubts that the Society played a tremendous part in promoting the development, creativity and quality of British microbiologists at that time.

The SGM

Donald Woods and Butch had both been enthusiastic founding members of the SGM and held office in it, so naturally, having been exposed to it as soon as I joined Woods, it became part of my professional life. I could not afford the subscription at first, but I contrived to attend a couple of its early meetings and was much impressed. As soon as I had a regular job I joined, and attended its meetings as often as I could - much aided by the fact that I could, given Butch's permission, charge my basic travel and subsistence costs to the Scientific Civil Service.

In the 1950s the Society would meet for two days twice a year, in the spring and the autumn. Later it would meet more often. The highlight of the Society's year was its Easter meeting at the Royal Institution in London, most of which would be dedicated to a symposium on some special area of microbiology. (The autumn meeting would be held on a university campus, usually outside London.) For the Easter symposium the Society's Committee would choose topics that would interest as broad an audience of microbiologists as possible and which also reflected the major directions of current scientific advance, so the proceedings were generally slap up-to-date, often exciting, sometimes even revelatory - yet sometimes controversial. Often I would come away feeling rather humble about how much I had still to learn, and only moderately cheered by the thought that most of those present knew as little about sulphate-reducing bacteria as I knew about their work. I could console myself that there was one tiny nugget of knowledge in which I was ahead of the game - even if I was made nervous by the prospect of one day having to talk to the Society about my work.

The Society's symposia rapidly became internationally famous, and after a few the Committee decided to publish them as books. Their well-intentioned idea was to require the contributors to provide written scripts in time for their contents to be printed and available to membership before the actual meeting. This obligation had two laudable objectives. Firstly, those like me who were unfamiliar with aspects of the topic could read, and if necessary bone up on, the material in advance; secondly, the contributor's oral presentation could be a commentary on, and up-dating of, the written text. Page proofs of the written scripts were circulated to the membership, so that revisions and discussion might be included in the published version. It was an idealistic plan, but it foundered for a mundane reason: participants made notes on their proofs and did not buy the book, so the Society lost money. So for several years the final book was made available before the meeting. Or it ought to have been; on a few occasions a laggard contributor or lax editor would foul up everything by missing deadlines, preventing the book from being printed in time. This would precipitate an embarrassing situation at the actual meeting because its quality would suffer as speakers perforce altered their planned commentaries at short notice, an especially burdensome problem for contributors from abroad. But when all went according to plan the meetings were superb.

Speakers were instructed to leave plenty of time for

discussion and Chairmen were enjoined to be severe with loquacious contributors, so there was usually a reasonable amount of discussion, to which I was generally far too timid to contribute.

I recall particularly the 1952 symposium, partly because it had a political dimension. The US authorities, then much influenced by Senator McCarthy's Committee on Un-American Activities, took away the passport of one of the principal scheduled speakers, a distinguished American virologist named S E Luria. It happened a couple of weeks before his planned flight to London and all necessary arrangements had already been made. At the meeting it fell to a young American post-doctoral researcher who was then visiting Cambridge, long-haired and scruffy-looking, to deputise for Luria as best he could. He reported one of the most important experiments of the decade. He told the meeting that a group in the USA had discovered that when a bacterial virus infected a bacterium, all it did was inject its own DNA into the host bacterium; very little protein got transferred the bacterium. This finding, which may seem obscure on its own, was a powerful part of the gathering proof that DNA was the stuff of genes are made of, because a feature of such a virus infection is that the unfortunate bacterium is caused to make vast quantities of new virus, complete with DNA and everything else that makes it up. We now take it for granted that genes consist of DNA, but this idea was then regarded with widespread scepticism. Sadly, Luria's stand-in was a terrible speaker; his diction (head down, reading mainly passages from a letter in not the easiest of mid-Western accents) was such that few of those present grasped what he was talking about. He was rather unhappy about his cool reception. But his news duly spread by word of mouth and the impact of that meeting among British microbiologists was considerable.

The young post-doc was James Watson. Ten years on, with Francis Crick, he would be awarded the Nobel Prize for the elucidation of DNA's double helix structure.

Another memorable symposium took place in 1953, also epoch-making in its day. It concerned adaptation in bacteria, the subject of my research with Hinshelwood, and it included contributions from Hinsh himself and from leading critics of his views, bacterial geneticists such as Jacques Monod from Paris and Sol Spiegelman of Illinois. It was a gentlemanly clash of titans, with Hinsh defending his corner brilliantly but ultimately ineffectively: regulation at the genetic level mediated by DNA was superseding Hinsh's physico-chemical equations as far as interpreting bacterial adaptation was concerned.

In contrast to those heavyweight though courteous exchanges, I was not the only person present at the 1956 symposium to be startled by the vehemence of an attack by C F Robinow on E D DeLamater's evidence from microscopy that bacteria possess a chromosome. We now know that they do, but the evidence then available was fuzzy and in truth neither side was really convincing.

Not all the decade's symposia were quite so action-packed. The 1954 symposium was about the industrial potential of various microbes and it so happened that Butlin and I had been prevailed upon to contribute, which meant that I, to my horror, would have to address the Society formally. The meeting took place over a Friday and Saturday, and mine was the final contribution. I had prepared my paper meticulously and had a verbatim script; I found myself addressing an audience that had dwindled from some 250 to about seventeen, mostly my own colleagues and a few committee members. Clearly the British weekend break was of greater moment to members than my topic, the economic importance of autotrophs (a specialised kind of bacteria). Ah well! I don't think the Society ever again scheduled a weekend symposium.

Apart from the symposia, at every meeting there would be paper-reading sessions, at which members read short research papers to such of the society as had assembled to hear them. These sessions were in a way the nitty-gritty of the Society's activities, because they reported the very latest research news, whereas the symposia collated both new and old research. Abstracts of the papers were published rapidly in the Society's Journal, so, for the authors, they offered a quick and relatively painless route for preliminary publication of important work - or work which the authors felt was important, which was not always the same thing. Speakers would be assigned fifteen minutes: ten minutes for the oral presentation plus five for discussion. Presentation of a paper was a salutary exercise in brisk and concise communication. Regrettably a few members were prone to loquacity: despite alarm clocks, coloured lights which lit up as the minutes ticked away, and the best efforts of even so formidable a

Chairman as Professor B C J G Knight, contributions which over-ran their time were far from rare.

Although variable in quality and reaching fluctuating audiences, the paper-reading sessions in those days provided a valuable platform for exciting new research. But again a mundane reason gradually undermined a good idea. Teachers of microbiology, both lecturers and professors, realised that they would also serve as an ideal platform for giving their graduate students experience of public speaking, so more and more papers proved to be hesitant reports of thesis material: virtuous no doubt, but less than compelling as stop-press stuff. The Society's paper-reading sessions were in due course abandoned.

One other formal event was the Annual General Meeting, for which an Agenda of reports from the committee on finance, meetings, Journal etc., had been scrupulously circulated beforehand. Today it is sparsely attended, but in the early years the AGMs attracted much interest; some 250 members were present to demand that the President protest to the US State Department over the refusal of Luria's visa (which he did, to no effect whatever), and on other occasions complaints and suggestions were voiced to the committee. I tried unsuccessfully to persuade the Society to hold occasional summer school in microbiology since I had found those of the 1940s so useful.

The Society's more formal activities could be a little intimidating, especially for younger members such as myself, but the compensating advantages of its meetings were tremendous. Not only did they reflect the excitement of a new discipline which was racing forward, but there were many opportunities to meet and talk casually with leaders of the subject, from home and abroad, at coffee breaks and meal times. These were very informal. One evening at each meeting would be dedicated to a Society dinner held in a university dining hall or sometimes at the London Zoo's restaurant; dress would be casual and there was a rule was that there would be no formal after-dinner speeches. Actually, that rule was not followed literally because, in the first place, the President rightly felt called upon to say a few words of thanks to those who had organised the day-to-day aspects of the meeting, and in the second place, Bill Bunker was usually present with his remarkable fund of jokes which he would tell with engaging modesty. So a kind of counter-tradition developed whereby the President, after duly conveying his thanks, would remind the Society of the 'no speeches' rule and then invite Bunker to tell a few stories - these being a 'non-speech'. It was a very popular custom, which began around 1950 and persisted for many years.

The Society for Applied Bacteriology

For all its friendliness and studied informality, there was a certain austerity about the Society for General Microbiology, perhaps because it was concerned primarily with rarefied and fundamental aspects of microbiology. Its atmosphere certainly contrasted with the jollity of its smaller sister society, of which I also became a member, the Society for Applied Bacteriology (SAB for short). 'Sister' is perhaps the wrong word because the SAB under an earlier name pre-dated the SGM and a few of its members did much to initiate its formation. This Society was firmly concerned with practical matters, and one felt that the members had come to meetings hot-foot from their pathology labs, food laboratories, dairy laboratories, breweries, abattoirs, veterinary stations or experimental farms, kicking off their boots or discarding their aprons or gloves, laughing, scratching and slapping each other on the back. Meetings were in fact quite as serious as the SGM's and, for me, they kept my rather academic feet on the ground. And the SAB always had time for a boozy dinner, usually culminating in a folksy singsong - in which I would join, and sometimes be lent a guitar to strum. In later years I would take along a soprano saxophone and usually find some fellow musicians with whom to play some jazz, which would generally be well received. For years the SAB had been concerned with microbes in general, not just bacteria, and in the 1990s it grasped the nettle and changed its name, to become the Society for Applied Microbiology, or SfAM.

The Institute of Biology

The Institute of Biology was a rather different body from the SGM and SAB. Founded in the later 1940s to guard and further the interests, education and professional standards of biologists of all kinds, it also awarded professional qualifications, sometimes by examination and sometimes for experience. Bill Bunker and Butch were both members, and in fact I contributed to one of its earliest symposia around 1953, with Butch of course, a paper on our Libyan excursion. I became a member as soon as I could afford to, because I judged it to be a Good Thing, but I played little part in its activities in subsequent years, the SGM and SAB being more than sufficient distractions from the laboratory bench.

I was therefore much surprised when, in 1965, the Institute made me a Fellow, an honorary rank conferred upon distinguished biologists. Naturally I was pleased and flattered. I could now add the letters FI Biol. to my name! Even more astonishing, in 1982 I was asked to be its President, even though I had little idea of what it did.

I demurred, but Dax Copp, the Institute's General Secretary, assured me that his administration was well organized and highly efficient, and that I would spend a year on Council as President Elect which would enable me to learn about presidential duties and the Institute's activities and needs before I took over, and anyway he would be there to advise me where necessary. He added that they operated an informal rota of subjects and it was time they had a microbiologist as President. How could I refuse? I didn't.

He was right. The Institute had expanded and become respected in high places since the fifties, with Divisions, Regional Sections, representation on Government and academic committees and a finger in European biology. And its administration, closely managed by Dax, was marvellous. Lamentably, just as I took over, Dax retired. A new General Secretary had to be engaged who had yet to learn Dax's administrative talents.

I floundered. I found the Institute in a financial crisis over the purchase of new premises, expensive work having been approve without proper consultation, the detailed administration seemed to have collapsed. Meetings were called without proper papers, all sorts of detail went wrong or remained undone. I found myself fielding complaints about this and that. I wish I could say I was a firm and far-sighted President, but I guess I was little more than a figurehead.

But the Institute and its finances have survived and flourished. It is now renamed the Society of Biology and is the true equivalent of its sister Professional Institutes in Physics and Chemistry

All research scientists need their regular society as a kind of intellectual or professional anchor. Of course, I attended meetings of other societies during my career, and naturally I participated in numerous international gatherings abroad. All active scientists have to do this in order to keep up with developments and meet workers in neighbouring disciplines. But for me the SGM and the SAB provided contrasting infrastructures for my own intellectual development as a microbiologist. In later years I would be elected to the SGM's Council, edit its Journal (more of that later) and, many years on, would become its President (what a terrifying thought that would have been, had it entered my head in the 1950s! Happily I grew up over the years).

And for the SAB? I did very little but contribute some rather basic stuff to several of its symposia and play them quite a bit of jazz. How kind each Society was to make me one of its few honorary members after I retired in the later 1980s!

Writing papers

Meetings, symposia, conferences and the like may promote ideas, clarify thought and stimulate further experimentation, but the ultimate reason for scientific research is to add to the sum of human knowledge. This means that the state of science must be recorded permanently somewhere, in a published form where it will be constantly accessible to everyone interested. After all, scientists seek to understand nature - this is what motivates research workers. Understanding nature also plays a part in motivating the agencies that support research, but these bodies are generally more concerned with exploiting nature and are interested in such technological consequences as might follow science's contributions to knowledge. This distinction between understanding and making use of knowledge epitomises the formal difference between science and technology. Most, probably all, research scientists combine scientific and technological motivations to different degrees and use similar research procedures. A researcher tries firstly to learn something new, and secondly to ensure that the new information is made available to, and accepted by, fellow scientists. A few self-absorbed, secretive or greedy scientists disregard the second objective, and some regimes (political and commercial) constrain their scientists to secrecy. But the vast majority of research scientists want to contribute to mankind's further understanding of nature, knowing that such understanding is essential to the wise exploitation of nature.

However, though adding to knowledge may be pleasing, it

rarely satisfies human aspirations. Individual research scientists wish also to be recognized for their contribution(s), preferably with a mite of applause, with further research support and, of course, with a living. For all these reasons, therefore, scientists must publish their research. To dismiss in a capsule what is in fact a very complex issue, commercial or political secrecy in research may be transiently valuable for those benefiting from whatever is being concealed, but ultimately the secret must emerge or the knowledge will be lost.

In practice this means that the first observable product of scientific endeavour is almost always a scientific paper. During the second half of the twentieth century the amount of scientific research done in developed countries increased enormously, and with it has grown the output of scientific papers. So an elaborate system evolved dedicated to ensuring that scientific papers be original, correct factually, and comprehensible to fellow scientists; to ensure, too, that if they include theoretical matter, this too, be comprehensible with a sound experimental base.

In outline, the system works like this. A scientist has completed a piece of research - say a description of a new type of microbe: how and where it lives; what it has to consume to multiply; what it does that is of interest. The scientist may have mentioned the work at a scientific meeting, published a preliminary note about it, or even posted an account of the work on the Internet, but the time has come to prepare a definitive account to be published for posterity. A hundred years ago, when scientists were few, such scholarly papers could be long and discursive, often with personal digressions and asides. Today the form of a paper has to be fairly rigidly prescribed: impersonal but for the author's name(s), with as informative a title as possible; a brief, crisp introduction; an equally brief account of the techniques; an account of the results obtained; perhaps a brief discussion of their significance. All must be backed up with references to other relevant publications, a summary and key words for indexing and computerization. The emphasis is necessarily on telegraphic precision and rigid adherence to the point.

It is very rare for a scientific paper to follow the chronology of the research reported, simply because research rarely progresses in a straightforward manner. For example, two-thirds of the way into a research project a scientist may well discover something which invalidates or alters all his or her earlier work; then previous work must be repeated, replanned, perhaps even rejected. Such hiccups and back-trackings are normal in research but, however fascinating - or exasperating - they are to the researcher, they are of no scientific interest. Manuscripts for publication must be presented in a logical, not chronological, order.

Once the writing problem has been surmounted (and problem it is, because good scientific writing is very laborious, as well as quite different from regular literary creation), the next hurdle is peer review. The Editor of whatever journal the scientist has chosen will send copies to two or three scientists familiar with the research area, the referees, who read the paper and to offer an informed opinion on its scientific quality and clarity. The Editor will also take his own view of these matters, and will communicate the upshot to the author: the paper will either be accepted for publication, generally only after modification in the light of editorial criticisms, or it will be rejected, and the author must take the reasons to heart and try elsewhere - or do some more research and submit a thorough revision.

The referees are, or ought to be, the scientist's peers as far as the science is concerned. As you may imagine, peer review easily leads to resentment, especially when criticisms are felt to be pernickety or unjust. Referees are usually anonymous and it is the Editor who has the thankless task of communicating criticisms or rejections to indignant authors. But just as motorists hate traffic wardens but need them, so most scientists dislike peer review but agree that there is no substitute for it. The reason is simple: scientists are as bad at self-criticism as anyone else and without peer review the scientific literature would be cluttered up with confused writing and downright rubbish.

A few would argue that it nevertheless is. Like all elaborate regulatory systems, peer review is less than perfect. Rubbish occasionally gets past referees and is published; other scientists soon recognize its rubbishy nature and it is forgotten or contradicted. Peer review is also supposed to prevent unnecessary duplication of work published earlier, but 'rediscovering the wheel' (as it is known to cynical older researchers) does occur when authors and referees are both slapdash. Sadly it is becoming increasingly common, because earlier work easily passes unnoticed among the mounting deluge of new scientific papers. Much rarer are instances of deliberate fraud and plagiarism in scientific writing, and they rightly generate a big fuss. Cheating over priority or attribution is also known, but such malefactions are sooner or later found out.

Despite shortcomings, the peer review system that has evolved for sieving scientific research is remarkably robust and effective, and a major reason is that it is largely voluntary: the primary sieves, the referees, like the majority of editors, work willingly as a duty to the science.

There is a further point to be made about the system. It cannot, indeed it could never, ensure that the findings reported, and the interpretations put upon them, are ultimately true. A good, well-refereed paper will be as sound as contemporary knowledge and techniques allow, but no more. Once it is published - and this is a really important reason for publication - its substance is displayed for other scientists to confirm, amend, modify, or sometimes refute. Which is as it should be; criticism, refutation, even falsification, of established knowledge, as Karl Popper pointed out long ago, comprise the main routes by which science advances - and sometimes retreats.

The lure of print

As I told in chapter 2, my fellow student at Balliol, Christopher Longuet-Higgins, had upstaged his contemporaries by publishing, with Ronnie Bell, an original paper during his second year as an undergraduate. My work with Hinshelwood, in my fourth year, had yielded a very minor paper (though I had been very proud of it at the time).

My work with Woods had yielded nothing publishable - because, as I also told earlier, Donald was very firm about rounding off research before publication, and a draft manuscript based on my thesis remained in one of Donald's desk drawers while he 'thought about it' until his untimely death in 1964. So my first really original publication arose from my tiny nugget of knowledge regarding the effect of selenates on sulphate reduction, which I mentioned in chapter 7. It was a clear, new set of observations and I had no problem with peer review, though I had several weeks of silent anxiety while my manuscript was in the hands of *Nature*. No one else was working in my area - the most recent publications of that time on selenate toxicity referred to plants and fungi - and the work stood on its own. Indeed, I had the whole field of the biochemistry of sulphate-reducing bacteria almost to myself for two or three years, for Jacques Senez in France had barely started his research. My papers of the early 1950s were certainly severely edited, but none was rejected. Moreover my experience with my doctoral thesis had taught me humility regarding my own writing; I heeded the editings and quickly acquired the ability to write with the precision and brevity necessary for publication in a good quality journal.

I encountered a quite different aspect of scientific publication when Professor Egami visited me in 1954 and brought me the news that Ishimoto had discovered what came to be called cytochrome C3. Suddenly I faced a major dilemma, one that most research scientists can expect sooner or later. I learned that I was not alone in doing this exciting new work; I had a competitor, one who would certainly publish and who might do so ahead of me. What should I do? The fact that Butlin and I had included mention of the cytochrome in our paper to the Rome congress in 1953 spared me the chagrin of having someone else announce its very existence to the scientific world before I had done so, and on reflection the fact that there was a co-discoverer gave me extra confidence in what I had done; nevertheless Egami's revelation came as something of a shock. I now know of many scientists who would have responded by becoming secretive about their own work, sometimes paranoically so, lest their rival learn something that will put him or her ahead. But Woods had trained me well; he had taught me, with illustrations, that such hyper-competitiveness soon becomes a counter-productive blight on scientific progress, benefiting no one. The world of biological research is fraught with sad examples. As far as Egami's visit was concerned, I suppressed any such inclinations and talked freely to him. But the problem of what to do next remained, for scientific reputations undoubtedly depend very much on original and reliable publications.

In the event, I decided not to rush into premature publication but instead to press on with my research until I had found out as much as I could about what cytochrome C3 was and what it did. Then I would write a comprehensive paper, I hoped a substantial one, on the whole matter. In that way I could also follow up related questions, such as the other substance that could be seen in the spectroscope. Yet total silence would have been detrimental to my own scientific reputation, so on the way I would publish bulletins of my progress, as communications to meetings or short notes, simply to indicate to those concerned what aspects I was working on.

Ishimoto (whom I never met, though we exchanged rather formal letters) chose a different way. It took me three years from my discovery of cytochrome C3 to publish, in 1956, my 'definitive' paper, which was quite long, during which time Ishimoto's group published four papers, short but complete, on various aspects of the cytochrome. Though his group used a different strain of sulphate reducer, our approaches and findings were essentially similar. In the event, that was fine. As far as the wider scientific world was concerned, when my long paper came out we had collectively learned a lot about cytochrome C3 and its accompanying green pigment (the substance responsible for that extra band in the spectrum, which we had both extracted and partly purified), and almost all that information had perforce been double-checked on opposite sides of the world, with different strains of related bacteria. Honours were about equally divided. In the long run I think my policy paid off slightly: since almost all of the accumulated information was to be found conveniently in my one paper, which included citations of Ishimoto's group's papers. My paper, thirty years later, had become listed as a 'citation classic': the paper most often cited in its particular research sphere.

Being an editor

In the 1950s, the *Journal of General Microbiology* was Britain's leading journal for the publication of basic microbiological research. It complemented a rather older journal concerned with applied microbiology, then called the *Journal of Applied Bacteriology*; microbiological papers had also appeared in medical, botanical, zoological and technical journals for some decades. The *Journal of General Microbiology* had been founded in 1946 by the Society for General Microbiology to bring papers on fundamental microbiology under one umbrella, so to speak; it was non-commercial, so its academic and literary standards were very high, and it rapidly acquired a formidable reputation. After I had succeeded in having a few of my papers accepted by it, I was flattered when one of its joint Editors in Chief, Arthur Standfast, asked me to referee papers for it regularly. I took my duties seriously. I applied to the papers sent to me the lessons I had learned from my thesis and my own earlier papers, effectively (with Standfast's encouragement) acting as a sub-editor myself. Whether the unfortunate authors were best pleased to find their written English anonymously devastated I know not, but Standfast and his colleague B C K G ('Gabe') Knight stood the rap, and were pleased. Around 1960 - I have no note of the precise year - they made 'an honest editor' of me: the *Journal* had by then an Editorial Board, and on it appeared the name of John Postgate. At last I had laid the ghost of my rejected thesis.

It did not make getting my own papers published any the

easier, I might add. Editorial criticisms and comments on my own efforts were just as severe, but more than usually frank.

My editorial duties with the *Journal* showed me something quite unexpected. I had thought that I had been alone in having difficulties, by then largely overcome, with scientific writing. I was amazed to discover that I was far from alone. The *Journal* rejected more than half of the papers submitted to it on grounds of 'poor presentation', which effectively meant bad writing. That did not mean bad literary style, which was acceptable - even preferable if it made for clarity. What it meant was convoluted and obscure sentences, often fraught with redundancies and abstract nouns, and poor or non-existent attempts to present material in a logical sequence. For some reason, I realised, once Britain's scientists had decided to commit their findings and thoughts to paper, they felt compelled to write as if they were translating from indifferent High German. I recognized the syndrome very well because I had once done the same thing myself; like a moralistic ex-smoker, I felt uncommonly strongly against it.

Arthur Standfast and Gabe Knight felt just as strongly as I did about clarity in scientific writing. Knight had become Editor of the Journal (with A A Miles) at the time of its inception and almost at once the Journal's editorial severity had so offended one senior British microbiologist that he never published in it again. Standfast replaced Miles in 1951. He was actually a garrulous, yet slow-talking man, and Knight was a formidable personality of great literary sensibility; together they maintained a tight editorial regime throughout the 1950s and '60s, and dedicated an enormous amount of their time to the *Journal*. I came to know both of them well. To authors they seemed high-handed and inflexible, almost as if they derived a sort of sadistic enjoyment from tearing into hard-working researchers' manuscripts - yet nothing could have been further from the truth. They wanted the Society's Journal to be clear and straightforward, an intellectual flagship for the Society. Their editings and demands for modification were all directed towards clarity of whatever science was being presented; they fell over backwards to avoid unnecessary alterations, and also to explain those that they did require. But they were resigned to receiving few thanks, and were gloomily amusing about the lamentable level of literacy among Britain's scientists.

I learned from them certain 'red flag' phrases which tell an editor at once that a manuscript will need what Gabe called 'drainage'. A list would be tedious, but allow me two examples. The first will be familiar: a scientist writes that he/she did something for "a period of 5 minutes". The phrase "a period of" is a red flag: it can be removed without affecting the sense at all. Again, nine out of ten manuscripts will include somewhere the words "it has been shown that....."; scientists seem to find that particular phrase irresistible. It can almost always be deleted, because if 'it' had not been shown, the writer would not be making whatever statement follows the phrase. Both examples are symptoms of verbosity, phrases that add no information to the paper. In contrast to the second example, "Bloggs has shown that..." is quite acceptable, because it tells the reader something. An editor soon learns that an amazing number of little phrases exist which trip lightly off the pen and convey nothing whatever. And in scientific writing they matter, not only because they cost money in setting type but because they usually distract the reader from the main sense of whatever has been written.

In fairness to the British, let me add that the problem of obscure, puffed-out scientific writing transcends language: Germans themselves do it in German; Americans are often appalling at writing straightforwardly; and so are the French. Scandinavians and Dutch are better and this is significant. I am sure it is because they always publish science in English and, because it is not their native language, they are compelled to think carefully about each word they use. And if any young scientist reads this, let me slip in a distillation of those years of experience. Firstly, always write simply, logically and grammatically. When you think you have got a bit right, look again at what you have written, imagining yourself to be Japanese, with little English, trying to make out the sense by translating each word. You will be amazed at (a) how many of your words and phrases are not only unnecessary but actually distractions, and (b) how many ordinary English words are ambiguous.

As the 1970s approached, Knight, and shortly afterwards Standfast, felt it was time to retire. In 1969 I was eased into their place. Some members of the Society for General Microbiology's Council (of which I was by then a member) welcomed their departure, resenting what they felt were dictatorial attitudes on the editors' part, and looked forward to a relaxation under my control. But my predecessors' training had taken effect: an editorial colleague, reminiscing many years later, wrote of being "an editor under John Postgate's firm hand".

Being an editor takes a tremendous amount of time, and a working scientist has to find it out of his spare time. By 1969 I was in charge of quite a large research group as well as doing my own research; I recall an occasion in the late summer, shortly before I took over, when Standfast had gone on holiday, Knight had departed, and I was in charge alone. University vacations are good times for writing papers and a deluge of manuscripts had come to me, with most potential referees on holiday. I had edited and drained several papers in the preceding fortnight or so, and I stood in my office one morning, a manuscript in each hand and three on the floor, after my secretary brought in two more and left. I found my brain had stopped. I simply could not think what I was doing with all this paper, even what it was all about. If I tried to concentrate on one, I could not assimilate a single sentence. So I left my office and went for a walk.

I recovered quickly, but I realised that I must not allow things to reach crisis point again. I decided that the *Journal* could no longer be run by two or three volunteer editors. When I took over, Council agreed that I might revise the editorial machinery so that we had an Editor-in-Chief (me), three Senior Editors and a substantial Editorial Board. That was fine - the position is essentially the same a quarter of a century later - but how does one prevent editorial standards dropping when so many are involved? My solution was a gimmick we called the 'training loop'. When a new member joined the Editorial Board, he would be given an averagely awkward paper to edit (in pencil), then one of the senior editors would re-edit it, explaining in detail all his or her changes - including 'red flag' phrases, 'in house' conventions and so on. They would get the idea quickly, usually after a couple of papers, because they had no personal involvement in what had been written, and they could see the sense of the editings without resentment. At least one new member, who had submitted a manuscript just before joining the Board, anxiously withdrew his own manuscript after going through the training loop, in order to revise it himself.

On the other hand, some missed the point. One, whom we had to dismiss, was immensely slow, taking months to deal with a manuscript, and then would cover it with inked alterations, many unnecessary, and send it to the senior editor recommending outright rejection. If ever an author had good cause to protest! At least one awful paper got published because I could not bear to return the mangled manuscript after such a delay. But the system did give the editoriat a degree of consistency, and it worked without driving everyone batty. And of course, I, as Chief, received the usual flack from resentful if verbose authors - including a startlingly rude letter from a distinguished medical microbiologist of my own generation because the manuscript of an American guest researcher in his laboratory had been 'drained'.

Sixty to seventy per cent of manuscripts were either rejected outright or needed some, often much, editing because of poor presentation. The rest? Well there are some scientists who can and do write good papers; whose minds work clearly, who can express themselves economically and logically - and who bother to read the 'Instructions to Authors' and so get symbols and abbreviations right. What a blessing they are! They usually prove to be outstanding researchers, too, and I am convinced that the two go together. Someone who writes clearly also thinks clearly, and clarity of thought is what science is all about.

I retired from the Chief Editorship of the *Journal of General Microbiology* in the mid 1970s, consigning the *Journal*, with its revised editorial structure functioning reasonably smoothly, to the tender care of my successor, microbial geneticist Stuart Glover. The Society for General Microbiology's membership when I left the Journal the membership was around 3000, reflecting the growth of the subject not only in Britain but also throughout the world. And not only did most of those members want to publish papers in their 'house' journal, but so did many microbiologists from overseas. To cope with an ever-increasing flood of manuscripts, the *Journal of General Microbiology* under Knight and Standfast had spawned a sister organ, the *Journal of General Virology*, to take all papers on viruses; in addition several commercial journals had become established, which published papers, often more rapidly and less carefully edited, in newer branches of microbiology such as biotechnology, microbial genetics and molecular biology. Partly because of this diversification, the *Journal of General Microbiology* developed rather a stuffy image among younger researchers and in 1993 it changed its name (to *Microbiology*).

Throughout this book, I have written about things as they were in the second half of the Twentieth Century. New editorial problems have arisen in such areas as the conservation of important but space-consuming information, such as maps of genomes, detailed protein structures and exhaustive statistical data, which not only must not be lost, but which must be rapidly accessible to those who need to know. Information storage and retrieval is a global problem in all areas, one to which microfiches, the Internet, memory sticks and the like are palliative but impermanent solutions. What is clear is that conventional printed journals can no longer cope in the twenty-first century. But I firmly believe that, as microbiology grew and flourished in Britain during the later decades of the twentieth century, the *Journal* and its editors did an enormous amount not only to conserve the reputation of British microbiology, but also to sustain its quality by making people think about what exactly they were writing, and therefore about what exactly they had been doing.

My doctorate examiners and my wife were the people who put me in a position to make my exhausting contribution to this beneficent effort. Yes, I am grateful. Now.

CHAPTER TWELVE

Travellin'

"Join the Navy and see the World," said a widespread recruiting poster in my childhood. Well, "become a scientist and see the world," could be an equally apt slogan. The analogy fits in some detail, because, as in the Navy, someone else prescribes the parts of the world that you get to see. Congress organizers, host universities and the locations of congress centres, in place of the Admiralty, determine where you go.

International scientific congresses are an important part of the give-and-take of research, and sooner or later researchers will find themselves travelling. Non-scientists tend to regard congresses and overseas meetings as opportunities for enjoyable trips to exotic places at someone else's expense – "boondoggles" in US American - and it would be idle to pretend that a boondoggle element does not enter into the matter. Conference organisers do indeed try to select nice places for meetings because, other things being equal, the Leaders of Research are more likely to find time to come than if they are invited to a gloomy, or even dangerous, industrial or inner-city area. And more subtly, pleasant surroundings, preferably remote, make for more relaxed discussion and exchange of information. But an element of tourism is always there.

My first encounter with the international 'set' took place in 1952. I had been at CRL for some three years; an International Congress of Biochemistry was due to be held in Paris in July; I had some biochemical findings on pyruvate metabolism in sulphate-reducing bacteria which I believed would interest the congress; with Butlin's support the DSIR agreed to finance my attendance. Suddenly I was among the *élite* of biological chemistry: Roger Stanier, my old friend Chain, Linus Pauling (whom I had known briefly as a visiting Professor at Balliol), Bernard Davis, Ben Volcani, Elizabeth Work, André Lwoff, Jacques Monod, A Prévot, Donald Woods - specialists will recognise the names of the giants of the era. Of my own generation, Jacques Senez, Ben Nisman, Georges Cohen, Bruce Newton, Peter Mitchell and many others were around. Distracted by nervous tension until I had given my own contribution, I nevertheless had a wonderful time talking science with all and sundry, wandering with other scientists about Paris and being taken by Nisman to visit Jacques Monod in his lair at the Institut Pasteur. Monod was a great microbial physiologist, a father-figure of molecular biology, and the largely American queue to pay homage to him was long; I was shyly conscious that his interest in sulphate-reducing bacteria was likely to be marginal at best, so I sneaked away after a polite word or two.

I recall talking with Senez about life, politics and science in the small hours of the morning on the Champs Elysées after a rollicking banquet... and on another occasion being 'put down' by a lesser giant, American V Cheldelin, whose work on selenates and plants which he had published a few years earlier I wished to query. He told me to go and read his papers. Actually, I had read them, and still had some queries, but he did not stop to listen. I made a mental note never to do that myself to aspiring young scientists myself in later life, and I hope I lived up to my ambition. But they were heady times and the science was exciting, and though I have forgotten what the major scientific highlights of the meeting were, I recall that the principal papers were very good and that I benefited enormously from the formal proceedings, and even more from the 'extra-curricular' contacts and conversations.

My next foray abroad took place a year later when I went to Rome to contribute to an International Congress of Microbiology organised by Chain, who was now at his purpose-built research laboratory there; as I told in chapter 4, he had invited Butlin and me to talk about the practical uses and activities of sulphur bacteria. As things turned out, it proved to be a somewhat less serious, and funnier, event than the Paris meeting. This time I had a major talk to deliver, on behalf of both Butlin and myself, and putting it together had been somewhat stressful. Butch's idea was to leave out most of the biochemistry, while mine was that biochemistry should be its main emphasis. But we compromised without serious argument and some two months before the meeting the version to be published was ready, I had written my script (I spoke strictly from a script in those days - a bad practice, but essential for one as nervous as I was), and the slides needed to illustrate my talk were ready: about fifteen of the heavy three-inch square glass objects which lecturers used in the days before 35mm cardboard transparencies (now widely displaced in their turn by PowerPoint).

I planned to bring Mary along - we ought to have enough money if we lived cheaply. Jacques Senez had written to suggest that Mary and I meet him and his then wife Gillou in Marseilles a few days before the meeting, so that they might drive us to the Congress, sight-seeing and relaxing on the way; in return, I should work in his laboratory for two weeks after the meeting, to show them such things as cytochrome C3 and a method I had devised for enumerating sulphate reducers; and, for my part, to see what they were doing. Butch strongly approved - he was all in favour of the boondoggle element - and the laboratory's directorate were pleased that one of their staff should be invited to Marseilles. They too agreed, and that took care of my expenses, though not Mary's. No matter; we were ready to go long before departure date. Realising I should have a lot of luggage, I even had the foresight to post my slides for my lecture, carefully packed in a slotted wooden box, to Chain's laboratory in Rome, sending them off a month in advance so as to be sure they would be there in time.

A post-war Italian congress, then Marseilles

The first hint that things would not go smoothly according to plan occurred almost immediately after I had sent off the slides. The whole French railway system went on strike. This meant that we could not travel by rail, by far the least expensive way, but would have to go by air. But it was summer, and everybody in Britain seemed to want to fly either to France or across it. British European Airways - as the national carrier was then - took our names, and a deposit, and told us to be ready to fly at 24 hours' notice. That is why, somewhat dazed, Mary and I arrived in Nice, with luggage and no hotel booked, two weeks ahead of the Congress.

It was lovely. We found a pleasant, not too costly, hotel on the Quai des Etats Unies, telephoned the Senezes and told them we would meet them in Nice, which was on the way to Rome, and settled into a 10-day sunshine and seaside holiday on the Riviera, my own expenses refundable. Boondoggling? Well - it wasn't our fault, was it?

In due course the Senezes met us and we set off for Italy in their car. We continued our agreement, established when Senez had worked at Teddington, that we should speak English when the topic was science and French otherwise; it worked very well and benefited our linguistic abilities all round. I could, and still can, speak voluble and inaccurate French with an English accent, one which non-anglophobe French find quaint. Once my audience is acclimatized, I usually make myself understood. Mary, in contrast, spoke more limited but excellent French with a high-class Parisian accent, generating surprise, almost reproach, that she was not actually French.

However, French-style driving, exacerbated by the bends of the *Grande Corniche*, was something quite unfamiliar, especially to Mary; within an hour she was carsick. Senez prescribed Phenergan syrup; we bought some in Menton and it worked, albeit making her drowsy.

We made quick touristic visits to Genoa, Orvieto and Viterbo; Mary and I found Italy new and exciting, and the Senezes who, like many of the French intellectual Left, took a rather colonial view of Italy and its inhabitants, enjoyed showing us round and found our Anglo-Saxon reactions amusing. We had not allowed for our hosts' superior life style: seeking an hotel in Siena, Gillou Senez homed in on the most expensive and pronounced it adequate. Though it was fun to be in a huge bedroom with its own marble bathroom and gilt fittings, at that standard Mary and I would soon have been broke. Happily that was our only overnight stop on our way to Rome, where Chain had booked both us and the Senezes into an economical boarding house, the *Pensione Athena*, close to the University, where the congress was to be held.

"*C'est une maison particulière?*", asked Gillou in dismay as we arrived.

But it was clean, sunny and welcoming, and she became reconciled to it. Mary liked it at once, and especially delighted in being woken up of a morning by the room maid drawing the curtains: "*Buon giorno, bella signora!*"

In Rome I went straight to Chain's laboratory to collect my slides. Fate's second blow: they were not there. So by tram to Rome's central postal sorting office and customs, accompanied by Mary with Italian dictionary at the ready. After much hand-waving and pidgin Italian, I made my problem understood and a search was instituted. My package was not there. It had been delayed by the French railway strike. I waited a couple of days, hoping, but then matters became urgent. Being due to talk the following day, I spent a morning in Chain's lab with drawing equipment and my script, drafting, from my memory of what my slides had contained, sketches and tables for use with an old-fashioned epidiascope. Thus my first major conference lecture was supported by largely imaginary data! Some months later my package reappeared at Teddington: every slide was smashed and useless, so the story might not have been much different had it arrived in Rome on time.

Scientifically, the Congress papers and lectures ranged from pretty good to very modest indeed. That was the way with such big international meetings in those days: anyone who could rustle up the necessary expenses and had something to communicate could expect to be allocated 15 or 20 minutes in which to present a short paper, and an abstract the work would be published as part of the Congress proceedings. Such conferences could offer an opportunity to establish priority in making some important scientific advance, but more often the offered papers were means of obtaining expenses, because administrators and research directors were, and are, much more likely to provide their staff with travel money if the name of the laboratory is going to receive some publicity by appearing in print. The invited lectures would be a more serious matter; sometimes they might deal with burning scientific issues of the day, and lead to memorable debate; more often they would be useful *résumés* of progress in their designated scientific area. As with all scientific meetings, the major benefit to the assembly would be meeting and talking with fellow scientists from distant lands.

It is a reflection on my frivolous outlook more than on the programme, I fear, that my clearest memory from the Rome meeting (setting aside my own stilted performance) is of a short paper from a Singhalese scientist who claimed to be able to influence bacterial growth by mental power. He had inoculated jellified cultures with similar numbers of bacteria, set half of them aside and concentrated on the rest for half an hour, willing them not to grow. After subsequent incubation, it seemed, fewer bacterial colonies appeared on the cultures on which he had concentrated. I had to miss his presentation, but I was told that he became understandably indignant when some in his audience took his claim seriously enough to suggest that the results had been fudged, perhaps unwittingly (much the most likely explanation, in truth, and easily done). Yet he could hardly have expected that a claim which promised to undermine the whole of experimental microbiology would go unchallenged.

Some at the Congress felt that his paper ought to have been disallowed as wasting valuable time. Like Chain, I did not, and still do not, agree. Certainly nothing further was heard of the work, but research was relaxed in those days, there was room for cranky papers and their presenters might even benefit from criticism. Today the pressure of offered contributions at such meetings is enormous, and any organising committee would certainly exclude his paper as being too implausible.

Scientifically, Rome may have been so-so, and I cannot be sure that age has not altered my recollections appreciably, but socially it was splendid. Not only did I meet many old colleagues, visitors to Butlin's group or participants in last year's Paris meeting, but I met new people, including the great Robert Starkey, one of the pioneers of research on sulphate-reducing bacteria. And the official receptions and excursions were marvellous: a rather select and alcoholic reception at Chain's Istituto Superiore di Sanità, a vast official reception in Rome's Campidoglio, and a day trip to the Villa D'Este and Tivoli. All were marvellous experiences, though the latter two were rather slimming: at the Campidoglio it was a long walk through the fascinating building to the exterior, where a marvellous spread was available. Unfortunately for many foreign visitors, the Italian microbiologists had not only brought their families along but had got there first: by the time the British and Americans, at least, reached the tables there was nothing left.

I remember standing by an empty table with Donald Woods, Sidney Elsden, Ernest Gale and their wives, all chewing the bones of a cold roast calf which looked as if vultures had got at it. Actually, none of us really blamed the poor and hungry Italians, still recovering from their wartime defeats. But when a similar problem occurred at Tivoli, more alert this time, we formed a team: some kept seating while others foraged for food. Mary even got us some Italian ice cream; but polite Americans such as Claude ZoBell starved again. Occasional austerities left room for delicious meals at Rome's many *trattorias* in the company of fellow scientists, and there was no problem at the splendid final banquet. As a concession to foreign visitors, the formal speeches by our hosts were given in Latin; a kindly gesture, which defeated even the Latinists among us since they, not unreasonably, pronounced the language as if it were Italian.

It was the first truly international congress of microbiologists since before the Second World War and despite almost comic mishaps and absurdities the nationalities present rejoiced in rediscovering each other. So, regrettably, did the pickpockets on the Roman buses - but misfortune and muddle were rapidly swept aside by general goodwill and pleasure. A bizarre image of international conviviality still remains with me: a jolly American had chosen to wear a joke tie to the Campidoglio reception, one which he could cause to rise in the air by pressing a concealed bulb in his pocket; there he was: large, middle aged, and roaring with laughter while three small Italians gazed in wild surmise, as much at him as at the tie.

Congress over, we managed a spot of tourism in Rome itself - the Sistine Chapel, St Peter's, the piazzas and Roman excavations. Mary had fitted in quite a lot of sightseeing while I had been at meetings - and warded off several would-be helpful young Italian men. Then the Senezes took us back by a scenic route: Perugia, Assisi, overnight in Ravenna; Padua, overnight in Venice (including the obligatory gondola ride); Verona for lunch, overnight in Gap, in the French Alps, and so to Marseilles.

There Mary and I were the guests of the CNRS laboratory where Senez had his little research group. The laboratory had a fairly spartan guest room - the showers were some distance away and were so covered with algal slime that we rarely brought ourselves to use them. No food was available, but there was a heater and Jacques Senez's technician Maurice Dupont brought us fresh croissants and milk for coffee each morning. We lunched at a local restaurant patronised by business people called Chez Soi. Often we would be entertained for dinner by the Senezes; once they gave *un cocktail* (a cocktail party) for us at which I borrowed Gillou's guitar and 'plucked and whined' (ie: sang the blues and other sad jazz songs over elementary guitar chords). The guests expressed enjoyment of the music, and of Gillou's eggnog, but they did not understand about the cocktail hour. They did not go home. Hour after hour passed and they remained. Gillou, baffled but ever polite, produced a steady supply of drink, but she did not have food for so many; Mary and I became hungrier and hungrier until, at about 11 pm, we made our excuses and left, stoking up with a sandwich at a bistro on the way home.

The Senezes drove us to Provençal beauty spots and even, thoughtfully, gave us an overnight *congé* on our own in a holiday apartment, which they owned at Cassis.

At the laboratory I was busy, passing on some of the techniques and discoveries I had made, discussing and even setting up experiments, and Mary enjoyed sightseeing in Marseilles - then a very safe town for tourists. Everyone made us very welcome, and we slipped easily into the daily life of

Marseilles, lunching regularly at a local restaurant and feeling almost part of the community. It would be foolish to pretend that there were not occasional stresses; I was again conscious of Senez's barely contained envy and his sense that I was a threat to his status - for I was still ahead of him scientifically and was something of a rising star - and I was always careful to be admiring of his work and arrangements. Attitudes and habits jarred at times, and Mary found his need for applause notably difficult to like. But young and dedicated people are tolerant of each other's foibles and, at least as far as Jacques and I were concerned, our joint obsession with sulphate-reducing bacteria overrode personality problems. At the end of my scheduled stay we departed with sincere regrets, and Mary and I were abidingly grateful for the Senez's goodwill, generosity and enthusiasm for showing us around. Gillou was unexpectedly moved to tears on the day we left.

We visited Mary's brother Robert at Fontainebleau on the way back to Britain, talked English, and had a welcome hot if shallow bath.

Back home I busied myself with research once more, developing cytochrome C3 in particular but keeping some other themes going too. I travelled to scientific meetings in the UK, usually of the Society for General Microbiology, once or twice a year - our laboratory budget wisely allowed for such excursions - and after 1953 I went to meetings abroad, in France and Belgium for example, almost annually, but, to my regret, my two weeks in Marseilles were my only working visit to a laboratory in Europe.

CHAPTER THIRTEEN

Go west, young man

By the mid 1950s I was a familiar figure at microbiological meetings in Britain and I had joined the international circuit. However, for the up-and-coming scientist there was another hurdle to surmount: though I had a higher degree and a doctorate, I did not have my BTA.

What that? BTA was an imaginary degree of the 1950s. The initials stood for 'Been To America'. After about 1950, almost every budding British research scientist emerging from a university with a decent degree would spend a post-graduate or post-doctoral period, usually a year, doing research in the USA. Funds to support such visits were fairly easily come by from research and educational trusts, and the experience was greatly valued by both the visiting researchers and their British supervisors or employers-to-be. In general, too, British visitors were much esteemed by their US hosts, because in those days the intellectual standard and level of education of British post-graduates and post-doctorals were generally superb, especially by local US standards. (In later decades they declined in Britain and rose in the USA.) But there were social problems: austerity had made a few young Britons into scroungers and even petty thieves, as I would later learn; they might 'nick' laboratory equipment for home use, or charge personal costs (eg long-distance telephone calls) to the host laboratory's budget. However, on the whole transatlantic goodwill survived occasional misbehaviour, and perhaps the British were not unique in this respect.

By graduating in the late 1940s I had missed my 'BTA'. The chance to restore my status came when, in 1957, I received a wholly unexpected offer of a $300 fee if I would come and address a symposium, sponsored by oil companies in up-state New York, on the physiological chemistry of sulphate reducers. The subject of the symposium was 'Sulphate-reducing bacteria, their relation to the secondary recovery of oil'.

What is secondary recovery of oil, you ask? It happened that I knew: it is the collective name for processes whereby oil wells which have been used-up, in the sense that ordinary pumping extracts no more oil ('spent' wells in the jargon), can be treated so that more oil becomes available. I knew because ZoBell had written about the topic: it seemed that sulphate-reducing bacteria could actually promote the release of residual oil stuck to shale deep down in such wells. Of course, I knew nothing else about secondary recovery and had never seen an oil well. ZoBell had once sent Molly

Adams a couple of cultures from deep down in oil wells and that, in truth, was the full extent of my, and Butlin's group's, contact with oil microbiology.

What self-respecting scientist would be discouraged by such ignorance? By now I possessed a compensating wealth of fundamental knowledge about sulphate-reducing bacteria; I felt I could tell them what was what, and here was an opportunity to learn something new about the activities of my microbial pets, as well as to get my 'BTA'. Intellectually I jumped at the chance.

Intellectually, I said. As bad luck would have it, my health was poor and, though I concealed my feelings from my colleagues as best I could, the prospect of a lone safari into mid-century USA greatly alarmed me. I did go - but before I retail the story I must digress once more into my health problems, boring though such matters are (except to those who have or have had with comparable problems), because they coloured the whole of my visit.

Medical interlude

The duodenal ulcer which had troubled me in the early 1950s had gone, or at least become quiescent. But bouts of excessive anxiety continued to plague me and, in 1957, I was in the thick of one. My brother called my condition the 'screeching willies'. I looked anxious, I was jumpy; my movements and speech were often tremulous. I was always weary, would palpitate if I had to run for a bus, and I slept badly. I felt rather as if I had a constant hangover from too much alcohol, though in fact I rarely drank at all. I feared crowds: I could have the greatest difficulty in concealing sensations of panic in, for example, a large department store, and on at least a couple of occasions found myself impelled to leave without buying whatever it was I went in for. I dreaded sociability, unless it be with family, or old friends with whom I was wholly at ease; and my 'normal' fear of public speaking was intensified. Only my passion for jazz would move me to go somewhere unfamiliar of an evening or weekend, and at jazz clubs I would skulk in the background as best I could. If I got to play, as I steeled myself to do once or twice, I would play badly and hesitantly. However, doctors could find nothing somatically wrong with me.

Fellow sufferers will recognise at once the symptoms of the condition called anxiety neurosis or endogenous depression, depending on how protracted and/or debilitating it is. My current bout was not helped by the domestic stress of adjusting to life with our two daughters, Selina, at two and a half years old a cheerful, healthy infant, and her sister Lucy, aged almost one. I have since learned that identifiable stresses make little difference to one's situation once dread has started to close in. In the 1950s, diagnoses of neurosis or depression carried overtones of hypochondria, even malingering, among both doctors and their patients. "It's all in the mind, snap out of it!" said my mother, typifying a widespread attitude. And anyway, even a sympathetic family doctor could do little about the condition. Mine prescribed phenobarbitone, which at least ensured sleep of a kind, plus zombie-like sloth when awake. I could still keep working like a beaver, and I lived from day to day.

How could I face the USA in this condition? My upbringing and sense of duty triumphed: I would load up with phenobarbitone and face it. With Butlin's approval, for he was delighted with the glory reflected on his group, I entered into negotiations with the DSIR.

America

Negotiations with the DSIR were needed because, though HQ was also well pleased at my invitation, as a Civil Servant there was no question of my keeping the $300 fee. That must be surrendered to the Department, and I would travel using the expenses and allowances appropriate to my rank. The meeting would be hosted by St Bonaventure University, a small foundation then noted for its baseball team; it was near a town called Olean, the centre for the New York State oil industry. However, $300 could buy a lot of travel in those days, much more than was needed for a week's meeting in upstate New York. HQ agreed that I should plan a more extended stay in the USA, bracketing the symposium, and I did so. I arranged to take up Professor Van Niel's invitation to spend two weeks at his laboratory in Pacific Grove looking at his special cultures of sulphate-reducing bacteria, with a brief side-trip to see the microbiologists at Berkeley outside San Francisco, then to go to my meeting near Olean, taking in Sidney Rittenberg's laboratory in Los Angeles.

After the meeting I should visit Professor Starkey at Rutger's, New Jersey, call into New York City for some visits, then to the Canadian Research Council's laboratory in

Ottawa, to which I had been invited, before returning to Britain. A preliminary stop at the U K Scientific Attaché's Office in Washington, was obligatory; days off gained by weekend travel would enable me to visit my brother-in-law Robert, now moved to Kentucky. Altogether a mighty zigzag across a substantial chunk of Northern hemisphere, with a lot of flying - which still terrified me. I should be away from home for about seven weeks. I had negotiated substantially more than $300-worth of travel, at which Butch and my laboratory colleagues were delighted. As for myself, I felt quite ill at the thought of it, but I smiled bravely, prepared my talk and bought quick-drying travelling clothes.

In 1957 the British Treasury still regarded air travel as exceptional, at least for its lower-ranking officers. An exception was made within the USA because of the huge distances usually involved, but once an itinerary was settled, actual flights were booked for one, and subsistence dollars provided, by the UK Scientific Mission's office in Washington - hence my obligation to call in personally. But it meant that I could cross the Atlantic by sea, which I preferred.. So I duly boarded the *Queen Elizabeth*, cabin class, at Southampton on Wednesday September 18 after a discouraging rail journey during which a lady with a Southern US accent talked incessantly and gruesomely to her companion about her operations.

On board I discovered to my dismay that single travellers were obliged to share a cabin with a stranger. My companion proved to be Mr Katz, an elderly non-anglophone rabbi in a black smock and round hat, travelling from Israel to a Jewish religious congress in New York. He, too, was astonished, and even more upset, to find himself obliged to share, and he protested at once to the Purser - in vain, of course. He proved to be an unusually unsatisfactory cabin-mate, because his religious duties obliged him to read regularly from the Talmud and not to eat outside the cabin; on the first night he opened a tin of sardines clumsily and covered the cabin 'desk' and sink with fishy oil, which he spread around rather than mopped up with newspaper. He read until 2.30 am, left the light on, snored in his brief sleep and woke up at six to read some more. Happily the cabin steward was horrified by the mess, and by my hollow-eyed account of my night, and he promised to exert pressure on the Purser. I had to remain for another interrupted night, then I was offered a change of cabin (to Mr Katz's apologetic relief). My new companion was Dr Douglas, a dentist from South Carolina who was friendly, racist, and largely unable to understand my accent. I decided that there was no point in trying to disabuse him of the friendly belief that it was anti-Semitism that had caused me to arrange the change. Instead I gritted my teeth and let him grumble to me of the iniquities of US labour unions, who obliged employers to pay 'illiterate niggers' normal wages. His prejudices were truly awful by my standards, but in other ways he was a kind and sympathetic man. I remained hypocritically silent and we managed well enough.

The *Queen Elizabeth*, launched in 1940 and refurbished from wartime service as a troopship, was Britain's pride among the trans-Atlantic liners: a floating, first class hotel with glorious 1930s-style decor. There was little to do but lounge on deck and then eat abundant but rather ordinary food. Given peace, I would have enjoyed that but, presumably because of my doctorate, I was accorded the unwelcome privilege of being placed at the Surgeon's table for meals. The Surgeon was pleasant enough, but at least two of our company were painfully uncongenial and the conversation was banal or, when it verged on the political or the social, offensive. Nor did I enjoy the two gala dinners, the funny hat parade, mock Derby race, bingo and so on. The QE proved not to be the place for a solitary self-conscious intellectual of leftish prejudices; happily I had by then learned the wisdom of silence and equivocation. But I enjoyed moments of jazz played by the ship's band between more ordinary dance music, and I spent quite a lot of time in the ship's cinema. My distant hope that a restful, relaxing cruise would enable my poor health and anxiety state to recover came to nothing.

The slow approach to Manhattan by sea is one of the seven wonders of the modern world. Appearing first as a tiny but familiar backdrop, the skyscrapers of New York look like a cluster of stalagmites protruding from the edge of the sea, light and beautiful. Then they grow, grow and grow again until they are huger than anything one has ever experienced, dwarfing the giant Cunarder like grotesque follies; the Statue of Liberty, beside them, is tiny. In dock one raises one's eyes to see their tops - and goes on raising them until one's neck aches. It is an astonishing sight, and one which has lifted the spirits of wave after wave of European travellers, immigrant or visitor, for much of the Twentieth Century.

The sardonic let-down of actual arrival on the quay at

New York was something I would not learn of until my third US visit some five years later. On this first visit, an unexpected advantage of being a civil servant suddenly revealed itself. I was met by a UK representative as I stepped off the boat; my luggage was collected and I was whisked through customs and immigration in no time. Within about an hour I was waiting on Pennsylvania Station for my train to Washington, 'Parlour Car' ticket provided by Her Majesty's agent (I had actually come with an air ticket, too, but that was easily cancelled by telephone). I was bemused and delighted by trivia: the box-like advertisement in the centre of Penn Station which advertised a hair dye while playing *Bluebird of Happiness*, the dial-a-coke machine (I dialled myself a Coca Cola), the helicopter flying in between skyscrapers. It dawned upon me that the scenery as we travelled south through New Jersey was less than lovely, mostly derelict-looking railroad lots, but even the train itself was fascinating and large.

The journey took several hours, with time for lunch in the restaurant car, and the outlook improved as we left the East Coast megapolis behind. In Washington, advised by an English lady passenger, I used a 'group tariff' cab to get to the Gralyn Hotel, quite a pleasant bed and breakfast cheapo that the UK Embassy used for low-ranking impecunious British officials. Seeking supper at a local drug store that evening I had an attack of nerves and departed, my plate of 'prime-burger' and fries (= chips) unfinished; I had had too many new impressions for my already anxious condition, augmented by travellers' diarrhoea. I wanted milk (a reversion to my ulcer regime) but the Gralyn had none; I retired early and slept fitfully.

A blow-by-blow account of my travels and struggles with health problems would be tedious. Suffice it to say that I visited the UK Scientific Mission and collected dollars and air tickets, I saw a doctor and got a new kind of drug called a tranquillizer (which, regrettably, I abandoned before I had really given it time to work), as well as a reserve prescription for phenobarbitone which, redeemed in San Francisco, carried me through my trip. I also managed some reasonably tranquil sightseeing (the White House, Washington Monument, Lincoln Memorial) before flying next day to Kentucky to spend a pleasant couple of days with brother-in-law Robert Stewart, his French wife Jacqui and their new second offspring Mary-Frances, in their then current home at Fort Knox.

My first official rendezvous was due to be with Van Niel at Pacific grove on the Californian coast. To reach it from Kentucky I flew to St. Louis, staying overnight in an average hotel located in a rather depressed area. I vaguely hoped to seek out some jazz on the evening of my arrival, and after dinner I set out for a walk; very soon I noticed several sinister characters lounging around in doorways, and I returned rapidly to my hotel. Next day I flew to Dallas, Texas, for a change of plane, then to San Francisco for a stop overnight, then a connecting flight to Monterey, the airport that also serves Pacific Grove. It was a slow and roundabout route by more recent standards, but by the time of my delayed flight to San Francisco, which was smooth and pleasant, my fear of flying had receded considerably. The scenery as we flew across the Rocky Mountains was breath taking, as was the sight of pinky-white saltpans as we approached SF international airport.

Sadly, the screeching willies returned when I went for a walk that evening from my hotel, so I did not explore. Next day I did better and walked around, admiring San Francisco's cable cars and attractive hilly layout. I felt quite safe - unlike in St Louis - and discovered a strange fact about downtown San Francisco: one should not stand near the kerb if wondering where to go next, because the traffic in both directions would courteously stop, assuming that you wished to cross the road. Reciprocal politeness forced me to cross the road unintentionally two or three times before I learned to retreat into a doorway to consider my next direction. (Can this still be true? It was certainly so in 1957.) But I did not do much sightseeing, because I had decided that my tranquillisers were not working and I arranged to use my reserve prescription for phenobarbitone, which took a little time. Thus equipped, I made my way to the airport and, with quiet confidence, flew to Monterey.

Arriving at the San Carlos hotel, with its ornamental palms outside, in glorious sunshine, I felt a lightening of the spirit. It was an enchanting town and the hotel looked over house roofs, seeming quite Spanish from above, to a bright blue ocean. Sadly the food was less attractive, but I was becoming accustomed to standard US catering: fibrous half chicken, almost tasteless turkey vol-au-vent, strangely bland salt beef and cabbage. Only later, instructed by Van Niel, did I learn that local US cooking could be very good indeed.

Next day Van Niel collected me from the hotel and took me to his laboratory in Pacific Grove. Actually, Pacific Grove was indistinguishable from Monterey, because the two communities are contiguous and so, too, was a third township, Carmel, where Van Niel had his home. All three occupied a beautiful rocky peninsula protruding into the Bay of Monterey, covered with largely wealthy dwellings, pines and golf courses. His laboratory, part of the Hopkins Marine Station, was actually on the seashore facing a rock peopled by brown pelicans and smaller sea birds. A beautiful outlook, and I at once regretted that I had not brought swimming trunks. But my regret was short-lived: I learned that the locals never even contemplated bathing, because the water was always frigidly cold and even the most dedicated bather emerged again within seconds.

On my way to the laboratory we collected a young Norwegian microbiologist, Kjell Eimjellen, who had arrived with his family the day before me for a two-year stay. We talked microbiology for most of the morning. The fascination of doing so, for Van Niel was a mine of information about exotic marine microbes, ameliorated my disappointment with the scene around me. Because the laboratory was a mess. It was untidy to the extent of being ramshackle, had almost no modern equipment, and no one seemed to be working there. Van Niel's tiny office was a shambles with only a deckchair for visitors. Yet here it was that, once a year, the *élite* of U.S. microbiologists, plus a few lucky Europeans, would assemble for a summer school in microbiology, which was famous for its quality throughout the microbiological world.

Later we had lunch at a good restaurant on Monterey Pier, and inspected Cannery Row, a street that was already becoming a place of pilgrimage for admirers of John Steinbeck's novel. Appropriate bogus memorabilia were on offer from enterprising traders. Then Kjell rejoined his family and I was on my own at the laboratory. I cleared myself some bench space and set about preparing culture media wherewith to revive the rather old strains of sulphate-reducing bacteria which Van Niel had kept for me, and also to grow a new type which Molly Adams had isolated at Teddington, called the Singapore strain; I wanted to show it to him. With luck my fortnight would be just time enough for me to get those two things done.

I settled into a daily routine at the laboratory easily, moved from the hotel into nearby lodgings and began to enjoy life, though the willies were never far from the surface.

Van Niel was always slightly formal to me: I was "Dr Postgate" and he, naturally, was "Professor Van Niel" to me. It was a pleasant change from the immediate first-name address used by most U.S. citizens. He and his wife were excellent hosts. They drove me around sightseeing - the breath-taking beauty of the Californian coastline was wholly new to me - and entertained me often at their home in Carmel. Here is an example of Van Niel's special courtesy: E F Hartree, the assistant of Dr Keilin to whom I had shown cytochrome C3, visited the laboratory for a day while on a tour of the West Coast (I think he was a little dismayed to find no one but Kjell and me there). Van Niel invited him and me to an excellent dinner at his home, with good Californian wine; during post-prandial conversation, the somewhat jet-lagged Hartree fell asleep. We all paid no attention and went on talking. After about three minutes, totally unaware of what had happened, Hartree woke up and continued the conversation from where it had been three minutes ago. With immaculate smoothness Van Niel switched us all back to the earlier theme and the evening proceeded as if nothing odd had happened.

Van Niel soon discovered that I had acquired some of my father's interest in food and wine, and that I was not impressed by my gastronomic experiences in the USA so far (he did not know of the excellent cooking of my brother-in-law's French wife in Kentucky). So he made a point of introducing me to good West Coast food - sea bass, abalone, T-bone steaks and so on - and teasing me about my knowledge of wine. Californian wines were then represented in Britain by a very modest product called 'Big Tree Burgundy' and I had not bothered with them; Van Niel provided, and made me pronounce upon, some of the vintage products of California's better vineyards. Of course, I got them wrong, thinking they were superior French clarets or burgundies and, of course, when he produced a genuine, classy, French claret, I got that wrong, too. I pretended chagrin, but I was pleased to learn. After all, good Californian wines were still uncommon, and little known even in the USA, in 1957.

I learned one very useful health hint from the Van Niels. My habitual anxieties had been made worse by a new problem: the shakes. If I exerted myself at all I became all trembly and breathless, and my heart palpitated; it had been quite embarrassing one day when I had walked briskly up a hill with Kjell and had to pause and pant at the top. Then one day, in general conversation, one of the Van Niels mentioned that, on their trip of a year or two ago through France, they had developed trembling and palpitations because of the strong coffee. Once they cut coffee out all was well again. It quickly dawned on me that, being in the USA, I was drinking mugs of coffee four, five, even six times a day. It was difficult not to, because it was offered both at and between meals almost automatically. The solution, for an Englishman (in 1957 a rare species on the West Coast), was easy and socially successful: ask for tea. The request never failed to delight my hosts, because they were anxious to please and tea was just what they expected the English to want; almost always they could rustle up an old tea bag and some tepid water, wherewith to make an innocuous, almost caffeine-free yet warm and wet drink. I consumed much pale brown tea during the rest of my trip, to the quiet pleasure of my US friends, and my palpitations rapidly disappeared. To this day, I rarely drink coffee in the USA.

(A digression about tea. Some ten years later, by then a seasoned traveller in the USA, I was flying from Atlanta to Chicago and my fellow passenger, pleased to discover an Englishman beside him, talked of how they sometimes drank tea in his family because a grandmother had come from England. He went on to tell me of a special heirloom he had at home, a sort of ceramic "kettle" with an elegant swan-necked spout and a handle, which one warmed and made tea in. I slowly realized that he was describing an ordinary earthenware teapot, certainly a rarity in the Middle West. I assured him that such devices were not unfamiliar to me, and that they made especially good tea.)

My lodgings, to which Van Niel had introduced me, were economical. There were no meals - I could use the kitchen to prepare breakfast and otherwise ate out - but my landlady Mrs Hilder and her husband, a retired clown, were very kind and fascinated by the many foreign lodgers Van Niel brought them. If I came in at odd times they might offer me cookies and buttermilk (very good) and we would talk of England and other distant places. I learned that they regarded Van Niel as a sort of guru: his way of fixing one with an intense gaze and talking slowly had much impressed them. Mrs Hilder had dreamed some verses which she felt were of deep philosophical significance and she wished to discuss them with him. She enjoined me to ask him to call in sometime, which I undertook to do and indeed did. It seemed from Van Niel's reaction that I was not the first to convey the invitation (I doubt that it was ever taken up).

Cultures of sulphate-reducing bacteria take some days to grow, especially if the parent cultures are at all old so, once I had set up my cultures I had time to spare. I had arranged to visit Berkeley, part of the megapolis of San Francisco, where a section of the University of California housed some of the most distinguished of US microbiologists, including Roger Stanier, of whom more later, and the world's leading authority on anaerobic bacteria, Professor H L Barker. Stanier, whom I knew well, had invited me, so, with slides and seminar prepared, I transferred myself for a couple of days from the quiet calm of Pacific Grove to the powerhouse atmosphere of one of America's most prestigious university campuses.

My seminar, given in a state of obvious alarm, provoked little discussion - it was one of two or three seminars offered to the laboratory that day and the audience was saturated. This sort of situation is still usual in most US universities. I was passed from researcher to researcher, including some distinguished names from the period, and we would talk for a while, again a somewhat mechanical process unless one found real common ground to discuss. Happily I did so with Barker: he was interested in my work on enumerating sulphate-reducers, and I found his studies of the even more difficult methane-producing bacteria fascinating. The two types of bacteria inhabit similar environments in nature, and Barker found it difficult to rid his cultures of unwanted sulphate reducers.

Daytime was a whirl of scientific talk, with a brief refuelling at lunchtime. On my first evening the Staniers entertained me at their lovely house overlooking San Francisco Bay, where we drank Californian Muscat as aperitif and had a lovely European meal prepared by Germaine, his French wife (also a well-known microbiologist). On my second night I was entertained by Ben Volcani and his wife, an Israeli microbiologist working as a Fellow at Berkeley. There I was introduced to the American Martini, a near lethal drink composed of 95% chilled strong gin, 5% ice and a touch of vermouth. It hits one behind the knees after about

10 minutes... happily my Oxford training served me well: I heeded my senses and refused more than one.

That evening was a little frustrating for me, because I would much like to have gone to a 'joint' called the Hangover Club, where Earl Hines (one of the top three jazz pianists of all time) and Muggsy Spanier (a jazz cornettist of great distinction) were playing, and the Volcanis were planning to take me. But a fellow guest reminded the company that the British biochemist Lord Todd was giving a seminar on a co-enzyme at the University that evening. The party's priorities were different from mine, and they had the transport. I went to the seminar with good grace.

Berkeley was a great experience. A scientific powerhouse certainly, but also a highly cultured, liberal and forward-looking society - as best I could judge in my brief visit. I was very lucky to see it before drugs and student militancy made a mockery of its liberalism in the 1960s. But it was exhausting, and I was happy to return to my now familiar lodgings in Pacific Grove. My Singapore culture had grown, and Van Niel was duly admiring of this seemingly new type of sulphate reducer; his acetate-utilising cultures revived one at a time, but all were clearly a mixture of bacteria. In no time, it seemed, my three weeks were up - but I had done what I set out to do. I sealed up four of Van Niel's cultures to take back home with me for further study, said my farewells to Kjell and his family; next day I ate a farewell breakfast of bacon steak and hominy grits very kindly provided by the Hilders, and was duly transported to Monterey airport by the Van Niels to continue my travels.

Los Angeles

Los Angeles was to be my next stop. The air hostess en route, observing that I was English, sat beside me to discuss the Little Rock episode for much of the flight (which was happily calm). That episode had occurred a few weeks earlier at Little Rock, Arkansas, and had tested the sincerity of the US Government's policy of desegregation. The State Governor, Orval Faubus, had disobeyed the Supreme Court's rulings over segregated education, and President Eisenhower had ordered the Federal Guard to escort a group of black American children through jeering segregationist crowds to attend a previously segregated High School. All America was talking about it. (The segregationists' attitudes "make me ashamed of the colour of my skin", Mrs van Niel had said to me during my stay at Pacific Grove.) I sensed something of my Air Hostess' bewilderment. She was a white Los Angelean, and colour prejudice had been an unquestioned part of her upbringing. She found it remarkable that my 'very best friend' at my preparatory school (when I was aged 8 to 11) had been a dark Indian, Nagu Ranganatha, and even more remarkable that he and his brother Ramu often visited my house for meals, and I theirs, and that once I had gone on a camping holiday with Ramu. I explained that my preparatory school had been multi-racial and that I had grown up with no intrinsic colour prejudice at all. But I also had to acknowledge, firstly, that my awareness of colour prejudice, particularly in the USA, had made me wary and uneasy in my casual relations with American Negroes;

secondly, that immigration into the UK from Pakistan and the Caribbean was beginning to generate comparable racism in Britain.

Ours was a superficial probe into a complex human problem, but frank for its day and place, and it was refreshing, after my South Carolina dentist on the Queen Elizabeth, to encounter someone trying to adjust to what was happening.

On a short stroll outside my hotel (the Mayflower) in LA, I decided I had caught 'flu. My eyes were sore and my nose runny. I also had a renewed attack of the 'screeching willies', noting in my diary that the further I walked from my hotel the shakier I became. However I was better next day when my primary host, Sydney Rittenberg of the University of Southern California, picked my up and we talked about sulphate-reducing bacteria with his colleagues Byron Mechalas and Ian Kaplan. They had been doing some interesting and original experiments which complemented mine, and were on the way to discovering a new type of microbial metabolism. My anxieties submerged.

I was entertained and shown round, too. My 'flu had receded out at the University and my hosts explained that it was simply the effect of the Los Angeles smog. One learns.

Syd Rittenberg drove me about LA on my first evening and, looking over LA from Griffith Park I saw it to be a vast urban sprawl, with no centre. It seemed unimaginably huge and impersonal; awful, polluted and noisy as a place to live in, its citizens floating a few feet above the megapolis night and day on pneumatic car tyres, never meeting casually, never walking (where was there to walk to?), never part of a community. Syd, a native of the city, assured my that I was utterly wrong, that it was a fascinating conglomeration of villages, of interesting, creative and neighbourly people, that there was nowhere else in the world where he would choose to live.

Julie Loewe and her husband Roland entertained me next evening and showed me the Mexican quarter centred on Olvera Street. Julie was a family friend from childhood in Britain, the daughter of Australian painter Stella Bowen and the writer Ford Madox Ford. Abetted by a Mexican bartender, the Loewes introduced me to tequila. To drink it properly one tips some salt into a groove on the back of one's right hand, licks it, then sucks a lemon slice briefly, before taking a gulp of what struck me as alcoholic sewage. My explosive reaction gave much pleasure to a crowd of Mexicans that had quietly assembled to watch.

On my penultimate day in LA, a Saturday, Byron Mechalas and Ian Kaplan, with their wives, took me on a sightseeing tour. It took in Knott's Berry Farm, an early 'theme park' where actors in Wild West costume acted out events and tourists drank the juice of boysenberries; Huntingdon Beach, fraught with oil derricks beneath which the pumps say 'two bits, two bits' night and day; Redondo Beach, with curious fish and tame penguins; to Byron's home for tea and doughnuts; to dinner at General Lee's Chinese Restaurant in Chinatown; then to Hollywood to stroll on Hollywood Boulevard (then a perfectly safe thing to do) and finally a drink among the starlets at Maxim's on Sunset Boulevard. The waitresses, and many of the clients, were indeed impressively good-looking. In all it was an experience to marvel at, and I had been allowed to pay for the lunch at Knott's Berry Farm but nothing else. All that time and hospitality out of regard for a fellow scientist whom they had met but two days earlier! This was, and probably still is, the American way with visitors. Would that my British compatriots were equally hospitable to visitors from distant and strange places. Few are.

St Bonaventure

The next day was not good. An 06:30 start to catch my flight to Buffalo went smoothly, if a bit rushed. Up and away over the Rockies in a noisy DC7 when after about an hour, to my relief, the engine noise eases and I can hear myself think. How pleasant, I reflect. Not for long, though. I look out of the window and observe that the port engine has stopped. Its propeller (it is a twin-engined prop-jet aircraft) is stationary and black oil is gushing out. As I take in the spectacle, a dead calm voice announces over the inter-com, "This is your Captain speaking. We have a malfunction of our port engine. We will return to Los Angeles, where a new plane will be awaiting you."

We do so. I have become strangely calm. After a net two-hour delay we are off again and a small sandwich lunch is served, unhappily just as we encounter tremendous turbulence over the Rockies. However, we bounce our way onwards - interminably, it seems, but it is only six hours, and we are allowed to undo our seat belts after Denver - and duly we arrive in Chicago. Here North American efficiency is displayed at its best: the connection for Buffalo has been held up for me. I am whisked off the LA-Chicago plane by an official and transported direct to that for Buffalo with, miraculously, my luggage. I arrive at Buffalo at 02:00 local time, though it has been a 20-hour day for me - somehow an hour has disappeared, but I am too nerve-wracked to work it out. By good fortune I had had the foresight to buy a sandwich at an all-night snack bar on Buffalo airport. I eat it, dazed, in my over-heated hotel room.

A new day - October 21st, 1957. I was sleepy but still alive. I had planned my trip so as not to be due to move on until late afternoon, because I wanted to see Niagara Falls. I allowed myself to be persuaded to take a $15 taxi trip; it seemed costly but was a good bargain in the event, because the taxi driver was friendly and I could be as quick or slow as I chose. The falls were indeed fantastic, with their eternal spray and rainbow; the autumn colours of the surrounding trees were beautiful, and there was a most impressive whirlpool further down the Niagara River. The approach had been rather sordid, but the site was well laid out and there were many tourists. I took less time looking around than my driver expected, so he insisted on including a scenic tour of Buffalo on my return - quite rewarding, because his idea of scenery was their new sports pavilion building, a 'skyway' road system, the downtown commercial area and so on. Not quite the usual Grayline tour.

That afternoon Dr Anderson and Professor Liegay came and drove me to St Bonaventure University, where the symposium, which had brought me to the USA, was to be held. The countryside that we drove through was beautiful to my eyes, though they told me that I had missed the best of the 'fall' colours by a couple of weeks. St Bonaventure was a modern neo-gothic campus site and I was housed in the Olean Motel across the road from its entrance.

My first surprise was to find that the staff were almost all monks, wearing brown habits. The explanation was that it was a Franciscan university. Apparently very few of these exist, the Franciscans not being an especially academic order. My visit to Assisi in 1953 proved to be a useful conversational ploy. My second surprise was to see occasional students, generally in clusters, wearing funny hats with cards hung from their necks. These bore abusive slogans such as 'I am a fool'. It was explained to me that these were freshmen, in process of being 'fazed' by their seniors. 'Fazing' was a cruel means of induction into the student fraternity to which the authorities turned a blind eye; I am told it also occurs in the US marines where it is called 'hazing'; comparable maltreatment of newcomers is not unknown in schools, British, American and Australian. I was quietly disgusted. My third surprise was my one-inch thick, six inches by five rib-of beefsteak, part of an excellent, basically Italian, dinner hosted by Father Mallachy (the Symposium organiser) at a nearby restaurant. It was my first direct experience of serious American meat-eating. I retired that night awhirl with new experiences once more, bloated with food, but fortunately tired enough to drop off as my head hit the pillow.

Next day, by invitation, I sat in on a meeting of the

American Petroleum Institute. Most of the symposium participants were members, and had come early for a discussion of the disinfectants that can be used to treat 'infections' of sulphate-reducing bacteria in oil well technology - they block and corrode pipes and generate unwanted sulphur compounds - and also to compare ways of estimating numbers of these bacteria. Here I encountered another cultural shock. Virtually all of the participants worked for private companies and presented papers about their company's new bactericides, which had trade names or even just numbers, and gave details of how effective they were. One substance seemed to me to be rather good, so I naively asked what its chemical nature was. The speaker, to no one's surprise but my own, said he was not able to reveal that information. I was astonished. How can a scientist evaluate a substance without knowing what it is? In fact, as I quickly realised, I had met the reality of commercial secrecy for the first time. No wonder the quality of the proceedings struck me as academically poor; they were all working in the dark. However, no one was offended at my innocent British aberration and later, when I could make a real contribution, my intervention on the technique of counting sulphate reducers was welcomed.

An unexpected test of my morale came later the same day. I was casually asked to do three broadcasts, two for the local radio station at Olean and one for the students' radio system; the third would be as part of a panel of all the symposium speakers. I was terrified. I refused at first out of simple stage fright, but then shamefacedly gave in. In the event they went off quite well and I managed to express sympathy for the freshmen in the taped broadcast for the students, as well as to bring in the odd English-type witticism. Anderson said encouragingly that I was "ready for television" now.

The symposium proper started on my third day there. ZoBell gave the opening survey, a wide-ranging talk on the distribution and activities of sulphate reducers; Robert Starkey, another father figure of research on these bacteria, reviewed their part in metal corrosion. Professor O B Williams of Austin, Texas, and Anderson of St. Bonaventure talked on the effectiveness of bactericides with little allusion to the basic science; Dr R Allred compared ways of counting sulphate reducers. My contribution, third in the programme, was the only one to deal with fundamental matters, their biochemistry and physiology, but that was what they had invited me for. Actually it was not widely heard because the sound system went wrong for me, but it was received respectfully. Professor Wolf Vishniac, an expert on sulphur-oxidizing bacteria at Yale, had come all the way across the state especially to hear me, and expressed himself well pleased, but I know that many in my audience were out of their depth.

There was a reception at which lashings of martinis were served. Our Franciscan hosts had been given a special dispensation to break their austerities and partake of martinis, but my experience in San Francisco had made me wary and I asked if they had any sherry. After assuring a monk that sherry was really my preference, that I was not just acting out of "respect for our cloth", some was sent for - I learned later that someone had dashed out to the motel to buy some. Thereafter a bottle of Harvey's Bristol Cream was produced at cocktail times especially for me. This was but one example of the thoughtful hospitality I encountered several times on this trip. They also got the message quickly that I preferred tea to coffee, so they sent for some tea bags and regularly supplied some instead of their customary coffee at meals, and the waitress at the motel brought me my rather un-American breakfast without my ordering after the first morning - useful, because once the conference was on I found myself surrounded by delegates as soon as I appeared in the motel coffee shop. It was a flattering but, at that hour, a constipating situation!

After four days it was over, and time to go. Handshakes and good wishes all round; confirmation of my plan to visit Starkey later in my tour. I had been given souvenirs, including a cigarette lighter, a 45 rpm recording of an address by the Principal and various documents; also my cheque, which I dutifully posted to Washington for transmission to the DSIR. I had been shown over the university by students, who wanted to be told about undergraduate life at Oxford, and who had enrolled me, ZoBell and Starkey in their alpha-kappa-mu fraternity. I had been shown the University's treasures in its library by the curator (an oddly random collection which included a model of the seminary in sugar, a page of the Gothenberg Bible, two Rembrandts, some Christmas cards made of postage stamps and a copy of my Postgate grandfather's *Sermo Latina*). In return I had passed out advice on handling sulphate reducers in all directions and shown Anderson and his research assistant, Sister Regina Lanigan (a Franciscan nun) how to work their newly-acquired spectrometer.

And the symposium? I had had star treatment - disconcerting over breakfast but good for the morale; the welcome and hospitality had been superb - Professor 'Frenchy' Liegay in particular had gone out of his way to ensure that all my wants were seen to. The surroundings had been, to me, an enjoyable revelation of a small corner of American life, and my fee of $300 was exceptional, in those days, for one of my relative youth. But on the scientific side - well, ZoBell and Starkey had gone over familiar stuff; Allred had described a culture medium for counting which was good - he had already published it and I had tested it at Teddington - but he had no clear idea why it worked and it remained for me to explain it in the discussion after his paper. The bactericide papers had barely been science at all (a pupil of Williams', who must be nameless because he became a very distinguished microbiologist at a far Western university), endeared himself to me for ever by hissing in my ear "a lot of hogwash" after his master's paper). Only my own contribution had been at all innovative. It seems churlish, even after forty years, to record that, scientifically, it was all pretty dim. But every scientist sums up meetings subjectively; I do not doubt that a majority of those present thought it wonderful.

New York, 1957

My next stop was New York City, where I was booked into

the Abbey Hotel, a cheapish hotel on the corner of Seventh Avenue and West 51st Street where the UKSM would put its middle-rank visitors. Nice and central but a bit scruffy: Bell Captain drunk one evening; woken up one morning at 07.30 by electrician wanting to mend the central heating in my room; cigarette ends and stink of tobacco in my room. But I made do and stayed a week, during which I made three scientific visits. At Columbia University I talked to Dr Krasna, a scientist working on hydrogenase, the enzyme that enabled bacteria such as mine to consume hydrogen. At the Haskins Laboratory I talked to Seymour Hutner, an ebullient anglophile lifeman, and his colleague Provasoli, about their speciality, marine microbes including sulphur bacteria. And I made an overnight trip to New Brunswick to visit Starkey at Rutgers University, where I gave a seminar with some aplomb. Starkey and his wife Florence were hospitable; they had a dinner party for me and next day he brought extra sandwiches for me to have lunch in the laboratory, which was their custom. It was my first experience of peanut butter with jam. As for the science, I do not dwell on it because, rewarding though much of it was, for me the local music dwarfed it.

Back in England I had planned for some spare time in Manhattan. It was still the fountainhead of jazz and most of the jazz greats were in good shape and working there. For a jazz lover it was a place of pilgrimage, a Medina to New Orleans' Mecca. Fortunately I was in fair mental and physical shape myself - my tremors, anxieties and dyspepsia were often dormant; I was buoyed up by social success as a scientist and, apart from occasional bursts of fatigue, I felt I had things reasonably under control. Moreover, the Metropole Bar was just round the corner from the Abbey, and it had continuous live jazz from early afternoon (midday at weekends) until the small hours of the morning. The band would be strung out in a line on a long, thin stage behind and above the bar, at which one could stand and listen for 45 to 50 minutes nursing a single weak beer; then one of the barmen would firmly hassle you into buying another. I spent a lot of time there, and consumed a lot of thin Knickerbocker beer. I also sought jazz further afield, at the Henry Hudson Hotel, and at Jimmy Ryan's on 52nd Street, and I came across an English jazz fan who showed me to Goodie's jazz record shop on the West Side.

I was a neophyte in a kind of heaven. I wrote up my experiences for the magazine *Jazz Monthly* (May 1958; the article reads a bit pompously now). Memorable high spots included Sidney de Paris (trumpet) playing with his brother Wilbur's band at Ryan's; Bobby Hackett (cornet) leading a multi-instrumental sextet at the Henry Hudson; and above all a quintet at the Metropole led by Coleman Hawkins (tenor saxophone) and Charlie Shavers (trumpet). That group was quite remarkable. The audience at the Metropole was usually noisy and the barmen habitually crashed empty bottles into a huge container below the bar, yet at one stage the quality of the Quintet's jazz brought everyone to attentive silence - until a philistine barman crashed the next bottle. "Did you have to do that?" asked Shavers, sardonically.

Only slightly less rewarding, largely because of their

somewhat rabble-rousing overtones, were groups led by Henry 'Red' Allen (trumpet), Tony Parenti (clarinet) or Sol Yaged (also clarinet) at the Metropole. I regretted having to miss drummer Gene Krupa at a club on 42nd Street, and I voluntarily missed trumpeter Miles Davis at Birdland, not liking his style. (All these names will be completely familiar to jazz enthusiasts; we rate Hawkins and Allen among the small pantheon of Great Jazz Originals, along with Louis Armstrong, Duke Ellington, Benny Goodman and Charlie Parker.) I found it a marvellous experience to hear musicians of that talent and calibre earning their daily bread. Sometimes their jazz sounded a bit routine, but quite often they were manifestly enjoying themselves, doing what they loved, and being admired and paid for it, and the Hawkins-Shavers group was superb, obviously in a thoroughly creative mode.

Jazz was my greatest delight in New York. As I said, it overshadowed everything else. But as well as keeping my scientific appointments I did a few other things. I walked around a lot (one could do so perfectly safely in those days) gazing in wonder at the traffic and people milling about in chasms bounded by ridiculously tall skyscrapers. In streets and eating-places I felt as if I had walked into a Damon Runyon story. People spoke in a sort of quick-fire vernacular; they liked to seem, and often were, hyper-efficient. They were disconcerted by my English habit of saying 'thank you' for ordinary services; they were generally unforthcoming, but friendly when bemused by my accent. They were also prone to widespread halitosis (due, I think, to a fad for garlic bread). I discovered the automat as a place to eat effortlessly: a room with a few tables and standing shelves, surrounded by slot machines vending various dishes, sandwiches and drinks. I visited the UN building, did a little shopping for records, spent a couple of hours in the Museum of Modern Art and, of an evening, peered into the strip clubs on 52nd Street, ready to move quickly if a tout saw me, for I wisely had no thought of going in. Like many before me, I fell in love with New York.

My trip was reaching its end. In the late afternoon of Saturday November 2, after checking the jazz at the Metropole once more (Hawkins and Shavers, playing *Lover come back to me* quite gloriously, unknowingly provided me with a marvellous farewell), I caught the plane for Ottawa via Montreal. It was a pretty bumpy flight which was aborted at Montreal because of the weather. I eventually reached my hotel, the Elgin, by train at 23:00, exhausted.

Sadly, I remained in a tired state for my three days in Ottawa. I do not think it was noticed ordinarily: the adrenalin flowed and kept me going in scientific discussions and general sociability, but I often felt faint in moments of calm and quiet, particularly when standing about in company (as tends to happen rather often on these occasions). However, I gave my seminar with reasonable aplomb, though aware that I had been more confident at St Bonaventure and at Rutgers. It was well received. Yet despite the hospitality of my principal host, Dr Norman Gibbons of the National Research Council Laboratories, and the friendliness of all the scientists I met, I was glad to leave on November 6 for Montreal, from whence my flight home was booked for next day. My morale was much improved when I discovered that I could change my booking and travel, actually by a rather more direct flight, that same day. There was just time to cable Mary, to buy presents her and our daughters Selina (two) and Lucy (six months), and off I went.

Mary had arranged for a local hire car to meet me at Heathrow. My diary records, "Selina wants presents and Lucy giggles." For my part, I quickly went to bed and slept for almost 48 hours, broken only by a two-hour break at about 24 hours when I ate a meal of some kind. I had been away for seven weeks.

Well, I had gained my 'BTA' at the cost of considerable fatigue; clearly I had tried to fit in far too much. Every first-time visitor to the USA underestimates travelling time, neglects the need for periods of solitude and quiet and forgets about the tiring effect of a constant stream of new impressions and faces. I thought I had been liberal with free time but, except perhaps in New York, I had not - and I had not started off in the best of health and morale. How had the USA of 1957 grabbed me?

All my preconceptions proved to be wrong. I had expected to visit powerhouses of scientific modernity, clean, up-to-date, furbished with state-of-the-art equipment. Van Niel's ramshackle, untidy laboratories quashed that idea - somewhat to my relief, in truth. Even Hutner and Provasoli's laboratories in that mecca of modernity, New York City, had a casual, old-fashioned atmosphere. There was a touch of the powerhouse about Berkeley, and even more about Columbia, but neither was intimidating and the people were busily doing just the sorts of thing I did at Teddington. I met commercial secrecy at the St Bonaventure API meeting, but otherwise encountered complete openness over scientific matters - or so I believed. Able to be completely open myself, I sensed no hint of the closeness, competitiveness and jealousy which I would meet in the USA in later decades, and which would in due course seep into British science. I also found the intellectual atmosphere immensely refreshing, even to being over-awed at times - happily cytochrome C3 served me well, being something of general importance which had emerged from an area few people knew much about. But I also encountered, sometimes with a touch of relief, startling ignorance and even dimness. Above all I had found numerous new friends and contacts, been applauded, and even offered jobs. For a young researcher it was, scientifically, a marvellous and rewarding experience.

So, too, was my brief experience of ordinary American life. I had left England with all the post-war British prejudices: a knee-jerk, leftish anti-Americanism. I had believed the USA to be peopled with money-obsessed and racist rednecks, greedy, unjustifiably wealthy, politically corrupt, commercially gangster-ridden and internationally domineering. All those prejudices were but fractional truths. I learned how Americans in all walks of life were deeply concerned about their society's problems, especially those of race prejudice, crime, poverty and corruption, and I was impressed by their ability to do something about these things, to haul their own society up by its bootstraps, so to speak. They had faults and blind spots; some of which, such as their ideas about state medicine and socialism, were idiotic and exasperating. But I simply loved the country; I wanted to get well and go back. I liked the people, their food and talk, their energy, their kindness to strangers, even their generally high level of education and political awareness as evinced by TV and newspaper reporting, even in casual chats while travelling.

I had set off with one set of prejudices and had them perforce replaced by a wholly new set, more soundly based if now a little starry-eyed. But they were open to modification in future. And also I saw with new eyes my familiar Britain, where by 1957 a society in which an attitude encapsulated by a nautical catch phrase, "I'm all right Jack, haul up the ladder", was rapidly replacing the post-war era of co-operation and social conscience. That, too, was an invaluable if dispiriting lesson.

A centre for economic microbiology

I must step back a few years, because my tale of cytochrome C3 has taken me somewhat ahead of the story of Butlin's team. Butlin had taken the first step towards achieving his ambition to build up a centre for the study of microbes of importance to industry and public welfare when, in 1948, he had persuaded his Director and the DSIR to appoint me to his little team. My kind of research meant more than working out ways of exploiting or controlling such microbes, it meant seeking to understand the underlying science as well: discovering what biochemical and physiological processes caused the microbes to behave as they did. I had been brought in: to find out what made sulphate-reducing bacteria tick, so to speak.

Butlin's ambition generated a semantic problem, one which might seem trivial but which is really very serious. How does one describe that sort of background research to the press and public, to industry, the DSIR, even other scientists? It was not simply applied microbiology, because that includes medical and public health microbiology, in which we had neither expertise nor professional interest. Moreover, that name tended to exclude the more fundamental side of the research. To call it 'industrial microbiology' would have been partly correct, but misleading. We expected to be of service to industry, and we were, but we were at pains to include, even emphasise, the non-industrial side of our microbiology: its involvement in areas such as pollution, deterioration, disposal processes and mineral formation. These were aspects that concerned the public good rather than just industrial production.

Gradually we settled upon the name 'economic microbiology' to describe our kind of research, and this term was widely adopted for a couple of decades. With the advent of genetic manipulation in the 1970s, it became subsumed into the term 'biotechnology' as it is used today.

The publicity surrounding our trip to North Africa in 1950 had given Butlin's plans a boost and, as I mentioned in chapter 8, I had produced a couple of papers which added to the team's academic respectability. By the end of that year he had been allowed to recruit further new staff to pursue research on the microbiological production of sulphide at Teddington.

It so happened that another opportunity, for diversification as well as expansion, arose quite soon. Dr S T

Cowan was the Curator of the National Collection of Type Cultures (NCTC), a collection of cultures of medically important bacteria on which hospital laboratories, university researchers and industry could draw, for a nominal fee. It also held a few fungi such as *Penicillium*, which were involved in the production of antibiotics. The Medical Research Council (MRC) financed it and, being both the best-known and largest microbial culture collection in Britain, it had also accumulated a variety of bacteria of general scientific importance but of little or no relevance to medicine. In 1950, Cowan announced to the scientific world that his microbial menagerie had become unmanageably large, and drastic action was needed. He proposed to thin it out by discarding all microbes that were not of direct medical interest. These would include many industrially-important bacteria, such as those involved in solvent production or food fermentation, in deterioration and corrosion, in mineral and effluent decomposition, as well as the antibiotic producers (which were mainly micro-fungi). If a home were not found for them within a year, they would be thrown away.

Microbiologists were dismayed: a safe repository for representatives of important types of microbe is absolutely necessary for the continuation of research. During the history of the subject, several important types had already been lost by accident or carelessness on the part of their discoverers, and their equivalents never rediscovered. Butlin saw his opportunity: he proposed to his Director, and to the DSIR, that his unit be expanded to take them over. The advice of leading microbiologists was sought (they were enthusiastically supportive), negotiations with the MRC took place, and in due course the DSIR agreed.

In this way, in 1951, the National Collection of Industrial Bacteria (NCIB) came into being, adding to Butlin's domain at Teddington. It was squeezed into a partitioned-off part of Butlin's large laboratory on the first floor of the main CRL building. W S Greaves was re-deployed within CRL's staff to be its curator, under Butlin's direction, and two young technical staff were soon recruited to help to handle the cultures.

Nursing a collection of living microbes is no mean task. If they are of the kind that forms spores when their cultures dry out, things are easy; one can prepare lots of little tubes of spores and keep them dormant, opening a tube as needed. But most bacteria do not form spores. And if they are kept too long in old cultures they die. Therefore, during the 1940s and earlier, new cultures (called 'subcultures') had had to be made at regular intervals. But each time you make a subculture of a strain of microbes, you take two risks: one is that you might contaminate your strain with extraneous airborne microbes, generating all the problems involved in recovering the original strain, not to mention notifying customers and so on; the other is that the more you encourage a population of microbes to multiply, the greater the chance that the strain will undergo biological variation or mutation, and so come to differ from the organisms originally deposited. (In truth, this kind of variation happened quite often in all collections of bacteria; usually the changes were minor as far as the user was concerned, but sometimes they were serious.)

A typical routine to minimise such risks would work like this. The microbiologist would receive a new specimen and after checking that it was what it was supposed to be, would make two subcultures. Call them P and Q. P would be used as the parent of any subcultures that the Collection might supply to customers. Q would remain untouched except when, in due course, it would become the parent of the next generation of two more subcultures. The original stock could be discarded only when these, its 'granddaughter' subcultures, had grown. That is the simplest possible routine; often more complex routines were needed. But whatever the routine adopted, it was an immensely boring and time-consuming operation and also one that absorbed lots of expensive culture media. And even though it might minimise contamination, biological variation or mutation, those risks still existed.

However, during the 1940s a procedure called freeze-drying had been worked out, which seemed to offer an escape from these problems. Freezing kills most active bacteria, though not bacterial spores. Microbiologists had recently discovered that even those that do not form spores stay alive if they are frozen in special gooey solutions rich in organic matter. A preparation made up of glucose and sterile blood serum was a particularly good life preserver. Moreover, if the solid frozen mass was then dried to a powdery clump, without being allowed to thaw - which meant arranging for the ice to evaporate off in a vacuum - they remained alive but dormant and, provided they were kept dry, they did not have to be kept frozen any more. Wetting the powder with a nutrient solution could resuscitate them.

Freeze-drying was a tremendous practical advance in this context (it is now used for a variety of purposes industrially, from preserving anti-sera in medicine to manufacturing instant coffee). Cowan was already freeze-drying all that he could of his medically important bacteria. However, it was a new process; no one quite understood why it worked, nor did anyone know for how long freeze-dried populations could be expected to survive. (By the 2000s researchers had learned that, if they survive freeze-drying at all, they usually last for several decades.) So Greaves and his helpers embarked on a process of freeze-drying all the organisms that the NCIB had received, as well as the new ones which began to arrive, while still keeping active cultures going, at least until his freeze-dried ones had lasted for a few years.

The freeze-drying operation was generally successful and it greatly simplified the day-to-day running of the collection. The little tubes, called ampoules, in which the freeze-dried cultures were sealed for storage were robust and, in apparatus that rapidly came on the market, it was as easy to prepare 100 such ampoules as one, so customers became accustomed to receiving vacuum-sealed ampoules of a dried powder rather than the living cultures they were accustomed to.

However, it rapidly became obvious that there was not enough room in the laboratory space allocated to the NCIB for testing, culturing, freeze-drying, storing and indexing the collection. Not that anyone was surprised by this situation, but in the DSIR one had to let things approach crisis point to get anything done. Representations were made, inspections took place, plans were considered, and in due course a substantial increase in laboratory space for Butlin's team was agreed. It would take the form of a prefabricated building, outside CRL's main laboratories, into which all microbiological research would move. The NCIB would expand to occupy Butlin's current territory within the main building.

Apart from acquiring the NCIB and being promised a purpose-built laboratory, there was another reason why 1951 was a great year for Butch: he was granted independence within CRL. The staff of that laboratory was formally divided into groups, each with its own head. Among these were a Radiochemistry Group, an Organic Chemistry Group, a Polymers Group and Dr Vernon's Corrosion Group. Butch had long hated being a part of the Corrosion Group. For reasons which I never really grasped, he felt strong animosity towards Vernon himself (who seemed a mild man to me) and took pains to have as little to do with him as possible; he had deliberately run down to a minimum his own team's experiments on microbiological corrosion, and he took little interest in them. CRL's Director, by then Dr D D Pratt, a chemist, was not sympathetic to this antagonism but bowed to circumstances. With the arrival of the NCIB he decided that Butlin's team could become an independent Microbiology Group within CRL's structure, with Butlin as its Head. Butch was delighted and gave a party.

Within a year of its inception, the NCIB was handling 1000 cultures. When new ones arrived the staff had to learn how to grow them, and this occasionally caused problems. Early in the 1950s Professor Kluyver deposited a number of cultures of *Acetobacter*, bacteria that form vinegar from alcoholic beverages. His instructions were that they be cultured on a continental type of beer. A modest but regular supply of this was therefore arranged. However, the bacteria required only a few millilitres of the beer and there were usual three or four bottles available. So occasionally, always of an afternoon, Butlin and I would be summoned by Greaves to his office in the NCIB because he had signified his intention to "subculture the acetobacters". The residual beer needed disposing of in a civilised fashion. It was very good.

The ceremony of subculturing the acetobacters started after the Microbiology Group's prefabricated laboratory had been built and the rest of us had occupied it. Over the next few years the Microbiology Group grew in size and its interests diversified. New staff including Sylvia Selwyn and Don Wakerley had been taken on to help with Butlin's own pet project, the microbiological production of sulphide; quite early in the 1950s a small team had been recruited and seconded to a Government laboratory called the Microbiological Research Establishment (MRE) at Porton on Salisbury Plain. More about MRE in the next chapter; for present purposes MRE possessed world-class expertise in the cultivation of bacteria rapidly and continuously, but it had never grown exacting anaerobes such as sulphate-reducing bacteria. Butlin's team, headed by P S S Dawson, was in fact the first to do this successfully. (As I mentioned in Chapter 9, when after about two years they returned to Teddington and set up their continuous culture apparatus in a little annexe to our pre-fab, the bacteria they produced in large quantities were invaluable to me in my research on cytochrome C3.)

A wholly new departure, which was initiated in 1952-3, was research based on the detoxification of phenolic effluents using bacteria. Several industries, especially the chemical, petroleum and gas industries, produce wastes, which are watery solutions of chemical substances called aromatics. Among these are the phenols. Many household disinfectants are based on phenols and they work very well because phenols kill all kinds of microbes. It does not matter if those phenols get washed down the kitchen sink and kill a few bacteria in the ordinary sewerage system, because they become so highly diluted by other domestic effluents that by the time they reach the sewage works they do no harm to the microbes that purify sewage. But factories produce vastly greater amounts, quantities, which could easily swamp a municipal sewage works and stop the whole purification process. And they cannot be released into rivers or the sea because the phenols kill the microbes at the bottom of the food chain and, if their concentration builds up, they kill fish and other fauna (but not plants, which generally tolerate phenols). However, special types of bacteria had been known for many years which could adapt themselves to feed on phenols, destroying them and actually multiplying at their expense - provided they did not have to cope with too much at a time. Indeed, in mid 1952 Monsanto, a multinational chemical industry with a factory at Ruabon in North Wales, proudly opened its own purification plant in which bacteria were used to destroy phenols in their factory effluents. It worked so effectively that the purified water could be released direct into the river Dee. They held a grand party at Ruabon, serving salmon from the Dee for a splendid lunch, for which they transported their guests to and from London (including Butch and me) in a specially chartered train.

Work in various parts of the world was showing that some of the chemicals formed by bacteria in the process of degrading phenols were very interesting to chemists, often difficult to make in the laboratory yet potentially useful to the chemical industry. Why not get the bacteria to make the phenols in these effluents into useful chemicals instead of destroying them completely? Such was Butlin's thinking, and he was much encouraged by the work from the USA which provided a quick and easy way of spotting intermediates in the bacterial breakdown of phenols and related substances. It was called 'simultaneous adaptation' and its details do not matter here: its principle was that if a bacterial population had adapted itself to use a certain phenol, it would be found to have adapted to utilise the intermediates in its breakdown as well. The inventor of simultaneous adaptation was R Y Stanier, then a Professor of Microbiology at the University of California, Berkeley, USA.

Roger Stanier

I had counted Roger Stanier a personal friend, although he was several years older and certainly more distinguished than me, since we had met at a Society for General Microbiology conference at Oxford in 1952. As well as discussing politics and literature, we had talked about adaptation, anaerobes and the then exciting new evidence that DNA might really be the stuff of genes. I had enjoyed his microbiological erudition; he seemed to know everything, and he possessed a devastating critical ability. However, he seemed to find Butch's and my ideas for the microbiological production of sulphur good, and was delighted by some of the more fundamental stuff about sulphate reducers that I was uncovering. He was actually Canadian; he had spent some time on a visiting award at Cambridge just after the 1939-45 war but had disliked it - I think he found ancient universities too self-absorbed and stuffy for his taste. At the time I met him, he was on sabbatical leave from Berkeley at the Institut Pasteur in Paris, where there was a flourishing centre for research on adaptation and on the ways in which bacteria regulate their physiology.

Roger was a tall, gangly person; he walked with a lope, like me, and he had a curious way of blinking his eyes at you if, in discussion, he thought you had said something silly or mistaken. It was a warning to expect a penetrating refutation of what you had proposed which, though it could be disconcerting, was rarely other than good-humoured. Like many a highly intelligent and sensitive person, he was shy and could seem austere, even forbidding, but he was actually friendly and good-natured. I warmed to him when he told me that he sympathised with my fear of public speaking, which he had once shared in some degree. As well as being an extremely knowledgeable microbiologist, he was widely read in history and general literature, he enjoyed paintings and was intensely aware politically; he also had good taste in food and wine - all features which endeared him to Butlin, too.

Hearing that he was in Europe, Butlin asked him to visit us at Teddington and see our research. We discussed, and he heartily approved of, our plans to start some research on the degradation of phenolics. In due course, Vic Knivett, a microbiological biochemist from Cambridge, and Stanley Thomas, a chemist from within CRL, joined the Group to initiate the research.

I must have encountered Roger at least three times in 1952, because he was also at the biochemical conference that I attended in Paris in that year. But I did not see a lot of him outside its meetings, perhaps because he had discovered Germaine Cohen-Bazire, a delightful scientist from the Institut Pasteur who later became a world authority on a group of alga-like bacteria called cyanobacteria. They married in 1956 and she emigrated to Berkeley to join him - as I told earlier, I visited them during my trip to Pacific Grove in 1957. In due course he became the delighted father of a daughter.

I met Roger on many occasions in later years. He remained staunchly Canadian and always kept a *pied à terre* on the Canadian West coast for holidays. He became increasingly critical of his adopted USA. The McCarthy trials of the early 1950s had upset him, for he was politically liberal, though hardly left wing by European standards. In the 1950s and '60s he was involved with several liberal causes in California, and was much dismayed by the student unrest at Berkeley in the early 1960s, which he regarded as self-centred and anti-social. He saw these young people wilfully going down a road in which crime, drug addiction, violence and the abuse of sex would flourish, against a background of an increasingly self-centred and reactionary political administration. And he had a much-loved daughter then approaching adolescence. As he once put it to me, in the USA there was nowhere for his offspring to go but downwards; he had to get out. He and Germaine were offered, and accepted, positions at the Institut Pasteur in 1969; there they remained for the rest of his life, both continuing their distinguished microbiological careers. We continued to meet. He stayed with us in Sussex for a couple of nights in 1972 and he and I went out hunting antiques (he quickly realised that many of the antiques which attracted Americans to the South of England were junk). Later I stayed briefly at their home outside Paris, on a bizarre occasion when I was summoned urgently, at Swedish expense, to a Sunday meeting in Paris to discuss biotechnology.

Roger was an inveterate cigarette smoker. He died in 1982 of lung cancer, after a debilitating period of illness. He received numerous honours from several parts of the world, including being elected a Fellow of Britain's Royal Society. He was a popular, likeable man, as well as one of the last great generalists in microbiology; today we are all specialists.

Stinking ponds and old wine

In addition to our ongoing research programmes, most members of Butlin's Group regularly undertook short-term research problems brought to us from outside the group by people seeking advice. Butlin and I did ad hoc research on water-pollution problems, some of which were quite curious.

For example, a flooded clay pit in New Malden, Surrey, turned black and began to stink of hydrogen sulphide almost overnight. Local residents were threatening the Council with legal action, and the local Medical Officer was anxious about health hazards. Back at Teddington samples of the water showed clearly that sulphate-reducing bacteria had become established in large number and were generating the stench. Most probably some fly-tipper had dumped waste organic matter into the pit to avoid the cost of disposing of it correctly. Such conventional treatments as we could suggest - filling in the pit, pumping it out, or pouring in masses of acid - would be slow and expensive. Then one day, before any of our remedies could be put in hand, the local Medical Officer phoned us: overnight the water had turned yellowish and stopped stinking - would we come and look? We came in haste and bewilderment. It was quite true. It transpired that another illegal dumper had come at night and tipped a lorry-load of soil contaminated with waste from a chromium-plating works into the water. Chromates are bright yellow chemicals, and some had obviously dissolved in the water. Could chromates have stopped the activities of the sulphate reducers? Back to the laboratory we hastened, and in a few days we had shown that chromates were indeed powerful inhibitors of bacterial sulphate reduction, effective at very low concentrations. Some miscreant had unwittingly cured the New Malden Local Authority's problem, and led us to discover a new and effective way of controlling such pollution.

As another example, the Twickenham Borough Council had access to several disused quarries, now watery lagoons, which it wanted to fill in so as to recover the land. It also had masses of domestic refuse, some incinerated to clinker, which it wanted to dispose of. But if it just tipped the refuse into the lagoons, sulphate-reducing bacteria would have had a field day: they would have generated a monstrous, actionable pollution problem on a vastly greater scale than New Malden's. The Borough Engineer, A S Knolles, devised a plan for dividing the lagoons into smaller ponds, making porous walls out of his clinker, and then quickly filling those ponds one at a time with raw refuse, before covering the lot with soil. We thought it would work, and it did. We monitored the ponds for sulphate reducers as they filled them; they were slow to start multiplying and, provided they had enough raw refuse to fill each pond within a day or two, it could be packed solid and covered with soil. No doubt the sulphate reducers flourished underground, but no smelly gas escaped: pollution was avoided and land was recovered.

We were consulted about all sorts of other practical problems, too. Molly Adams and Butch did some tests on corrosion of concrete and stone by sulphur bacteria; I no longer recall the precise context. A 'disease' was afflicting pyritic fossils in the Natural History Museum and might have involved acid-forming bacteria (we found that such bacteria were indeed present, but ultimately they proved not to be responsible); we examined a bloom on paintings at the National Gallery which might have been due to fungi (it was not); we advised on how to prevent sulphide pollution of wet petroleum which had made it unsuitable for aircraft in the far East (sulphate-reducing bacteria proved to be responsible, and our proposed palliative, treating the petroleum tanks with chromate, actually worked).

Not all problems proved to be microbiological. We inspected sediment in sherry, which a famous importer was anxious about. It was not microbes but 'Rochelle salt', a perfectly normal chemical deposit to find in a maturing wine. (Disobeying Civil Service rules, we accepted a bottle each to take home.)

In dealing with such ad hoc problems, of which there were many, we often did a few experiments to clarify the questions being raised and to judge if they had any new scientific implications (such as the chromate discovery had). But ours was a free service and, as a publicly funded laboratory, were careful not to trespass on the territory of professional consultants. Indeed many of these consulted us, especially Bill Bunker. By 1956, Butlin's Microbiology Group at CRL, with its NCIB, had become a flourishing centre for research and advice on Economic Microbiology, with a considerable national reputation. It was also gaining a reputation internationally as a reference centre and for its research on economically-important microbes, especially the sulphate-reducing bacteria. Its research programme was overseen by the special Advisory Committee on Microbiology mentioned earlier, to which the Group would report regularly and which would itself report to the Chemistry Research Board, the Steering Committee of CRL.

Sweden in 1958

A problem with writing about the ordinary life of a scientist is that one could easily become a travel bore. I could elaborate on how the 1958 International Congress of Microbiology, held at Stockholm in Sweden, gave me my first glimpse of that delightful and austere city, with its old town, its permanent exhibition at Skansen, its elegant buildings, and the marvellous vistas of its archipelago. But proper travel writers do that sort of thing much better than I could. More apposite just now is the international scientific comradeship that I encountered there.

Butch's group was riding high, and the DSIR readily agreed that he should give a paper on his sulphide-from-sewage process at the 1958 International Congress. I went along as his spokesman. It was summer, and Stockholm was looking beautiful. Although the meetings were generally well organised, there were inevitably occasional changes in programming and our paper happened to be rescheduled without our seeing the appropriate notice. We learned of the change too late. We were sitting in the cool afternoon sun in the courtyard of the *Tekniske Hogeskol*, drinking orange juice (provided free by one of the Congress' sponsors) and talking science with colleagues from several nations when Denis Herbert, a friend from MRE about whom more later, joined us; he brought the news that, at the session he had just been attending, our names had been called and we were not there. Butlin seemed unconcerned - and that suited me; no doubt the administrators at DSIR HQ would have been annoyed had they found out, but in fact we were probably better occupied meeting with and talking to our microbiological peers.

The Congress was a less elaborate affair than that held in Rome five years earlier, and though it was less well attended I met new colleagues and renewed acquaintance with microbiologist friends from all over Europe and the USA. Politically that year was one of partial remission in the 'cold war': Krushchev had taken power in the USSR, and Soviet politics, while unpredictable, was in an outward-looking phase. Several scientists from iron-curtain countries were present; I spent some time with my old friend 'George' Starka of Czechoslovakia and, with him, Butch, Denis and Denis' colleague Owen Powell (more about him later, too) I met Ivan Malek, a distinguished Czech academician.

Malek was a large man with a Slavic face, the Director of Prague's Institute of Microbiology. He was an expert on fermentation processes and an authority on continuous culture, which was being studied and applied in his own laboratory. He was known to all except me because his Institute had hosted an international symposium on the subject to which all the others had contributed; Denis had read Butch's paper for him. It was the first of several international symposia on continuous culture. (A symposium, by the way, differs from a congress in that it is a small conference on a specialised branch of a subject, with only invited speakers; it might be held independently, or one or more symposia might form part of a broader congress, conference or meeting.)

Malek was very forthcoming and friendly; one evening

we all dined in one of Stockholm's superior restaurants, and Denis and I had to dissuade Owen because he wanted us all to join in "a real Swedish *skol*"; this meant drinking each others' health rather noisily and was clearly not appropriate to that particular restaurant. Malek, according to Starka, had good relations with the Czech communist establishment and his Institute was well supported; despite his official position, he was later regarded by British Intelligence as safe enough to be allowed to attend, with a couple of colleagues, a follow-up symposium on continuous culture held at MRE in October of 1964. That visit generated an amusing if delicate situation, because the presence of Czech scientists actually within a military research institution thoroughly upset the local Security Officer, and he and his two colleagues were to be seen skulking around outside the lecture room, hovering at meal times and so on. It so happened that, on the day that MRE threw a party in the Officers Mess for the symposium delegates, the British general election results were announced; a narrow victory for Harold Wilson's Labour Party over Douglas Home's conservatives. Most of the British delegates, including those from MRE, were Labour supporters, and the party got very jolly. It was a reminder for Malek and his colleagues of democracy at work, and a source of even greater anxiety to the Security Officer, who feared that alcohol would loosen the tongues of his local scientists. Malek, albeit a model of verbal discretion in public, actually held relatively liberal political views. In 1977 he was one of the dissident intellectuals who signed 'Charter 77', a document protesting against the dictatorial regime imposed by the Czechoslovak authorities after the Soviets crushed Dubcek's "Prague Spring" of 1968. He was stripped of his office and remained in limbo until the disintegration of the Soviet Union.

However, considering the state of relations between the Soviet bloc and the West, perhaps most remarkable was the presence in Stockholm of Academician Kutzentzov, from the USSR itself, mixing freely with the delegates instead of moving around in a group with an 'interpreter', as Soviet delegates were wont to do. I had quite a long conversation with him in halting French as we both waited at a Stockholm bus stop. I was especially interested in the work of a young scientist called Sorokin who was studying sulphate-reducing bacteria in his Institute and who had uncovered a quite fascinating new aspect of their physiology. I cannot say that our exchange was very informative scientifically, but that it took place at all in that informal way was remarkable for those days. I got a hint that Sorokin was not all that secure in the Soviet hierarchy and was unlikely to be working in Moscow for long. This conjecture proved to be true, but Kutznetzov must have carried back my message of respect and greeting, for I later received a letter from Sorokin sent by way of Scandinavia - this was a period when personal communication between younger Soviet and UK scientists was rare and difficult.

There were not too many formal evenings at Stockholm, which was a good feature because one would dine in informal groups of delegates in one or another of Stockholm's many restaurants, as we had done with Malek. But a special

Congress banquet was held on the penultimate evening at the Stockholm town hall. It was accompanied by a curiously Swedish entertainment: a display of gymnastics by nubile adolescent schoolgirls. This, as Butch remarked, some middle-aged gentlemen among the delegates seemed to find strangely interesting. There was also a parade of national flags, each one borne by a goddess-like blonde of the sort of breathtaking beauty that Sweden seems to specialise in. Some French scientists had to be restrained from expressing their appreciation to the lady carrying the *tricoleur* because, as Dr Holme, sitting at our table, explained, "they wished to kiss her very thoroughly". On the last night there was an informal '*bierabend*' at the Hojskole, which was livened by a group who had been to a cocktail party at the Soviet Embassy and wished to sing community songs. It was all very jolly and beery; at the end Butch, Owen, Denis, Helge Larsen of Norway (of whom more later) and I crowded into the car of a Swedish Professor, Owen lying horizontal across our knees in the back and complaining weakly, to be driven across Stockholm to the Swedish Royal Automobile Club for yet more drinks. We dispersed at about 2:30 am; I retain a vivid memory of Helge shaking my hand, his blue Norse eyes shining, saying, "Good times!"

I must not give the impression that this Congress, or any other, was all boozing, eating and sightseeing, but these are always important on such occasions. They are a necessary corrective to what would otherwise become mental saturation. In fact both the meetings and the sociability were very serious, and the talk was all about science; one was working all the time, even when relaxing. Often the most useful scientific exchanges and insights arose during informal jollifications, and the contacts one formed were invaluable later. A truth well understood by working scientists, and rarely by administrators, is that the formal proceedings of scientific meetings are in fact a minor part of their professional value: they are a necessary framework, but it is the informal discussions and contacts that are really productive.

The group's demise

In 1958 Butch's dream of a centre for basic and practical research in Economic Microbiology seemed to be coming true. But already there were signs that all was not well. Changes had taken place in the status of CRL, which had been renamed the National Chemical Laboratory (NCL), and the anomaly of having a team of microbiologists in a laboratory dedicated to chemistry was bothering the laboratory's Directorate and the administrators of the DSIR. Moreover, Butlin's growing reputation, his success in getting new staff and funding, had aroused envy among senior colleagues. Just as he cordially disliked Vernon, there were others who cordially disliked him. But the crucial problem was external: the world sulphur shortage had moderated, partly because new sulphur sources had been discovered, partly because several industries had gone over to using iron pyrites as their source of sulphuric acid, thus bypassing native sulphur altogether and reducing the national requirement for it. Sulphur had become cheaper, and by mid 1958 the microbiological production of sulphide did not look nearly as promising a process economically as it had done in 1951, although it was approaching success. In addition, Government money for research, though still abundant by the standards of the 1990s, was becoming short. In the eyes of DSIR's administration the *raison d'être* of Butlin's Group was the sulphur project, and this, they considered, was not going to pay off. The other work, including the Group's world-famous fundamental research, was secondary. The Chemistry Research Board discussed the matter and late in 1958, against the advice of the Advisory Committee on Microbiology but with the Director, D D Pratt's, approval (his support of Butlin had always been ambivalent), the DSIR proposed disbanding the Microbiology Group, retiring Butlin and redeploying other staff in a more biologically orientated laboratory, its Water Pollution Research Laboratory (WPRL) at Stevenage.

Protests and acrimony ensued. I, who had been in a state of depression through much of 1958, came to life, so to speak. (There is a moral for psychologists here: if you have a patient suffering from endogenous depression, give him or her something exogenous to depressed about.) With Butlin, I set about lobbying contacts in industry and politics, urging them to write letters of protest to the Secretary of the DSIR and to the press. The Institute of Biology protested publicly on our behalf, and so did the Institute of Professional Civil Servants (our trade union); the Society for Applied Bacteriology and the Society for General Microbiology protested too (the Society of Chemical Industry vacillated and decided not to). Distinguished microbiologists from overseas wrote letters of support. Our Advisory Committee on Microbiology added its weight to the protests (before being thanked for its services and stood down); Bunker and a science journalist friend, Roy Herbert, ensured that the national press reported the matter. Butlin and I visited politically influential scientists such as Sir Harold Hartley (one of the father figures of biological engineering) to enlist their support. It may well have been Hartley who was behind a leader that *The Times* carried, supporting us. A question on our future was asked in the House of Commons - and received a bland answer. In all, there was quite a furore; St Bonaventure University got to hear of it and telephoned to offer me a position there. They were exciting times, with moments of intensive plotting and moments of optimism; my health improved remarkably, despite real anxiety - and lack of sleep.

We probably slowed down the process, but the die was cast. In the spring of 1959 Butlin's group was disbanded. Butlin was retired and the research programmes were terminated (though within a year sulphate-reducing bacteria again featured in part of the NCL's corrosion of metals programme). I had been offered promotion if I would accept transfer to the DSIR's Water Pollution Research Laboratory (WPRL), but I knew, and confirmed at an interview, that its Director was wholly unsympathetic to the sort of basic research that interested me. Indeed, F W Ochynski, who had joined our phenolic effluents project in the mid 1950s, had been transferred to us because of conflict with WPRL's

Director over just such issues. Not tempted by that particular promotion, I chose to leave early, as I shall tell in the next chapter. Most of my fellow research staff found other positions and in the end only one actually moved to the WPRL. The NCIB was moved to the Torry Research Station at Aberdeen, and in due course was amalgamated with their collection of marine bacteria to become the National Collection of Industrial and Marine Bacteria. It is still in Aberdeen.

CHAPTER FIFTEEN

The Microbiological Research Department

I mentioned in chapters 9 and 15 the small team which Butlin sent, in 1951, to study the continuous culture of sulphate-reducing bacteria at the Microbiological Research Department (MRD for short; later it became Microbiological Research Establishment or MRE) on Salisbury Plain. It was the Ministry of Supply's biological warfare laboratory located just outside the village of Porton, within the same barbed wire that enclosed a laboratory studying chemical warfare defence. In a military sense, both were defence establishments - but you cannot do much about defence without knowing a lot about offence.

Why did Butlin second a team to a military establishment? Because MRE actually undertook a lot of non-military research, and at that time it was a very distinguished microbiology research laboratory. It led the world in several areas, including the construction and use of continuous culture systems. Dawson's team sent from CRL in 1951 were able to learn the technique rapidly, and also to contribute something new, in that they accomplished the first-ever continuous culture of a really exacting anaerobe. They returned to Teddington after about two years with equipment and expertise to continue the project (and, as I was also told, to supply me with material wherewith to study cytochrome C3).

I had visited the CRL team a few times and was familiar with the set-up there. I knew several of the MRE staff personally, notably Denis Herbert and Owen Powell, with whom Butch and I had enjoyed a rollicking Congress in Sweden. I knew, of course, that biological warfare lay at the root of its research, but I was also aware that BW, as they called it, had become a minor part of its research programme. So when I realised that Butlin's Microbiology Group was really due to be disbanded, early in 1959, I wrote to MRE's Director, David Henderson, about a job. I did not feel able to take up St Bonaventure's kind offer because I was sure I should soon have problems with its Franciscan base; I had also been invited to apply for a newly-founded Chair of Microbiology at Queens College, Dublin, and went for an interview, but its founders, Guinness, wanted its incumbent to study the microbiology of peat and this aspect did not attract me. However, it happened that at MRE a senior scientist, Joan Powell, had recently died, and thus a vacancy existed at a senior level; Henderson had been on the Advisory Committee overseeing Butlin's group's work and he knew of me and my research.

One afternoon he phoned, tactfully calling my wife at home, and asked her to tell me that he "thought he could respond satisfactorily to my letter", and would I get in touch with him. I did. I could not expect to continue my research on sulphate-reducing bacteria but, because these organisms seemed to show exceptional longevity, I had already become interested, in theory, in the general problem of how long bacteria live and what causes them to die. By good luck the survival of bacteria in general was a subject into which Henderson wished to expand MRE's research; I was happy to tackle the fundamental side of the problem, so we quickly established contact at a scientific level. I was offered, and accepted, a position. I was to work among the more biochemically-orientated members of the laboratory, in a loosely-linked group headed by Denis Herbert, who had also taken over responsibility for MRE's research into continuous culture.

In the spring of 1959 I uprooted myself, sold my home and moved to Salisbury with my family, renting a nice 'Ministry' house in St. Osmund's Close. Within 18 months I had got on well enough to be promoted, so I had lost little and gained much by turning down WPRL.

Denis Herbert

I had known Denis Herbert from scientific meetings for some years before I joined him. He was slim, with dark hair smoothed back, and he had a bird-like, peering manner which was in fact due to myopia but which gave him an aristocratic demeanour. Basically a biochemist, he was a most intelligent scientist with a clear, logical mind. At scientific meetings he could seem formidable and remote, an impression enhanced by the effects of his short-sightedness. If at a scientific meeting someone presented poor quality research, Denis would rise to his feet and point it out with scathing precision. But in fact, although intolerant of affectation, he was friendly and forthcoming, and he loved to discuss both practical and theoretical problems of microbiology - as well as to talk of politics, cars, music and wine. He was never superior about his intellectual achievements, though he could be incisively critical when it was deserved. In informal circumstances he was a good-humoured and helpful person, who became a lifelong friend to me as well as a respected scientific colleague.

Denis had achieved fame as the first scientist to crystallise a bacterial enzyme, a protein called catalase, in the mid 1940s, and in the 1950s he did some useful research on a very dangerous bacterium (*Yersinia* [earlier *Pasteurella*] *pestis*) which is responsible for bubonic and pneumonic plagues; it was in later years that he became the world's leading authority on continuous culture.

A less well-known distinction, of which he liked to tell,

was that he was probably the only person ever to see the transmission spectrum of fully virulent plague bacteria. He told the story thus. Plague has possibilities as a biological weapon, and MRE worked on *Y. pestis*. Most such research was done with a carefully chosen non-virulent strain, to avoid the obvious risk that the researcher might accidentally infect him or herself. Fairly early in his career at MRE, a junior staff member helping with the laboratory's culture collection inadvertently supplied Denis with a culture of virulent *Y. pestis*. He grew several litres of a culture and, without taking any special precautions, poured portions into centrifuge tubes - which are open glass vessels, like fat test tubes - centrifuged them for over an hour in the open laboratory, collected and homogenized the paste of live bacteria which sedimented to the bottom of the tubes with a spatula. Finally he inspected the suspension in a hand spectroscope, a device that had to be held close to the face under a strong light. (This device was the precursor of the reversion spectroscope, which I used to discover cytochrome C3.)

It was at this stage in his day's work that senior safety officials discovered the mistake their junior had made. Two officers, bearing a disinfectant spray and encased in protective clothing, rushed into Denis' lab, stripped him and sluiced him down with disinfectant; his clothes were sterilised and the laboratory fumigated, including his notes. Then he was taken into the nearby Army hospital for observation while they waited for the expected pneumonic plague to develop. He remained perfectly well, unscathed, but for his dignity - which is a credit to his technique as a microbiologist (and perhaps to his good health at the time).

Denis was fascinated by apparatus and machinery, always designing and/or modifying gadgets. Such matters easily distracted him from the actual performance of experiments and his scientific output was less than it ought to have been from someone of his intellect. His published bibliography was small, with a high proportion of what he chose to call 'think-pieces'. He had no time for routine paperwork; his own manuscripts were always late, and he would leave letters, reports, manuscripts and the like to accumulate on his desk and, every now and again, throw the lot into the waste-paper basket. He argued that, if something in the heap really mattered, someone would telephone about it. This made him unpopular with (a) certain colleagues who were obliged by MRE regulations to have him approve their manuscripts for publication, (b) administrators, who liked a response to their messages, and (c) editors of scientific journals who might have innocently sent him a manuscript to referee.

As far as the third category was concerned, he soon got on to editorial blacklists. When in later years I became an Editor-in Chief myself, I had on at least three occasions to telephone Denis' junior, David Tempest, and ask him to recover from Denis' desk, and return, a manuscript which a member of my Board had unwisely sent him.

Denis' friends and colleagues, though sometimes exasperated, adjusted to these foibles, for he was one of the intellectual *élite* of British microbiology.

Outside science, he was sociable and had a wide circle of friends. He had, I believe, been briefly married in youth, but we never spoke of it. He was a socialist of a rather old-fashioned school (his father was Sidney Herbert, an early Fabian) and a freethinker. He loved high-fidelity recordings of classical, especially baroque, music; he was also a *bon vivant*. He was an addict of fast motorcars, which he drove with an almost manic glee, peering through his spectacles like Mr Toad of Toad Hall. I often wonder how he got home, because I early discovered that he had almost no sense of direction. But he managed.

MRE provided Denis with the right niche for his life's work. He easily came to terms with MRE's biological warfare remit; his employment was secure; the science was fascinating and of fundamental importance; and his bachelor life, centring on the Officers' Mess at Porton and his elegant apartment in Amesbury, suited his essentially unambitious, highly cerebral, personality very well. He spent his entire career there, retired nearby and, another unregenerate cigarette smoker, he died of lung cancer in 1989 aged 72. I was at his funeral in Salisbury which was, naturally, secular.

Domestic interlude

To return to my own affairs. Natural processes had augmented the brouhaha surrounding my departure from Teddington. Mary was pregnant for most of 1958 and almost simultaneously with the final announcement of the demise of Butch's Group our third daughter, Joanna Mary, arrived. She was born at home, in the customary small hours of the morning, and my principal memory is of incessantly boiling water downstairs, despite a plentiful supply in the tank upstairs, and making cups of tea for the Irish midwife. Much to that good lady's pleasure, Joanna arrived about twenty minutes before our doctor, so there was nothing for him to do when he came but partake of another round of tea.

Once I had settled on my next job, we had to plan our move to Salisbury. Mary, preoccupied with Joanna and dubious about the whole atmosphere of MRE, did not want to move, but she dutifully rallied. As I mentioned, we had to sell our house; the Ministry of Supply had an estate of tied houses on the outskirts of Salisbury and would rent us one, which saved a lot of bother at that end. I felt tremendously guilty because we sold our small three-bedroom semi-detached house in Twickenham for £2,700, £300 more than we had paid for it in 1952. (Five years later, I learned, the house sold for over £5000.) I suppressed my uneasiness over my rank profiteering, however, because I needed the money.

The move to the countryside meant that I must, belatedly, buy a car (I had used buses, trains or a bicycle until 1959). Helped by my colleague and friend from Butch's Group, F W 'Ocky' Ochynski, the profit enabled me to buy a second-hand converted Commer van, which served admirably as a family estate car for several years. I also had to learn to drive. Ocky, car enthusiast, amateur breeder of mink, and microbiologist, undertook to teach me. He had learned driving himself as a Polish soldier working with the Allies during the 1959-45 war, and his instruction, delivered in his unique Polish-English, was unconventional, spattered with "bloody fools", but generally very sound indeed. On fellow drivers:

"Always remember zat zay are dangerous bloody fools. Don't believe zaim when zay wave zair flippers" (ie: give a hand signal).

On a driver on the crown of the road:

"You see from zee back of 'is head zat ze bloody fool does not know what 'e is going to do. Keep out of 'is way."

Ocky's wisdom often returns when I drive, even today.

Moving day came. Ocky and I drove to Salisbury a day in advance to leave the car with emergency luggage in the garage and return by train; Molly Adams helped Mary take the children by train and I followed later, having seen the furniture removers off, shut up the house and given the key to the estate agent. I gloss over those first few days of fun and chaos; within a week we were installed in a lovely house built on a gentle incline in a secluded close. Our upstairs window overlooked a large, green open space called Hudson's Field, just across the usually quiet main road; there were cows in a field one house along to our right; Old Sarum, the ancient cathedral site and Roman camp, was a stone's throw away; there was a grassed area in our close where children could play. It was April of 1959, spring was well advanced and Wiltshire, always a beautiful county, was at its best.

I recall a moment when daughters Selina (four), Lucy (two) and I were upstairs, looking out of a window and rejoicing in our newfound home. For young town-dwellers, the farm animals, which we had seen on our explorations, had been a source of great pleasure, for they had rarely seen such creatures except in their picture books.

"Isn't it a lovely place", I said, "Real chickens, real horses."

"Real cows," they said.

"Real cows," I echoed, "real ducks."

"Real ducks," they responded.

"Real camels," said Selina.

"Real camels," I echoed, then, "CAMELS?"

"Yes, Daddy, look."

I looked out of the window. There, in Hudson's Field, were two camels, hobbled. It transpired that Chipperfield's Circus was in town and would set up in Hudson's Field, and that these were the very first arrivals, but it was some time before my daughters accepted that camels were not an ordinary part of the English country scene.

In due course that day elephants came lumbering up Castle Street, which was by then lined by Salisbury citizens and their children, the news having got around. By then we were waiting in Hudson's Field. There were six relatively small elephants, and they entered at a brisk trot, each elephant holding the tail of its predecessor by its trunk. It was an impressive sight, but it reduced Lucy to tears: until then elephants had been cuddly pink toys which people gave her as presents and these monstrous galloping pachyderms were just too much of a shock.

All our neighbours worked for the Ministry; many were scientists, most had young families. Our children settled in at once and soon found new friends; our neighbours were congenial and we formed several long-term friendships. The house was bigger and better designed than our Twickenham semi, and Salisbury was a lovely, relatively traffic-free, county town in which to live, with its long-established shops and a weekly market, and perhaps the most beautiful cathedral in England. I commuted out into the countryside to work, against the main traffic stream. Altogether it was an idyllic domestic setting for a young family.

Life among the germ warriors

My arrival at MRE was smoothed by the friendliness and helpfulness of the Assistant Director, Leonard Kent, as well as by another senior, John Morton (whose function was a little obscure), the Administrator John Lister, and, of course, Denis. I was assigned a nice-sized laboratory and was promised an assistant as soon as I felt ready for one. I had demurred from having an assistant right from my first day because I wanted to do some preliminary experiments myself - and make my own mistakes privately. Like any bench scientist, I needed to get the feel of what was, for me, a new kind of research.

I soon came to realise why MRE was, at that time, perhaps the major intellectual and research centre for Microbiology in the UK. Denis and his colleagues had put continuous culture on to a rational theoretical and practical basis and were demonstrating its power as a research tool; Owen Powell and colleagues were performing some of the first experiments involving the growth of single cells rather than populations; the late Joan Powell, and Dick Strange, had opened up the biochemistry of spore formation in bacteria; Harry Smith (my next-door neighbour in the Close at home) and his colleagues were elucidating, for the first time, the biochemical reason why certain pathogenic bacteria would attack one part of the body and not another; Jock Westwood's group was in the forefront of the culture of viruses in tissue culture. There were groups studying the preservation of live bacteria, microbial genetics and how infections happen. MRE was the only laboratory in which the physiology and biochemistry of dangerous pathogens and mixed infections could be studied in reasonable safety, and its Director was personally involved in such experiments; MRE also had what were, for the time, excellent mass-culture facilities, in the charge of Raymond Elsworth. It was, in fact, one of the earliest laboratories to adopt an inter-disciplinary approach to research, employing chemists, physicists, medicos, geneticists, biochemists and bacteriologists to bear upon its problems, and the success of this approach was impressive. In the distant background lurked the matter of biological warfare, and some of the staff were studying organisms that were potential biological weapons, but at the time I arrived the topic was rarely mentioned. As Dick Strange sardonically put it, biological warfare was almost a dirty word in those days.

Was this just mass hypocrisy? Not at all. Everyone was well aware that the British government financed the laboratory because biological weapons were a real military threat, along with nuclear, chemical and conventional weapons. So Britain needed to know about them if only for defensive reasons. But as I wrote earlier, you do not learn much about defence without knowing about offence too: about how to make, package and use such weapons. None of this implied anything other than disgust at the thought of biological weapons actually being used.

I recall an occasion when the Committee for Nuclear Disarmament staged a Mass March on MRE to protest against biological warfare. MRE's gates were closed, police were deployed around its barbed wire perimeter, and all but a select few of the staff were asked not to come to work that day in case of violence. It was cold and it poured with rain all day, and many of us felt sorry for the drenched and chilled demonstrators. How nice it would be if we could all forget about warfare and get on with the rest of microbiology! But, as Dick Strange again wisely observed, how infinitely more massive a row would there be if biological weapons were to be used on Britain and MRE's expertise were not available.

Sadly, degraded threats sometimes compel degrading compromises. But the powers that guided MRE took a civilised view of its role in these matters. They realised that you had to know a lot about microbes in general to be able even to think constructively about those, which might be used as weapons - and it is easier and safer to study less harmful organisms. Moreover, most potential biological weapons - plague, anthrax, some nasty virus diseases - occur in nature and cause disease anyway, so it was useful to have a centre of expert knowledge on their spread and control.

Finally, research over the previous decade had shown that, from the military standpoint of the time, microbes were actually poor weapons compared with, say, guns and atom bombs. All these considerations had led to biological warfare becoming a truly minor aspect of MRE's total programme, though everyone on the staff was expected to turn their minds to the subject when called upon (as happened about four times during my first three years) and some were happy to involve themselves more deeply in direct research on the subject.

I had arrived knowing that my research would be fundamental, remote from any military use. I was amused rather than dismayed to find several curious leftovers from the laboratory's military origin. For instance, vestiges of rank persisted. Staff were rightly forbidden to eat or drink in laboratories, so there were official refreshment breaks twice a day, in addition to the lunch break. Tea or coffee was taken in one of four separate common rooms: one for Scientific Grade staff, one for Experimental Grade, one for male industrials, one for female industrials ('industrials' was the term for unqualified assistants). My natural egalitarianism jibbed, despite Denis' assurance that the separate common rooms had been queried at one time and were positively desired by the staff. Then there were segregated lavatories: one set for Scientific staff, another for Experimental and Industrial staff. Being of a senior grade, I could enjoy another privilege, whereby senior staff (including Senior Experimental Officers but not more junior members of the Experimental Grade) could join an Officers' Mess close by, take lunch there and use its facilities - both superior to the more distant canteen. It did not escape my attention that I could lunch with certain colleagues but not take coffee with them, nor pee in the same loo.

A dangerous distraction was the lunchtime *aperitif* in the Officers' Mess. A 'school' of drinkers, including Owen Powell, John Morton and Mark Darlow (the Medical Officer of MRE), tended to assemble at the bar and it was easy to slip in for 'just one' on the way to lunch and later find that one had forgotten lunch and was woozy with gin and tonic, or sherry. One didn't even pay: one just signed one's mess bill. After a few lost afternoons I learned to go quickly past the bar to lunch unless the occasion was really special.

In the Mess, too, I soon gained an official function. The fame of Raymond Postgate, my father, as a writer and authority on wine had reached MRE. Soon after I arrived the Mess Committee decided it needed a Wine Committee and appointed me, Denis, Owen Powell and one of the military staff thereto. As luck would have it, Harvey's of Bristol, a long-established firm of wine merchants, were clearing out their cellars to receive new stock and almost our first act was to buy, extremely cheaply, several dozen bottles of quite excellent claret whose name I have now forgotten (it was a Bourg, I believe). The Mess was astonished and delighted at its new Committee's success. The wine sold out quickly. The Mess looked to us with quiet confidence to replace it with similar wine of comparable quality. We could not, of course, but we never quite lost the reputation we gained from that initial piece of luck. I, personally, learned a lot from Owen's knowledge of the wines of Alsace (I was then a claret man) and under our surveillance the Mess cellar was good for a while. But not to everyone's taste: we had a marvellous Château Latour, which David Henderson dismissed as "blackberry juice". He thus showed a discerning if undiscriminating palate: many decades of experience have gone into obtaining that highly esteemed flavour in which some find a hint of blackberries.

Coffee and tea breaks were, for me, the time for brisk interchange of ideas - political, social, cultural, sexual but mostly scientific - with my colleagues. Happily, the scientific competitiveness which I have since met too often elsewhere was absent. No one seemed to fear that his ideas might be 'pinched' by another. Ideas were common currency: if someone used one of your ideas, you might use someone else's. I rejoiced in these breaks, having become somewhat isolated intellectually during my ten years in a chemistry laboratory. Some British microbiologists, including one or two within MRE, resented the intellectual arrogance of the senior 'Portonites'. I was unaware of this and, since I had the good fortune to be accepted among them at once, I felt no such envy. I recall only some hurt surprise that no one had the least interest in my previous decade's research - though they accepted that it was fairly distinguished. There was no suggestion, for example, that I should give a seminar on it, and occasional good-natured allusions to my interest in 'autotrophs' showed that my new colleagues had but the faintest idea of its nature (some sulphur bacteria belong to a category of microbes called autotrophs; my sulphate reducers did not). I took this in my stride, helped by the fact that I hated giving seminars anyway. I now know that all really good research organizations are like this: obsessive self-absorption is usually necessary for good collective science, and work which is not relevant, no matter how distinguished, is a distraction. Immature scientists can find this insulting; I was a bit immature, I suppose; I still am, really, but I suppressed any such feelings.

I gradually learned that there were, in the common rooms, invisible barriers. The biophysicists tended to sit near the tea urn and remain silent. My particular chums - Herbert, Powell, Keith Norris, Strange, David Tempest, and Kent - tended to congregate near a certain window; the virologists would be across the room, the pathologists near the end. Such cliquishness, I now know, is common to all communities, but at MRE it was unimportant. We all had a roving brief if we wanted to discuss something that other groups would know about. I gradually learned, too, that there were the real live wires (who were busy getting as much research done as they could) and the sleepers (who were doing what needed to be done but were opting for a quiet life). The latter had clearly found it all too easy to relax, stop reading the scientific literature and plod on quietly with their research problems. A nine-to-five-thirty routine at the laboratory was favoured by its being eight miles from Salisbury, so bus time-tables, car pools - even the exceptionally pleasant countryside and fertile gardens at home - played a significant part in the planning of experiments.

Owen Powell

Owen Powell (E O Powell) has appeared a few times already. He was an outstanding scientist and a very British kind of eccentric, a good friend of Denis, Butch, me and many another. He dressed oddly; he never wore socks and his trousers were rather like the Oxford bags of the 1930s. He was tall and almost painfully thin, of indeterminate age, with a pale, ravaged face topped by untidy white hair. He had a monstrous tremor, especially of a morning: at the coffee break in the common room his cup would rattle and shake in its saucer as he held it unsteadily under the urn. For he was a cheerful alcoholic. He made no secret of the matter; he liked to drink a lot and tremors and hangovers were, to him, a small price to pay. Alcohol did not impair his science in any obvious way. He had, like Denis, an extremely penetrating intellect and an ability to think laterally.

Actually it was the death of Owen's wife Joan, herself a distinguished microbiologist working at MRE, that had enabled Henderson to take me on to the staff, and it was her old laboratory that was assigned to me. By then Owen lived an ostensibly bachelor life in the Officers' Mess, a situation which did nothing to inhibit his drinking. His combination of almost boyish enthusiasms with an air of depravity made him strangely attractive to some women, and this part of his life was a muddle; the rather closed world inhabited by Porton scientists made extra-marital liaisons rather easy, and appropriate rumours and problems were not uncommon. But he was private about his private life and I took it as none of my business. In due course, several years after my departure from MRE, he married again: the ex-wife of another colleague.

Owen was not a microbiologist by training; I think his background was in physics, but it might have been in engineering. He was a natural mathematician and before I came he had worked out virtually all the mathematical theory which underpinned MRE's pre-eminence in continuous culture. He had become deeply interested in what actually happens when a population of bacteria grows: how fast do the individual bacteria grow? When do they divide into two? In my time he was studying the distribution of such doubling times. It was an interest which, in a way, echoed that of my early mentor Hinshelwood, also a scientist with a strong physico-mathematical bias. But Owen had no time at all for Hinshelwood's ideas, which had been effectively superseded by then. His approach was more analytical: instead of working with bulk populations of bacteria, he had set about observing individual bacteria and timing their multiplication.

The way he did this was simple, but immensely laborious. With his assistant, Fred Errington, he had set up a microscope in a room kept at a constant warm temperature - a room-sized incubator - and he grew his bacteria, actually the same kind that Hinshelwood had used, on a thin membrane under which nutrient fluid flowed gently. Thus they were warm and well fed, so they multiplied. He and his assistant would inoculate a membrane at the beginning of the day and, having chosen, say, four cells to watch, would take turns at peering down the microscope with a clock to record the moment when each cell divided into two. This might take between 40 and 50 minutes. Then they would watch the eight daughter cells, which would always take a shorter time, around 30 minutes, to produce the 16 granddaughters. These would be watched as they divided into 32 great grand daughters. Since, as they expected and soon confirmed, their cells did not all divide at the same instant, the moments of division among the later generations became increasingly unpredictable; things became pretty chaotic as the fourth generation approached, cells dividing every few minutes. I don't think they ever got further down the cells' pedigree.

It was also tropically hot in that room; on days when they had a full-scale experiment on, Owen could be seen to rush wild-eyed out of the hot room, wearing nothing but his underpants and lab coat, in order to seize and gulp down a cup of coffee, and dash back to allow Errington a respite. No wonder he felt he needed a few drinks at lunchtime!

The actual manipulating of the microscope with its special stage was extremely tricky, but despite his tremor, Owen could perform such manoeuvres with the delicacy of a surgeon.

Owen was a dedicated and single-minded scientist who did science simply because it was fun. He pretended complete indifference to whether any research he did would be useful or not, a patently false posture which he adopted to provoke the more serious-minded of his fellow scientists. Equally he was proud to be the only senior scientist at MRE who was not a Doctor; doctorates, he would tauntingly maintain, were bogus Teutonic degrees. He liked to tease, and had himself an enormous capacity for enjoyment. He liked classical music, was witty and vulgar; predictably, he got on very well with Butch. In several ways he was an overgrown undergraduate: totally open and un-pompous, and a splendid foil to Denis' almost prim enjoyment of conviviality. He fortunately took kindly to me (although he took every opportunity to express his contempt for jazz, which he regarded as non-music) and I enjoyed his company immensely - I also found his comments on my research most valuable. At scientific meetings, Owen was always at the centre of hilarity and enjoyment.

A microbiological undertaker

Despite all these agreeable distractions, excellent research was being done at MRE, and my own got underway. What, I asked, caused bacteria to die when they did not form spores and had not been heated, or insulted with disinfectants, radiation and such agents? Denis, like Butlin before him, left me to plan my research programme entirely by myself - though I sought his advice and also talked to all of MRE's staff that had any interest in the question. I was quite aware of the relevance of my theme to biological warfare, which 'John' Silver (one of the few actually studying biological warfare) dourly pointed out to me at our first meeting: biological agents would not be of much use if they were dead, so MRE needed to study microbial death. But it was also a fascinating problem of fundamental biological importance, one which had rarely been touched upon during the history of microbiology: fewer than a dozen important papers had been published on the matter in the previous sixty years. In due course Janet Crumpton (I forget her maiden name) and John Hunter, in that order, joined me. Janet was young, friendly and meticulous; she also knew all about how to get things done in MRE - a tremendous asset. Hunter was a masterly career technician, utterly reliable and rather quiet, of a kind that 'Fultonization' would all but eliminate from the Scientific Civil Service as the 1960s progressed.

I chose an easy non-pathogenic bacterium to work with, an organism which had, and has, nothing to do with biological warfare. It was *Klebsiella aerogenes* (its modern name is the somewhat more alarming *K. pneumoniae*), the same species, and actually the same strain, as Hinshelwood had used under the name of *Bacterium lactis aerogenes*. Owen was using that strain, too.

I got down to work. Because of our preoccupation with bacterial death, Janet, John and I became known as the 'microbiological undertakers'. Everyone was friendly and helpful; only Dick Strange seemed curiously ambivalent. Several months later I learned the reason: he had been asked to study the same problem, without my being told and without Denis or anyone else telling him of my planned involvement. Not a good start, for Dick was a sensitive man and I was probably tactless when first I talked to him. It took well over a year for a kind of strain between us to vanish, but we had become good friends by the time I left MRE.

Obviously management was not always very effective at MRE - for I do not think it was deviousness. On other occasions I learned that feelings were sometimes hurt by inconsiderate decision-taking. This was odd, because with Leonard Kent, John Morton, John Lister, as well as research leaders such as Denis, there were a lot of managers about - too many cooks, I suppose.

Minor undercurrents did nothing to mar my happiness in having a good research problem, excellent facilities and stimulating colleagues, particularly as I was able to introduce a modest novelty of approach and thus put in my 'two bits' worth'.

This is the sort of work we did. Bacteria such as klebsiella multiply simply by growing large and splitting into two. There is neither a mother nor a daughter; at the moment of division the mother vanishes and the progeny are twins of identical youth. This fact had become well established during the 1950s. In no sense does the parent cell grow old and die; if the bacteria can keep on multiplying, they can be viewed as enjoying a bizarre kind of immortality, forever recapturing their youth - or, if you prefer, vanishing like the old soldiers who never die. This understanding raised some interesting questions regarding the nature of mortality, which I cannot go into here - it was good for a lot of coffee-time discussion.

But if for some reason klebsiellae can no longer multiply, do they become senescent and die in the way we do? That was one of the questions which interested us. The most common reason why bacteria cease multiplying is that they run out of food, so I decided that our first approach should be to study death by starvation.

Doing useful experiments on the nature of bacterial death is actually rather tricky because, as Owen Powell put it, one can only observe bacterial death retrospectively.

That needs explaining. It comes about because bacteria are so small and featureless that live and dead cells look identical. Therefore, to discover how many cells in a bacterial population are dead, a microbiologist has to take a sample of that population, count the cells in it, place it on the surface of a medium in which the living cells can divide, then incubate it for a few hours - usually overnight in a Petri dish - and some time later see how many of the original cells have taken advantage of the situation and multiplied to form colonies. Those which have not done so are presumed to be dead. The retrospective element arises when one asks, were they dead when the sample was taken? Or did they die afterwards? Or again, would they have survived and divided if the microbiologist had chosen a different culture medium? All a microbiologist learns at the end of such a test is that a certain proportion of the population was probably dead when the sample was taken. For most purposes that is good enough. But in truth there is no reliable way of saying, "that cell has just died"; one can only say "that cell was probably dead several hours ago".

There is still no really satisfactory way to get round this uncertainty. In the 1960s it was something one had to live with, but at least we managed to decrease the period of retrospection substantially. By growing population samples on microscope slides and counting corpses and micro-colonies under the microscope after incubation periods of one to three hours rather than overnight, we limited the uncertainties.

Together the three of us showed that some individuals die of starvation faster than others. And they did indeed go through an ageing process before they died: how long they remained able to multiply depended on how well fed they had been before they were starved. During starvation they actually consumed their own cell material (stored carbohydrate, protein and nucleic acids) and the more of these substances they had to spare, the longer they survived.

We also found that, when they had consumed about half of their expendable constituents, they started dying, in the sense that they had become unable to form colonies on a slide culture. Nevertheless, such cells still retained many of the characteristics of living bacteria: they respired, albeit slowly, they carried out various normal metabolic processes, and they were anatomically intact. It seemed as if they were not dead but senescent, like an elderly higher organism that is lively enough but can no longer reproduce.

(Some 30 years later, in the 1990s, comparable studies with other bacteria (not klebsiellae but rather different creatures called micrococci) cast doubt on this interpretation of our findings: starved micrococci become dormant rather than senescent and can actually be resuscitated. Not dead, just fast asleep!)

If I include Dick Strange and his colleagues, who were also studying bacterial death, we had the research field almost to ourselves - though a Dr Arthur Harrison in the USA had recently worked on the problem and we were in touch with him. We investigated some known phenomena such as Harrison's 'population effect' (within limits, dense populations die more slowly than sparse populations; it happens partly because, when bacteria finally die, all sorts of nutrients leak out, to be consumed by surviving neighbours: a phenomenon known as cryptic growth. It is a sort of passive cannibalism). We also persuaded Denis and his young associate David Tempest to collaborate in some very important experiments, which showed that, using very slow continuous culture, one could obtain populations which were multiplying so slowly that a proportion was always senile or dead. But a blow-by-blow account of our research would not be appropriate here; let it be sufficient to say that it was reasonably innovative and painstaking. Our major paper, published in 1962, remains the most systematic study of bacterial death by starvation in the literature. (Though, judging from subsequent papers in the research area, it is now rarely read - perhaps because it was long, and such exhaustive papers have gone out of fashion.)

Being a microbiological undertaker was proving to be as interesting and scientifically rewarding as I had hoped, but I had formed a sort of attachment to the sulphate-reducing bacteria, which was difficult to break. (I never did abandon them entirely, in fact.) There were questions left over from my days at Teddington which I wanted to finish. Indeed, as I have mentioned, I was able to do a few clandestine experiments at MRE - my own 'secret' research which Denis and Henderson viewed with cautious indulgence.

A somewhat musical interlude

Denis and Owen had no time at all for jazz. Denis regarded it tolerantly; Owen, as I mentioned, refused to acknowledge that it was music at all. However, I managed to find a few fellow aficionados in the Salisbury area and even formed a tiny group within MRE: cornet, clarinet, guitar and brushes-on-an-envelope (substituting for drums). We practised weekly in the lunch break. There was a Salisbury Jazz Club, which I attended regularly, but the truth is that my cornet playing was in poor shape (partly, I realised many years later, because of a dud instrument) and I did not get to play regularly. More often I played rhythm guitar with local 'trad' groups. For the turn of the decade was the era when traditional jazz reached the height of its popularity in Britain and all over Europe, with recordings by jazz bands such as Chris Barber's and Acker Bilk's in the Top Ten lists. The Beaulieu Jazz Festival down in Hampshire was a kind of traditionalists' jamboree, but I only got to it once because of other commitments. 'Trad' at variable levels of competence was played all over the country and the Beatles, who would soon displace jazz and introduce the era of rock music and its derivatives, were still a little-known quartet of Liverpudlian singers who seemed to have got themselves a gig in Hamburg.

As a jazz musician I was not doing well, but my love of jazz and my urge to write about it remained. In the 1950s there were several magazines devoted to jazz, and the most highbrow of these was called *Jazz Monthly*, edited from Lands End by an Irish anarchist called Albert McCarthy. It was a self-consciously intellectual publication - for several years it sub-headed itself, "The magazine of intelligent jazz appreciation". Some of its articles were puffed-up with semantic confusion masquerading as critical analysis, but others were penetrating and scholarly. I had been subscribing to it since 1956, and had submitted a few rather journalistic reflections on the jazz scene while at Teddington, which McCarthy had liked and published. So by the time I moved to MRE I had become a regular columnist, producing a few 'witty' paragraphs about jazz in general every two or three issues. Readers liked my effusions, and I remained a columnist ("Between You And Me - John Postgate") for about a decade, after which time I became a member of its panel of regular record reviewers. Every now and again I would write longer studies for the magazine about specific jazz musicians or jazz topics.

Once I was accepted as a regular contributor to the magazine, Mac, as we all knew him, would invite me to meetings of his contributors. These would take place three or four times a year at Long's Wine Bar off Oxford Street in London. There would gather the cream of the period's jazz writers and critics, gossiping, talking about jazz and getting slowly pie-eyed on wine at the expense of the magazine. Among names which were familiar to jazz lovers over several decades might be broadcaster Charles Fox, bearded and amiable, who would generally leave early; Max Harrison, who was also authoritative on classical music and was therefore immensely superior in manner and outlook; Paul Oliver, the world's leading authority on the blues; Stanley Dance, doyen of jazz writers, who soon emigrated to the USA to work in association with Duke Ellington; Alun Morgan, a celebrated critic with an encyclopaedic knowledge of recordings and musicians; reviewers and sleeve-note writers such as Michael James, Raymond Horricks, Jack Cooke and Ronald Atkins; musician/writer Brian Priestley, and blues expert Tony Russell - plus various interested non-contributors whom Mac would invite along. The company would usually divide spontaneously into two sub-clusters, Mac with acolytes at one table talking of more philosophical, political and aesthetic matters, Alun with another group talking more of recordings and news of jazz sessions. I would try to place myself within earshot of both groups. They were immensely friendly and talkative gatherings. As the evening wore on the *Jazz Monthly* crowd would displace all but the hardiest other customers, and when Long's closed the party would weave its way to a nearby Indian restaurant where Mac, a vegetarian, could rely on the food being meat-free. I managed the final part of the routine only once: for me real curry on top of lots of wine proved to be a sure-fire emetic.

We were a dedicated lot. We all believed that we were doing something to upgrade jazz criticism and writing, which was then at a dismal level as far as both grammar and content were concerned. We hoped we were widening appreciation of our beloved music - in the 1950s jazz was still regarded as rubbish by the musical establishment - and I think we had some degree of success. We needed to be dedicated because, apart from the pleasure of seeing our names in print occasionally, these parties were almost our sole reward for our efforts: over some 15 years of regular contributing I received about eight very small cheques from Mac. Not that he ever pretended to me that things would be otherwise - but I learned some years after the magazine's demise that payments to me featured much more frequently in its formal accounts. Mac simply pocketed them himself. Well, as an anarchist he believed firmly in "from each according to his ability, to each according to his need"! I did not resent it.

The conviviality and amiability of the contributors on these occasions contrasted with the bitter vituperation of their writings, for they had in common overt and unconcealed contempt for each other's tastes in jazz, views on jazz and writing styles. During the late 1950s and early 1960s almost every issue had an article by one contributor attacking another, and those Mac chose to publish were but a sample from those that were sent in. Mac had to prevent contributors from hogging the 'letters' feature with indignant retorts. The reason was that the 1950s and early '60s were a period of intense creativity and change in jazz: idioms that had been modern in the '40s, such as be-bop, were becoming absorbed, along with traditional forms and 'swing' influences, into 'mainstream' jazz. Purists were still exploring archaic New Orleans jazz and its popular variant, Dixieland, had enormous appeal. Be-bop musicians were tangling on the one hand with blues and gospel music and on the other hand with Latin-American influences. 'Free-form' jazz, in which the harmonic and euphonic foundations of the music were discarded, was emerging, out-modernising the modernists. There was a great deal to argue about as critics contended that their favourite styles were being neglected, corrupted, misjudged or commercialised; it made *Jazz Monthly* a lively and controversial, if rather inward-looking, publication.

In truth, however, *Jazz Monthly* was even then a literary anachronism. It was a leftover from the self-indulgent "little" cultural magazines of the 1920s and earlier: low-circulation, highbrow publications dedicated to art, poetry, political fringes and so on, most of which died in the First World War. The contributors were collectively dedicated to a cause, but rampantly divided within it. The magazine tolerated affectation and pretentiousness in its quest for critical standards; it was individualistic, but its anarchic editor rarely altered a word of a text. The magazine's integrity was ferocious: the idea of toning down or rejecting a poor review so as not to offend an advertiser, now commonplace, was unthinkable to all concerned. So was any suggestion of pulling one's punches because one was writing of a fellow contributor. It was a relic of a more expansive era of publication and, probably lethally as far as its own future was concerned, commercialism played no part in the thinking of its editor or its contributors.

For me, writing about jazz was no substitute for playing it, but it was great fun being part of *Jazz Monthly*, and a wonderful introduction into the jazz world. I carried on writing about jazz for many more decades. The magazine gradually lost advertising and readers during the 1960s, as rock displaced jazz in popularity.

In the early 1970s it foundered financially and Mac gave up the struggle. It briefly became *Jazz And Blues*, edited by Max Harrison, but that was soon bought out and engulfed by the longer-established *Jazz Journal*, a less overtly highbrow and more popular jazz magazine. It is happily still with us in the early 2000s.

CHAPTER SIXTEEN

More travel

Back to science. It had become quite commonplace for a scientist to visit the USA by the late 1950s. Not so Australia. But in the later 1950s that country was undergoing a scientific *naissance*, so to speak, sparked by its government's post-war investment in research, and arising in part from its successful applications of science in agriculture during the 1940s, and in part from government recognition of the importance of science-based technologies for serious economic development. Australia had a general policy that its professional research scientists should spend one year in every three working abroad, most often in the UK or the USA, and that enlightenment was paying off. Australian research was climbing the world's scientific ladder and distinguished savants from abroad were beginning to accept Australia as a place to visit. International collaborative conferences and research projects centred on Australia were becoming increasingly frequent, and Australian scientific journals were gaining in reputation. By the end of the century, Australian science would be totally accepted (and its funding cut drastically, as in every other country), but in 1959 it was still up-and-coming.

Cytochrome C3 had become my round-the-world travel ticket. A couple of months before I left Teddington to join MRE in 1959 I had been invited by the Australian Academy of Sciences to contribute to a select but high-powered conference which was to be held later that year in Canberra. It would discuss recent research on haematin enzymes - of which cytochromes were a group. Could I come and tell them about cytochrome C3? I had to find my own travel (and pocket) money but would be their guest in Australia. It was to be a most prestigious gathering and Henderson was properly impressed; even in our early discussions of my going to MRE he had agreed that I should go, and that MRE would provide the additional funding. I had even pulled together some unpublished research material from my Teddington days to make a contribution, which included at least something new.

So, after less than four months working at MRE, I left my assistants, Janet and John, to carry on with the microbiological 'undertaking' while I winged my way Down Under. The pleasures of family life in Salisbury, of my welcome at MRE, and the euphoria of having escaped from the DSIR, were all still upon me; I set off on August 14, 1959, in good health and spirits.

Crossing the world

At once one of the great advantages of working for a

paramilitary body became evident. Not for me the hassle of catching buses and trains; I was assigned an official car and driver to take me, with a refreshment stop, from my Salisbury home to London's Heathrow airport. However, once there I was in the hands of the British Overseas Airways Corporation (BOAC) for a 48-hour journey to Sydney in a piston-engined Britannia aircraft, an admirable if noisy machine which was then a source of national pride. It was very cramped (in that way no different from today's jet aircraft, of course) and required refuelling stops every few hours. Such stops would last for between 45 and 60 minutes, and each time all passengers had to leave the aircraft for a transit lounge because of the fire hazard presented by fuel vapour. In these days of long-haul jet travel its itinerary seems like a safari, and indeed it developed something of a social character as the travellers mingled stop after stop. Here is a telegraphic outline of the trip, edited from my diary:

Leave LONDON about mid-day. Stop at ZURICH for fuel and refreshment, then a fairly long haul with dinner to BEIRUT (where we are met by armed guards and virtually marched to the transit lounge). Another long haul to KARACHI for breakfast at BOAC's airport hotel. (Disgusted by two passengers, off-duty pilots, who think it funny to demand bacon of the hospitable Pakistani waiters; they don't get it. Also shocked by a nicely brought-up New Zealand girl who admits to being relieved that they wore gloves, or she would not have felt like eating anything.) On, with lunch in flight, to CALCUTTA, which is very hot and humid and serves us with cold coffee; then, with dinner served by a beautiful Indian hostess, to SINGAPORE, which feels even hotter (here the aircraft fills up, mostly with Australians, but I get a double seat and can doze). Thence to a somewhat cooler DJAKARTA (met by Indonesian soldiers who look like children but are armed with machine guns) for pineapple juice in the transit lounge. After breakfast in the air (accompanied by a certificate of having crossed the equator) our next stop is at DARWIN (in Australia at last; barramundi, a tropical fish, for lunch), then, managing to doze a little, a smooth flight to SYDNEY.

I arrived at 21:30 local time; my biological clock made it 12:30. Fortunately I was met by an old friend from Balliol days, Gordon Samuels, with whom I was to stay for a couple of days before the meeting, and visit again after it; he and his wife, Jackie, were most understanding and, after plying me with chicken sandwiches and gin, which did something to confuse the biological clock, they sent me to bed. It eased my transition, but for several days I would find myself annoyingly tired by day but alert and wakeful in the small hours of the Australian morning.

During my stay Gordon or Jackie, and sometimes both, drove me around Sydney, showing me the sights, took me out into the countryside, had guests in to meet me, and introduced me to Australian wines. I also fitted in a scientific visit to a biological laboratory outside Sydney at Cronulla. Despite my constant battle with my biological clock it was a wonderful glimpse of the area, which, once more, I must skim over for fear of boring the reader. As in California, I had a sense of enormous space everywhere. Here there were marvellous beaches, delightful inlets and fjords, wonderful countryside or 'bush'. Sydney Harbour was an especially beautiful location, centred on its magnificent bridge, impressive despite rain and an overcast sky (being mid August it was, of course, later winter). The Kings Cross area was a cosmopolitan shopping centre (I am told it has deteriorated since then). Australian wines were a revelation (my diary is full of tasting notes; in 1959 almost the only Australian wines to be found in the UK were 'plonk', or wines such as 'Emu Burgundy' marketed for its medicinal properties). Restaurant food, too, was excellent - as was that served by my hosts.

All too soon I had to take flight again, to Canberra. This was Australia's capital city, still under construction, separated within its own Capital Territory from all other Australian states. It was then an architectural mess: a huge building site with scattered pockets of completed houses, shops and offices, interspersed with shallow gouged-out valleys of bare soil, seemingly as if some grotesque residue of opencast mining was being rehabilitated. In one of the habitable enclaves was a large silver flying saucer surrounded by a moat: the home of the Australian Academy of Science. A walkable distance away was the Hotel Canberra where the congress delegates were housed; it was startlingly British in appearance but with central heating - to my great relief, for the weather was frosty. At dinner it was buzzing with variant forms of the English language, spoken by Australians, Japanese, Scandinavians, Americans, Belgians, native British and, when unavoidable, the redoubtable Mme Chaix of

France. In addition to Mme Chaix I met old acquaintances such as Martin Kamen, Egami and Phil Trudinger, and many new ones who had hitherto been names on scientific papers; it was certainly a well-selected gathering. That night the sky was bright and clear, and an Australian participant showed me the Southern Cross definitively - in truth a rather unimpressive constellation which I had been unable to recognize with certainty myself.

Next morning there was the inevitable chatty conference breakfast for which I, albeit somewhat bleary as always, was ready. I sat with Dr Bob Morton, who was one of the conference organisers, Professor Drabkin, Professor Egami and a couple of others. I have already told in Chapter 10 the tale of Egami and Professor Drabkin's kipper; Drabkin was happy and we all survived.

So by bus to the actual meeting. It was high-powered and hard work. Formal papers and discussions occupied the whole day, with meal and refreshment breaks, and in the evening there were scientific *conversazione*. Sometimes bored, sometimes excited, sometimes simply saturated, my major take-away lesson was how ignorant I really was about haematin enzymes, despite several years reading around the subject and despite having worked with an example. It was a great relief to discover that most of the others knew very little about cytochrome C3, so that my paper would be more new to them than I had feared. In the event, it was very well received, and some were astonished, because C3 seemed a very strange protein in those days (nowadays lots of cytochromes C3 are known and everyone is rightly *blasé* about them). Gradually I came to realise that we were all in much the same position: immensely up-to-date in our own tiny frog-ponds but startlingly unaware of what was going on in the puddle next door. Well, that is what such meetings are all about: there were no startling revelations and none had been expected, only consolidation and reassessment of the research area as a whole. I think all participants regarded the meeting as a success and departed with something new to think about.

A run-down of the science would be inappropriate here, but some of the peripheral activities and interactions were curious or entertaining. Australians like to be on first-name terms with their colleagues, a situation which caused me no problem. Not so Mme Chaix. Bob Morton, wishing to be friendly, elicited her first name, Paulette, and proposed to use it. "No, no!" cried Mme Chaix, all flustered by this familiarity, "Madame, or Doctor, or Professeur Chaix..." Fortunately Bob had the wit to realise that she was not being standoffish, just *une Française bien-elevée*. Because my French is generally fluent if not very accurate, I often ended up at meals with Mme Chaix, talking French - not quite what I had expected on a trip to Australia.

On the third evening of the meeting, somewhat euphoric at having given my paper and influenced by rather a lot of preprandial sherry, I escaped with Phil Trudinger, Martin Kamen and David Bonner (an American plant physiologist) to drink a couple of beers in a local pub. Phil, Australian himself but cosmopolitan, wanted us to experience an Australian pub. In 1959 it was quite an experience. An era of very restricted drinking hours, which legislation had in practice led to rapid binge-boozing, had not yet come to a close and the pub could only be open for three hours of an evening - a relaxation from earlier years when open-time was but an hour or so. For one used to comfortable, welcoming British pubs, it was a most discouraging place. The bar was a stark, undecorated room with yellow walls half-tiled, its floor was of concrete and the bar itself was tiled. There was nowhere to sit, and not even a footrest along the bar so that one could stand and lean. It was for all the world like a public lavatory: get in, use it and get out, seemed to be its message. But sturdy Australian drinkers, all male, took it in their stride and refused to be discouraged, and so did we. The beer, as I recall, was quite good.

On another occasion, after the main conference, an afternoon visit to some government laboratories was arranged for the conference delegates. I have, truth be told, never been very enthusiastic about visiting people's laboratories as a scientific tourist - unless, of course, I have something to discuss which I think would be mutually interesting. It is a sort of shyness; too often have I found myself uncomfortable, struggling to take an interest and conscious that my host would prefer to be getting on with his or her work. I am mistaken, for scientific tourism can be a most valuable source of ideas for all concerned, but my disposition is always to fear the worst. Anyway, I was tired as well and politely withdrew myself from the proposed trip and went for a walk around Canberra's administrative centre, observing the early spring blossom and colourful birds.

Returning to the Hotel about four, I discovered Dr Dickens, a distinguished older British biochemist, relaxing in the sun on a seat by the croquet lawn (another of the Hotel's British touches). He was a traditionalist who had no truck with informal dress: he always wore a dark suit and usually, as on this day, a stiff collar and tie.

He proposed that we order afternoon tea. The Hotel Canberra rose to the occasion splendidly. At a small table for two in the foyer it laid us a tablecloth and duly produced our tea: silver teapot, milk, hot water, tea strainer, proper china, sugar with tongs, little sponge cakes in ribbed paper cups with a glacé cherry on top - everything correct. Dickens was pouring me a second cup when the rest of our party returned from their trip. No one said a word, but as the Japanese, Americans, Australians, French etc walked past and we nodded and smiled, I saw the gamut of facial expressions: astonishment, bewilderment, delighted recognition. As a young American biochemist, Lucille Smith, said to me later, it was a wholly unexpected and utterly English scene for them to come upon. I do not think Dickens was in the least aware of the mild sensation we caused.

The conference continued uninterrupted from Monday to Friday. All of us were exhausted, except perhaps the Australians, who are remarkably tough in this respect, and the grand excursion arranged for our relaxation on Saturday was most welcome. In two buses the whole conference set off and, after a sight-seeing drive round Canberra, drove some 50 miles to the old Australian township of Goulburn, with its unspoiled colonial style buildings and its avenues of eucalyptus trees. There we had lunch. Then we had a long, dusty drive to the well-named Bungonia Lookdown, a cliff overlooking a magnificent gorge, surrounded by sub-tropical vegetation: macrozamias and 'grass trees'. Some of us, including a delighted Mme Chaix, caught sight of a kangaroo, but I missed it.

On the return journey our bus broke down and it took the driver an hour or so to patch it up. Meanwhile Bob Morton entertained us by making a eucalyptus wood fire, which smelled wonderful, and looking for poisonous spiders under the bark of a fallen log, which was a far from welcome enterprise. Happily he found none. Eventually the driver said "She'll do," and we re-embarked for a rather laboured return to Canberra. Dinner was well over at our hotel by the time we arrived - our colleagues from the other bus smiled at us sympathetically - but we were taken to an Italian restaurant in the city, which, albeit not too keen on this invasion of boffins, fed us, well. I recall a good clarinet-led quartet in the Benny Goodman style swinging nicely, which brightened my life but caused some of the Japanese exquisite agony.

After the weekend there was a nomenclature committee, where we proposed a systematic way of naming haematin enzymes, particularly cytochromes (it was officially accepted by an international biochemical body some months later). Then the conference began to disperse, most of them to visit a few Australian research centres before going home. For my part, after visiting the Australian National University and Trudinger's group at the Baas-Becking Institute (they studied thiobacilli, a group of sulphur bacteria), I flew off on the Tuesday for Brisbane, the next stop on my own circuit.

So far I had been in cosmopolitan company, among Australians who had mostly spent time in Europe and were used to European ways. Despite Mme Chaix's little problem about how she should be addressed, everyone made allowances for other delegates' national habits and customs. For example, the Japanese were still very unpopular among average Australians in 1959 as memories of Japanese treatment of wartime prisoners died hard, but the three or four Japanese at our meeting were welcome fellow scientists as far as all of us were concerned.

However, as the guest of Professor Skerman at the University in St. Lucia, Brisbane, I was deep in the Australian heartland, where I found the people immensely welcoming but strangely stiff. Partly my accent generated unease; I have an educated Southern English accent; old-fashioned BBC perhaps, with a tendency to talk quietly and in a self-deprecating manner. Loud, forthright Australians easily missed what I had said, a situation not helped on this visit by the fact that my host was very deaf. However, we managed well enough. I stayed at his home with, a luxury for Brisbane, my own shower and lavatory. Supper, preceded by a grace as were all meals, was distinctly strained, as his wife and teenage daughter did not feel it proper to speak unless invited to.

Afterwards he had invited guests from the University to meet me and take a glass of beer. As the party got started I noticed that all the wives were at one side of the room and the men were in a cluster on the other side. Politely I detached myself from the men and joined the ladies, asking the nearest what her interests were. Rarely have I generated such embarrassment. Fortunately a wife whom I'd met earlier, and who had spent two years in England, joined us quickly and took me over, gently manoeuvring the pair of us into the middle of the room, whereat her husband detached himself from the men and joined us. Very tactful.

A couple of days later, back in Sydney, the Samuelses explained my *faux pas* to me. This was the Australian way: at formal parties the men and women did not mix, even after formal introduction, let alone without it. However, I believe that my little solecism happened so quickly that I do not think Skerman noticed. At his command conversation ceased briefly as we distributed ourselves around the room on chairs, sofa and cushions, for what he planned would be a structured discussion about British versus Australian education. Again I unwittingly sabotaged his plans by talking party talk - about any old thing that seemed appropriate at the moment, not specially education.

My seminar next day was a general survey of the sulphate-reducing bacteria, though of course cytochrome C3 came into it. It went off perfectly well. But Skerman, doubtless too deaf to hear any of it, dozed off very soon after I started. Over the years I have become used to this happening. Heads of Departments have to sit through lots of lectures which are of little, if any, interest to them. However, as I finished he woke up - again, I have noticed many that many Departmental Heads develop that talent - and dutifully proposed a vote of thanks. It became abundantly clear that he had not only missed every word of my talk but had even got my subject wrong, because he thanked me for a very interesting talk on the thiobacilli, a quite different group of sulphur bacteria which I had at no time mentioned; he told some anecdotes of his experiences with them. Obviously his staff were used to this sort of thing. No one turned a hair, and such questions as were subsequently asked of me did actually refer to sulphate reducers.

Talking of national stereotypes, another seminar took place immediately after mine, before essentially the same audience, given by an American authority on haematins who was also travelling around after the Canberra meeting. Whereas I wore suit and tie, stood politely at a lectern and enunciated carefully from notes, he spoke extempore in a drawl, wearing open-necked shirt and slacks, half-sitting on the lecture bench with his hands in his pockets and a cigarette dangling from the side of his mouth. I thought him very bad mannered; I wonder which of us seemed the more alien to our audience? Me, probably.

But despite minor hitches, Skerman was very kind and hospitable, ensuring that I visited the microbiology and biochemistry departments of the University, where everyone was friendly and interested; he also drove me around the countryside to see the sub-tropical scenery and vegetation. But uninterrupted science was wearing me down and on the afternoon of day three I was not displeased to return to Gordon and Jackie's haven in Sydney for a brief respite.

By now I could get around Sydney on my own, which was fine because Gordon and Jackie were both busy working people, he in his law office, she as a television personality. I could be reasonably independent. I used the Sydney rail system to visit the laboratory of the Royal North Shore Hospital, which was a centre for research on haematins. (I was duly alarmed by notices on the local station platform warning passengers to beware of poisonous 'Red Jockey' spiders, which are restricted to that tiny area of Australia. They are seemingly prone to bite people's bottoms in outdoor privies, having roosted under the seat.) I had brought from England a crude preparation of desulfoviridin, the green protein that accompanied cytochrome C3 in my sulphate reducers, for the hospital's haematin specialists to see, and I demonstrated some of its properties before giving it to them. We had a useful discussion about what its chemical structure might be. I also made my way to the University of New South Wales, where I had been booked to lecture about sulphate reducers in general.

But despite being busy, Gordon and Jackie contrived to make much of my 5-day stay a holiday from my scientific tour, with dinners, a picnic trip to the Blue Mountains, seeking out a local jazz band, more research into the quality of Australian wines, and so on. On one occasion we met for lunch at a nice place called "The Bistro", near the centre of Sydney. Gordon introduced me to the proprietor as an Englishman with a taste for wine. The proprietor, however, did not think much of Poms, especially not their taste in wine: "We wouldn't drink the wine we export to you!" But he made a gesture of friendliness and invited me to taste a white wine he was serving. Ever polite, I responded, "It's very nice, but not really to my taste."

"Y're right." He interrupted, cuffing me on the shoulder, "It's lousy."

Evidently I had passed a test, for he then brought us a very nice Rhine-type wine and we chatted with him about Australian grape varieties over lunch.

All too soon I had to become a proper travelling scientist again, a little fragile on the early morning of my departure because we had been up into the small hours on the previous evening, after a slap-up dinner (hosted by me) and a visit to a nightclub. But doziness probably helped me survive the rather bumpy three-hour flight to Adelaide, which was to be my last port of call before returning to Britain. By early afternoon when I reached Adelaide's Strathmore Hotel, colonial style and balconied, I was more or less myself and, happy to have some spare time before my visits next day, I did some present shopping and sight-seeing. I marvelled at the black swans on the river (I bitterly resent the fact that, by the 1990s, black swans have been imported all over Europe and are now quite commonplace: another little travellers' joy has been ruined). Adelaide was a centre for immigrant Italian-Australians: the shops in the town centre were quite European in appearance, with salamis and cheeses and pavement displays of greengrocery; more Italian than 'Strine' was being spoken in the streets.

The Strathmore's breakfast menu was classic Australian. Among a huge choice of dishes was steak with two eggs, but even after an early night my effete digestion could only face my regular travelling diet of orange juice, toast and tea.

Whenever clusters of people move around, whether on package holidays, tours or scientific conferences, there is always someone who is late or gets things wrong. I consider myself to be efficient; I never thought I should be the awkward one. But at Adelaide I was. My host was Bob Morton, of the Waite Institute of Agriculture. My visit had been finalised at Canberra, but it transpired that he had expected me to turn up the day before, and to stay at a different hotel. Apparently a dinner for me and Egami had been arranged. I knew nothing of this; my stay at the Strathmore had been booked for me from England. I was duly contrite, was forgiven, and embarked upon my programme of visits and talks within the Waite Institute. All went well, with me shepherded from group to group by Bob, until something cropped up and he had to ask the Director of the Waite's Wine Research Institute to take me to lunch. We became engrossed in conversation about wine, and he invited me to come and see his laboratories and procedures, which I found most interesting. Be informed, by the way, that we tasted not a drop. However, an hour or more later a breathless Bob appeared at the door, having been searching for me all over the place: apparently the Chemistry and Animal Husbandry departments were still on my programme and expecting me. I never did get to see Animal Husbandry; I do hope they were not disappointed, but I do not think we should have had a great deal to talk about. Again I was forgiven; Bob had arranged a pleasant dinner at his home for Egami, me and some of his colleagues.

Next day I visited the University of Adelaide's Biochemistry and Microbiology Departments. I believe they had had eight or nine scientific tourists since the Canberra meeting and were getting tired of us. Nevertheless, they were civil but brief - which suited me. As I wrote a few paragraphs ago, these duty conversations between visitors who are not really interested and hosts who would rather get on with their work are the bane of scientific travel. However, and this is the sort of thing which negates what I have written, among those I was scheduled to have a word with proved to be biochemist Dr A B 'Sandy' Roy, whom I had long wanted to meet because he studied certain enzymes which interact with sulphates. These are called sulphatases; they react with sulphates in organic compounds. I had not found them in sulphate reducers, which attack inorganic sulphates; nevertheless it was likely that the sulphate reducers used something of the sort.

Happily Dr Roy decided that our discussions would be much more civilised if conducted in his car, driving round the countryside, with which plan I heartily agreed. It was a most agreeable way of spending a couple of hours of the late afternoon and I suppressed a guilty feeling that I ought perhaps to be at the Waite's Animal Husbandry Department. Back at his home for sherry, after a most enjoyable tour and talk, I discovered that Sandy was alone: his wife was still in hospital having just produced their first baby, a daughter. So I invited him to dine with me at the Strathmore, where we drank the wine of one of the vineyards we had driven past, Chateau Reynella. As I recall, it was a fairly old vintage, rather unusual among Australian wines in those days; certainly it was one of the best Australian clarets I tasted on my tour.

It was a very suitable end to my tour round the sub-continent, much less exhausting than my 1957 race round the USA, thanks partly to my earlier experience but equally to the hospitality of Gordon and Jackie Samuels. But my adventures were not over. The next day I set about my return to Britain, this time in my capacity as an employee of MRE. The RAF would fly me in a Comet, one of the earliest types of jet aircraft, from Edinburgh airfield outside Adelaide, and next morning an official car duly came to the Strathmore to collect me.

I found myself part of a flight in which everyone seemed to know each other: serving personnel, relatives and offspring commuting between Australia and Britain. I was introduced to a pleasant adolescent schoolboy, Nigel, on his way back to school in England, with whom I would apparently share accommodation at the overnight stop-over near Singapore.

A ride in a real jet in 1959 was an experience rarely vouchsafed to civilians. I was terrified as the machine took off at a steep angle like a rocket, and hurtled towards Darwin. We were there in a surprisingly short time and rocketed once more towards Singapore. As we approached Malaysia things got bumpy and I began to feel very uneasy. Then, suddenly, came the one thing everyone dreads: the aircraft jolted a couple of times and then plummeted like a pancake. It did not point its nose down; it just fell, leaving my stomach somewhere up in the sky and my heart in my mouth. Quite as suddenly there was a crashing sound and sensation as if we had hit ground - but we hadn't. We had just bottomed out of a downdraught. It was incredible to me that the aircraft survived the bump. (I later learned, and happily did not know then, that all our Comets were by that date showing signs of metal fatigue.) Soon afterwards the pilot emerged from the cabin and walked down the aisle. "No casualties?" he asked merrily. It transpired that we had touched the edge of a monsoon.

Changi, the RAF's transit stop near Singapore, had been wartime Japanese prison camp. It was now a bazaar for the sale of duty-free Asian clothing, watches, transistor radios, binoculars, cameras and other optical equipment to its itinerants, in shops where you were given a Coca-Cola to soften you up the moment you crossed the threshold. They had marvellous bargains. Advised by the more experienced Nigel, I bought Mary a tiny transistor radio - in those days something of a rarity. The mess was a stark but fascinating room, with a large, slow-moving electric fan on the ceiling and lizards on the wall; supper was ghastly (cauliflower soup, fish, an orange and condensed milk); the overnight accommodation was cell-like, with a shower but no soap or towel. It was exhaustingly hot, too hot to sleep, so I did not mind the 04:00 call for our 05:30 flight out. Before we embarked an RAF Sergeant assembled us on the airfield and called the roll, to ensure that we were all present.

"Wing Commander Postage?" I heard.

A double take from me, and then, "Present."

Of course, I realised, as a Principal Scientific Officer at MRE, my equivalent RAF rank was indeed Wing Commander. On the ground I probably out-ranked the pilot. And Postage is a common misreading of my name (I have a collection of at least 28 others). For some months, back at MRE, I was known as Wing Commander Postage.

At least we had had time for a quick breakfast at Changi. We were also served breakfast on the Comet as we flew to Katumazaha in Ceylon where, because we were flying due west and the clock had gone back two hours, we arrived neatly in time for our third, not unwelcome, breakfast. Then there was a long flight to Aden, during which a snack meal of indeterminate character was served and the clock slipped back another couple of hours. In Aden it was 12:00 noon local time and 125° Fahrenheit, so hot that no question of a meal arose; no one had the energy to move. We were passed orange juice and dry biscuits in a decrepit lounge set in sandy desert, while Arabs peered at us through the unglazed windows. And there we remained, inert and passive, for an hour. When at last we re-embarked the aircraft was like an oven; in the 10 minutes it took us to take off and ascend to 1000 feet I soaked my shirt and its collar with sweat.

The aircrew had changed and they all had a wild look about them, but it went as the plane cooled down; apparently this was the effect of their having been stranded for 24 hours in Aden waiting for us. Our next stop was at El Adem in Libya, where I got a nostalgic glimpse of scrub desert, familiar from my 1950 excursion with Butlin, and was served a breakfast-like meal of bacon and eggs. Then we were off to Lyneham airfield in England. I managed to doze despite a garrulous lady who had joined us in Libya and I was somewhat revived by coffee and biscuits over Paris. My 30-hour day seemed to have consisted almost entirely of breakfasts. Luxuriously, there was an official car waiting at Lyneham to deliver Wing Commander Postage, with cuddly koala, kangaroo and platypus for the children, home to Salisbury at 02:00 local time. My biological clock took some days to adjust to Greenwich Mean Time.

Chicago, 1961

Conferences such as the Australian gathering, which was small, highly selected and specialized, are the most effective ways of exchanging and collating scientific information; they provide enlightenment and stimulation to all involved. They are also very hard work: the oral presentations are usually too good to miss, the discussions well informed and constructive, and the conversations during breaks and intervals straighten out one's thinking. After a couple of days, however, even the most enthusiastic brain saturates, which is why wise organisers leave long gaps between sessions and break up the programme about mid week with a big touristic excursion. It compels participants to think about something else for a while - or perhaps just sleep.

In contrast to that intellectual intensity, the annual meeting of the Society of American Bacteriologists (later to become the American Society for Microbiology) to which I was summoned a couple of years later, in 1961, was an intellectual mish-mash. The visit came about because the US Office of Naval Research (ONR) sponsored a symposium on marine microbes in association with the bacteriologists' meeting. Sulphate-reducing bacteria are important in the sea and in marine sediments; I had published some work on how they adjusted to the saltiness of sea, so they invited me.

Henderson, albeit far from enthusiastic about my continued attachment to "sulphur bacteria", had no serious objection: the ONR would pay all my expenses and fly me over, my research was going well and I could safely leave things in the hands of Janet and John for the couple of weeks I needed to be away.

That is how I came, in mid April, to be flying backwards across the Atlantic from the US air base at Mildenhall, Suffolk, en route to Trenton, NJ, with a stop-off in Harman Airfield, Newfoundland. Backwards? Yes. The seats in US Military Air Transport Service aircraft, on which the ONR had booked me, all faced the tail. Apparently this arrangement was normal: it greatly diminished whiplash injury if a crash or an abrupt forced landing occurred. I am told it ought to be adopted by ordinary commercial airlines, but they are convinced that their passengers would not stand for it.

The aircraft was full of US servicemen and their families returning 'on furlough' from Europe, mostly from Germany, all delighted to be going home. The trip was like a rather restrained family party.

My glimpse of Newfoundland was a dead loss: there was a wall of snow too high to see over on either side of the path leading to the transit lounge. I was told that they had just had 194 inches of snow.

My visits to the USA and Australia had taught me wisdom. I had planned to arrive a day early, so I was able to do a little leisurely sightseeing, even to visit Chicago's superb art gallery, in between resting to allow my biological clock to catch up with the time zone. By the time the participants began to assemble later on my second day, I was in good form to greet old friends and meet new ones.

The whole meeting was held in a huge Chicago hotel, The Morrison, with a vast auditorium with a balcony surrounding it, numerous smaller 'conference' rooms which were used for paper presentations, and a gigantic foyer with shops and counters, including a big coffee shop, which offered a 24-hour service of fast food. It housed over 2000 delegates; a few stayed elsewhere in Chicago. I discovered that at night a watchman patrolled accommodation floors to ensure that everyone had locked their door - I had forgotten to lock mine. A relic from Chicago's gangster days, I innocently surmised.

The ONR symposium preceded the main Society meeting and was middling-to-good scientifically; some of the contributions were rather bland, but there was reasonably constructive discussion. I had been able to make a decent contribution out of some unpublished experiments Ochynski had done under my guidance at Teddington, rounded off (in some degree) by some extra ones I had done 'secretly' at MRE in between working on bacterial death. Henderson had obligingly turned a blind eye to my 'Sunday' experiments on sulphate reducers; Denis was aware of them and had even helped me to find an obscure piece of physical equipment which I needed.

Then came the main meeting, and I discovered that the contributed papers were its least important function. Most delegates, especially the young ones, were obliged to present a paper in order to get expenses from their funding bodies, but nobody felt any obligation to listen to them and they were very sparsely attended. (Contributed papers, I remind you, were a feature of all mid Twentieth-Century scientific meetings; they were later displaced by poster presentations). Instead, the foyer and corridors, which were liberally provided with comfortable seating, were abuzz with microbiologists talking and gesturing. Some were exchanging gossip; some exchanging research results, or concealing them if a scientific rival was within earshot; some were setting up collaborative research projects. Above all, young microbiologists were seeking new or better jobs, and older ones - deans and professors from universities, or representatives of industry - were sounding out potential candidates for positions. Sometimes they were actually interviewing them. The meeting had become a vast labour exchange, and this was completely accepted: there was a huge notice board advertising new posts in the foyer, constantly being consulted.

Well, informality is a fine thing and so is the American urge towards self-advancement. But it certainly ruined the plenary lecture, also sponsored by the ONR. That lecture was dedicated to an invited European scientist, and it opened the conference. On this occasion it was given by Jacques Senez in the large auditorium, but so noisy was the background chatter that only those close to him could hear a word. (It was, in truth, an example of flagrant communal bad manners. Many years later, when invited to give the ONR lecture myself, I have to say that memories of the unfortunate Senez were a major reason for my refusing.)

However, the meeting was by no means a scientific write-off. There were a dozen or so symposia, miniature versions of the Australian meeting, given by invited speakers, and many were very good indeed. Moreover, for me the 'chatter' was very rewarding, because I met and talked to a couple of dozen scientists whom I knew from publications or correspondence but had never met, and I also renewed acquaintance with numerous old friends from my 1957 peregrination round the USA, and from international congresses.

The Morrison Hotel was like a kind of enclosed, futuristic metropolis. Everything one might want - doctors, travel agents, medicines, food etc - was available in the foyer and there seemed to be no actual reason why anyone should wish to emerge. To go out into the street at night was, for an overseas visitor, to enter another bizarre universe. The senses were assaulted by bright, moving lights advertising food joints, shops and cinemas, and by cars, trucks and taxis weaving about with headlights ablaze, and lights saying 'Walk' or 'Don't walk'. Police cars, sirens screaming, zoomed past, pedestrians bustled along with their heads down.

One evening I met in the foyer Professor Sebastiano Genovese, from a marine biology station in Sicily. We had corresponded about sulphur bacteria and this was his first trip to the USA. I suggested we dine together. He agreed, but with one stipulation: that we remain in the hotel. He could not bear to go outside; the flashing lights, noise, bustle and movement were too much for him. The Morrison Hotel had become his bolt-hole, the only place where he could feel secure. I concurred, and we had a pleasant, relaxed meal in the coffee shop.

On another occasion I saw in a local paper that there was a jazz club some 24 blocks away so, one evening I set off on foot, thinking it a trivial distance, a straight walk to the East according to a map I found in the foyer. Very soon I found myself in an ill-lit zone of the City, utterly silent, with no traffic and no one about, surrounded by towering, totally dark buildings. Down the far end of a street someone was staggering; I heard a distant shout. The hairs on my neck stiffened like a tom-cat; I walked on a bit, saying "nonsense" to myself, but gradually realised that blocks were much bigger units than I had thought, and that I had another twenty or so to go. I turned back, and covered the return journey to the hotel pretty quickly, scared by absolutely nothing but the silence, the stillness, for there was no traffic at all, and that weird shout. How right, in retrospect, I was! In those days I did not know, but I soon learned, that one did not walk alone at night away from the lights of downtown Chicago: one took a cab.

But I did hear some good jazz. On another evening one of the few coloured microbiologists in the USA, whom I knew as 'Camp' Campbell and who worked for some industrial corporation, took me and a couple of other jazz enthusiasts to the Sutherland Hotel on the South Side. This proved to be in a black quarter. Pianist Jodie Christian was playing with a quartet, which included a be-bop trumpeter whose name I did not discover. It was not my favourite kind of jazz, though I enjoyed it. But I found the environment less encouraging. I sensed that we were tolerated because our host was black. I, who had genuinely had no sense of colour prejudice in my earlier life, had become painfully aware that it existed, and was coming to feel it in reverse. Salutary, I suppose. Another evening I heard Bob Scobey's band playing Dixieland jazz, by then very popular but rather routine to my ear.

A curiosity. Sometime during the meeting I came across Sister Regina Lanigan of St. Bonaventure University, a Franciscan nun to whom I had explained the workings of the spectrophotometer on my visit in 1957. She asked to discuss some experimental results with me and invited me see her notes in her room in the Morrison Hotel. I duly went at the appointed time, and found her quite twittery. It dawned on me that she was fussed at having an unchaperoned man in her room. However, we discussed her work; I think I made some useful suggestions and, as I left, she very kindly blessed me. I still hope her blessing will count in my favour if I am mistaken in my atheism.

Yet another surprise. Claude ZoBell invited me to dine with him and his wife in the penthouse restaurant at the top of the hotel, 48 floors up in the sky. With us was a microbiologist consultant to the oil industry. It was called the Carousel Restaurant, and the waitresses wore extremely scanty skirts, tiny pinafores and black fishnet stockings. They were meant to look '*ooh-la-la*' Parisian, which would have been lovely had they been young and beautiful but, as in a drawing by George Grosz, they were all rather old and scrawny.

Anyway, all was going well until the room began to move gently. I had a terrible feeling of nausea: was it an earthquake? Was I having stroke? Was the building collapsing? But no one else seemed to notice, so I clutched the table with both hands and became silent and, no doubt, pale. Slowly I understood: we were in a rotating panoramic restaurant. Every ten minutes or so the whole room rotated by a few degrees so the diners got different views over Chicago as their meal progressed. No one had thought to tell me, and I had missed the clue of its name - I wonder how Genovese would have fared had he ventured up there?

Incidentally, I knew that ZoBell was a Mormon. Our fellow guest did not know, and made several anti-Mormon jokes. Altogether it was not the most unstressful of dinner parties for me.

Oh dear, there were so many oddities. Such as another evening with a gang of younger scientists at a German-American diner, where everyone drank American beer out of steins and ate steaks or sausages, and both customers and waiters sang dog-German songs while a Tonmeister pointed out the words on a huge board: "Ist das nicht gut für Schweine Stew?" Diners, loud: "Ja, das ist gut für Schweine Stew." Again, three French Canadians wanted to discuss sulphate-reducing bacteria with Senez and me. We went to one of their rooms and, aided by glasses of bourbon whiskey, did so - in French. That was fine, my French was adequate. But Senez's contempt for their Canadian French knew no bounds: "*Ces pauvres cons qui pensent qu'ils sachent parler Français!*" he exploded when we had left their company.

The conference's informality paid off for me. Over drinks I met another fellow researcher on sulphate-reducing bacteria, Leon Campbell. He was a youngish (my age group) cigar-chewing Texan who worked at the University of Illinois at Urbana, some 100 miles south of Chicago. About three years earlier he had made an important discovery, one which made sense of some perplexing observations I had made before I left Teddington. The story illustrates rather nicely how scientists can innocently delude themselves, and others.

Hot and cold bugs

Since the 1920s, microbiologists had known that sulphate-reducing bacteria could grow in very hot water at between 55° and 75° Celsius. These temperatures are too hot for normal living things to bear. The heat-tolerant sulphate reducers could be found in hot springs, compost heaps, central heating systems and so on. Not all sulphate reducers grew in such hot places, and those that did grew very, very slowly, if at all, at ordinary temperatures. So the question arose, were the hot-water ones, called thermophiles, the same species as the temperate ones, called mesophiles? In the 1930s, scientists working in Holland published evidence that they were the same because, using the sort of training process I had exploited with Hinshelwood, they could 'train' mesophiles to grow at temperatures favoured by thermophiles, and train thermophiles to grow at low temperatures. Both Bunker and Butlin had repeated these experiments and agreed with the findings.

I must add that there was something very odd about all the work: the thermophiles formed spores but the mesophiles never did; however, Professor Starkey, working with the Dutch in the mid 1930s, had evidence that spore formation could be gained or lost by training.

Almost all my work at Teddington had been with mesophilic strains, but we had had some cultures of thermophiles. I could not find any cytochrome C3 in them, nor its companion desulfoviridin. I asked myself, would they learn to make these if I trained them to become mesophiles? Equally, would a mesophile lose the ability to make cytochrome C3 when trained to be a thermophile? Such changes would strike most microbiologists as quite extraordinary, but so was the reported ability of the two types of organism to acquire or suppress spore formation. I set about a programme of training cultures to find out.

My cultures simply would not train. Even strains which Butch, or to be accurate Molly Adams and Margaret Thomas, had used a decade or so earlier did not perform. I went on trying for several months. What could be going on? Then Leon Campbell's paper was published: he had used serology, a technique which is much used in medical bacteriology to identify pathogens, and had shown quite unequivocally that his thermophilic and mesophilic sulphate reducers had nothing in common serologically. They were quite different species. Moreover, the thermophiles were identical with a food-spoilage thermophile called *Clostridium nigrificans*, which was well known in the food industry: it caused a kind of spoilage in canned food called 'sulphur stinker' spoilage - a significant name in retrospect.

To cut a long story short, I got myself a couple of authentic cultures of *C. nigrificans* and assured myself that he was right: they did reduce sulphates. I re-read the old papers, I checked Molly's notes, and Bill Bunker let me look at his, and light dawned. The earlier researchers had been mistaken: it was a question of cross-contamination. In the thirties microbiologists were not as expert at getting pure cultures of sulphate reducers as Molly later became, and everything pointed to the workers in Holland having started their training experiments with populations that were mixtures of both thermophiles and mesophiles. Molly and Margaret's own cultures were probably pure, and Bunker's may well have been, but their tests were done very casually because they had no reason to doubt the earlier work. In particular, they did not check whether their 'trained' strains actually went on growing at their new temperatures. In retrospect I could be confident that they were dead or dying.

I imagine I would have got there in the end had the Teddington Group's disbanding not loomed, but Leon Campbell had solved the enigma. I mentioned earlier that Molly had isolated, and we had together identified, a new type of sulphate reducer which was a mesophile but which formed spores - it was the one I showed to Van Niel in 1957. It too fell into place: at MRE I had been able to check it by serology and it seemed to be closely related to Leon's *C. nigrificans*. But it was definitely not a thermophile.

We had much to talk about and, as I shall tell later, our contact was very productive. Among other things we were able join forces and confirm, by the rather crude DNA analyses available in those days, that the thermophiles and mesophiles were genetically unrelated and that, on the other hand, Molly's and my mesophilic spore-former was indeed related to *C. nigrificans*. I was well pleased by all these developments.

New York again

After the Chicago conference dispersed I fitted in a few days in New York, staying briefly with my cousin Jane Abraham and family who lived outside the City at Great Neck, Long Island. I also visited New Haven and Boston to talk to various scientists about death or sulphate reducers. I got to Manhattan a couple of times to feed my other obsession: I heard trombonist Jack Teagarden's Sextet at the Village Vanguard Club - another legendary figure; I checked on the Metropole again (it was less exciting this time) and went to Eddie Condon's Club on East 56th Street, where I had a rather overawed chat with another great trombonist, Vic Dickenson. I bought him a drink, and felt greatly privileged. Afterwards, at about 2 am, I walked diagonally across New York back to my hotel at 50th and Broadway with no incident other than someone trying to sell me a ring on a street corner. Imagine doing that in the 1990s! Next day I even managed to squeeze in some present shopping for Mary and the children at New York's Macy's before my return to England. Altogether it was a more relaxed and enjoyable visit to the USA than my 1957 trip had been, and my morale and health were good throughout - largely because I had learned my lesson and left myself time to spare between my commitments.

A coda

Cytochrome C3 had a lot of mileage left in it yet. Early in 1962 I received a transatlantic telephone call from my new friend Leon Campbell, then a Professor of Microbiology at the University of Illinois at Urbana, Illinois. If I could get leave from MRE, he could finance a year's visiting Professorship at Urbana; could I come?

I was both delighted and terrified. I had never taught anyone, and was scared of lecturing; how could I possibly do what was required of a Professor? Yet the opportunity to live in the USA for a while, and to finish off some of the leftovers from my sulphate-reducing days, was irresistible. It was a great honour, but would Henderson stand for it?

The short answer was no. But he agreed that I might go for three months if I could leave Janet and John with a precise research programme. I could, and Leon agreed to a shortened visit. In the event, I extended my visit to seven months. To go with my family and live in the Middle West of the USA, to become, albeit briefly, part of a new community was a fascinating and delightful experience for all of us and deserves its own chapter.

CHAPTER SEVENTEEN

A home in the West

So, letters were exchanged, travel arrangements were made, luggage was assembled and trunks were sent on ahead (necessary because our hand luggage had to be as light as the exigencies of three young daughters - then aged four, six and eight - permitted). Farewells were bidden, in person and by telephone. Excitement mounted and, on Thursday September 6, 1962, a kind neighbour drove us from our Salisbury home to Southampton docks. There we embarked on the Queen Elizabeth, Joanna, our youngest, solemnly wearing a cardboard Huckleberry Hound mask.

Airlines had by then become the carriers of choice to the New World for single, business or professional travellers, but they were still not an option for a family, unless one was seriously rich, and transatlantic liners still departed every few days with a more-or-less economic quota of passengers. And for a small family they had great practical advantages: they were palaces of delight for children, with their playrooms and child-care facilities, elevators, parties with prizes, cinema shows, plentiful food and relative freedom of movement.

The voyage lasted for six days. It had occasional lows because Mary was a poor sailor, and spent much of the time prostrated by seasickness. Also the children, over-stimulated perhaps, occasionally became fractious, but it was a memorable experience for all.

As the morning of the following Tuesday progressed the Manhattan skyline appeared on the horizon, to grow gradually to its awe-inspiring height: an overwhelming spectacle which few travellers see today. Disembarkation, delayed by a longshoremen's strike, was slow, but the customs officers were friendly. Everyone had to 'tip' a longshoreman $2 to recover their hold luggage - a flagrant scam about which we had been warned - and such was the crowd that Mary, now recovered on dry land, had to walk some distance into New York to find and bring back a taxi while I guarded the luggage and children. However, by late afternoon we were being driven between the skyscrapers of Manhattan to the Commodore Hotel into which Cunard had booked us. At a stoplight a group of tawny-faced young boys caught sight of the trio of pretty young English girls in the cab and pressed against the window, making kissing and swooning gestures at our bewildered daughters. "We start young in New York," said our Puerto-Rican driver amiably.

Our hotel room proved to be a dismayingly expensive suite. Moreover, on checking on our train, scheduled for next day, I found that it was fully booked, which drastically scrambled my travel plans. Happily I also learned that one was going to Chicago late that evening, and had a sleeper reservation available. A quick change of plan, a $10 'use rate' fee to the hotel to buy our way out of our suite, check forwarding of our trunks, send a cable to Leon Campbell, grab a quick sandwich-type meal in a nearby Automat (a room one side of which was a wall of glass-fronted slots with a fantastic variety of ready-to-eat food in them, to the delight of the children), and by ten-thirty that evening we were in a family sleeper compartment on a train, shortly to depart westwards. The kindly Negro steward had solved the problem of which child should have the top bunk by having them draw straws, and soon all, even the anxious father, were fast asleep, lulled by the train's gentle movement.

The Great American Railroad System is wonderful, and the way the population of the USA allowed it almost to vanish was one of the minor tragedies of the 20th century. They were a major part of their country's heritage, for it was railroads that opened up the continent during the 19th century. The huge locomotives were - still are - marvels of engineering, and the carriages are luxurious by European standards. Yet even in the 1960s the railroad system was in economic decline and fast disappearing. But our train, on a route still much used, was a delight - and our cabin was a miracle of compression. While we had our breakfast in the diner car, the steward converted our bedroom into an air-conditioned 'parlour', from which we, still dozy from our travels, could gaze at the passing countryside all day and get a sense of the sheer vastness of the USA. We had passed through Buffalo in the night, but we saw great plains, then the vast sprawl of Cleveland, and we were for long stretches of time beside water: Lakes Erie and later Michigan. In the late afternoon, one time zone away from New York, we arrived in Chicago.

To step out of our air-conditioned compartment onto the platform was to enter an oven: the heat and humidity were breathtaking. I thought I understood why: as we walked past the huge locomotive that had hauled us so far, it was radiating heat. But I was wrong. The whole of Chicago was hot, like a sauna, in the warmth of the early fall. But we adapted, and duly caught the Illinois Central Railroad, far less wonderful than the New York-Chicago service, for a rather cramped ride to Urbana-Champaign. Our journey was eased by a pleasant couple of fellow passengers, apparently from the University of Illinois, who pointed out scenic wonders to the children. Two hours or so later, after travelling through hectare after hectare of corn stubble, we arrived, to be met by Leon Campbell and Ralph Wolfe, bearing a tiny 25 cent bottle of 'Mogen David' wine as a joke gift to tease me about my fondness for good wine. They had installed us in the Lincoln Lodge Motel for a few days where, thanks to air-conditioning, we all flopped out once more, me intermittently a prey to restless anxieties.

Next morning was Thursday, and our priority was to settle ourselves into the Midwest for the duration of our stay. We needed to find ourselves a home, a car (there was no public transport and distances were far too great for walking or cycling), a school for the older two girls and other domestic details, as well as to install myself with the University's administration, fix up pay, insurance, and so on. Ralph was a tower of strength in these exercises; he acted as guide and chauffeur. His first act was to take me to the University, fix up my salary details. It transpired that, because payment was monthly in arrears, I should get no pay for six weeks, though an advance could be, and was, arranged for slightly over two weeks hence. The few dollars I had brought from England, already seriously depleted, would have been manifestly inadequate. So Ralph, unsurprised, took me straight to a bank to take out a substantial bank loan.

"This is the American way, John," he explained, as my puritanical reservations about a loan surfaced. "You must learn to live on credit."

How right he was. The bank employee with whom I was arranging an account took down details civilly enough and finally said:

"And how much will you be depositing, Dr Postgate?"

"Nothing," I replied, "I should like a loan of $1500."

He brightened up immediately. "Certainly, Doctor."

And so it was fixed. How different from the UK, where even a small overdraft then required a headmasterish interview with the bank manager! In the event, I was able to pay off the loan out of my salary by the first of January.

By Thursday we had found a nice-looking three-bedroom ranch-style house in South Prospect, a street in a suburb of Champaign. (Urbana and Champaign are contiguous communities and I was never clear where one ended and the other began). Ralph said the rent was too high but I had no real choice; I agreed to it. It would be available in a couple of days and on Saturday morning we left our Motel and moved in. I said it was "nice". So it looked, outside; but inside it proved to be a tip, filthy with the sort of academic squalor one can encounter in University towns all over the world. The oven, refrigerator, cutlery and utensils had a patina of grease, and the sink was dirty. Discarded garments, or parts thereof, turned up in unexpected places. Dirty shower/bathroom; dust everywhere, vacuum cleaner full; rubbish still in the kitchen trashcan - and so on. Mary and I embarked on a high-speed spring-clean and were dropping with hunger by the time we walked to a nearby supermarket to find food for lunch. But it all came together in time; we had found a nest with breathtaking speed and were very happy there once we had cleaned up, bought and borrowed essentials, and our trunks had arrived - two weeks late.

Accounts of hard times grappling with domestic fittings in strange places can be tedious, and I shall not record all the minor things that went wrong, or just askew. But one episode had its slapstick side. For the first time in our lives we had an electric dishwasher. Wonderful, we thought, for we had seen them in advertisements. One had to programme it - and there were no instructions. Crucially, it needed non-foaming detergent, and we did not know that detail. The first time we used it, we filled it with greasy dishes and cutlery, added some laundry detergent and sat back to relax. It gurgled and snorted gratifyingly, but very soon froth came out of the front and spread over the kitchen floor. We had nothing at all with which to stem the rising flood of foam, so we tore down some of the curtains to contain it. We were in the grip of the machine. How to stop it? I pressed various buttons and only succeeded in reprogramming it to do a second run. Another, if lesser, flood of froth ensued. But eventually it all ended. The dishes were now clean, and the curtains had needed a wash anyway - we came to love it, just as we came to love the deep freeze in the garage. After our return to England we obtained both as soon as we could.

We settled reasonably easily into Midwestern domestic life. The Welcome Wagon came, an unashamedly commercial but pleasing enterprise, delighting the children with its gift of six free 'donuts', and me with its free plastic fly swat. Morning television was fine for children; programmes were adjusted to age, becoming increasingly young as the older ones went off to school. We enjoyed the open plan, spacious street with cornfields in the distance; came to recognise the dawn wail of a distant train, which acted as an alarm clock for us. The neighbours and assistants in the supermarket were friendly. The local school welcomed our children and they formed friends almost at once, despite their alien accents. Selina, our eldest, retained her English accent throughout the visit; Mary overheard one child say to another as they waited for her outside the house - and you must imagine this a childish Midwestern drawl: "Selina's OK, but she only just came and don't speak English so good."

Lucy, on the other hand, soon acquired the Midwestern inflection, and she lost it just as rapidly when we returned to England.

The hunt for a suitable family car was proving less

successful. Ralph and I had visited a couple of used car dealers, but after about ten days the son-in-law of a professional baby-sitter (another valuable feature of US academia: fee 50 cents per hour, minimum four hours) came round with a choice of two for us. We fell for a Ford Fairlane automatic with a Thunderbird engine - a white, sportive gas-guzzler that served us marvellously well. Mary had day-to-day charge of it and would ferry me to and from the University as necessary. It cost $400, which by British standards was amazingly cheap, and was in good condition except that its speedometer needed fixing. Automobiles are so much a part of ordinary life in the USA that used cars are generally cheaper and more trustworthy than in the UK and odd jobs, such as fixing a speedometer, can usually be done while you wait. I could use my British driving licence, but car insurance was expensive: I was a foreigner and my driving was suspect - probably rightly, because Europeans then, as now, drove aggressively and much too fast. Midwestern drivers, even most students, were models of sobriety, obedience to signs, and common sense. However, after a brisk drive round the town and University precinct in the company of David Tempest, a fellow visiting scientist from England, I was ready for the US life.

The laboratory

The Microbiology Department of the University of Illinois occupied much of a large building called Burrill Hall, and Leon's laboratory was somewhere on its upper floors. It took me several weeks to find my way around the building, but I soon learned the essentials: the routes from the car park to the lab, to the library, to the Union Building. The working hours kept by the researchers were something of a shock to me, conditioned as I had been to a nine-to-five routine for the past dozen years. Leon was in the laboratory by 8 am, and his senior assistant, working for his doctorate, would have arrived soon after seven. Work, interrupted by coffee breaks, teaching duties, lunch at noon and fairly frequent seminars, went on until about 4:30 pm, when most Americans would return home for dinner, only to return at about six and be there until 10 or 11. They would be in the lab for most of Saturday, unless a big ball game was being shown on TV, and for much of Sunday, too. The upshot was that everyone worked slowly. I found it impossible to adapt, but my new friends were understanding. After all (I assume they thought), I was new and settling in, I was subject to the exigencies of a young family, there were many new things for me to see, and anyway the British had a reputation for not working very hard. I felt quite awkward at first, as I bowled in regularly at about 8:30 am and, though I left about 5 pm, I rarely appeared in the evenings and my weekend appearances would only be for the odd hour or so. But I began to feel better as I realised that because I had the habit of working fast, I was getting as much research done as anyone. Indeed, one afternoon Leon's senior doctoral student confided in me that he envied my working style. Sometimes, he said, he would find himself working steadily and unable to think exactly what he was doing. He might find himself setting up an experiment that he had done a few days ago, having completely forgotten both the fact that he had done it and the result. Or he would think up a bright idea for a new approach, only to discover from his notes, too late, that he had tried it already.

It is perfectly true that a tired mind can play all sorts of tricks, one of which is to erase memories completely (even in the young). I remembered the lesson several years later when a graduate student of my own was enthusiastically overworking and beginning to enter a repetitive cycle mentally - in his case I insisted he take a three-week holiday and banned him from late-night work in the lab. He cheated a bit, but the message got through and his thesis was excellent. Years later he was elected a Fellow of the Royal Society.

Another unfamiliar feature of life in the lab was the abundance of seminars. Most lunchtimes there would be a seminar on some aspect of microbiological science, given by a researcher from the lab or a visiting scientist. (I use the term 'microbiological science' rather than 'microbiology' because the seminar might be on any topic, which had a bearing, remote or immediate, on microbiology. Genetics, biochemistry, marine science, ecology, straight chemistry, pathology and so on were all grist to the seminar mill.)

Postgraduates were especially encouraged to come along, so they were well attended - *habitués would* bring sandwiches and eat during the talk - but I wondered how much of this deluge of information sunk in. My postgraduate colleague's opinion was "very little". More senior staff, including me, were selective simply to avoid being 'seminared out'. So around noon a group of us would more often go for lunch to a local café - I have forgotten its name; we called it 'The Greasy Spoon' and we would have such National delicacies as a hamburger with trimmings, followed by apple pie *à la mode*, washed down with coffee or Coca-Cola. Today widely dismissed as junk food, in 1962 I found it a good and highly nutritious diet.

I settled into my own routine and integrated myself reasonably well into the pattern of Leon's research team. It was a pleasure to be back among the sulphate-reducing bacteria, with their (to me) homely smell of bad eggs; I got a few experimental themes under way, and made some positive progress, and was able to relax a little from my inevitable visitor's tension and look around me.

Leon and Ralph

Leon Campbell was a big man. A Texan with a slow drawl, he thought before he spoke, and what he said was usually cogent, and often decisive. He was not one for quicksilver repartee, but he missed nothing and had a great enjoyment of irony. In common with several of my new friends at the University, he seemed to find my Englishness a source of constant entertainment - not just my accent and idioms but also the way I worked. As I have indicated, I tended to work as fast as possible, to get an experiment set up as quickly as I could, ignoring or putting off interruptions as best I could; sometimes I would make a mistake, swear, and have to start all over again. Leon would work slowly and deliberately, chewed cigar at the ready, seemingly welcoming interruptions, and get it right first time. Some said he was tough, even severe, in teaching and administration, but I found him easy-going, helpful and patient - as well as sensitive, especially about his own scientific achievements. He had been greatly pleased by the fact that I had independently confirmed, and acknowledged, his rationalisation of the thermophilic types of sulphate-reducing bacteria. He was a friendly and generous host. As well as being almost inseparable from a fat cigar, he displayed a tremendous capacity for laboratory-brewed coffee. Leon later became a leading light of the American Society for Microbiology, an Editor of that Society's Journal, and the President of a University in Delaware.

Ralph Wolfe, my co-host, was as complete a contrast as you could imagine. A thin, wiry Virginian, quick of movement and thought, he was not surprised by my Englishness, having spent two years on a sabbatical with Sidney Elsden in Sheffield. He was certainly one for quicksilver repartee, and we often enjoyed a sort of sparring conversation which would have Leon chiding us for "talking all that malarkey." He seemed to me to be a bundle of nerves at times, but so was I, so that made for fellow feeling.

Like Leon, Ralph was generous, hospitable and immensely helpful. He was a dedicated scientist; he told me once that he had never read a novel. Some said he was very secretive, because he had had some of his research pirated by a rival research group a year or two before I came, but the only inkling I had of that was his cynicism about openness in science, which, sadly, he communicated to at least two of his graduate students. But the pressure of US competitiveness must have been at the root of his refusal, to my surprise, to be a co-author or read the draft of my manuscript when I came to write up my research on the sulphate-reducer from that duck pond. "I'll read it when it is published," he said. So I am happy to record that he had his day a couple of decades later: he was a co-discoverer of the Archaea, a huge group (a 'Domain' in biologists' jargon) of living things, all microbes, all fundamentally different from all other living creatures. They are present-day representatives of a very primitive kind of life. That discovery kick-started a revolution in general biology.

News, politics and day-by-day affairs

The family joined in the life of a university town - the two older girls were still being made much of in their local school and the youngest was fast becoming a TV addict. Mary and I were invited to a University reception, and to little dinners with new friends and colleagues; the children were invited to parties and picnics. At weekends we drove to outlying parks and communities for family outings in the autumn sunshine. The rolling plains of Illinois were so vast and the skies so huge that one could see a storm brewing on the western horizon yet know that one still had four or five hours of fine weather to go on a trip and return. The weather was utterly predictable and the forecasts on TV were completely reliable: all so very different from our life in Britain.

As I hinted earlier, Urbana-Champaign was an inward-looking community, but it was by no means isolated from the world outside. Early in October the political talking point was a racial segregation crisis in Oxford, Mississippi. The University of Mississippi ("Ole Miss") had been obliged under the new anti-segregation laws to enrol a black student, one James Meredith. On his first morning, September 30, white segregationists had stormed the campus to block his enrolment and a riot had ensued, resulting in many injuries and three deaths. The Governor had sided with the segregationists and called in State Troopers. Kennedy had sent in Federal Marshals, who enforced Meredith's admission and enrolment. But the standoff continued and he had to be shadowed by Marshals to attend his courses. All this was widely reported nationally and internationally, and some TV interviews from Oxford, Mississippi, were shown on National TV networks, which I found horrifying. One southern senator broke down in tears on TV. A girl student (a "co-ed" in the jargon) was due to follow Meredith. Most depressing to me, a majority of the students of Ole Miss, who ought to have been relatively progressive, opposed Meredith's enrolment. But our local TV and the newspaper took a liberal view of it all, and indeed everyone I knew or overheard was on Kennedy/Meredith's side; the consensus seemed to be that this was a nasty hiccup on the road to a more civilised social order - though Urbana-Champaign then had fairly segregated housing and job opportunities, as well as a quota of racist bigots, even among the students.

But as if to cheer up the nation, on October 3 a US astronaut circled the earth five times before returning safely, in the right place, and with fuel to spare.

I became fascinated by Californian wines, which at the time were almost unknown in Britain. I write 'almost' because I remember advertisements in London Underground trains in the 1930s for 'Big Tree Burgundy', which could well have been Californian because its label carried a picture of a big tree with a tunnel cut through it, through which a car could be seen driving. Many years later I saw a giant sequoia in Northern California cut so that one do just that; naturally I drove through it.

My oenological father had no time for American wines of any kind and hardly acknowledged their existence, so I was amazed to discover how mistaken he was. The local liquor store kept a wide range of French, German and domestic wines, the latter labelled with varietal names such as cabernet sauvignon, pinot noir, zinfandel and chardonnay. Varietal names were then almost unknown (on labels) in Europe, where regional names were obligatory (except, curiously, in Alsace). Sadly the bottles were stored upright and illuminated in a store centrally heated to over 20°, so a pricey chateau-bottled French claret was often ruined by bad storage. However, the Californian wines were tough, and for a dollar one could buy a bottle of decent *ordinaire*; splash out $1.50 to 1.70 and you could buy a wine with a vintage year.

My investigations remained centred on the local liquor store, tasting branded names such as Louis Martini and Almaden; my diary records, for example, that Martini's cabernet sauvignon 1956 was comparable in style and quality to a middle range Pauillac, and favourable comparisons with European wines appear at intervals. I was so impressed that towards the end of my visit I telephoned Louis Martini's firm in California to ask if they would export a case to my father for me - but they felt unable to, which is probably just as well because it could have been a very expensive exercise. In fact a mild anti-alcohol ambience pervaded the whole of this mid Western community - it was the Bible Belt and drinking was still widely regarded as sinful. The University was 'dry', which means that, being an educational institution set up in the nineteenth century on Government land (a 'land-grant University'), no alcohol was allowed by statute on its campus. University receptions were teetotal, with fruit cup replacing the European *vin d'honneur*.

(Almost a decade later, having forgotten this detail, I would greatly embarrass Ralph. I had remembered that he had become fond of Guinness while spending a sabbatical year or two in England, so, arriving unexpectedly, on a passing visit to Urbana-Champaign, I went straight to a classroom where he was preparing for a lecture. I presented him with two bottles of Guinness, which I had carried across the Atlantic for him. Fortunately he and I were the only people in the classroom at that moment, because his response was rather as if I had slipped him a naughty magazine: he thanked me furtively and hid the bottles in a cupboard as quickly as he could.)

Most of my immediate hosts and colleagues had little interest in wine; they drank it rarely and in small amounts, probably only when entertaining a European. Nevertheless those friends would have the occasional beer, off campus, and usually provided a generous supply of bourbon whiskey and a bowl of 'rocks' (ice) when they entertained visiting scientists in their homes. I know that I educated some of my friends just a little, because where they might earlier have bought a costly and probably inferior French import to serve to wine-bibbing guests, they began to serve Californian wines instead.

Of course, there were a few real oenophiles around. A distinguished and senior biochemist, 'Gunny' Gunsalus, whom I met later, proved to be very well informed about Californian wines, their vineyards and vintages, and was politely, dismissive of the brands I had discovered for myself: there were even better ones to be had if one paid attention to the proprietors and vineyards, as well as vintages. He was quite right, as I later learned.

By the second week in October I had been in Urbana for little over a month, yet I found myself being headhunted. It came about this way. Ivor Robinson, an old friend of both Mary and me from our undergraduate days at Oxford, now had a Chair at Syracuse University on the East Coast. He came through Urbana and stayed with us on either side of a dash to give a seminar at Notre Dame University, South Bend, Indiana. We were delighted to see him, and consumed a fair quota of Californian wine while chewing over old times and recent politics. It transpired that he was in the process of abandoning Syracuse for an appointment at an Institute of Advanced Studies then in process of being founded in Dallas, Texas. It was to be an élite, research-based institute, providing only postgraduate teaching for the region, the South-Western Universities' answer to Princeton's Institute of Advanced Studies on the East Coast, which had undoubtedly set standards for its neighbouring universities. They were recruiting appropriate staff and they would welcome a reputable microbiologist: they had suggested that, during his visit, Ivor sound me out for a position there. It was well backed financially, mainly by the oil industry, it would pay astonishingly well by British standards, and the prospect of working in an academic *milieu* with substantial research time and minimal teaching duties was immensely attractive. Moreover, I no longer had any problem with élitism in education (I had reluctantly recognised that Britain's comprehensive education system, which I had once naively welcomed, was dumbing down rather than upgrading the educational standard of its pupils). In addition, I was already becoming uneasy about the biological warfare side of MRE's programme, though it had so far impinged hardly at all on my current research area. I was seriously attracted, but the approach was tentative and informal, and we left it that I would reflect on the matter.

A TV world

Life in Urbana-Champaign centred on the University. The talk of the town was the new Assembly Building then under construction, a monstrous structure which would seat 16,000 round a central arena for sports, concerts and the like. The arena could seat another 2000. Its progress was regularly reported by the local TV station. This was a comparable focus of community life as well as a regular source of conversation, criticism and opinion at the lab.

At home local TV was a boon for the children, as I have already said. Of an evening we followed ball games (I developed quite an enthusiasm for basketball matches, despite my normal disdain for sports of all kinds, and found myself rooting for the University's team). The local channel's news became a 'must'. It was divided into three five-minute items: local news, national news (which reached as far as Chicago) and world news (which rarely went beyond New York). It bemused us, and enhanced our sense of remoteness from Europe, yet once we understood how important a part of life in Urbana-Champaign it was it greatly helped us to feel part of the community. Naturally we also watched the national networks; we had the choice of NBC or CBS. We quite enjoyed personality programmes (Jackie Gleason and Jack Benny were stars of the period) but we found the general quality of programmes unimpressive (slick, certainly, but at the intellectual level of an eight-year old, I wrote in my diary). Moreover the constant interruptions by commercials soon wearied us - their quaintness of their banality quickly ceased to amuse - and for some time we felt quite affronted when a star or presenter would break into a commercial plug. I quote from my diary:

"Sunday 21st October... M points out that the commercials embarrass her, particularly Mr Roberts of the weather report when he switches to "Meadow Gold" Orange Juice or "Manhattan Rotisserized Coffee". I feel the US is too busy to realise the degradation involved in requiring people to behave like this - like those unfortunates who actually sing the commercials; but I am probably overgenerous. Jokes about cripples and midgets are still good for a laugh here ...a sort of medieval lack of identification with a performer exists which enables the sentimental American still to laugh at deformity and accept the degradation of commercial TV. Nothing really touches him."

A pompous reaction on our part? Yes. But back in Britain Mary and I had not been TV watchers: we had only possessed our own TV for a few months, largely for our children's amusement, so we were not yet inured to commercials - even Britain's regulated variety. For us, relief from commerce, and better overall quality, could be found in occasional serious or informative transmissions on the Public Service Channel, which was free of commercials - and it offered good jazz programmes now and again.

In fact our day-to-day judgements on US television were too austere. I say this because there were occasions when the American TV showed real, indeed outstanding, quality. The date October 24, 1962, is now but a minor footnote to the history of the Cold War between the Western democracies and the Soviet Union. It was the day on which the Cuban Crisis reached its peak.

The background was this. Fidel Castro's communist Cuba, supported by the Soviet Union, had long been at loggerheads with the USA, but had so far been little more than a minor irritant in the Cold war. However, a year or two earlier Cuba had granted the Soviet Union permission to build bases for long-range missiles on its territory. The US President, John F Kennedy, a Democrat, had naturally objected strongly. Nikita Khrushchev, the Soviet leader, paid no heed and, once the missile sites were ready, he started to ship the missiles to Cuba, escorted by Soviet warships. Kennedy responded with an Address to the Nation, explaining that he had ordered a naval blockade of Cuba with instructions to intercept the Soviet ships and, if necessary, to sink any ship suspected of carrying missile parts. By October 24 the Soviet convoy was well past the halfway mark, and the US Navy was lying in wait close to Cuban waters. Everyone realised that war was closer than it had ever been. At the laboratory the atmosphere recalled for me Britain on September 3rd, 1939, when the nation waited by the radio for the news that World War 2 had begun. Every hour at the laboratory we would stop work to cluster round a transistor radio, which somebody had brought in, and listen to the news bulletin. The Soviet convoy seemed to move ever more slowly and, as each broadcast ended, we would return to work without comment, or talk briefly of day-to-day things. The atmosphere was electric, for Urbana-Champaign was close enough to Chenout Air Base to be within the perimeter of an early missile target; our tension was well founded. It is impossible to generalise about attitudes, but, with the exception of the University's one regularly anti-establishment liberal, almost everyone seemed to be solidly behind Kennedy, not only in the University but, Mary told me, in the shops and among our neighbours near home. This was remarkable, because many were as scared as I was, and most of Illinois outside Chicago was staunchly Republican.

Our local trepidation must have been felt nationwide. In response, both NBC and CBS took the momentous step of dropping commercials at peak viewing hours for the duration of the crisis, and devoted themselves instead to reporting of a most brilliant and intelligent kind. The debates at the United Nations were televised almost without interruption; interviews with sometimes bewildered senators or representatives brought alive the self-doubt of US politicians in the face of the exigencies of the outside world; the factual knowledge displayed by TV's star newsmen proved to be immense. A third world war threatened, and commercial TV momentarily became a source of strength and sanity. Momentarily, because it lasted for less than 24 hours; Khrushchev blinked, so to speak: the Soviet convoy paused, then turned back - and the rest is history.

As I recall, there was a collective sigh of relief, but no one celebrated. Life returned quickly to normal, TV to its usual uncultured insipidity. Yet to be fair, US TV's potential for quality did occasionally break through at other times. A programme by one of NBC's star telecasters, David Brinkley, was shown sometime during the Cuba crisis, entitled "The Other Face of Dixie". It revisited Little Rock, Atlanta and Clinton, sites where the American Negroes' struggle against racial barriers had been initiated in the late 1950s, to report on how far racial barriers had successfully been breached. In the aftermath of the then recent affair of James Meredith at Oxford, Mississippi, it was a heartening experience. Earlier that month we had seen and heard students at "Ole Miss" mouthing the sort of racism I had last heard from Nazis. Yet Brinkley's interviewer assembled a few students from Little Rock High School, which by then included 14 Negroes, and both coloured and white discussed how they had got on during the last few years. The naive surprise expressed by both colours at finding each other human, and their attempts to explain their discarded attitudes in terms of their upbringing and backgrounds, reflected a real change in attitudes from 1957.

I found this change wherever I went in the USA in 1962-3. In 1957, the white racism which I encountered in private homes or travelling was either passive or positive, sometimes even vehement; with few exceptions (entirely in university or jazz *milieux*) the topic was either brushed aside or people talked about daughters being raped by black men. On this visit I found almost everywhere a passionate sense that the race problem must be solved; I even met some southerners falling over backwards to overcome their conditioned reflexes.

Mostly the support for integration arose from the highest of motives, because Negro militancy had not then reached a sufficient pitch to frighten white America seriously. But occasionally, and sometimes comically, I encountered slippage: a typist at the University supported integration because "otherwise all those Negroes will come north and we don't want them here."

Brinkley's programme was honest. It made no bones about the slow pace of integration, about how isolated the Negro pioneers of integration felt, about how far from real social integration they really were. It was a salutary and encouraging programme for its time, if rather sad from a twenty-first century perspective.

Another impressive memory of TV dates from December

17th, 1962, when Kennedy gave an hour-long interview to a three-man panel from the three major TV networks, NBC, CBS and ABC. Each network put up its star reporter, with the result that the questions were penetrating, well informed and, though polite, pulled no punches. For a whole hour Kennedy answered them, plainly and directly, and discussed without evasion Cuba, China (which had recently invaded India), his taxation policy, unemployment, price regulation, colour prejudice and so on. In retrospect, that interview was an astonishing contrast to the side-stepping and obfuscation which confrontational twenty-first century interviewers force upon politicians by their loaded and often tendentious questions - not that European politicians have not learned to play the tendentiousness game equally enthusiastically - for I had, and subsequently have had, no reason to think that the questions or topics put to Kennedy were prescribed or set up. It all seemed to be a model of twentieth-century democracy really working, of the press doing its job properly for once. Yet only fifteen minutes earlier we had watched a newscast in which Billy Graham, an extreme Christian evangelist, addressed the assembled top brass in the Pentagon, eyes protruding like Joseph Goebbels (Hitler's propaganda minister, if any of the younger generation should read this), while he mouthed hogwash about how the finger of God had intervened as the Soviet ships sailed towards Cuba. My diary comments: "What kind of a country is this, whose President talks common sense for an hour, yet which turns a religious maniac loose among the men who will press the buttons?"

The real world

By October the fall had begun. But the weather remained mild for another month and, in such spare time as we all had, we took the children on excursions, to marvellous, imaginative playgrounds, of which there were several, or out for family picnics, and, of course, supported their social round, as well as engaging in our own. Halloween, then almost unknown in Britain, came at the end of October, and our children delighted in a party with pumpkin pie, followed by the ceremony of "trick or treat", in which small (and carefully supervised) gangs blackmail adult neighbours into rewarding them with sweet and sticky candies, packs of which had been on sale in supermarkets for several days. They came home with a bagful each, which, despite their protests, we had to commandeer and ration. Winter was actually signalled on November 7, when the 'song' of the crickets, which had until then filled the evenings, ceased abruptly. A few days later bright red finches visited the campus in substantial numbers, like Red Cardinals without crests, and in a couple of days they were gone - I never identified them. But even then the weather was bright and sunny, if cool, for most of that month.

At the laboratory I was more or less accepted as one of the gang, albeit one with an odd accent and idiom. I gave a seminar on starvation and survival in bacteria to the research staff, one on the effects of cold and freezing on bacteria, to the biology students, and also three or four rather tremulous lectures on sulphur (sorry, sulfur) bacteria to Leon's class of

401

50 students. Later Leon asked me to set a question based on my lectures for their finals examination, which I duly did. When I came to mark ('grade' in U.S. parlance) the answers a month later I discovered that only two students had any real recollection of my three lectures; another six had remembered a few fragments and the rest were patently floundering. Dismayed, I talked to Ralph about it. He was sympathetic, but thought I had pitched my lectures at a higher level than they were used to. However, he added that my grades conformed to the general trend in the other questions in the finals.

My teaching was thus unimpressive; happily my research was progressing well, partly because I had topics, left over from my days in Butlin's group, which I could wrap up efficiently because I knew exactly what needed doing, and also because Leon and I had discovered overlaps in our research interests which enabled us to share experimental questions and settle them quickly. One of these matters was to sort out, with a few new experiments, the proper classification of Molly Adams' spore-forming strain, which I mentioned in earlier chapters. This led us to set up a new classification scheme covering all of the types of sulphate-reducing bacteria then known; our scheme was useful for about fifteen years, when several entirely new types of sulphate reducer were discovered and it needed thorough revision.

Ralph Wolfe, who worked in a laboratory just down the corridor, also handed me a problem to sort out. In his own research, which was principally concerned with the bacteria, which make marsh gas (methane), he had come across a quirk of microbial physiology which seemed to involve sulphate-reducing bacteria. The details are in the scientific literature and do not matter here. He invited me to sort it out. It involved visiting, in Ralph's car (sorry, automobile), a pool in the neighbouring countryside, which was much polluted by the excrement of ducks, the biochemical pathway of the decomposition of whose excreta was then incompletely understood. Not, perhaps, a glaring gap in our understanding of nature, but scientists tend to be obsessive in their quest for detail. I duly took samples of pond sediment, carried them back to the laboratory for examination and by the end my stay, which had by then been extended to six months, I had solved that problem to our common satisfaction. As Ralph had foreseen, a new type of sulphate-reducing bacterium proved to be responsible for the missing step. Thus I would make a salient if minor contribution to the total edifice of scientific knowledge. Perhaps I should add that not all my research at the University of Illinois was quite so abstruse!

Visitors and visits

The seminar trail was, and probably still is, an integral feature of US science. Scientists circulate constantly, travelling from their home laboratory to visit other laboratories, where they will give an account of their recent research to the local postgraduates, plus a proportion of the Department's staff and senior researchers. Before and/or after that seminar they will normally make time to discuss their work, in their own offices or by their benches, with those researchers who have a special interest in the topic, and they will usually stay overnight, as a guest of a faculty member or of the Department, to be entertained informally by some of the local scientists. Then they will collect a fee plus travel expenses, and travel on to the next University or Institute. Like a modern version of the medieval troubadour, as we used to say, they sing their scientific song at rewarding centres all over the country. The fee - the reward - is variable; one can judge one's standing in the world of US science by the size of the fee one is offered. Though sometimes little more than a tedious formality to over-exposed postgraduates, seminars and their associated contacts can be a most effective source of intellectual cross-fertilisation, especially the informal talk of an evening The visiting seminar routine is a major reason why the USA has become world leader in research despite its huge size, for every established researcher expects to spend a good portion of his or her time flying around the continent on the seminar circuit, and in a major university several departmental seminars will take place every day, often, as I indicated earlier, over lunchtime. ("Seminaring" is much less common in Europe because most universities and institutes pay no fee, and rarely offer expenses; happily, most visiting Americans are generously unsurprised.)

The Microbiology Department naturally had its quota of visiting seminarists and I was fortunate to hear many and assist in their entertainment. I recall, for instance, the visit of Jacques Monod, from the Pasteur Institute in Paris. He was one of the outstanding molecular microbiologists of the later twentieth century, and he spoke perfect US-inflected English.

(His mother was American). His speciality was deciphering the means by which the information encoded in the genes of microorganisms was decoded by the cell and translated into appropriate physiological activity. His research was historically related to the kind of work on adaptation in bacteria that I had done almost twenty years earlier with Hinshelwood, whose theories had, as I told in Chapter 3, been undermined by later discoveries in bacterial genetics.

Monod was one of those primarily involved in such later work, and the subject had raced ahead since then. Host to Monod on this occasion was Professor Sol Spiegelman, who worked on the floor above Leon with a team of largely Japanese post-doctoral researchers. Sol's work paralleled that of Monod in many ways. He too was a leader in that field, and he was intensely competitive over his research. After Monod's seminar, several others and I went to Sol's house to drink bourbon on the rocks and talk science. It was a weird experience. Scattered around the large drawing room were a dozen or so scientists, with Monod and Sol half facing each other. Every now and again, someone would get up, put a couple of ice cubes in his glass (we were all male) followed by a shot of whisky; this would be sipped slowly as the ice melted. (I rather dislike whisky, but as the evening progressed I kind of warmed to it, if that is the right verb to use) The talk was highly technical, and my ageing memory has long erased the details, but the striking feature for me was the caginess of both Sol and his guest. They were like two boxers sparring. They seemed to talk freely, as courtesy required, and conversation in the room flowed adequately, but we were all attentive to their words. But both avoided mention of anything really new or unpublished unless, perhaps by allusion to some third party's work, one of them realised that the other already knew of it. Being myself prone to blurt out everything I knew to visiting scientists, I was much surprised, and one of my illusions about scientific openness was shattered that evening, but my US friends were mainly amused. I later learned that such rivalry was, and is, common in the USA (and within a few years it would become widespread in Europe).

Yet in day-to-day relationships, Sol was a friendly, hugely intelligent and highly amusing regular of the Greasy Spoon luncheon party. I got on well with him, because my sulphate-reducing bacteria offered no threat. In his eyes (I suspect) they were a suitably harmless occupation for a bright if effete Englishman. Sol was the only scientist I have ever known who talked openly of expecting to receive a Nobel Prize in due course - sadly, he did not, but two or three years later Monod did.

Another molecular microbiologist who came through was Martin Pollock from England, whom I knew well. He also worked on bacterial adaptation, but was much less of a rival to Sol than Monod. At the party for him Sol was amused by our very English accents and conversational style; at one stage, discussing British reluctance to pay fees for seminars, Martin asked him whether he would do a lecture for the modest fee of £20. "Make it guineas," joked Sol, "And I'm your man!"

Guido Pontecorvo, whom I knew well from Butlin's

Advisory Committee, came through to talk about the genetics of moulds. I have forgotten who was his University host, but I took him home to dine with Mary and me. Though he disapproved of my having joined MRE, because of his aversion to its biological warfare connection, he sympathised with my wisdom in escaping from Teddington before the axe finally fell on Butlin's group, and we were, and remained, firm friends.

Sometimes visitors from abroad had jet lag problems. One who shall be nameless came as Leon's guest to give a seminar on the subject of bacterial spores, another of Leon's scientific interests. He had flown in direct from Australia. He had a very monotonous lecturing style, and embarked upon what proved to be a very dull talk, one that he had clearly given many times before. After about 30 minutes he began to speak more and more slowly, leaning against the wall by the blackboard, and then paused, as if thinking carefully over his next point. The pause got longer, longer, and longer... abruptly he shook himself, repeated his last sentence and carried on for another 30 minutes. I have encountered many a lecturer who bored the audience to sleep, but this was the only time I have known one to bore himself to sleep as well.

I, too, had a modest turn on the seminar circuit, but the shortness of my visit and the exigencies of the Midwestern winter restricted me to two brief excursions. My first was in mid December, to Nashville, Tennessee, for most of the world the location of Grand Old Opry, the home of Country & Western music, and also of a then rising star called Elvis Presley. But for me it was the site of Vanderbilt University, which housed the laboratory of one Art Harrison. Art was the only scientist in the world apart from Dick Strange and me who was studying death of bacteria by starvation at that period. He had embarked upon the subject with Professor Hinshelwood at Oxford, more than a dozen years after I had worked with Hinsh, and I had come discuss our common research, not to give a seminar. I had not met him before; he proved to be friendly, open about his work, and hospitable. After a flight via Chicago and Indianapolis he met me at a chilly, almost snowbound Nashville airport to drive me to the motel where I was to stay. The roads were sheets of ice, and his car's heater had broken down; rarely have I had such a freezing ride. It was alarming too; chatting as we drove smoothly down a hill towards an intersection, he said, almost casually, "I hope no one's coming across here - my brakes are full on". We had been unintentionally tobogganing! Happily the crossing was indeed clear.

After I had settled in, he collected me for a drive to dinner at a steak house in downtown Nashville - an even more frigid journey - where we were to dine with a Professor Jones and the representative of a scientific instrument company which hoped to sell an expensive scientific instrument to the Professor. I was so cold I could hardly converse until I had rather slowly thawed out. Nashville's drink laws forbad the public sale of hard liquor in restaurants, but this establishment had a "bottle bar" to which customers would bring their own bottles and, for a modest charge, have portions dispensed with appropriate mixers. There seemed to be certain communal democracy in the matter of whose bottle was which; Professor Jones had invested a bottle of bourbon whiskey at the bar, which enabled the management to supply me with a stiff gin and tonic, which much assisted my thawing-out process. No doubt some other customer partook of Professor Jones' investment.

After a somewhat alcoholic meal Harrison took me home to his house for conversation with some of his fellow scientists, lubricated by bourbon. Later came a frigid drive back to my motel, me somewhat anaesthetised from the cold by alcohol. If Nashville's drink laws were intended to promote sobriety, they were not impressively effective.

My diary records that after breakfast, where I renewed acquaintance with that southern speciality grits (an almost tasteless porridge), with egg and bacon, I was somewhat dopey for scientific conversation, but it was relaxed and unexacting. In the afternoon we slipped in some tourism: Art drove me some 30 miles out of town to see Andrew Jackson's antebellum house, The Hermitage, with its slave cabin. Built in 1819, it looked absolutely charming in the winter sunshine, snow everywhere, with fat robins hopping around. Thence a quick dash round Nashville, including obeisance to the outside of the Grand Old Opry Theatre, followed by a stop to admire a full size reproduction of the Parthenon in yellow concrete which housed a garish war artists' exhibition; outside it were a large number of frosted Christmas decorations and statuary, illuminated, with constant recorded carols playing from partly hidden speakers. Glorious US Christmas kitsch!

I moved about with American speed, of course. After a

brisk supper with Art and his wife, he took me to the airport to catch an evening plane for a short flight to Knoxville. My ill luck held: the plane had defective heating, and the flight was frigid. So was Knoxville, where Harry Peck met me with his car, to drive me to Oak Ridge. Happily his heater worked, but I was both tired and chilled. I had to refuse Harry's invitation to stop for a drink at his home as gracefully as I could, and he took me to my motel, to flop out for the night.

Next morning Oak Ridge Biology Division seemed to be a ghastly place, a kind of industrial plant converted into laboratories, but it was a busy hive of research activity and scientific discussion was brisk and intense, distinctly wearing after yesterday's full programme. But Harry was an enthusiast, and he had recently made a serious advance in understanding the earliest stages in the reduction of sulphate by our bacteria.

After I had been introduced to the Director, a friendly Dr Hollaender, Harry and I talked all morning. Harry was a big fellow, with something of a weight problem; we got on well and I enjoyed the gleam of pleasure in his eyes when I was able to tell him something that had a positive bearing on his recent work, or if we both saw a way of pushing the work forward. I sensed that he regarded Leon Campbell as something of a rival, but like Leon, he seemed to have no such feelings about me, and I had no such problems with either of them. He had brought some diet drink for his own lunch, but also some sandwiches in a bag for me, and we talked right through the mealtime. In the afternoon I met some of the other researchers in the Division and discussed with them wider matters of common interest, such as freezing bacteria, bacterial growth and bacterial DNA. My seminar later that afternoon, on starvation and death in bacteria (my work at MRE), bore upon the interests of several researchers at Oak Ridge, and was well received. After dinner *en famille* with the Peck family, they had a son and a daughter, a dozen or so researchers came in for beer and informal chat. We talked on and on, and it was not until well after midnight that Harry delivered me to my motel, happy but intellectually wrung out.

I wish I had been on better form for the further two hours of talk in the laboratory next morning, particularly as my last stop was to meet a somewhat loquacious if distinguished microbiologist who was still in full flow when the airport limousine arrived for me at about 11:00. But someone rescued me, and after brisk farewells I was off. I caught my plane from Knoxville back to Champaign/Urbana via Cincinnati and Chicago - with delays due to the wintry weather but no more cold problems.

Obviously I neither received nor expected a fee for my visit to Vanderbilt, since I gave no seminar; only later did I discover that Oak Ridge, being a Government Establishment, did not pay seminar fees. Ah well! Thus did I miss out on an enviable feature of the US seminar circuit - an experienced scientific troubadour would doubtless have fitted in some paid university seminars as well.

My second trip took place in mid January. I had met Bill Finnerty, a one-time colleague of Harry Peck, in Chicago a couple of years earlier and discovered that he was a fellow jazz enthusiast and that he also played jazz trumpet. He worked at the University of Indiana on bacteria which attack oil hydrocarbons. His laboratory was in Indianapolis, some three hours' drive from Urbana, so he invited me to visit, give a seminar and stay overnight. He and a colleague wished to visit the University, so they drove over, collected me after lunch and took me back in their car. Very convenient for me - no hassle about catching airport limousines and so on.

I stayed with Bill, his wife Marge and their five children, but their house was large I even had my private bathroom. It was a pleasant change to spend most of the evening playing jazz records. Next day, however, serious science was resumed, but gradually, because my first stop was to be introduced to the head of Bill's Department. He was a Morris dancer and was perceptibly disappointed that my knowledge of English folk dance was negligible, but I managed to sustain some conversation on old English folklore. Then I talked microbiology with various members of the staff, had lunch with Bill, and gave a seminar in the afternoon on my MRE work. It provoked much discussion. I also met again 'Camp' Campbell, who had taken Bill and me to that modern jazz joint in Chicago. Bill held the customary drinks party with various of the staff at his home evening, when a fairly vigorous scientific discussion later gave way to some more general talk about life in Indianapolis.

I had noticed that Bill locked his office when we went to lunch; apparently the Department was almost in a state of siege, being located in an impoverished part of town and being regarded by the local miscreants as a source of saleable objects to steal. They would take almost anything: forceps, spatulae, glassware, stationery, personal property and so on. He locked his car doors as we drove round town, explaining that when motorists halted at stop signs, thugs had been known to throw open the door, jump in and mug them. In the first seven days of that January Indianapolis had recorded 167 crimes of violence, rape, assault or murder, and each day a column in the local paper headed "Our Streets Of Terror" reporting the most newsworthy examples. At that period it was a rough city. (When I told all this to my chums back at Urbana, they seemed largely aware of it; one of the Professors remarked, "If you wished to give the USA an enema, Indianapolis is where you would insert it").

The party went on until well after midnight and, in a most un-American manner, both Bill and I overslept until about 09:30. I had no scientific duties the next day, so Bill took me on a tour of downtown, where I respectfully noted a remarkably ugly war memorial at its centre, and then in the mid afternoon it was time for me to catch a plane back to Urbana. Alas! An ice storm in Illinois had grounded all aircraft going in that direction; there was nothing for it but to take instead the long-distance bus - a stopping journey of some three and a half hours, which would deliver me to Urbana around midnight. So Bill drove me to Indianapolis bus terminus to await the next bus. I sat on a bench in a damp, dismal, yellow-painted brick waiting room, and after the previous night's conversation my company seemed distinctly sinister - at least, those who were awake did. But I kept my eyes lowered, pretended to doze, and hoped I didn't look too alien. In the event no one bothered me, I caught the bus, and apart from an occasional controlled skid the journey was uneventful and quite comfortable. The roads were sheets of ice, so Mary had no intention of meeting me in our car; I had to take a fairly costly taxi home - happily I had earned $75 expenses for my seminar.

Fragments of the Midwestern scene

Next day I had a proper sight of the effects of the ice storm. It was breathtakingly beautiful. Every tree, every twig, every blade of grass was covered with a 2 mm film of ice, a glassy coating which glistened in the bright morning sun amid a snow-covered suburban landscape. Despite its brilliance, the warmth in the sunshine was insufficient to melt the ice in the frigid air. I have no record of the temperature, but it was certainly some 10°C below freezing and no one in their senses went outdoors, even well wrapped-up, if they could avoid it.

By then Urbana-Champaign was blanketed in snow. The roads were icy sheets of impacted snow, with walls of snow on either side, often five or six feet high, where snow ploughs had thrown snow to one side or the other to keep the way clear. Numerous cars were buried in snow and would not be recovered by their owners until the thaw (who they belonged to I never discovered - the offspring of multi-car families, I suspect).

Coming from a wet, temperate land, I was fascinated by the efficiency with which local life was geared to the hard winters of a continental climate. Our house, like most others, had an integral garage, and it shared our warm-air-ducted central heating system. Thus one went from a warm house into a warm car, the numerous cylindered, gas-guzzling engine started without cold-induced trouble, and its heater cut in almost at once. One drove away without ever being exposed to the elements. A short dash through the cold air would normally be inescapable, to get from the car park to one's destination - shop, university or other building - but that would be warmly air-conditioned. Mind you, not everyone was in a position so to elude the climate: the local news media reported a handful of premature deaths from hypothermia in outlying rural settlements during our stay. I gathered there were a few such deaths each winter, mostly associated with poverty, despite social security and relief services.

Once we had come to terms with the snow we were greatly pleased with ourselves, and wrote letters back to England boasting about the hard winter and telling of the ways in which we coped - for we were remarkably free from winter ailments despite the cold. Sadly, our families and colleagues at home were less than impressed: 1962-3 was the coldest, snowiest winter in Britain for about a century, and our letters were received with bleak familiarity.

Driving with confidence on impacted snow for over two months was a technique I had to learn. In the first place, everyone changed their tyres to so-called snow tyres, with deep treads designed to give maximum grip on a frozen surface. But even so, imagine a snake of cars commuting into town along South Prospect Avenue; not bumper-to-bumper in the British way, but sensibly spaced out for the slippery conditions. At the Avenue's end comes a 90° right turn, narrowed by walls of snow. Bear in mind that you have automatic transmission; bear in mind, too, that you may only brake very gently, if at all; and bear in mind, finally, that if you come to a standstill you will have difficulty in starting again, let alone in moving in the direction you want to go. The timorous driver slows down to a crawl and creeps tremulously round the corner, thus infuriating all the regulars and risking an accident. The expert trick is to use a controlled skid. You start your turn, give a very gentle kick on the throttle, your rear wheels start to skid, you turn into that skid and - bingo! - you've done a right angle turn, and you are on your way. And you have not used your brake. It was fascinating to observe car after car perform the manoeuvre of a morning. On the second day of permanent snow I took time off from the lab that afternoon and drove to a snow-covered yard in front of an unused silo, where I spent some two hours mastering the controlled 90° skid in my Ford Fairlane. Never were two hours better spent - I could then join the commuters with some degree of confidence.

The automobile is an extension of an American's home and a lifeline to the outside world. Naturally parking loomed large in the daily routine of Urbana-Champaign and was strictly regulated. Metered parking, private or rented parking, customer free parking, short and medium term parking zones, some free and some metered, were widespread, and carefully monitored. Only once did I fall foul of the parking regulations. For some reason which I failed to record I parked illegally one morning and received a 'ticket' requiring me to report to the local JP's office "within 72 hours" with my licence. I had to go home and collect my letter from the US Secretary of State's Office permitting me to use my British driving licence. I went that afternoon, and it was closed. However, it soon opened, and I was received by a spotty, pregnant secretary of about 19 years old who asks me how I got the ticket. I explained, with English vagueness, and she said, "Be more careful next time" and let me off. How nice that such discretion is in in the hands of a JP's secretary!

Another case of devolved discretion eased a domestic crisis for us. During our stay Mary's father became seriously ill, and by late February it became likely that he would die soon. Mary dropped everything, so to speak, left me to look after the children, and took a flight to from Chicago to London to see him. He was by then in hospital, alive, but very unwell. She stayed for two whole days before taking a return flight to Chicago. She arrived at Chicago airport towards midnight, and there trouble started: the Immigration Officer pointed out that her visa was valid for just one visit to the USA and had thus expired. Neither Mary nor I had noticed this; visas for both of us had been arranged by MRE and my visa was for an indefinite number of visits; I still do not know why Mary's was for a single visit. A further complication was that Mary's passport, though British, quite correctly gave her birthplace as Perth Amboy, New Jersey, USA, because that was where her parents (both British) had been living when she was born. How come a US citizen by birth was re-entering the USA on a British passport with an out of date visa?

Mary explained the circumstances as best she could - that she had been obliged to rush suddenly to visit her dying father, and was now returning to where her husband and three

417

children, living on an academic visitor's visa, awaited her. The Immigration Officer turned aside to a colleague and said, quietly but audibly, "I'm inclined to believe her." He let her through, with a polite injunction not to do it again.

Mary's trip was timely. Her father died at the beginning of April, while we were actually in New York on our way back to Britain.

Being accustomed to Britain's brick-built houses, I was surprised by the warmth, elegance, variety of design and apparent sturdiness of the almost universal wooden frame houses. The use of wood explained the prevalence of fire hydrants in downtown, and why fire precautions, Fire Chiefs and Fire Engines were an important part of the local *mythos*. A compensating virtue of wood was the speed with which houses could be demolished. One day, in a street outside the University, I watched, transfixed as a truck carrying an enormous grab drove up to a quite substantial but empty frame house, parked beside it, and the grab just seized chunks of the house and literally tore it apart, all in less than an hour. It was a curiously satisfying procedure; by evening nothing was left but a concrete slab and some stopped-off pipes.

An oddment. Shortly after I arrived Ralph took me on a visit to Kikapoo, near the border between Illinois and Indiana, to seek, and fail to find, a salt spring that might have yielded some interesting microbes. Kikapoo was an exhausted strip-mining area, totally devastated by opencast mining, that had been rehabilitated and beautified most effectively and was now a most attractive area of undulating grassy mounds. Nearby we talked to the custodian of a graveyard; he knew nothing of a spring, but informed us "I've got seventeen

Indians buried here - don't know anything about them of course." Nearby was Andy's Live Bait Store. This was truly rural USA.

Mary was invited to a festive lunch for "Ladies Of The Press" on the strength of her few reviews of spoken word recordings back in Britain. A proviso was that everyone should wear a funny hat, and she dutifully composed one, symbolising a life centred on domestic chores and children's toys (ie sporting a saucepan, a baby's bottle and a small plastic brontosaurus). It earned an honourable mention and a prize LP on which the University of Illinois Choir and Orchestra sings a programme of student songs.

The grand new auditorium was sufficiently completed to be opened formally at the beginning of March, and celebrated with an open-house invitation to all the citizens of Urbana-Champaign to walk round and through it freely. Uninterrupted entertainment was provided all day in the central arena, with superb amplification. Naturally Mary and I took the girls along, to be regaled first by a then popular voice and guitar Duo, Les Paul and Mary Ford, followed by the jazz trombonist J J Johnson, supported by a band consisting of seven more trombones and a rhythm section. Great fun, even though Mary and I were for various reasons exhausted. The enormous building, which effortlessly managed 40,000 visitors on that day, was curiously beautiful, as if a huge grey flying saucer had landed downtown. (Some years later I returned to Urbana-Champaign, to find that it had been covered with white plastic, making it look even more like a Hollywood science fiction set.)

Reminiscence of J J Johnson at the auditorium brings up

the matter of jazz. In fact, I was somewhat starved of jazz, and I had not brought an instrument to play myself. There was no indigenous jazz in Urbana-Champaign proper, though there was a rather modern-styled student group, which I listened to a couple of times and found rather uninteresting. The saxophonist Stan Getz came through town and gave an enjoyable concert in the University's Concert hall in mid February, attracting a large audience, but mainly I listened to the radio - a regular Budweiser programme from a Chicago station, and a Sunday afternoon broadcast from Mattoon local radio - or watched occasional jazz programmes from National Educational Television put out by the University's own station. That series was in fact very good, presenting fashionable talents from the period including Sonny Rollins, Dave Brubeck, Dizzy Gillespie, The Modern Jazz Quartet, Cannonball Adderley, the traditionalist Turk Murphy and the singer Carmen McCrae; I wrote a short report of it for *Jazz Monthly*.

Leaving the lab for lunch at the Greasy Spoon. University of Illinois, early 1963.
L-R: John Postgate, Ralph Wolfe, Sol Spiegelman, Leon Campbell.

Farewell

The thaw began abruptly on March 3, with a gushing of water along the storm channel in front of every dwelling in South Prospect. Snow fell off roofs, icicles grew on eves and vanished again, cars emerged from their snow blanket by the roadside. Our time was running out and there was much to be done at the lab, experiments to be checked and sometimes redone, unfinished manuscripts to be discussed, farewells to be spoken.

In all, my stay generated six scientific papers, all but one (those ducks) shared with Leon, and some with other collaborators as well. American scientists were more obsessed than the British with accumulating scientific publications in those days, so my US friends were impressed: an average of one decent paper a month seemed notably productive for one who arrived late and sleepy at the laboratory each morning, and was not often around at weekends. But for my part I knew well that luck and my leftovers from Teddington days, plus Leon's input, had made a major contribution.

At home packing had to be done, the treasures and essentials collected over six months had to be sorted and a trunk sent on. The car had to be sold, the tenancy of 1911 S. Prospect needed to be terminated, travel tickets were to be checked and so on. And, as friends, colleagues and neighbours realised that our departure was really imminent, we received a small deluge of social invitations, several of which we simply had to refuse. On one of our last few days Ivor flew in again, this time with a senior professor from the new Institute at Dallas, to discuss a real offer of a post at their Institute of Advanced Studies. Obviously I could come to no decision then, but my reflections on the matter needed suddenly to become serious. My friends at the University were enthusiastically in favour of my moving to Dallas - but to complicate things I had since received a personal letter from Donald Woods, telling me that the British Agricultural Research Council was seeking an experienced microbiologist to help direct a new and interesting research group; would I like to meet the Director Designate in New York on my way home? More of that story in Chapter 19.

Greatly helped by the Tempests and Ralph Wolfe, we departed by train for New York, via Chicago, on April 2, 1963, seen off by Ralph and a valiant, 'flu-ridden Leon. We were sad, because we had all been immensely happy in this very different but welcoming world. The children, especially, would have warm feelings towards the USA in years to come; even when most details of their life there had been forgotten, something of their happy experience would remain. We had all become, in a catch phrase of the day, mid-Atlantic citizens. For my part, on the many occasions when I travelled to the USA in later years, I would feel a perceptible lifting of my spirits, a slight sense of coming home.

We broke our journey for a few days to stay with my cousin Jane and her family at Great Neck, during which time I managed to take the adults to Eddie Condon's for dinner, to hear an excellent jazz quintet led by the clarinettist Edmond Hall. In due course we took the SS United States, a fast but noisy liner, for the five-day voyage back to England.

Mary spent the voyage barely awake, the side effect of a big daily dose of seasickness remedy; the girls vacillated between being sick themselves and having a boisterously exciting time. I coped, more or less, and we arrived in Southampton on April 14th, a cold, damp Sunday morning.

What did we miss most of all once we were back home? Central heating!

CHAPTER EIGHTEEN

Departure from MRE

Civilianization

The circumstances surrounding the demise of Butch's group at Teddington had made me very conscious of the political side of British science. I was still convinced of the merits of economic microbiology: especially of those aspects of the science which could do much for the public good but which, translated into research projects, were too long-term to interest university researchers and too basic to attract industrial research.

As I explained earlier, the name "economic microbiology" covered all economically-important processes in which microbes were used. It included production processes such as brewing, food preservation, manufacturing antibiotics and, of course, agricultural microbiology, for there is hardly an aspect of farming that does not involve microbial activity of one kind or another (that is an interesting story which I must set aside just now). And it also covered less immediately profitable matters including corrosion, deterioration, waste disposal and the like.

It was this side of economic microbiology which was being neglected, largely because its profitability was far from obvious, and the demise of the Teddington Group had removed the last publicly-funded centre for basic research of that kind. My continuing interest in this matter had become known among microbiologists, and because of this I had become secretary of a Joint Working Party on Economic Microbiology which had been called together by the Society for General Microbiology, the Society for Applied Bacteriology, and the Society for Chemical Industry's Microbiology Panel. These were the UK's three main microbiological Learned Societies. The Working party was considering the state of Britain's research effort in Economic Microbiology.

In 1961 the Joint Working Party produced a report which, once approved by the parent Societies, was sent to the Royal Society. That Society approved it and sent to the Minister of Science (then Lord Hailsham). The report stressed the neglect of basic economic microbiology within the Government's research programmes and it recommended setting up a National Centre for Research in Economic Microbiology, and proposed an outline programme for it (largely, in fact, an extension of the programme of Butlin's Teddington Group).

The report all but nominated MRE as the appropriate centre for such research, for it had become obvious to all that MRE was a very British absurdity: a well-staffed and well-serviced laboratory admirably suited to undertake high-quality research in economic microbiology, especially bearing in mind its bulk fermentation facility and expertise in continuous culture, yet dedicated to biological warfare, a topic which much of the staff seemed to disregard for much of their time. Of course, this was an outsider's half-truth. The 'biological warriors' of MRE, those doing research closely related to biological warfare and protection therefrom, took their task seriously and were dedicated to it. Nevertheless there was a strong surge of feeling within MRE favouring its civilianization.

Not least among the supporters of that view was its Director, David Henderson, with whom I had several informal talks during 1961, in my capacity of Secretary to the Joint Working Party. He was well pleased with the Joint Working Party's report and was willing to give house room to any research group, which might be started. It would be a step towards civilianization and, like any good director, he was not averse to expanding his establishment. But quite reasonably he did not want to let MRE become deeply involved in what he called "sewage and sulphur"; it did not suit his medical background and it would have been an absurd waste of MRE's ability to handle very nasty pathogens and so to contribute to medical microbiology.

Moreover, for all his benevolence, there was a tricky administrative problem. MRE was at that time under the

Ministry of Defence. If it were civilianized it would have to leave that Ministry. Where should it go? Henderson disliked and distrusted the DSIR, which he felt, quite reasonably, had shown incompetence over Microbiology; and he would not tolerate being "under those chaps at the MRC" (Medical Research Council). The Ministry of Health seemed unsuitable if the laboratory's programme was to include a substantial amount of non-medical research, and there was no other home, especially for an establishment with an annual budget of around £1m at 1960 values. Henderson wavered from enthusiasm for civilianization to gloom at the prospect of new 'masters'. Yet by early 1962 matters seemed to be arranging themselves smoothly: the Minister had pronounced himself broadly in favour; the Chairman of the Advisory Board responsible for overseeing MRE's research (Sir Charles Dodds) was known to be well-disposed, too; the Ministry of Defence seemed unconcerned at losing MRE; the possibility of an autonomous Institute was not ruled out.

I departed for the USA for what ended up as the seven-month stint at the University of Illinois, which I described in the last chapter. In 1962 I returned to find a changed, sadder laboratory. Henderson, whom I had left in a vigorous, optimistic and decisive mood, received me with a sort of leonine gloom. I learned that the international nuclear stalemate had revived US interest in biological warfare; that this interest had fed back to the Ministry of Defence; that the Scientific Adviser to the Cabinet, Sir Solly (later Lord) Zuckerman, had personally intervened to discourage the civilianization of MRE; that MRE's financial estimates for the next five years had then been agreed, and that though these allowed for a modest expansion, it was earmarked exclusively for the 'practical' side of the work. This meant research bearing directly on biological warfare.

The gloom had affected several of my colleagues. Moreover, while I had been away, the laboratory had suffered two serious accidents. In one, an experienced staff member working on virulent plague had caught the disease and died; everyone was still shocked, the more so because it was still not clear how it had come about. The second was less humanly disastrous but quite as devastating: the virology group had made a very public and crass scientific mistake, caused by getting its tissue cultures cross-contaminated. These events had lowered morale, too.

Along with many others, I felt that biological warfare was something we as a community needed to understand and know about, but I could not agree that it should occupy the major resources of the country's best-equipped microbiology laboratory. I saw my own future as constrained and became dispirited myself. I felt that it was time to move. With the help of Donald Woods I found a new job in 1963 - more of that in the next chapter - and departed quietly.

In the same year seven or eight other senior research scientists left, and more departed in 1964. Many were those live wires I wrote of earlier. Denis and Owen remained, but MRE certainly lost much of its pre-eminence in UK microbiology.

Almost twenty years later, and over a decade after David Henderson's death, part of our early dream came true: MRE metamorphosed into a non-military institute of biotechnological research, part of the Public Health Laboratory Service. It became the Centre for Applied Microbiology Research (CAMR for short) and began to recover the respect with which it had been regarded in the 1950s. I, by then a Professor at the University of Sussex, had a pleasurable sense of vindication when, in 1981, they asked me to give its first David Henderson Memorial Lecture.

From sulphur to nitrogen

The unit of nitrogen fixation

I came upon my new job in a roundabout way. In 1960 an important scientific advance was published which was to have a dramatic effect on my career, and to explain it I must say a little more about nitrogen fixation. It is a process in which bacteria are deeply involved, so I had followed its progress with interest, but it was, at the time, remote from my own research experience. I mentioned it a couple of times in Chapter 10, notably in the context of Professor Burris' visit. Here is a slightly more extensive run-down.

Nearly 80% of the atmosphere consists of nitrogen, a gas that is chemically very inert. That means that it rarely reacts with other substances except in harsh conditions: within an electric discharge such as lightning, or with a catalyst at a high temperature and pressure. On the other hand, all living things contain compounds of nitrogen in the form of proteins, nucleic acids, hormones, vitamins and so on. The vast majority of living things cannot make their nitrogenous matter from nitrogen gas itself; their raw material comes as pre-formed nitrogen compounds in food, and those compounds come ultimately from plants and a few plant-like microbes (such as yeast in bread). These creatures in their turn make their nitrogen compounds from nitrates: simple compounds of nitrogen that they find in fertile soil. The nitrogen compounds in living things are constantly recycled: animals eat plants and each other; we eat both animals and plants. Excretion, death and decay feed bacteria and fungi, which pass nitrogenous compounds back to the environment, where bacteria convert them to nitrates for plants to reuse. This cycle keeps life going, but it leaks: certain kinds of bacteria exist that convert nitrates to nitrogen gas, and this escapes to the atmosphere, whence neither plants nor animals, nor yet the majority of microbes, can make use of it. It returns to being an inert diluent of the oxygen in air.

Were that the whole story, life on this planet would be in a poor, nitrogen-starved state. Happily a special class of microbes called nitrogen-fixing bacteria can bring nitrogen gas into chemical combination at ordinary pressures and temperatures, and they have topped-up the nitrogen cycle for millennium upon millennium, offsetting the leakage.

Nitrogen fixation is thus fundamental to world agriculture, and in the last hundred years farmers have begun to supplement that bacterial input by spreading nitrogen fertiliser made industrially from the atmosphere. The manufacturing process is elaborate, requiring a complex and expensive factory. Industrially, the usual procedure, called the Haber Process, is to prepare completely dry, oxygen-free nitrogen, and also hydrogen, compress them together to pressures of some hundreds of atmospheres, and expose them to special catalysts at a few hundred degrees centigrade. Only then would they react and form ammonia, and even then the reaction was always incomplete: a lot of nitrogen and hydrogen was left over at the end. Yet the bacteria responsible for the biological process manage to do it in air at normal temperatures. How they do it has been the subject of intense research since their discovery in 1886.

In 1960 Drs Carnahan, Mortenson and Castle in the USA cracked a problem: they extracted from a species of nitrogen-fixing bacteria the enzyme, the biological catalyst, which conducted the first steps of the process. It was called nitrogenase, and within the bacteria it bound nitrogen gas from the atmosphere and reduced it to ammonia.

Naturally I was aware of, and impressed by, their achievement. Especially so because around 1961 Butch came to visit me at MRE to talk about it, and in particular to discuss the biochemical inwardness of it: why and in what ways was it so important? He told me that the multinational petrochemical company Shell had commissioned him as a consultant. Stimulated by Carnahan's group's advance, they wished him to look into and report upon the state of the art in nitrogen fixation research, especially the chemical and biochemical side.

Why should Shell be interested at all? Because

Carnahan's group was actually employed by a rival chemical company, the Dupont de Nemours Chemical Corporation of the USA, a giant multinational centred on Wilmington, Delaware. And it had been published from Dupont's prestigious, and often secretive, Central Research Laboratories. Why, worried the executives of Shell, was Dupont devoting research effort of obvious quality to so fundamental a scientific question? Was there a possible industrial application that could be of interest to Shell?

So Butlin, fully recovered from the traumas of having had his Teddington Group disbanded, and positively enjoying his enforced retirement, made MRE almost his first call. Shell had equipped him with a business-type expense account that he wished to try out, so Denis, Owen and I were treated to a memorable lunch, even though we could only talk about the wider biochemical and microbiological contexts of Dupont's research. Butch also visited the four major research laboratories in Britain which had some expertise in nitrogen fixation: Rothamsted Experimental Station at Harpenden outside London (where P S Nutman headed a group working on plant-microbe associations); Long Ashton Research Station near Bristol (where D J D Nicholas, after studying such matters as the nutrient requirements of nitrogen-fixing bacteria, had initiated work on the enzymology of the process); University College, where G E Fogg was a leading authority on nitrogen-fixing blue-green algae (later called Cyanobacteria); and Imperial College (where E R Roberts was seeking intermediates in nitrogen fixation using isotopic nitrogen). All four laboratories received financial support from the Agricultural Research Council (ARC), and the programmes of the two research stations were naturally slanted towards agricultural questions. As far as basic chemical and biochemical research was concerned, very little was taking place in Britain.

A trip to the USA was necessarily part of Butch's programme, to his great delight. Among other places, he visited America's fountainhead of research on nitrogen fixation, the University of Wisconsin at Madison, where he renewed his acquaintance with Bob Burris and met another father figure of the subject, Perry Wilson. He also visited Dupont's at Wilmington, there to meet and talk with Carnahan, the senior member of Dupont's team (Mortenson had by then left for a University job). He was made welcome everywhere, and I learned later that he had made a tremendous impression despite his stammer: his good humour and open friendliness delighted everyone. Carnahan took to him sufficiently to show him his private hobby: after the conversation had turned to generalities he proudly took from his desk drawer, and displayed to Butch a set of photographs of a female nude taken by himself. Apparently they were highly professional.

"M M-M-M-Mrs Carnahan is a very beautiful w-w-woman", said Butch politely - a response which went into nitrogen fixers' folklore and was still good for a laugh at nitrogen fixation meetings over a decade later.

Butlin had conducted a brisk survey of the then current state of basic research on nitrogen fixation in Britain and the USA. He had realised that there were substantial technical difficulties in working with nitrogenase; it was destroyed by brief exposure to air, so all manipulations had to be carried out in the total absence of oxygen. At that date Dupont's was the only laboratory in the world to have worked out how to do this, though the knowhow was already being passed to Wisconsin and thence to other laboratories. As far as elucidating the nature of Dupont's interest, he had uncovered nothing dramatic: they had undertaken their research partly because to be seen to have advanced fundamental knowledge of a process so crucially important in agriculture was good for the Corporation's public image. In addition, they had hoped to learn enough about the enzyme to be able to imitate its action commercially, to patent procedures for making agricultural fertiliser more cheaply, or perhaps new methods of making valuable chemicals containing nitrogen. However, they had already concluded that their development was unlikely to affect the fertiliser or fine chemicals industry in the short or medium term and were planning to move into research involving the special types of nitrogen-fixing bacteria that associate with plants.

Butlin reported to Shell accordingly, in a brief but informative document that was, of course, confidential, though he actually slipped a copy to me. He recommended Shell to make a substantial investment in biochemical research on fixation, since a serious possibility still remained that understanding how nitrogenase works might enable industrial chemists to mimic the process or develop new processes. The company could do this either by setting up its own dedicated research team, on the lines of Dupont's, or by supporting university-based research. For the second option he recommended substantial support, including postdoctoral and postgraduate Research Fellows, for Dr Nicholas, who was thinking of leaving Long Ashton for Edinburgh, where a centre for research in microbiology and genetics was being established, as well as support for Roberts and Fogg.

In the event, Shell decided that the prospects of profitable fallout from such research were too remote. Nevertheless, they felt, research on the subject in a more open laboratory than Dupont's would be to everybody's advantage. So they passed the report to the then Secretary of the Agricultural Research Council, Professor E G (later Sir Gordon) Cox, a chemist with a special interest in structures of molecules and in X-ray crystallography. Cox was well aware that the process of nitrogen fixation was something of a chemical enigma. The Dupont group had shown beyond any doubt what had hitherto been known only circumstantially: that nitrogenase made ammonia from nitrogen. In living cells, other enzymes mopped up the ammonia as fast as it appeared, but it was truly the first identifiable product. But, as I indicated earlier, to make ammonia from nitrogen gas in the laboratory was difficult, and industrially the procedure is complex. Nevertheless, a huge, sophisticated and capital-intensive industry called the Haber Process, had grown up during the 20th century, supplying farmers all over the world with cheap ammonia-based nitrogen fertiliser.

The chemical enigma was that, in soil, nitrogen-fixing bacteria converted nitrogen to ammonia not only at ordinary temperatures and pressures, but also with both water and air abundant. It seemed to be a chemical miracle; how could they possibly do it? And what if it could be done industrially? Would not even cheaper nitrogen fertiliser then revolutionise world production of food, wood and fibre?

It was a research problem in basic economic microbiology with both fundamental and agricultural overtones. It was just the sort of thing the Agricultural Research Council had been created to support and, indeed, some felt that it reflected poorly on the Council's research planning that around 1960 there was no centre in Britain in a position to pick up and extend the Dupont group's findings.

The Council, urged by Cox, decided to set up a dedicated research group to study the problem. Nicholas was the most plausible British scientist to head the Unit, but his ideas did not match Council's: he wanted to study all the organisms of the nitrogen cycle, not just the nitrogen-fixing bacteria, and he also wanted to bring in research on plants which associated with nitrogen-fixing bacteria. Cox took the view that plants and other nitrogen bacteria would be a distraction. He wanted a more tightly focused research effort, and to him the question was fundamentally one of chemistry. There had been good, if circumstantial, evidence for many years that the element molybdenum, a metal, was involved in some essential way in nitrogen fixation; there was a good chance that it played a direct part in the actual catalytic process conducted by nitrogenase. What better than to have the research directed by a chemist whose speciality was complexes of organic compounds with metals, many of which were active catalysts of known chemical reactions?

It so happened that, as Cox's plans neared fruition, just such a chemist was available. Joseph Chatt, a distinguished inorganic chemist and Fellow of the Royal Society, had recently (1962) left ICI's industrial research laboratory near Welwyn, and was thinking of taking a Chair at Yale University, USA. Cox discussed his Council's plans with him, and Chatt decided to remain in Britain to become Director of the ARC's proposed 'unit for research on Nitrogen Fixation', yet to be established at a University or Research Station. Chatt's experience with ICI had accustomed him to think big: the Unit would be considerably larger than any Butlin had envisaged. It would have ten senior scientists (five chemists and five biologists) with some 15 support staff, and its remit would be to study the fundamental chemistry of biological nitrogen fixation without regard, at least in its initial programme, to other steps of the nitrogen cycle, to associations with plants, or to immediate problems in agriculture. Facilities would be available for taking on graduate students to do related research for their doctorates; Chatt's Assistant Director would be an experienced microbiologist.

Again an obvious choice for that position would have been Nicholas, but he had made it clear that he did not share Cox's and Chatt's outlook on the problem and the question was not overtly raised.

Britain had at that time no other scientist with experience of nitrogen-fixing bacteria combined with an appropriate background in microbiological chemistry. However, Donald Woods, then a member of the Council, knew of my disenchantment with the situation at MRE, and my background in chemical microbiology was appropriate. However, my extensive experience of sulphate-reducing bacteria was not obviously relevant. Nevertheless he put my name forward. As Chatt would put it to me much later, to chemists, sulphur is sufficiently close to nitrogen in the Periodic Table of the chemical elements - one across and one down - for them to expect a microbiologist who could handle sulphur bacteria to be able to cope with nitrogen bacteria. Cox and Chatt had Woods sound me out. I was tentatively interested and Chatt resolved to see me.

By coincidence, in the spring of 1963, I was returning from my stay at the University of Illinois, Urbana, just as Chatt was setting off for a three-month sabbatical at Pennsylvania State University. We arranged to meet as we both passed through New York City, travelling in opposite directions. That is why, one chilly morning, I came into town from Great Neck, where my family and I were staying a couple of days with my cousin's family on our way home to Britain, and arrived at his room in the Abbey Hotel. His wife, Ethel, tactfully left minutes before I arrived (years later she told me of her first sight of me in the corridor: a tall man, obviously English, who had come for interview wearing sandals).

Chatt I found to be a rather shy, stiff gentleman with toothbrush moustache and a gammy leg. He had a light northern accent and showed little animation except when talking about chemistry. He told me of his proposed unit, which sounded more and more ephemeral as I learned that it had no place to go and no staff, and did not actually exist. What kind of impression I made I do not really know; later, when we knew each other better, he indicated that he found me "somewhat bohemian" (I am still not sure what that meant; a combination of my embarrassed flippancy and the sandals, perhaps). What I am certain of is that we were each ambivalent about the other. Only later did I decide that we would probably get on reasonably well, and that the opportunity to start from scratch, coupled with his ignorance of microbiology but benevolence towards the subject, could be an advantage. I decided to give the job a try. Likewise he later wrote to Cox, as Woods reported to me: "Postgate seems to be the sort of man I could work with."

Those distinctly guarded opinions on both sides were the beginning of almost twenty years of exceptionally productive collaborative research, but many bridges had to be crossed before we could actually get down to it.

Changing horses

Cox interviewed me on my return. I was dismayed to learn that he had been on the DSIR Committee that had decided to abolish Butlin's Group, but the interview was otherwise encouraging because he seemed to know that my interests lay in the direction of basic research, and he was absolutely clear that the Unit was being founded to do just that. Our job was simply "to do good science" (Cox's own words): to choose the most amenable research material and to combine microbial biochemistry with pure chemistry so as to find out how biological nitrogen fixation worked. We should pay no heed, at least in our research plans, to applied and economic aspects of the matter: these would be taken care of by the ARC in other ways.

Cox had reinforced what Chatt had told me. I, too, was convinced of the value of interdisciplinary approaches to research and confident that work at a very basic level would generate technical fallout that would benefit agriculture in future, albeit in unforeseeable ways. (Would that Cox's words represented the attitude of Government research today!)

I applied formally for the job. I was more senior than the Treasury had agreed to - I would cost more - but I was told informally that that could be fixed. So now I had to disentangle myself from MRE. That was, in fact, one of the most difficult manoeuvres of my career, because Henderson was an emotional man and would take my wish to depart as a criticism of himself and his laboratory. That was the last message I wished to convey, given the goodwill and speed with which he had picked me up as Butlin's group disintegrated. In addition, I was in a tense state, suffering again from one of my periodic bouts of anxiety and depression. However, I forced myself - steeled myself would be the wrong metaphor - to fix an appointment with him and in a tremulous voice told him of my intention to leave - volubly assuring him of my gratitude for the opportunities he had given me, my respect for the MRE's research and so on. I think my obvious embarrassment and state of nerves startled him. He heard me out with gruff calm and said he would think about it. That was my first hint that he could, under the Ministry's regulations, have obliged me to stay. However, within hours Leonard Kent and Denis came in turn to me and told me that Henderson, accepting that I was perhaps under-extended and not entirely happy at MRE, had decided to release me.

Less traumatic was the situation regarding the invitation I had received while in Urbana to take up a post at the South Western Institute for Advanced Study at Texas. I had not turned it down and it was still in the pipeline; indeed, in that spring of 1963 I was still undecided between Texas and the ARC post. However, it had met with an obstacle: my Visiting Professorship at Urbana had entitled me to a non-immigrant educational visa, perfectly usual for visiting academics because it was relatively easily obtained and carried tax benefits in the USA. However, it bore the proviso that the holder should not seek employment in the USA for two years after he/she returned home. I simply could not wait two years. So I telephoned Cox and accepted his post, confirming in writing. Within a couple of days I had a phone call from the South Western Institute urging me to accept no other job, because it had connections with the State Department through whom it was making a special case for me, but this would take time. But I was by then committed. Some months later I felt better about my decision: on November 22, 1963, John F Kennedy was shot dead in Dallas, and suddenly Texas seemed far less attractive as a place to live.

London

I left MRE quietly in the late summer of 1963, having politely refused Leonard's offer of a sending-off dinner in the

Officers' Mess - I still felt badly about quitting MRE and was still too much troubled by my depression to face jolly sociability. My parents had converted the top part of their large Victorian house in Finchley into a self-contained flat and this was available at an economical rent. I and my family packed up, quit St Osmund's Close and moved in. What with changing schools and getting used to town life in a suburban flat, it was a pretty drastic time for the family. But grandparents were nearby - my parents were in the rest of the house below and Mary's now widowed mother lived a few miles to the North - and there were the sights of London to see, buses and tubes to ride and so on. We all adapted quite quickly. I took up my post with the ARC in the early autumn, after a few weeks' holiday.

An early question was what Chatt's Unit should be called. The ARC Nitrogen Fixation Unit would have been the ideal name, but in no time it would come to be known, at last within the ARC, by its acronym, the NFU. That would cause untold confusion in Head Office since the National Farmers' Union, with which they often had dealings, was well established as the NFU. Effectively the only alternative name was Unit of Nitrogen Fixation, unsatisfactory because it had a precise scientific meaning: a unit of nitrogen fixation was a number, a measure of the amount of nitrogen fixed by a unit amount of cells, enzyme or catalyst in a unit of time. However, common sense overruled strict logic and Chatt and I agreed to the name, commonly abbreviated to the UNF.

The UNF was going to be the biggest unit in the history of the ARC. However, at its outset it consisted of just two people, Chatt and me: the Director and his Assistant. We were accommodated in temporary offices at the ARC's HQ in Cunard Building, near Piccadilly in London - I was given a desk in the waiting room. Butlin, in touch with my activities, had donated his collection of 300+ reprints to the Unit-to-be; commuting on the Northern Line underground from Finchley Central to Piccadilly every weekday for some three months, I was able to read every one (all praise to public transport - I should never have managed them otherwise).

Chatt and I spent most of our days telephoning or writing to scientist colleagues, seeking temporary accommodation where we might get some research started. However, research scientists are always short of space. They will make tremendous efforts to accommodate visiting workers who wish to join in their research projects, even if the visitor wishes only to learn some technique and will later apply it in another context, but they are less enthusiastic about visiting researchers starting up wholly unrelated projects on their territory, particularly in large numbers. I received many expressions of goodwill, but all my friends' microbiological laboratories proved to be overcrowded already. Chatt, too, had difficulty finding temporary research space.

We combined our search for temporary space with visits to places where the new unit might be built. These including Rothamsted Experimental Station at Harpenden, where a barn-like building might be made available, and some disused laboratories of the Government Chemist just off Clements Inn in the Strand. There the smells generated by our chemists would certainly have provoked litigation from the lawyers in neighbouring offices; central London was certainly not the right place for the sort of chemicals Chatt used. But a new research unit was quite an attraction to any university and Queen Mary College, located in London's Mile End Road, put in a bid for us, so to speak, by making Chatt a Professor of Chemistry and offering him temporary research space in their Chemistry Department.

During my search I had approached a veterinary microbiologist, Professor R Lovell, whom I knew well. He had been a neighbour when I was a boy, and later I had encountered him again as Treasurer of the Society for General Microbiology for several years. He was at the Royal Veterinary College in Camden Town and, though neither he nor the college had the slightest interest in nitrogen fixation *per se*, he knew an opportunity for expansion when one came along. His proposition was that, if the ARC would pay for the conversion of the caretaker's flat - essentially two attic rooms - into laboratories, we could, for a modest rent, start microbiological work there for as long as it took to get our own building built, provided the labs then reverted to the College, free of charge.

A typical university academic's proposal. The ARC, familiar with such ways, agreed to both plans. Within a few months Chatt had moved to Queen Mary College, and taken on a secretary, and also Dr Ray Richards, the UNF's first senior researcher after me, and a couple of graduate students as research staff, in order to get the chemistry started. My move to the Royal Veterinary College was a little slower - I had to oversee the conversion - but eventually I moved into

445

a nice little lab and office, took on a secretary and technical assistant, and was joined by Dr Michael Kelly. Together we started some microbiology. The UNF had got going, albeit as two sub-units separated by about five miles.

Butternut Lake

About six months after I moved into the Royal Veterinary College an official in the ARC's headquarters learned, from the British Embassy in Washington DC, that a high-powered meeting of leading US researchers on nitrogen fixation was to take place in September, sponsored by a US research foundation, the Charles F Kettering Laboratory. Attendance was by invitation only, but the ARC was able to wangle one for me, as Assistant Director of its new Unit of Nitrogen Fixation. So in September 1964, I was off on my globetrotting travels again, this time on what seemed to me rather slim credentials, since the Unit barely existed. Michael Kelly remained behind to keep the lab going.

The meeting was to take place at a holiday resort in upstate Wisconsin, led by Perry Wilson, joint World leader, with Bob Burris, of nitrogen fixation research. Wilson had offered to drive me there from the University of Wisconsin at Madison. I duly arrived at Madison Airport by way of Chicago, where Bob kindly met me and settled me into the University Union for a couple of nights, thus leaving a clear day for visiting the laboratories and giving the customary seminar (on sulphate reducers, because my cytochrome C3 work had overlapped with Bob's research interests). I was somewhat jet-lagged and woke up at dawn next morning to discover that, experienced traveller though I was by then, I had packed the wrong adaptor for my UK electric shaver: the one in my travel bag was for France. (UK electrical fittings are consistently different from those overseas, and battery-operated shavers were not then as effective as they later became). A breakfast unshaven, a helpless prowl around the environs, then I find a janitor whose friend "knows there's a shaver shop in State Street". I walk there; the shop is open and can sell me one. Triumph! I'm shaved by 08:30. Respectable, in that detail at least, for my date with Wilson, whom I had never met. So later that morning I made my way to the Bacteriology Department for our rendezvous.

Perry - in the American way we were Perry and John within seconds - was a buoyant, laughing personality. A big, fair man with, to me, a remarkably young face and demeanour for one who had been an active, distinguished scientist some 30 years before our meeting. Years had clearly not withered him. He was most welcoming. He also, I gradually realised, seemed to find my Englishness slightly comic - perhaps because he had spent an enjoyable time at Cambridge in the late 1930s, so he told me. He quoted back to me a letter I had sent him during my period at ARC Headquarters in which I had introduced myself as "the Assistant Director of a British Research Unit that has neither staff nor laboratory, like an Admiral in the Swiss Navy". He still found the simile amusing. But I had done a lot of reading around the topic of nitrogen fixation and we had a lot of serious stuff to talk about, notably my ideas on the future programme of the Unit, on which particular species of microbe we should choose to study and how our work might complement the projects in hand at Wisconsin. Perry, it seemed, would be my host for this part of my trip.

There followed a couple of those days familiar to almost any experienced scientist traveller. Even though I had come for the conference, here in Madison the seminar routine was followed - I gave a talk on the sulphate-reducing bacteria to an assembly of staff and students, some of whom chomped lunch while I talked; afterwards I met and talked with many of them. Exhausting, but I strutted my stuff adequately. The evening before our departure for the conference I was a dinner guest at Perry's home, along with a fellow conferee, one Harold Evans of Oregon State University. I had not met Harold before. He was a specialist on the nitrogen-fixing bacteria which colonise the roots of legumes. We stayed the night, sharing Perry's guest room, so as to be ready for a quick departure next morning.

Perry duly drove Harold and me northwards into upstate Wisconsin, an all-day drive through pleasant, largely agricultural, scenery to reach, in the late afternoon, Frook's Blue Echo Resort, a holiday bungalow establishment with its own general store set in woodland. The leaves of the trees were already mellowing into their autumn colours. It was a charming site, apparently popular among hobby fishermen because of nearby Butternut Lake. Each bungalow accommodated four people; mine was shared with Perry, Harold and Ralph Hardy - another new acquaintance to me. He was from Dupont de Nemours in Delaware, now in charge of the laboratory where nitrogenase had first been extracted.

So we settled in. Beds were assigned, bags unpacked, provisions checked. Perry mischievously decided that, as an Englishman, I would naturally need marmalade with my breakfast. Innocently I agreed. So he took me to the local general store to buy some. Of course, they had none and the storekeeper was bewildered by the request; marmalade was unheard of in rural upstate Wisconsin. But Perry's friendly teasing broke down any doubts others may have had about my somewhat alien presence, and everyone was amiable and welcoming.

After a brief wander round I joined the rest for supper. Then Perry gave an orientation talk: he said the proceedings would last for two whole days and that they would not be published but only briefly reported for the scientific press. They would be wholly informal and with no special timing. Contributors would talk about their latest findings and discussion would be free-ranging. (I was appointed to give my summary impressions of the meeting at its end - which, I had to agree, was only fair since I had no serious research to report. But it was an unexpected challenge).

Then I spent a happy evening meeting scientists whose names I had encountered on published papers and chatting about nitrogen fixation. In addition to my bungalow colleagues, I knew Bob Burris well, of course, but not Dr Len Mortenson, who had kicked off the enzymology of nitrogen fixation by his extraction of nitrogenase; Drs Bill Bulen and Dick Burns of the Charles F Kettering Foundation, biochemists studying a nitrogen-fixing bacterium called *Azotobacter* (the Kettering Foundation was actually financing the whole conference); Dr Warren Silver, an authority on those non-leguminous plants which possess symbiotic nitrogen-fixing bacteria, such as alder trees; Dr C C ('Con)' Delwiche, a specialist on the nitrogen cycle in general; or Dr Mike Dilworth, an up-and-coming researcher on symbiotic nitrogen fixation from Australia. Plus perhaps a couple of others; it was a remarkably small gathering. Most became my long-term friends. All were curious about this British plan for a new fundamental research unit, so for my part I was happy to tell them what Chatt and I had in mind - though my main reason for being there at all was to clarify in my own mind how best to plan the Unit's future biological research so that it complemented rather than competed with current research elsewhere in the world. A naive, even utopian, ambition, it transpired over the years, but I was innocent, too, of the tremendous force that ambition and competition had become in US science.

Anyway, at the time everyone seemed to be very open about their science and ready to welcome a new research team, especially one that encompassed both chemists and biologists homing in on the problem. The first evening was indeed one of stimulus and goodwill.

The next two days centred on the most intensive, yet informative and constructive science sessions that I have ever attended. Topics were of various lengths, many innovative. Bullen and Burns produced the 'hit' of the meeting: they had managed to extract nitrogenase from *Azotobacter*. The scientific importance of this was that Mortenson's nitrogenase, obtained from a bug, which would not grow at all if air were present, was irreversibly inactivated by exposure to air. Bulen's and Burns' preparation was from a bacterium which would only multiply in air, and the form in which they extracted it, as a micro-particle, could be handled in air without damage. This finding had long-term consequences for the science, which it would be too detailed to go into here, but it exemplifies the quality of the proceedings - several other reports were of comparable value. Yet we had time for relaxation, and excursion to a local pine-lodge restaurant for a festive dinner, even a stop-off to look for bears round a rubbish dump (none appeared). And some of the group, like good Americans, fitted in time for a little fishing. Yet it was not exhausting - all were dedicated scientists, too excited to tire.

It was a truly fruitful meeting, for me especially but for everyone else too. And at the end they accepted a clumsy, ill-digested and over-brief summary from me with good humour. As I remember, it was followed by a brief sessions in which several took turns at telling jokes - a bit like returning to school.

A final detail. The sponsoring Foundation was much impressed by the scientific success of the meeting and decided to sponsor comparable, less private, international meetings on nitrogen fixation in various countries every few years. In contrast to the dozen or so participants at Butternut, attendance rose to over 3000 by the century's end. Clearly it had been a seminal meeting in more than one respect.

On Day 3 it was get up for early breakfast, handshakes

all round and dispersal. Burris drove me back to Madison, and after lunch and a rest at his home we set off together to the University of Illinois at Champaign-Urbana, where he had academic business and I wished to talk to my old friends of a few years earlier, Leon Campbell, Ralph Wolf, and all. It was a delightful journey and reunion, but this section must not develop to far from the world of science. Yet I cannot resist two little items.

1) I arrive at the Microbiology Laboratory building. The secretary I shared with Leon greets me amiably in the cool Western manner and we exchange a few words, "How are you?", "How've you been?" etc. There is a new typist in the reception room, gazing and listening with total fascination. I am introduced:

"I just love your accent!" she bursts out, "Do you always talk like that?"

"Er, yes, actually" was the only reply I could muster. Rather limp, I fear.

2) My return transatlantic flight is overbooked, and I'm late enough to be assigned a complimentary First Class, seated next to a quiet but pleasant man of coloured complexion. The staff is attentive and much liquor is offered in flight. He is teetotal and abstemious, but is not bothered by my partaking; I have no intention of drinking a lot, anyway. After a while we get talking and he tells me he is John Woodenlegs, Chief of the Northern Cheyenne Indian Tribe, and he is going to London on this, his first, flight abroad, to help promote John Ford's film *Cheyenne Autumn,* then having its London premiere.

He expects to meet Winston Churchill, whom he admired, (unlikely, for Churchill was not at all well that year) and probably the Queen; he looks forward to seeing London - so I politely suspend disbelief and we talk of English and Amerindian things. But as we approach Heathrow he asks me to help him robe, for he had promised to arrive in full Chieftain's regalia. What I should do would be stand by the men's toilet while he changed his outer garments appropriately, me holding ready the long feathered head-dress and halter for him to put on easily.

We leave the operation to the last moment, as the plane bouncily begins its final descent, because once robed he can no longer sit down (a stewardess has allowed us a dispensation to ignore the seat belt sign). So, with the toilet door half open, I was helping fit and adjust the head-dress, when a large Texan, having much drink taken, struggled up the now steeply down-pointing and wobbling aisle towards us, to answer a call of nature. Catching sight of a fully-feathered Red Indian emerging from the toilet, he emitted a loud cry of "Jesus!!" and stumbled speedily back to his seat, into which a stewardess snappily buckled him.

The Chieftain and I stood where we were until the plane had landed and come to a standstill. By prior arrangement nobody was allowed to get off, not even first class passengers, until Chief Woodenlegs had alighted, because the press wanted him to appear first in the arrivals hall, where they and their cameramen awaited. But the Chieftain insisted that his newly found friend and valet accompany him - which naturally I did.

So it came about that an astonished Mary saw me arrive from the USA, travel bag in one hand and a large, feathered Redskin beside me, the two of us strolling together across an almost empty arrivals hall. (Did she think, "I knew he'd bring some kind of souvenir, but this is ridiculous?" I like to imagine so.) The Chieftain's arrival is documented in *The Times* for 14 October 1964, but I'm not in the photo.

Sussex

The message of that interlude is: if you want a really good and productive scientific discussion, collect a dozen or so obsessive researchers, pack them off together to somewhere nice and remote (both of those things), with food, drink and accommodation, for a few days - no more - and leave them to it.

Now back to the Unit. Chatt's and my little groups remained divided between the two colleges for about twelve months, during which time our proposed new building got into increasing difficulties. It soon became clear that Queen Mary College actually had no feasible space available for us at ground level and that the only serious prospect would be to build the new unit on concrete stilts above the College's boiler house. This caused cost estimates to leap abruptly, and both the Treasury and the Finance Office of the ARC became anxious. Meanwhile the newly-formed University of Sussex, just outside Brighton, had begun to take an interest, largely because its first Professor of Chemistry, Dr Colin Eaborn FRS, knew Chatt well. A little belatedly, it too offered Chatt a Chair, in Eaborn's School of Molecular Sciences. There was plenty of building space on the newly-growing campus and, most tempting, free space was available immediately in its newly-completed chemistry laboratories, sufficient for both sides of the UNF to be temporarily accommodated. Delicate negotiations were conducted and the upshot was that Chatt resigned his Chair at Queen Mary and moved to Sussex with his chemists and secretary very early in 1965. That spring, Kelly and I joined them, having handed our laboratory suite over to a well-pleased Royal Veterinary College.

At the University of Sussex half of the campus was still a confusion of mud and builders' rubble. Most of the faculty's offices were in prefabricated huts, and so were ours, so we got muddy, and often wet, going to and from lab and office. One got wet and muddy going to the library, too. But it was good fun being in a new university and the laboratory space provided by Eaborn's School was large and well found. The UNF had now come together, with chemists and biologists working side by side. Soon we were joined by Mr Ken Baker as the Unit's Chief Technician, whom Chatt had met and engaged while at Queen Mary College.

Moscow

Here I shall insert yet another travelogue, not only because it encompasses some of the most bizarre experiences of my scientific career but because it illuminates a near-comic side of the "Cold War" which followed the Second World War. For nearly 20 years that confrontation had rendered the Soviet

Union effectively a closed society as far as most of the non-communist world was concerned. International communication and co-operation in science had become stultified, along with political relations. There were indeed scientific meetings in the USSR, but scientists from the West could rarely attend unless they were fully accredited communists. However, since the Cuban crisis mentioned in Chapter 17, political relations between East and West had shown signs of thaw, and, in 1964, the veils on science began to lift. In that year an International Congress of Physics, I think it was, was held in Moscow. Rumour had it that Westerners attending the proceedings had found the organisation chaotic, because the State tourist agency, called Intourist, had little idea of how to handle a sudden influx of a couple of thousand Westerners, linguistically challenged, unpredictable and all plausibly capitalist spies. Nevertheless a precedent was set, and in 1966 a comparable International Congress of Microbiology was organised, also in Moscow. In the event, some 5000 microbiologists planned to attend. Three special sessions on nitrogen fixation were scheduled, so it seemed natural to the ARC that Kelly and I should be there too.

A full account of the meetings would be inappropriately long, so I shall just present a few scenes from our visit.

* * * *

Michael Kelly, Dr Geoff Coleman from Leeds and I are in a transcontinental train. We have chosen to travel by rail rather than air or sea, to see something of the countryside. We are on a rail package tour offered by the British travel agency, Thomas Cook (at the time the USSR only accepted travel agency parties). We have survived a rough sea voyage to Ostend and found the Soviet carriage of our multinational train to Moscow. It will slew off carriages to West and East Germany and to Poland en route. We are seated in a narrow compartment, on a bench seat facing backwards from the direction of travel opposite a wooden wall. This unfortunate arrangement comes about because it is the last compartment in the coach, half-sized, accommodating three rather than the usual six passengers. We have also survived several passport checks around East and West Berlin, and our train is trundling through East Germany towards Poland. The scenery proves mind-numbingly dull: mile upon mile, hour after hour, of flat strip-farmed fields. We are running out of conversation, except to consider, every hour or so, whose turn it is to go along the corridor and, for a few kopeks, purchase three glasses of warm black tea (*chai*) from the Steward's samovar - the only refreshment available. Meals, in an adjacent restaurant carriage, provide neutral rather than welcome intervals, because the food is so nasty - though our admirable courier, a Mr Free, assures us that it is superior by Soviet standards.

As night approaches and supper is over, out of boredom we demount our bench, draw down our tiered three bunks, and retire to sleep.

That was a mistake. For roughly at midnight, at Brest-Litovsk on the Polish - Soviet border, the train has to transfer from European narrow-gauge rails to Soviet wide-gauge track. This involves an extraordinary feat of engineering, conducted under arc lights, in which all the carriages are lined up on a special stretch of line, one which includes both gauges, beside mechanical arms which lift all the carriages at once off their narrow gauge wheels, which are then pushed out from underneath by a suitably low-level motor, Then a new set of wide-gauge wheels is pushed underneath to replace them, the carriages are lowered again, fixed in place, a new locomotive takes over and the journey can continue. Geoff and I hop out of our bunks to watch proceedings from the corridor, but Kelly, already fed up by earlier frustrations of the voyage, remains angrily in his bunk - the bottom one.

That is another mistake. Before the operation actually starts, a burly Russian comes into our compartment and, with a friendly "*Ein Arbeit*" (German is clearly his *lingua franca*) he lifts up a hatch in the floor of our compartment, thus confining Kelly to his bunk whether he likes it or not, and unscrews a huge, black, greasy bolt from beneath, which he places on the floor on an oily cloth. It seems that this releases the wheels below. In due course, amid clatter and shouts, Geoff and I feel the carriage rise and, an hour or so later, descend. There is no question of Kelly sleeping, and he can't get out, so we shout doubtless unwelcome progress bulletins to him.

Eventually our friendly Russian reappears, restores the bolt to its place beneath the hatch, removes the cloth, wishes us "*Gute Nacht*", and departs. After a further delay the train actually moves off, leaving us to make the best of the remaining night's sleep as we trundle towards Moscow. Next day the scenery is as dull as before, but for gangs of muscular women labouring on the railway track.

* * * *

We are in Moscow Byelorussia station. There is an Intourist desk to receive Congress delegates. The receptionist assures us that we are not expected at all. Sadly, I am by then afflicted with the scourge that became known to all Western delegates as "Stalin's Revenge": food-borne travellers' diarrhoea. (I had been too nauseated to eat my spiny fish stew at lunch; the matronly waitress cuffed me round the shoulders and said "*Essen!*" but I managed to indicate stomach-ache and she relented.) At the station I dare not leave the party to seek a lavatory lest the rest vanish while I'm away. A huge effort of containment preoccupies me. However, after two uncomfortable hours the resourceful Mr Free manages to get us transported by bus to Moscow's Hotel Ukraina, a monumental building in the Stalinist style near the Moscow river. Happily our arrival is accepted. As we queue for our rooms at the receptionist's desk, an innocent American lights a fat cigar. Misfortune! This is a symbol of The Capitalist. The receptionist severely reprimands him for smoking over her and asks him to desist. He looks forlorn and hides the cigar behind his back; his apology is ignored.

When my turn comes I find that a double room has been provided for Kelly and me. Since I have paid extra to have a single room, I remonstrate and, persisting through several *nyets*, I am assigned a single room. It proves to be huge, with a large bath and - joy - a lavatory. I exploit both. The bath lacks a bath plug but, forewarned, I have brought a universal one (which I still possess). I learn later how lucky I am to get a room at all; some delegates scheduled for the Ukraina end up at a hotel 25 miles out of town and spend ages getting to and from the meetings.

* * * *

Later on Kelly and I, washed and somewhat restored, meet to seek some dinner in the impressive hotel restaurant. Most tables are taken, but we find one occupied by a solitary, rather large, gentleman, of uncertain nationality with an expression of abiding melancholy. We indicate that we'd like to occupy the two spare places; he seems unforthcoming, but grunts assent.

Waiters scurry past us, both male and female, and pay us no attention whatever. We study the menu, which happily includes an English translation. All our sterling currency has been taken from us at Brest-Litovsk, and replaced by roubles and kopeks (we are assured that the equivalent of whatever Soviet currency we have remaining will be replaced with our national currency when we return home). But much of our expenses have been prepaid, and Thomas Cook has provided us with Intourist vouchers of designated rouble values wherewith to pay for meals, taxis etc.
Soon we realise that our Intourist coupons do not fit in with the prices at all. Kelly and I discuss the matter, and conclude

that we must either overpay enormously in coupons or top up with our roubles. As we grumble about this, and about the inattention of the waiters, our table companion breaks his silence: "Just swing with the punches," he says.

Introductions all round. He proves to be Professor Mortimer Starr of California. We knew each other by name. He has been waiting for 30 minutes already but is resigned, having been in the hotel three days early. He had come early for pre-Congress organisational Committee meetings and seems kind of shell-shocked. He advises us always to choose a table served by waitresses, as the waiters tend to accept either vouchers or currency, but not both. He assures us that the Congress organisation is frustrating and bewildering but there is no point at all in trying to resist or amend it; the Ukraina's inefficiency is just a minor pinprick in the grand non-scheme of things.

* * * *

I am in the main hall of the University, having yesterday been given a quick tour of Moscow, registered and attended the Congress' opening ceremonies and speeches, culminating in half of *Swan Lake* by the Kiev ballet. (Half? Yes. There was an interval. but owing to a mistranslation a good proportion of the delegates, including me, thought it had ended and departed. Later I learned that it had not. But we got our dinner faster than usual). Anyway, this morning I am trying to find out from a number of cryptic notices where the scientific sessions I am interested in are taking place. Often I am interrupted by anxious, pale-faced Westerners asking where the lavatories are, for of these there is no sign. Perhaps the Soviets, in a strange prudery, consider them unmentionable. I do not know, and as my bowel problem has receded I am more or less stable, but Stalin's Revenge afflicts almost every Western delegate sooner or later. (In due course I do manage to find some wholly unsignalled lavatories.) Though the signs on the doors of the auditoria do not always match those given in the official programme, I manage to find some scientific sessions relevant to my interests. Oddly, no matter what the topic the large audiences consist mainly of women, mature ladies who listen, seemingly undiscriminating, to anything. Microbiology would seem to be a feminine pursuit in this country. I attend a meeting on nitrogen fixation but after a few trivial papers the interpreters announce that they must go home now, so the Chairman, Academician Mishustin, suspends the session altogether. No great loss, really, but some who travelled thousands of miles to say their pieces must feel aggrieved.

* * * *

I am standing outside the Hotel Ukraina, waiting for who knows what, watching a group of American tourists embarking on their bus to continue their tour of the Soviet Union. The wives have visited the hotel's gift shop, spending their most welcome hard currency on souvenirs. An infuriated husband is addressing his stubborn-faced wife so: "Jo-anna! You drive me mad!"

Why? Because she is carrying a neatly wrapped souvenir, a long and thin package with a triangular base, slightly taller than herself. It is clearly a bass balalaika, which awkward-shaped object she is determined to add to her luggage and carry home.

* * * *

I ought to be at the special symposium of nitrogen fixation - after all, that is why the Agricultural Research Council sent me to Moscow in the first place - but actually I am with a party on a fascinating Intourist visit to the Kremlin. I had risen early and had a solitary breakfast (miraculously I negotiated some toast) so as to get to my meeting in time. I was the first passenger to settle into a bus outside the Ukraina labelled "Symposium, Nitrogen Fixation".

What I failed to notice was that, after a discussion among drivers outside the bus, our driver changed the notice on the outside of the bus to "Kremlin Tour". He did not tell the handful of passengers already in the bus, nor did anyone else. Perhaps an alert Postgate ought to have observed an unlikely preponderance of delegates' wives among passengers who arrived later? I didn't. Nor have I ever regretted my guilty error: the Kremlin is a wonderful *mélange* of extravagant grandeur and absurdity, but I must refer the reader to the many guide and travel books describing its wonders. At one stage I got separated from my party, and I shall forever regret that I therefore failed to visit Lenin, embalmed in his tomb outside the Kremlin walls (apparently the party marched in ahead of an enormous queue of Russians, a privilege seemingly not resented). But I regained my party later, in time to be transported back to the Ukraina. My nitrogen fixation symposium was well over by then, of course.

* * * *

A day of meetings over, the organisers have laid on some early evening sightseeing tours of Moscow, and I have acquired a ticket for a two-hour boat trip on the Moscow River. It starts at 5:30 pm, so I ought to be back in time for dinner, which gratifies Kelly because he has invited a French couple to dine with him and wishes me to join the party because he speaks no French and they speak no English.

I duly embark on the appropriately-labelled bus with other delegates. Rather surprisingly, since the river is close to the hotel, the bus drives for nearly an hour towards the outskirts of Moscow, and we disembark by a waterway. No fewer that nine riverboats are lined up; many busloads of people are embarking on them, and I learn that this is not the short tour of the Moscow River at all, but a four-hour sightseeing excursion along the Moscow Canal. Apparently this excursion has been much over subscribed and, instead of restricting tickets, the Russians have recruited extra riverboats. I am told that food and drink will be provided. The fact that my ticket is for a different trip bothers no one; I am assigned the last boat, along with two microbiologist friends from my MRE days, Harold Zwartow and David Tempest, and two Dutch microbiologists. We five are its sole passengers.

As dusk falls, the flotilla sets off, headed by a large riverboat decorated with lights and flags, its band playing, and I learn later, with plentiful refreshments. Boat number 2 is also gaily illuminated, but the rest are dark but for ordinary deck and cabin lighting. Our boat is last. The seats are wooden, it is chilly on deck, and none of us has any idea what we are to see, other than rather uninteresting canal-side warehouses and cranes. Nor does it matter much, because pitch-black darkness soon falls and we can see nothing of the banks at all. Sometimes as the waterway bends we can glimpse the brightly-illuminated leading boat way up ahead, and hear fragments of its music. So we sit in the main cabin and talk.

Fairly soon we get hungry. One of the Dutch people, who speaks fragmentary Russian (both speak excellent English, as most Dutch do) goes down some stairs to a kiosk to enquire about refreshments. It transpires that we can buy plain cheese sandwiches - no freebies on our boat. However, there are also some bottles of wine for sale, green label and yellow label. We buy a bottle of the yellow label to share. It is a white Muscat, probably about 15% alcohol, and tastes like imitation sherry. The kiosk has no glasses, however, only waxed paper cups. The alcohol content of the wine is sufficient to soften the wax, and the lower parts of the cups soften and bulge under the weight of the liquor. But we dismiss anxieties about how much dissolved wax we are ingesting. We begin to feel caught in a Kafka-like trap, nothing much to eat, drink or see, but the wine undoubtedly cheers us up.

For one and three quarter hours we sail along, total

darkness outside, then, suddenly, piped Russian music comes out of a previously unnoticed speaker. Also, the leading boat turns round, followed by the rest of the flotilla; as it passes we see dancing and hear sounds of music and jollity. On the second boat there appears to be community singing. We feel so notable an event as an about turn requires another bottle; we try the wine with the green label. It proves to be identical to the previous wine in every discernible respect. Our piped music stops. Duly the wine begins to take effect, for we begin to see the humour of our situation. Not only are we absurdly cheerful, but we also develop mild headaches - as if we are getting drunk and having our hangovers all at once. But it sustains us for another one and three quarter hours of nothing much happening until we are returned to our starting quay.

We walk with careful dignity to our bus. (I learn later that those on the lead boat had a riotous party with excellent food and drink; two American delegates were carried off senseless). It is well past midnight and our driver wishes to get home. He hurtles across Moscow, the potholed roads causing us to bounce a foot or so out of our seats in unison, as in a movie cartoon. Such is our manic glee that we all find this hilarious, while we nurse our aching foreheads in our hands.

Delivered at last to the Ukraina, we find an infuriated Kelly waiting for me in the lobby. Why? Because this reprehensible tale has a subplot, involving his dinner guests. It seems that he had rather fancied the Frenchman's wife, but only learned that she had a husband after having issued his invitation. Being unable to speak any French at all, he had been relying on my reasonably good French to sustain communication. He had even bought her a corsage. In the event my absence had caused a delayed, awkward and embarrassing meal. He is not in the least mollified by our explanations, for David, Harold and I keep giggling like idiots. He would not speak to me for the next couple of days.

"Man, you sure look as if you lived it up last night!" says a friendly American microbiologist at breakfast next day. I felt that way, too.

* * * *

To the best of my unreliable recollection my room was on the fourteenth floor of the Ukraina. Kelly's was one floor above. On each floor, by the elevator, was a formidable matron at a desk in charge of the floor. There was also a mini-café, offering light refreshments. I am idly awaiting the oft-delayed lift to descend around nine in the morning, and I notice in the mini-café a citizen with typical Mongol face sharing a substantial bottle of vodka with another Soviet citizen. Each tosses down a shot, then my lift arrives. Some six hours later I return to my room. They are still there; seemingly sober, and the bottle is approaching its end. No wonder alcoholism was - and still is - a problem in that part of the world.

* * * *

The reception after the concluding ceremony of the Congress, held in the magnificent Palace of Congresses, was a party to end all parties: all possible liquors as well as excellent food and company - including many friendly young ladies who cannot, surely, have all been microbiologists. Many delegates felt that it made amends for the confusion and muddle of the previous week. For my part, I am enjoying myself, chatting and drinking cautiously, so I am less than prepared for two burly Russians who come up on either side of me and say, in tones that brook no refusal, "Come!"

Whoever I was talking to has vanished, so I obey. My two companions, who have no English, escort me away from the party, down three flights of stairs to the ground floor, then, so help me, down two more flights to a sub-basement. I remember the dreadful stories I have read of the Soviet secret police and their ghastly interrogation treatments. Have they discovered that my father was a renegade communist? Or learned of my social democratic background? Or that I once worked in a biological warfare laboratory? There is a flickering blue light in the corner of the huge cellar we have just entered and a silent crowd - not very reassuring.

We reach that corner, and light dawns. All are watching one of the few television sets then available in the Soviet Union. This is the last 15 minutes of the final match for the World Soccer Cup, and England is ahead of Germany. Germany had beaten the Soviet Union in the semi-final, and the one thing the Soviets desire above all else is that the Germans should not win! My erstwhile companions have collected as many English delegates as they could find to join the group to watch it and, despite my indifference to football, I sense the excitement as the game progresses and goes into overtime. And in the event the English win. Soccer fans still speak with awe of England's 1966 World Cup victory. The delight all round is extravagant and noisy; being an Englishman, my hand is shaken sore; I am bear-hugged by a huge Yugoslav, and many are the congratulations on my part in this great victory(!). I later learn that Kelly, arriving back at the Ukraina, was hugged and kissed by his floor matron for the same reason (no matter that he was of Irish extraction).

With relief I acknowledge the applause, express thanks and duly depart, opting to return to the Ukraina rather that to the party, which is still in full swing.

* * * *

The return journey had its confusions, too. An event resembling an episode out of a spy film took place when an Iraqi passenger, who had for some seemingly legitimate reason obtained a cheque from a naive English delegate, was escorted away by police at the next station. After the train had resumed its journey, the Englishman, observing that the Iraqi had left his case behind, opened it with the intention of returning it. It was full of wads of US $100 bills. He shut it at once and passed it to the steward, and it was taken away by police at Brest-Litovsk. What was going on? Your guess is as good as mine.

At Brest-Litovsk our hard currency confiscated on the inward journey was returned - or sort of. I received mine as some loose change in real sterling plus a US $1 bill and a Soviet travellers cheque for £10 (which some months later yielded £8, when I found a British bank which would cash it).

* * * *

Well, those were some glimpses of the International Congress of Microbiology, Moscow, 1966. Despite their frivolous content, I did get to a substantial number of the scientific presentations, but the standard of the contributions was not impressive. Though I learned very little microbiology at the Congress, I certainly discovered that alcohol was an ingrained and essential part of Soviet hospitality, but that efficient organisation was not their speciality. Even ten years later, microbiologists at meetings would reminisce about the muddles, confusions and misfortunes that they had experienced. But few regretted the experience; though it was stressful at the time and "Stalin's revenge" was the joker in the pack. But the kindness and good intentions of our Soviet hosts were unquestionable.

The unit grows

Back at Sussex, Chatt, Ken Baker and I planned purpose-built laboratories to be built beside the Molecular Sciences building. Ken and I dealt directly with the architects, much helped by a buildings office at the ARC's headquarters; it was an exhausting task, because the architects had no understanding at all of the needs of research scientists. My own research came to a virtual standstill for some 18 months, but in the end our buildings got built. The Unit moved into its own building in 1968, and after we had knocked down a few walls and rearranged the odd doorway, it served us very well for many years.

Actually, it had cost somewhat more than the estimates for laboratories on stilts at Queen Mary, but the Sussex Downs were a much nicer place to be than the Mile End Road, and there was room for expansion. Whatever the Treasury officials might have thought, none of us regretted the move.

From the Unit's outset, Chatt and I had agreed that, to start with, we should plan and lead the chemical (his) side of the research and the biological (my) side independently, keeping each other informed, of course. Our expectation, like that of Gordon Cox, was that, as our two threads progressed, they would come together, homing in on understanding the basic chemistry of the biological phenomenon of nitrogen fixation.

I completed my professional career in the Unit, another quarter of a century, during which the subject mushroomed, as more and more scientists throughout the world took up the topic. The details of how scientists' understanding of nitrogen fixation was transformed during that period would doubtless fascinate a historian of science, but is probably too arcane and technical for the general reader. (It has been documented an historical Royal Society symposium of 1986, as well as in scientific publications and reviews over the fourth quarter of the 20th century.) But we contributed substantially to those advances and I ought not to quit without providing a quick rundown on what the Unit got up to.

In outline, the Unit became internationally pre-eminent in basic research on nitrogen fixation, and was widely admired for its interdisciplinary approach and its co-operative way of working. This meant that chemists had to learn to understand the thinking of biologists, and biologists had to accustom themselves to the hard, down-to-earth outlook of chemists. The two disciplines differ markedly in the way their practitioners think. Chemists like their science to be precise; they like, for instance, to purify, crystallise, and determine the exact physical parameters of a new chemical. Biologists, in contrast, have to make the best of biological variation, and work with sloppy mixtures derived from biological material. Chemists like to explain chemical processes in terms of exact kinetic or thermodynamic equations, while biologists muddle along with statistics, often guessing processes from kinetics. I was lucky in a way, having been trained as a chemist and turned to biology, and I could to some extent straddle the two sides. Chatt had greater problems. I recall with amusement an occasion when I drew his attention to a paper in his area that I thought might interest him. His normal polite caution slipped for a moment as he remarked dismissively: "That's the sort of stuff biologists publish."

But once we were all at Sussex the two sides slowly began to gain respect for each other's work and real interactions began.

Here is an early example. Before the Unit started, scientists had learned that the nitrogen-fixing enzyme system somehow took up nitrogen gas from the atmosphere and attached hydrogen atoms to the two nitrogen atoms which make up the nitrogen molecule, a process that converted them into ammonia. This was the stuff that fertilised soil -

just as when you buy ammonium sulphate to fertilise garden plants. Mindful of the way over a decade earlier I had fooled the sulphate-reducing enzyme of sulphate-reducing bacteria by 'feeding' them selenate, so blocking the enzyme (I remind you that selenate molecules are very like sulphate molecules in shape and they stuck to the functional part of the enzyme), I wondered whether was there a chemical that would interact in a similar way with the nitrogen-fixing system. Not to block it (a few that did that were known already), but to be transformed into something we could measure easily and quickly.

Biologists bounced the question off chemists. Several suggestions proved to be known already and of no obvious use, but Kelly, Richards and I thought up a substance called methyl isocyanide, a liquid. Richards prepared some, and Kelly tested it. It worked marvellously: the enzyme converted it to methane, which could be measured rapidly by gas chromatography. Nitrogen-fixing activity could thus be assessed in three minutes or so compared with the 24 hours needed by the quickest analytical method then available. The serious flaw was that methyl isocyanide is very poisonous to humans, though this mattered less than you might think because it stank so horribly that no one could bear to be close to it long enough to get poisoned. That meant it had to be handled in a so-called fume cupboard, which sucked its vapour up a chimney and disgorged it into the Sussex countryside, where it soon dispersed and decomposed. Nevertheless, we used it for a few months, until we learned that Mike Dilworth, who had been at the Butternut meeting, had developed an equally quick gas chromatographic assay using the much less smelly gas acetylene. We adopted his acetylene test with some relief, as in due course did most nitrogen fixation laboratories the world over.

That is just one example of the sort of interaction that developed within the Unit over the years. Much of our research also involved collaboration with other research centres here and abroad and we attracted postdoctoral and sabbatical visitors from many parts the world. Several came again and again - one or two so often that they became more or less honorary members of the Unit.

We also had a steady throughput of postgraduate students who registered for a higher degree at our host university. They were especially valuable because, apart from bringing fresh, young minds to bear on various questions, they could also be given projects to investigate which were peripheral to our official programme rather than part of it - provided, of course, those projects, properly done, would achieve their hoped-for degrees. The Unit made several celebrated contributions to the science, 'breakthroughs' in journalese, in all of which students or visiting workers participated; an early instance was the preparation of a new and complex organo-metallic chemical which would bind a nitrogen molecule and then stick hydrogen atoms on to it - a primitive model for what the nitrogen-fixing system does. It was especially interesting because we all knew that a metal atom was deeply involved in the biological process. But the development that attracted wide publicity was our creation of new species of nitrogen-fixing bacteria by genetic manipulation - a very early example of genetic engineering, and the way it happened illustrates rather well how the Unit worked.

By around 1970 the biologists had done pretty well purifying and studying the nitrogen-fixing enzyme system extracted from a bacterium called *Klebsiella*, and it seemed to me that it might be helpful if we knew something about the genes that told this bug to make that enzyme when even closely-related cousins couldn't. But genetics was certainly not part of our programme. I tried to do a few relevant experiments myself, and soon realised that I simply didn't know enough about the techniques of bacterial genetics to make serious progress. It needed to be done properly, full time. Happily a graduate student trained in such techniques, Ray Dixon, came along and was willing to have a go as a research topic for a doctorate. After a rather frustrating year trying out ideas for making mutants of nitrogen fixers he had success with *Klebsiella*, obtaining mutants unable to fix nitrogen as well as other mutants with useful mutations. He then cured a nitrogen fixation negative mutant by introducing undamaged nitrogen fixation genes donated by a non-mutated *Klebsiella*, using a well-known process called mating, stimulated by a genetical element called a plasmid. (That is a simplified but correct account of what he did.) Meanwhile, quite unknown to us, a graduate student working with Professor Valentine in California had done very similar experiments, but he corrected his nitrogen-fixing negative mutant of *Klebsiella* using a bacterial virus to bring in the 'healthy' genes from a donor *Klebsiella*. After a brief moment of jealousy, we realised that this was wonderful, for we had each confirmed the other's findings, but in different ways and independently. And because the experiments showed that nitrogen fixation genes could be moved around, our work opened up the field of the genetics of nitrogen fixation for anybody to tackle. How many genes were there? Whereabouts on the bacterial chromosome were they? How were they regulated? Could they be isolated? And so on.

The genetics of nitrogen fixation soon became a hot research topic in laboratories all over the world and it blossomed over the next two decades - kick started by two graduate students half a world apart!

That was an important advance, but our spectacular one came after that. Both my student and Valentine's had found evidence that the nitrogen fixation genes lay close to a gene known to enable the bug to make an amino-acid called histidine. Every living thing has to have histidine. Dixon had the bright idea of getting a histidine-requiring mutant of a bug distantly related to *Klebsiella* called *Escherichia coli,* which never fixes nitrogen, and to correct its histidine mutation using a plasmid carrying the histidine gene from our *Klebsiella.* His hope was that the nitrogen fixation genes would be carried into *E. coli* along with the histidine-making genes, thus creating a genetically-manipulated nitrogen-fixing species hitherto unknown in nature. The experiment worked. Our letter to *Nature* in 1972 describing the nitrogen-fixing *E. coli* generated a mini-sensation and for a few weeks we had our taste of fame: media interviews and - real celebrity stuff this – we achieved mention in both *Time* and *Playboy* magazines!

Why the excitement? Because it raised the possibility, less plausible now than then, of putting nitrogen-fixing genes into any creature, most notably into food crops which would then manage without needing nitrogen fertiliser. (Hold on, you ask, why was *Playboy* interested? Because it involved mating, silly.) More seriously, the scientific community was deeply impressed and plasmids carrying nitrogen-fixation genes were invaluable research tools. Dixon's were used in laboratories all over the world.

THE UNF GENETICS TEAM, JANUARY 1976

L - R: The author, Christina Kennedy, Frank Cannon, Ray Dixon

The ARC, not knowing that we had started some genetics, was perceptibly bewildered and slow to react, but in 1974 our full-time staff complement was increased by half, largely so that we could develop our pioneering work on the genetics of nitrogen fixation.

The Unit's building was also enlarged - actually this happened twice during its tenure at Sussex. At its peak in the early 1980s, with an 'official' staff complement of about 45, there were actually over 80 people working in its building, the remainder being self-financed visiting scientists of one kind or another. Most of the Unit's senior workers became world authorities in their special fields and several of its staff and students went on to achieve university professorships. Martin Buck, a molecular biologist, became a Fellow of the Royal Society in due course; so, too, did two of my post-graduate students, Ray Dixon and Howard Dalton, along with two of Chatt's chemistry researchers. Howard, indeed, was knighted after becoming Chief Scientist of a Government Department concerned with Food and Agriculture. The Unit was quite a good incubator of scientific talent.

When Chatt retired in 1980, the ARC (by then renamed the Agriculture and Food Research Council or AFRC) departed from custom and did not disband his Unit, but transferred it to me instead, agreeing that I appoint our most senior chemist, Professor G J Leigh, as my Assistant Director to take charge of the chemistry. It was a reversal of the original pattern, but still sustained the spread of our interdisciplinary approach. By that time the chemistry side had expanded its research into electrochemistry, which is the study of chemical reactions forced, as it were, by passing an electric current through the reactants, and also into X-ray crystallography, the determination of chemical structures from the way in which the compounds scatter X-rays.

As a Director, first of the biologists, later of the whole Unit, I made a point of never directing. I would urge, cajole and lean on my research staff so as to keep the research on a co-ordinated and co-operative course, but in the end I expected them to know better than me what needed doing, and to get on and do it. If I had tried to manage them the bright ones would have departed and I should have been left with the mediocrities, of whom we had happily very few.

I like to think that my leadership echoed in some degree Duke Ellington's approach to his orchestra. He never managed his musicians: he had a collection of brilliant, disparate and individualistic soloists, and he gave them their heads musically. His contribution was simply to co-ordinate them, which he did in so masterly a fashion that he created the greatest jazz orchestra of this century - some say the greatest orchestra, jazz or classical.

For my own part, I managed to combine bench work of my own in the Unit, while directing a generally headstrong but also generally talented staff of scientists. In my own research I specialised in the physiology of nitrogen fixation, evolving later towards its physiological genetics as colleagues uncovered the basic genetics of the process. In 1956, after the Unit had been at Sussex for a couple of years, the University had made me a Research Professor, which gave me a useful handle to my name and enabled me and my colleagues to supervise postgraduate students. Sometime early in the 1970s, after our genetical advances had begun to get publicity for the Unit and I was becoming known outside the sphere of microbiology, the question came to me by way of Chatt - would I like to be considered for a Civil Honour? To my wife Mary's disappointment I politely declined: it would have been too much for the anti-establishment sentiments generated in me by my experiences at Teddington and with MRE. I was much more interested in achieving the scientific recognition of becoming a Fellow of the Royal Society (I knew some Fellows had proposed me). Happily, in 1977 the Royal Society did elect me a Fellow.

I travelled abroad most years for scientific meetings or to lecture and also spent a whole sabbatical year in the USA. I was active within the Society for General Microbiology, served on its Council, editing its *Journal of General Microbiology* and in due course I became the Society's President. I was also frequently present at meetings of the Society for Applied Bacteriology, sometimes as a speaker, sometimes just a participant. In the early 1980s I became President of the Institute of Biology. I wrote lots of research papers, some technical books, and somehow I found time to write *Microbes and Man,* a long-lived 'popular' book about microbes, and later a complementary book on microbes, *The Outer Reaches of Life.*

That's enough about me for the time being - some more in the next chapter. I retired in 1987 and the UNF became an outstation at Sussex of the AFRC's Institute of Plant Science Research (centred on the John Innes Institute at Norwich) headed by our senior biochemist, Barry Smith, later Professor Smith. Its name was changed to the Nitrogen Fixation Laboratory (NFL), but everyone still called it 'the Unit'. In 1995 it quit its by then rambling and obsolescent building at Sussex, and the bulk of the research staff moved to new purpose-built laboratories, the Joseph Chatt Building at Norwich. In the early 2000s the NFL was disbanded as a research group and its remaining staff were assimilated into the Institute's main staff complement.

I can recall lots of curious and interesting problems, people, places and events during my quarter century with the Unit, but to report on them all would render this chapter more like a school report than an insider's perspective on the scientific scene. For though we operated with enviable financial and bureaucratic freedom, the scientific scene was changing. As my time in the Unit drew to a close we were becoming an anachronism, and within a few years a new era would be upon us with accountants dominating government research, senior scientists deflected from their benches to write reports and project proposals, universities bidding for industrial money by setting up companies and science parks, and market forces conditioning scientific research policy and imposing secrecy, the antithesis of scientific progress. The Golden Age of science for the public good was grating to its end. And though I myself have inevitably featured prominently in my story, it is that Golden Age, not me, that these chapters have really been about.

The run-down

Yet I suppose I ought to sign myself out, as my preface served to sign me in, so this last chapter is more overtly autobiographical than what came before. What became of me?

I hinted towards the end of the last chapter that, as the end of my years with the UNF approached, the administration and nature of Government science changed drastically, in my view for the worse. Through all my tenure the UNF managed to sustain its relative immunity to bureaucracy. But the changing situation did not make for the happiest of retirements. The AFRC was under pressure to cut its expenditure, and to facilitate this it required Directors of its research stations to divide their research programmes into projects, which could be separately closed if necessary. Although Chatt and I had correctly maintained that the Unit's research programme was a single, multi-disciplinary project, in my last three or so years I was repeatedly bothered by paperwork from AFRC Headquarters asking questions such as which parts of the Unit's research programme would I close down in the event that a cut of 10%, say, or 15% was called for? Was the chemistry part of our programme necessary? Who of my permanent staff were expendable in the event of a staff cut of, say, two officers? I was able to delay, obfuscate and dispute, but it was time-consuming and sometimes childish.

We had almost no internal bureaucracy within our Unit, but there were two notable exceptions to this convention. One was set up to ensure that everyone in the Unit had some idea of what everyone else was doing, because in a dedicated research team good researchers can easily become so obsessed their own fragment of the research that they lose sight of the big picture. So all manuscripts intended for publication in learned journals had to be circulated to everybody before submission, for information and, if appropriate, amendment. The second was that our senior staff were obliged to prepare one or two page summary reports on their research progress every six months. They were allowed up to about 500 words, a valuable corrective against their tendency to loquacity. Published work should be omitted because the manuscripts had been seen already. Copies would then be pinned together and supplied to everyone in the Unit as a Progress Report. Every year the Unit would more or less stop work for a day in order to discuss the year's progress, as indicated by its latest publications and the last two progress reports. These reports, manuscripts and in-house meetings were a valuable, indeed essential chore; they often threw up new ideas and certainly eased collaboration - and they delighted visiting research workers even if they bored some junior staff.

Courtesy copies of the report were naturally sent to the AFRC"s headquarters. It so happened that the reports were originally grouped under Chemistry, Biochemistry, Physiology and Genetics, representing the principle academic disciplines underlying individual reports, though everyone knew well that our studies in all four disciplines were interrelated and overlapped. Then I discovered that HQ was regarding research in these disciplines as distinguishable research projects, one or more of which could be closed without seriously affecting the others. This was nonsense, conflicting directly with the intention that our research should be multidisciplinary. So I revised the headings to notional teams: Enzymology team, bioinorganic team, *Klebsiella* team and *Azotobacter* team (the latter names reflected the principal microbe being studied by that team). A given scientist's work might feature in one, two or even three teams' reports, re-emphasising the fact that the Unit's research programme was a network of multidisciplinary approaches. The change in no way altered what people actually did at the bench.

Coping with such bureaucratic pinpricks was dispiriting and irritating. I did not resent the visitors, staffing, supplies and maintenance problems that I had to cope with as well, helped by an effective secretary, Brenda, and a small in-house administration team. And I had an able technical assistant, Helen Kent, with whose help I managed to get into my own laboratory to do about three days' research a week at the bench. Chatt had done no bench work. But I was becoming stressed; as my sixty-fifth year approached, when retirement would finally be mandatory, I began to feel depressed and ready to go: my influence with HQ was perceptibly waning, and both HQ and my colleagues were becoming increasingly preoccupied with what would happen to the Unit when I retired. Who would direct it? Might it be moved from Sussex? Or, perish the thought, would it be disbanded?

All was not gloom, however, in the run up to my departure. The research had its momentum and there were farewell celebrations. The chemistry researchers, Chatt's erstwhile staff, invited me and Mary to a farewell dinner, and later the Unit as a whole set up a wonderful mass dinner party for us at Michelam Priory, in the Sussex countryside, with gifts and expressions of goodwill. Finally, on the eve of my 65th birthday, I shook hands all round, collected my briefcase and left my office and lab for the last time. Next morning, as planned and prepared, Barry Smith moved into my erstwhile office and took over the Unit; Helen retained possession of my lab for some months to finish off a project I'd started her on, watched over by Martin Buck.

Once I had retired I slept like a log for about 14 hours on three successive nights. Then I realised that I must find something to do, preferably something entirely different. Ten years earlier, Mary had embarked upon a biography of my father, Raymond Postgate, whom I mentioned briefly in my introduction. But for diverse reasons she never got beyond drafting the first three chapters, dealing with his childhood. She agreed that I might take over the task. It was a bit belated, because he died in 1971 and the public had had sixteen years in which to forget his name - and fame. So I buckled down to that as my main occupation.

Happily the University had made me an Emeritus Professor, which meant that I could park my car there and use the University library and many of its facilities. To use the library to look up recent historical and political matters was a new experience for me, as I got used to an unfamiliar system of referencing and learned what sources were available. I also learned that history, especially recent history, was a bizarre subject to a scientist. There was little or no corpus of consensus comparable to the edifice of scientific knowledge; the subject was fraught with prejudice and preconceptions. For instance, labour historians (of which my father was one), Marxist historians, economic historians and classical historians would offer very different takes on events. Most curious - do they ever achieve concordance?

In the UNF it had been my habit to tell Brenda where I was going if I left my office, and for roughly how long. It might be to my own lab, or to the library, to have coffee, or lunch, to visit the biochemists' lab, the geneticists' lab, the stores or whatever. This was so that she would know where I was in case she needed to reach me quickly. I had difficulty in breaking the habit. During my first few weeks of retirement, to her mild amusement, I would tell Mary what I was about to do: going to dig the garden for a while, to walk the dog, to write in my study, to wash the car, to go to the University, even to have a siesta. Mary was very patient; she assured me gently that she didn't really need to know, and gradually I stopped and learned to become more of a free agent. Mary and I had to get used to spending whole weekdays together - and soon found that we rather liked it, going on walks, drives and excursions together. I also played more jazz in the first few months of my retirement than I had since my student days. Very relaxing - and my playing improved

The rather unhappy situation that had underlain my retirement had left me with a depressive reluctance to do anything concerned with science, and I turned down invitations to a lecture tour in India, a meeting in Hungary, and a short-term 'Distinguished Visiting Scholar' post in the USA. But my past science did not leave me entirely alone. A symposium which I could not avoid, and indeed did not wish to, was the Society for General Microbiology's 42nd, held at Southampton in January 1988 to celebrate my retirement both as a professional researcher and as President of the SgM. Its subject concerned my major research specialities, bacteria of the nitrogen and sulphur cycles. Most learned societies would have called it a *festschrift*, with my name on the cover and photo inside the subsequent publication, but the SgM Council had no time for such fripperies. Nevertheless it was a great meeting, and I was happily able to make a real if modest research contribution myself since my final laboratory work had drawn both themes together, my topic being nitrogen fixation by sulphate-reducing bacteria. Also, most contributors dedicated their papers to me, in print as well as on the platform.

After a good and vinous dinner and a speech I was able to add a third strand of my life's interests to the frolic: the organisers had kindly invited the jazz band which I led at Sussex University, the Sussex Trugs, to the dinner, and we played jazz to the sometimes bemused but mainly delighted company for a couple of hours, while many of them danced. As the evening ended, some distinguished senior microbiologists had perceptible difficulty in remaining upright.

In the spring of 1998 I was also persuaded to contribute a plenary lecture of about 30 minutes on the evolution of nitrogen fixation at an international conference in Bonn, and I roped in my erstwhile colleague Bob Eady to be co-author. Space was made for me in the Unit's library to work on my talk and use the Unit's reprint collection. In the event, my contribution, through no fault of my own, had elements of slapstick comedy. My presentation was scheduled for the first morning, to follow upon the opening ceremony, at which distinguished civic dignitaries of the City of Bonn and the University were to make speeches of welcome to the delegates. It transpired that these worthies all tended to verbosity, and collectively they overran their time by about one and a half hours. This brought proceedings to well past the time for lunch, which was waiting half an hour's bus ride away from the conference hall at the University campus.

I offered to postpone my talk, but dear Hermann Bothe, the Conference Organiser, by then almost beside himself with anxiety, would have none of it. So I duly mounted the podium and delivered my paper to a somewhat restless audience, doubtless with rumbling tummies, abbreviating it wherever I could. My slides - for we used 35 mm slides to illustrate lectures in those days - were being projected on to a big screen behind me, so I had to turn round to see them.

All seemed to be going well until the last five minutes or so, when people started laughing at intervals. Perplexed, I soldiered on, pointing out at one stage that I was not joking. Then I glanced at the screen and saw the reasons for their laughter. What was being shown bore no relation whatever to my talk. They were distinctly informal slides of me at various earlier meetings, with familiar figures from the nitrogen fixation world. It transpired that international friends from other labs had collected these pictures and persuaded the projectionist to add them to my package of slides, to be shown after my talk, while Professor Len Mortenson would present me with a gift of wine. But the projectionist, presumably anxious about lunch, had raced my slides ahead of my talk and was projecting the joke slides before I had finished. Those in the audience who were following my talk, and not worrying about their next meal, must have found the illustrations bewildering. My friends' intentions were of the kindest - and I got the wine. But, oh dear, I wonder still what my Teutonic audience made of it! And we all had a distinctly late lunch.

My final contribution to the cutting edge of my science was, so to speak, thrust upon me by the Royal Society. The Society has a number of prize lectureships awarded to distinguished scientists in certain fields, and the microbiological one is called the Leeuwenhoek Lecture (in memory of the 17th century Dutch microscopist who first observed bacteria, Antoni van Leeuwenhoek). It carries a money prize and the obligation to give a publishable lecture to the Society, and to repeat it at least once elsewhere in the

UK. They appointed me to be Leeuwenhoek Lecturer for 1992. It was a singular honour, actually, but I remember reading the Society's letter of appointment with a certain curmudgeonly resentment: I've retired; I have no lab. Leave me alone! But my depressive feelings soon dissolved, to be displaced by anxiety: what could I talk about, with no new research to offer? I solved the problem by choosing to give a another talk about the evolution of nitrogen fixation, longer and in greater depth, including its bearing on the possibility of extending the ability outside bacteria, even perhaps of creating nitrogen-fixing crop plants. Fortunately it was a timely success.

A couple of more happy, painless episodes also stemmed from my scientific career. In 1990 the University of Bath decided to confer upon me an Honorary Doctorate, and in 1997 the University of Dundee conferred on me an honorary Ll.D (Doctor of Laws). Both honours gave me - and Mary - great pleasure; the Ll.D had additional piquancy because a lifelong friend from Balliol days, Gordon Samuels (see Chapter 16), had become one of the most distinguished lawyers in Australia, as well as a University Chancellor and later on Governor of New South Wales. I was able to write and inform him that, now I had a legal qualification, I was able to offer him, as a colleague, such advice as he might require at a preferential fee....

Actually, I recovered from my transient allergy to science quite quickly and began to broaden my horizons. I attended numerous Royal Society Discussion Meetings, not necessarily on microbiological topics. I was elected to the

Society's dining club, which had wide-ranging and often fascinating discussions after the dinners. I served on various Royal Society Committees, dealing with its library, a membership committee, two editorial boards (for *Science and Public Affairs* and *Notes and Records of the Royal Society*, the latter dedicated to the history of science), and I represented the Society for some years on a body concerned with cataloguing the archives of scientists.

An aspiring author

But my main pursuit in this period was to get on with Mary's and my collaborative biography of my father. I revised the three opening chapters which she had finished before she abandoned the book in the 1970s and wrote the remaining twenty-one, which she checked over and modified. Considering how difficult collaborative writing can become we managed pretty amicably. I also wrote more 'popular' science, such as a sequence of articles on microbiological topics for the *New Scientist* around 1987 - 91 and a few for *The Times* and *The Times Educational Supplement,* and for a couple of decades I reviewed science books, popular and technical, for a variety of journals, newspapers and magazines. Of course, I also wrote about jazz and reviewed jazz records, though in a more parochial magazine - more on that later. I gained a brief but pleasing reputation as a polymath when two of my reviews were published in the same issue of the *Times Literary Supplement,* one on a book concerned with microbes which thrive in extreme environments, the other a book on early ragtime. Both reviews were reasonably authoritative.

I wrote articles on science in society, morality, population, eugenics and religion. One on the latter topic, advocating agnosticism because the vast majority of recent wars and incidences of civil strife and terrorism have had religious origins, earned me an Honorary Associateship of the Rationalist Press Association, a humanist body. For that, my anti-religious father would have been proud of me!

In fact I rather fancied myself as a writer, and joined the Society of Authors. I was encouraged by the success of my first full-length book, *Microbes and Man.* It was commissioned in the summer of 1965 by the Penguin Publishing Co, which had ridden to success on its series of pocket-sized paperbacks in the mid century: the Penguin, Pelican and Puffin paperbacks. They originally cost 6d each, pre-war. My book was intended to be a survey of microbiology with emphasis on the impact of microbes on daily life, written in a manner accessible to the general reader, which meant using the minimum of technical terms and concepts. It was to be popular science, a genre that was quite rare in Britain at the end of the 1960s, and it would be part of their Pelican series. I wrote it during 1965-6 and delivered the script, scrupulously sub-edited by Mary, in the spring of 1966, but for reasons unexplained it was not published until 1969. I believe it largely achieved the commissioning editor's intention, but when it did ultimately emerge in print, it did so in the same batch as Penguin's paperback edition of John Updike's novel *Couples.* In the furore caused by the latter's sexual frankness, I fear my *opus* passed almost unnoticed by reviewers and booksellers. Nevertheless, it was not a failure. It caught on gradually, largely because it was seized upon by teachers of biology as a painless introduction to microbiology for sixth formers and first-year university and polytechnic students. I had not intended it to be a teaching aid, but I certainly had no complaint, and it did seep out to a general readership. In effect it sold quite well. It went through two reprintings until, in 1986, a complete update was needed.

Unfortunately, during the 1980s feminist censorship of putatively 'sexist' language reached a peak, especially in the publishing trade, and feminist 'language police' had come to dominate Penguin's copy editors. My use of '*Man*' in the title, in the traditional usage: a collective noun that encompasses men and women (as 'dog' encompasses dogs and bitches) must have been taken as provocation. It was certainly disapproved of, but it was too entrenched as a well-known title to be altered. However, they had expunged it from the text. And page after page of my revised manuscript had nit-picking alterations: "mankind" changed to "the human race", "every schoolboy" to the less accurate "every schoolchild" and so on, and for good measure, stilted grammatical and syntactical alterations had been introduced. More examples would be tedious, but precisely three out of some hundreds of sub-editorial amendments were acceptable to me.

Backed by Mary, who was firmly supportive of feminism but not of feminist newspeak, I threatened to withdraw the script altogether unless it was published as I had originally submitted it. Penguins duly gave in, but in the end the ladies exacted a mean-spirited revenge: the publicity signalling its release in *The Bookseller* did not mention that it was an updated revision at all, just that it had a new cover. Foreseeably the revised version was taken to be simply a repackaged reprint of the old one, so it sold rather poorly. That was not wholly a disaster, however, because it meant that after a couple of years I was able to recover my copyright from Penguins and could offer the book, further updated, to the Cambridge University Press (CUP), which accepted the offer willingly. That third edition emerged in 1992. It sold well once more - and went to a fourth revision in 2000. However, by then the feminist mafia's tentacles had reached into CUP and it got its claws into my manuscript again. After a milder dispute than I had had with Penguins, my own version was published. In all it was a bizarre if rather black comedy, after which I abandoned any thought of a fifth revision. By then the book had gained something of a global reputation and had been translated into nine foreign languages: Polish, German, Czech, Greek, Portuguese, Japanese, Chinese, Korean and (pirated) Russian. It is still in print as I write, in 2013.

Notwithstanding its turbulent history, *Microbes and Man* had done well. But as far as other books were concerned, I was less successful. Mary's and my biography of my father, A *Stomach for Dissent*, was completed around 1990, but biography was not then very commercial. Only after twenty-two rejections did I find a publisher: the newly established Keele University Press accepted the manuscript. It ultimately reached print in 1994 and, despite excellent reviews, it took off like a lead balloon. Apparently the novice KUP had no distributor arranged. That meant wholesalers did not offer it to high-street bookshops, so browsers never saw it; if anyone learnt of it and ordered a copy, the bookseller needed to order one from the publisher or, most often, advise the customer to do so. It sold few copies and was soon remaindered, because a larger academic publisher bought out the company. The copyright was in due course returned to me and is now dormant.

In the early 1990s CUP commissioned my second popular science book, about microbes that live in environments hostile to most forms of life. I mentioned it in the last chapter; it was called *The Outer Reaches of Life*. That did better because CUP was well established. Comically, at least one bookshop classified it under 'Philosophy', not 'Biology', but it sold steadily and is still in print in 2013. Later I wrote a short biography of my great-grandfather, an earlier John Postgate, a Victorian reformer who famously campaigned against food and drug adulteration but is now almost forgotten. The book was called *Lethal Lozenges and Tainted Tea*, but once again no publisher wanted it. Happily the Royal Society's History of Science fund gave me a grant to bribe a publisher to accept it, but despite a couple of good reviews it aroused little interest.

I also wrote a couple of books on jazz; one was yet another comic failure, the other a modest success - more about those later. Ah well! Seemingly I was not cut out to be a successful author. In my ninth decade both my inspiration and aspiration shrivelled, discouraged.

Another sort of travel

My scientific research had taken me to many parts of the world, for meetings, conferences, to give lectures, even for sabbatical stays. It had been, as I have written elsewhere, a marvellous experience to be part of the global community of scientists. It meant that one was welcomed into people's lives, often into their homes, and participated in day-to-day living in a way a tourist rarely does. And my host(s) usually showed me the touristic features of the area, but unless I took *congé* from my work I could rarely explore the location in any depth. And I had no real choice regarding where I travelled to; my destination was determined by my work, even though I could usually fit in one or two quick side-trips. For instance, if I found myself with a few hours to spare in a new town or city, my first act - if I were lively enough to take any action at all - would be to take the Grayline or similar tour of the place, just to get a glimpse of the major sights. But I have no complaint; it was a tremendous advantage to see bits of the wider world with my major travel and living expenses paid for officially.

When our children had grown up, Mary was able to leave them at home to look after the house and dog and come with me on some of my official trips (though not at official expense, of course), to Oregon (twice), to Mexico, to Egypt, to India, to Greece, Spain and several other countries in Europe. She would have a good look round, often escorted, and find new friends in distant places while I worked. Our first visit to Oregon was a year's sabbatical at Oregon State

University, Corvallis, OR, in 1977-8. A wonderful sojourn in a wonderful State with its glorious, varied scenery, tall, welcoming people, and a peaceful University - but I'll say no more as there have been enough travelogues in earlier chapters. With my retirement we accepted that those glorious opportunities had ended. Though we could now choose our destinations, we'd have to pay our way. Travel looked like becoming a rare treat on my pension, decent though that was.

But we were delightfully wrong. In the early 1990s Mrs Thatcher's Conservative Government oversaw a monstrous wave of economic stagnation and inflation in Britain, which its Chancellor, Nigel Lawson, attempted to contain by increasing the bank rate - which determines the cost of borrowing money. It rose to exceptional heights, around 15% if I remember correctly. I did not understand the underlying economics, but the upshot was that my retirement savings, which were in ordinary savings accounts, started earning substantial rates of interest, and that, coupled with the fact that my popular science articles and books were doing rather well, enabled us to travel in a most painless way: by commercial cruises. During the 1990s Mary and I managed to go on seven Swan Hellenic cruises, including escorted visits to most of the major, and some minor, archaeological and historical sites bordering the Mediterranean, as well as to Malta and the Greek Islands, and also Spain and Portugal, with a digression into the Baltic as far as St Petersburg. The Swan Hellenic cruises, originated by archaeologist Sir Mortimer Wheeler, specialised in conducted visits to the antiquities of the Eastern Mediterranean Basin, visits preceded by appropriate on-board lectures by scholarly experts. The cruises eschewed Bingo, cabaret and such trimmings of more popular cruises, and neither the crew nor the guides expected tips - all that was included. It was package tourism at its best.

Most of the passengers knew something about ancient history, and for me the cruises were a marvellous mental relaxation, in that the lectures and visits helped me to catch up with fragments of art, architecture, mythology and history, and to sense echoes of my classicist father's interests - areas of knowledge which I had drastically neglected during my research career. Mary, better educated in these matters, shared my enjoyment of what our children called "looking at old stones", ie seeing at first hand the remains of the cradles of western civilisation at Olympia, Mycenae, Ephesus, Knossos, the Island of Delos, the Parthenon of Athens, Pompeii, Carthage etc etc. The ship, *Orpheus*, and its Greek crew on the first five trips retained a touch of the amateurism of Sir Mortimer's early cruises. *Orpheus* was perfect, even though it was tatty, a bit of a rust bucket. It was comfortable and, being relatively small (about 300 aboard), it could moor at ports inaccessible to cruise liners carrying thousands (which would have to put sightseers ashore by tender or miss the sites altogether). There was a genial informality about life on *Orpheus*. One would usually find oneself sitting at meals with interesting and knowledgeable strangers.

The waiters were chummy. "What you want choose Windsor soup for?" said one to my wife at dinner one night, "Is only brown water!" But the food was good in a Greek manner and there were nice, economical, Greek wines. Many of our fellow passengers seemed to be regulars - as, for almost a decade, Mary and I were - and were remembered by the crew. There was dancing of an evening to a small, swingy band; Mary and I usually danced and on a couple of occasions I got to borrow a cornet from the band and join them in a little jazz.

I sit in on a borrowed cornet with the Manhattans in Orpheus, April 1992

Sadly, the company was taken over by the travel giant P & O for our last two cruises, with a new ship, *Minerva*, and though the intellectual quality of the tours remained, and although the ship was nicely planned, the friendly informality of *Orpheus* vanished; *Minerva* became, in the words of its brochure, a floating country hotel. Hell! Who wants a stuffy country hotel at sea? Mary and I tried two more cruises, but were put off and didn't cruise again. Anyway, the bank rate fell to a more normal value and we didn't feel all that wealthy any more.

The University of the Third Age

I discovered this admirable organisation, less pompously known as the U3A, in the late 1990s, when its meetings secretary, then a distant acquaintance, asked me if I would give the local branch an elementary talk on jazz. The U3A is simply a nationwide organisation for the elderly in which the members arrange courses and lectures, on an immense variety of subjects, given by speakers or tutors, mostly from among the membership, though sometimes from outside. It has no political, social, religious, charitable or medical objective; just learning, helping to keep each other's ageing brains active. No special expertise is required among tutors, lecturers or members - though in practice it is surprising how much expertise is revealed among all three.

My talk, actually a recital with taped recordings, would be part of a course on interesting hobbies. My fear of public speaking having vanished some decades before, I was intrigued by the idea, and by the possibility of giving a presentation which avoided the conventional historical approach. I did; it was a reasonable success. I joined the U3A and attended arts courses - literature, travel, economics, and history - as well as assisting for several years with an annual course on science and technology. For example, to celebrate the forthcoming millennium, for the year 2000 I roped in various old colleagues from the University of Sussex for a five-lecture course on scientists who, in the last few centuries, had altered the way we see the world: Galileo, Newton, Dalton, Faraday, Darwin etc. Though I thought nothing of it at the time, it came about that every speaker was a Fellow of the Royal Society, a remarkable programme for a local U3A group. It was a good series, and well attended. The intellectual level of the talks was pretty high but, being old and experienced, the speakers knew how to pitch their talks at a level which was comprehensible to and enjoyable by non-scientists. This was true of most of our U3A's courses, because there were two universities within the catchment area of Lewes. For my part I found the non-science courses especially useful and interesting because, just as the Swan Hellenic tours had done, they dealt with matters I wished I knew about but hadn't had time to study. They were also relaxing, because I was under no obligation to remember any of it!

And the jazz?

In my non-scientific persona I had become well known as a reviewer of jazz records, mostly in *Jazz Monthly* (which failed in 1971), *Jazz Journal,* and the more classically-orientated magazine *Gramophone*, for which I reviewed jazz issues for nearly 25 years. My stint with *Gramophone* came about in a flattering manner. Its regulars were the then aristocracy of Britain's jazz record reviewers, Charles Fox, Alun Morgan and Brian Rust. There was very little that one or another of those three didn't know about jazz. I was known through *Jazz Monthly* as a literate but rather flippant amateur of jazz, yet one day, when I was actually distinctly unwell with winter ailments, I received a letter from Charles inviting me to join the panel, as Brian Rust was departing. I made a miraculous recovery; we met for lunch, and it was settled. With *Gramophone* and the specialist magazines I have lost count of the hundreds of record issues I reviewed over some 45 years, LPs and EPs, cassettes and later on CDs. I also wrote a dozen or so articles about aspects of jazz.

However my attempt to write a book on jazz for a wider audience met with another bout of near-comic misfortune. My *A Plain Man's Guide To Jazz*, lovingly prepared in 1972-3, when no satisfactory elementary guide to jazz was available in the UK, was beset by a farcical set of circumstances. The publisher, having lost the corrected proofs, published the uncorrected script, replete with errors, typos and strange pagination, and almost immediately went bankrupt. The whole edition, if it can be called that, was seized by the Official Receiver and, though a few review copies had leaked out, none reached the shops. Thus, though it was well reviewed despite its typographical mess, it was a commercial failure. The Official Receiver invited me to buy the several hundred copies seized, but I had neither the money nor any idea what I could do with them, especially with all those maddening typos. So I did not. A few years later I saw copies of my beloved book being remaindered in London's Charing Cross Road and I sneakily bought myself a few. Today it is largely obsolete. But many years later I wrote, with discographer Bob Weir, *Looking for Frankie* (2003), a decent bio-discography of the jazz trumpeter Frankie Newton, and this sold well among jazz lovers for so specialised a book.

As a musical autodidact I toyed with the soprano saxophone but did not get far with it. However I had become a passable mainstream jazz cornettist, albeit still musically illiterate, playing fairly regularly at the University as an 'emeritus' member of that band of academics the Sussex Trugs, which I had earlier led. The Trugs played mainstream jazz at occasional university parties, and regularly once a week in its sports pavilion, sometimes to an admiring audience, sometimes to almost nobody. The Trugs became quite good when they played well, and could be abysmally awful when they didn't.

I played at other venues when opportunity permitted. For instance, early in 1980 I had taken my cornet with me to a pub in the outlying village of Chiddingly, the Six Bells, where a semi-professional jazz trio performed twice a month on Sunday lunchtimes. Semi-pro and sometimes professional jazz musicians would often drop in to play along with them; sometimes an exuberant jam session would develop. There was usually a substantial audience, with many regulars who enjoyed the quality and spontaneity of the music. At the invitation of the leader, pianist Bob Mitchell, I had shyly 'sat in' to play a few numbers. There were other musicians playing, too, but I don't recall whom. It was marvellous to play over a proper semi-professional rhythm section of piano, double bass and drums. That was the beginning of a 20+ year association with Bob; I became a regular at Chiddingly and played a small number of other gigs with him. I never got paid - as an amateur I didn't want to be - it was simply a pleasure to be tolerated, and occasionally complimented, by the many real musicians who joined in Bob's sessions. It was good experience, too. I played alongside, and adapted my jazz style to, modernist musicians whose roots lay in be-bop, other modernists who followed the contrapuntal West Coast style, die-hard followers of early New Orleans jazz and others whose jazz centred on the blues. My playing improved markedly and my nervousness eased as I learned to relax somewhat. It helped that the audience, and remarkably the bar staff too, seemed to like my playing. Now and again the publican would reward the visiting musicians, including me, with a bottle of his house wine.

In jazz 'sitting-in', or participating in a jam session, involves certain conventions, which are really just a combination of good manners and common sense. We were sometimes bothered by mavericks or self-centred musicians who hogged solos, or didn't know when to stop, who fooled around and spoiled a number, or doodled during other people's solos, but mostly the musician visitors were adult enough to behave sensibly and the jazz was good. Bob Mitchell died in 2005 and the drummer kept the sessions going, but soon afterwards I ceased being a regular since I realised that, by then in my early 80s, age and family problems were taking toll of my musicianship.

Meanwhile, however, a pianist from the past, Norman Day (see the end of Chapter 10), had got in touch with me. From a career in the Patent Office he had retired to Bexhill, on the Sussex coast, some 35 miles from my home in Lewes. We met, we both lamented the shortage of opportunities to play, and we agreed to meet weekly in Eastbourne, at a private music academy Norman knew of which would rent us cheaply a practice room with a piano. We would play some duets just for amusement and to keep in practice. Very soon a drummer joined us, then a clarinettist and later a trombone, bass and guitar, all retired or close thereto. We had grown into a small jazz ensemble composed of senior citizens. After a couple of years the academy decided to have an open day and asked us to perform for an hour. Suddenly we needed a name, and thus Norman Day's Eastbourne Academy Jazz Band came into being. We put up quite a good performance. Over about seven years, with some changes of personnel, we developed a repertoire of over 150 songs and became quite good on good days (I have CD recordings of some), playing mainstream and traditional jazz. That open day was the nearest we came to playing in public, but that suited us and we enjoyed ourselves. In 2007 Norman had to give up playing, the Academy had been sold and its new owners were converting it into a student hostel. We could no longer rent our practice room, so the 'Geriatric Stompers', as a visiting musician had once called us (disrespectfully if accurately) dispersed. Subsequently, some of us would meet and play occasionally.

Mary

In the 1990s Mary had begun to be bothered by forgetfulness. That's nothing new for people in their late 70s, and we laughed it off. But by 2000 she was clearly having more than usual trouble with memory lapses and confusion. Intellectually she was still fine, active and useful as a reserve magistrate, getting her record reviews written on time (just about), doing her bit as a trustee and school governor, as well as the daily chores - with which I helped. Again we laughed at her 'senior moments'; I suffered from such moments, too - notably in remembering people's names. By 2004, however, it had become clear to all of us within the family - except to Mary herself - that something was seriously amiss; she was losing her ability to use gadgets such as the record player, her special cassette player for listening to spoken word cassettes, the CD player and her word processor, and she never really came to terms with a new clothes washer and dishwasher. And she had become prone to delusions and illogical rages. In due course she consented to being seen by a specialist, who diagnosed moderate dementia, mainly Alzheimer's disease but with a vascular dementia component.

She was furious and in denial. For several months she managed social occasions remarkably well, and also came to the U3A meetings, but then really serious decline set in. I kept a log, a chronicle of misery too dismal to record here. Dementia is a ghastly disease for both sufferer and carer, utterly relentless. Faculties and memories dwindle, resurface a couple of times only vanish completely, on and on towards imbecility and physical incompetence. Ultimately some vital function in the brain disrupts and death follows, the final cause often being a normally trivial infection. Dementia's one redeeming feature is that the sufferer is rarely fully aware of what is happening - a feature that actually makes things worse for the carer, who can only watch helpless as the sufferer makes pathetically futile efforts to bring sense into what is to them an increasingly baffling scene.

In her last three years I did indeed become Mary's full

time carer, albeit helped by our two local daughters and a specialist domestic help agency. I proved to be a good carer, and I held to a promise I had made to her, in one of her moments of lucidity, that I would not let them put her into a home. But it was a steep and exacting learning curve, and to carry on I gave up reviewing jazz records and ceased all other writings. I stopped going to the Royal Society or its dining club, managed to give only one talk to the U3A and neglected the garden. My research became a distant part of my younger life, though I tried to keep up with the help of the Internet and *New Scientist* magazine. My musicianship deteriorated and I gave up Chiddingly, though I struggled on with Norman's band for a while.

For me there were two major crises. The first was when I had to break my promise: I could no longer manage her hygiene problems and she had to be taken into care. I knew she would not come back, but found that difficult to come to terms with. The second was some months later, in January, 2008, when several of her physiological faculties failed at the same time. She was taken from her care home into hospital, where she died. I was shattered. *Non sum qualis eram bonae sub regno Mariae*, I wrote, distorting a line from Horace.

I have skimmed through this melancholy story. The upshot was that I found myself bereaved and suffering from a variety of stress disorders, some of which slowly ameliorated, though misery and accidie remained.

Coda

But time does heal somewhat. In due course I was joined by Pamela Silvester as partner, widow of my old jazz-loving friend from Oxford days (Jim, see Chapter 8). Jim had died a few months after Mary and we chose to come to terms with our respective bereavements together. Now in my 91st year, I have regretfully felt it necessary to give up music making and communicating science because, though in fair health for that age, I am, in the words of William Dunbar, *feblit with infirmitie.*

Lewes, spring 2013